PRESIDENTS, PARTIES, AND THE STATE

Dominant theories of regulatory choice privilege the goals and actions of district-oriented legislators and organized groups. *Presidents, Parties, and the State* challenges this conventional frame, placing presidential elections and national party leaders at the center of American regulatory state development. Long the "out-party" in national politics, the Democratic party of Grover Cleveland, Woodrow Wilson, and Franklin Roosevelt confronted a severe political quandary, one that pitted long-term ideological commitments against short-term electoral opportunities. In short, Democrats were forced to choose between enacting the regulatory agenda of their traditional party base or legislating the programs of voting blocs deemed pivotal to the consolidation of national party power. Coalition-building imperatives drove Democratic leaders to embrace the latter alternative, prompting legislative intervention to secure outcomes consistent with national party needs. In the end, the electoral logic that fueled Democratic choice proved consequential for the trajectory of American state development. For, under the pressure to build a new majority party, an agrarian party with long-standing antistatist and antimonopoly commitments turned its governing power to the buildup of national administrative power and the consolidation of corporate capitalism.

Scott C. James is Assistant Professor of Political Science at the University of California, Los Angeles. His doctoral dissertation received the 1994 E. E. Schattschneider Award, presented annually by the American Political Science Association for the best dissertation in the field of American politics. James has published articles in the *American Political Science Review* and *Studies in American Political Development*.

PRESIDENTS, PARTIES, AND THE STATE

A Party System Perspective on Democratic Regulatory Choice, 1884–1936

SCOTT C. JAMES
University of California, Los Angeles

CAMBRIDGE
UNIVERSITY PRESS

PUBLISHED BY THE PRESS SYNDICATE OF THE UNIVERSITY OF CAMBRIDGE
The Pitt Building, Trumpington Street, Cambridge, United Kingdom

CAMBRIDGE UNIVERSITY PRESS
The Edinburgh Building, Cambridge CB2 2RU, UK   http://www.cup.cam.ac.uk
40 West 20th Street, New York, NY 10011-4211, USA   http://www.cup.org
10 Stamford Road, Oakleigh, Melbourne 3166, Australia
Ruiz de Alarcón 13, 28014 Madrid, Spain

First published 2000

Printed in the United States of America

Typeface Sabon 10/12 pt.   *System* QuarkXPress [BTS]

A catalog record for this book is available from the British Library.

Library of Congress Cataloging in Publication Data
James, Scott C., 1955–
    Presidents, parties, and the state : a party system perspective on
Democratic regulatory choice, 1884–1936/Scott C. James.
        p. cm.
    Includes bibliographical references.
    ISBN 0-521-66277-X (hardcover)
        1. Democratic Party (U.S.) – History. 2. Presidents – United
States – History. 3. United States – Politics and government – 1865–1933.
4. Administrative law – United States – History. 5. Interstate commerce –
Law and legislation – United States. 6. United States. Interstate
Commerce Commission. 7. United States. Federal Trade Commission.
8. United States. Securities and Exchange Commission. I. Title.
JK2316.J36 2000
324.2736′09′034 – dc21   99-37782
                                                                              CIP

ISBN   0 521 66277 X   hardback

TO MY PARENTS,
CHARLES HAROLD AND
TEREZINHA DE LOURDES SANTOS JAMES

Contents

vii

Acknowledgments

Some things are simply a pleasure to write. I have incurred numerous debts in the course of this journey and I am pleased to have this opportunity to acknowledge them now. As an undergraduate in the politics department at the University of California, Santa Cruz, I was fortunate to come under the tutelage of Wendy Mink, a wonderful teacher and scholar. Because of her I developed my ongoing interest in political parties, the American state, history, and development. Wendy also imparted to me, as her research assistant, an early sense of efficacy: a belief that I was cut out for academic life and could perhaps be successful in the field of political science. What more could an undergrad ask for? Most seminally, she also introduced me to Stephen Skowronek's *Building a New American State*, a brilliant book, the substance of which I have been in near continuous dialogue with for the last eighteen years.

It was in the graduate program at UCLA where I learned to be a political scientist, and as a faculty member of that same institution my education continues apace. From John Zaller I first learned the value of statistical analysis — even to an APD-type like myself! John Petrocik showed me, in addition, that data grubbing could be an exhilarating experience. More importantly, JRP also deepened my understanding of electoral processes and political parties as organizations, further instilling in me a keen appreciation (which I have not always followed) for clear thinking and clean writing. However, my greatest professional debt is to Karen Orren. First as teacher and dissertation director, and later as colleague, Karen has been my toughest critic and my strongest booster. This book simply would not have been possible without her innumerable contributions. She is a scholar's scholar, and her intellect, craftsmanship, and pure love of learning have been a constant source of inspiration (and awe) – qualities I continually strive to emulate. She is also a friend's friend, and I am profoundly fortunate to have such friendship in my life.

Along the way, a number of people have been kind enough to read various versions of this book, as conference papers, dissertation chapters, articles, or portions of the "final" manuscript. In alphabetical order, they are: Peri Arnold, Richard Bensel, Gerry Berk, Amy Bridges, Alan Dawley, Ken Finegold, Paul Frymer, John Gates, Paul Kleppner, Greg Koger, Eileen McDonagh, Eric Monkonnen, Bill Niemi, Karen Orren, John Petrocik, Gretchen Ritter, Pam Singh, Steven Skowronek, and John Zaller. At Cambridge University Press, Alex Holzman's early interest and sustained confidence in this project buoyed my spirits at critical stages in its development. As copy editor and production editor, Arun Das skillfully shepherded the manuscript through its final stages, while Pamela Dean's efforts produced an index for the book infinitely more professional than any I could have concocted myself.

One of my largest debts is to Pam Singh. Pam has generously read more versions of this book than probably either of us would care to admit. Her honesty, judgment, and unflagging faith in the merits of the project have made this a far better book than it would have otherwise been. As I write, we have been married for ten days. She is the love of my life, my best friend, and my partner in everything good.

Finally, I have dedicated this book to my parents, Charles and Terry James. They compliment each other perfectly. Early on, my mom instilled in me the belief that I could be anything I wanted if only I had the will to imagine it. Quite a bit later, my dad helped me to realize that after imagination comes discipline; after enthusiasm, hard work; after passion, patience. My parents are my heroes.

It goes without saying that any remaining errors of fact and interpretation contained in this book are my responsibility, and mine alone.

Scott C. James

1

Introduction: Parties, Presidential Elections, and Regulatory Choice – A Party System Perspective

[American political history affords] striking illustration[s] of the strategic position that may be won by minor parties and of their potential influence on the programs of the major parties. . . . Not every minor party can club a major party into acceptance of its policies. To do so the third-party must have its strength concentrated in close states, and the nation-wide contest as a whole must be regarded by party leaders as close. Otherwise, the splinter group carries no threat to the fortunes of either major candidate.

V. O. Key[1]

For many Americans of the late nineteenth century and early twentieth century, social anxiety and economic vulnerability were the most tangible fruits of industrial-capitalist modernization. "We are unsettled to the very roots of our being," wrote Walter Lippman in 1914, crystallizing this turmoil and so much more.[2] Several transformations seemed to be taking place at once. The penetration of competitive markets into once remote "island communities" strained social bonds and overturned established ways of life; while laissez-faire, with its cycles of boom and bust, aggravated economic uncertainty and militated against efforts at rational planning. As well, the passage of American capitalism from "proprietary-competitive" to "corporate-administered" stages brought forth indictments against the monopolistic practices of economic Goliaths; while, on a different foot, new forms of social organization and the spread of science and technology reordered basic human relationships.[3]

1. Key, *Politics, Parties and Pressure Groups*, 294–5.
2. Lippman, *Drift and Mastery*. Quoted in Kloppenberg, *Uncertain Victory*, 298.
3. Hays, *The Response to Industrialism*; Wiebe, *The Search for Order*; *1877–1920*; Archon, *The Invisible Hand of Planning*; Sklar, *Corporate Reconstruction*.

Such crises occasioned searching critiques of the American political economy. Alternative visions of America's programmatic future, rooted in differences of interest and ideology, were devised and fiercely contested. Populism, progressivism, and socialism challenged the hegemony of nineteenth-century liberalism. In the process, they raised fundamental questions about the legitimacy of the corporation, the rights of labor, and the place of the small producer in the American economic order.[4] In similar fashion, states' rights advocates, defenders of patronage democracy, and champions of bureaucratic expertise squared off over the degree and the character of popular oversight to attend the reorganized political economy: that is, whether collective ends would best be secured by reliance on local units of authority, the perfection of national party government, or the delegation of complex policy decisions to administrative experts.[5] Translated into concrete policy proposals and platform planks, these alternative visions were carried into the stream of national politics, where government leaders, balancing group demands against their own political needs, chose from among the leading contenders. These developmental choices were of profound moment for participants, and they carried with them lasting implications for the future conduct of American economic, social, and political life.

This book examines three episodes in the development of the American regulatory state between the years 1884 and 1936, initiatives undertaken during the Democratic administrations of Grover Cleveland, Woodrow Wilson, and Franklin Roosevelt. The cases examined are the Interstate Commerce Act of 1887, the Federal Trade Commission Act of 1914, and the Public Utility Holding Company Act of 1935. Each has been hailed as a signal achievement in the battle for national business controls that punctuated American politics from the Gilded Age to the New Deal. As well, in each instance the desire of Democratic party leaders to retain control of the presidency was the principal motivation behind the particular regulatory choices made.

In the chapters that follow, I will elaborate a party system perspective on the development of American regulatory institutions, one in which the imperatives of national party competition for the presidency are at the center of regulatory choice. The Democratic party in power confronted a severe policy quandary, one which I have termed the "Downsian

---

4. Goodwyn, *The Populist Moment*; Ritter, *Goldbugs and Greenbacks*; Mowry, *The Era of Theodore Roosevelt*; Link, *Woodrow Wilson and the Progressive Era, 1912–1917*; Weinstein, *The Decline of Socialism in America, 1912–1925*; Salvatore, *Eugene V. Debs*.

5. Skowronek, *Building a New American State*.

dilemma" – a reference to Anthony Downs's seminal work on two-party competition and the pivotal role of the median voter.[6] In essence, the Democrats faced a difficult choice between their long-term ideological commitments and short-term electoral opportunities, between legislating the deeply held regulatory aspirations of their agrarian party base, or abandoning those goals for the policy preferences of pivotal voting blocs whose support was deemed crucial to the consolidation of party power.

I will argue that coalition-building strategies to amass an electoral college majority imposed strict limits on the range of regulatory alternatives politically acceptable to Democratic party leaders. Such limits, I intend to show, prompted party intervention in the legislative process to secure regulatory outcomes consistent with these coalition-building needs. To be sure, interest-group pressures and the demands of congressional constituencies set parameters on party influence in the policy process. Nonetheless, I conclude that party intervention was largely successful. And while successful intervention did not always result in the perpetuation of Democratic governing power, the national electoral logic that drove policy choice did prove consequential for the trajectory of American regulatory state development. For under the pressures of building a new majority party, an agrarian party with longstanding antistatist and antimonopoly commitments would turn its governing power to the buildup of national administrative power and the consolidation of corporate capitalism.

Studying American Regulatory State Development

The subject of regulation is highly charged. Substantively, regulation redistributes both rights and income between different economic actors: between elements within the business community, between business and labor, and between business and consumers. Symbolically, it is often held to represent the subordination of unbridled capitalism to a democratically defined public good. Because it is laden with such significance, students of American political development have repeatedly sought to map the dynamics of American regulatory state development. Indeed, the intensity of the battle for interpretive supremacy itself suggests that something more is at stake than a simple desire to "get the story right." Should we understand the development of national business controls in the United States as signifying the triumph of "the people" over "the interests?"[7] Or, is it better understood as a victory

6. Downs, *An Economic Theory of Democracy.*
7. E.g., Beard, *The Economic Basis of Politics and Related Writings,* chs. 10–21; Schlesinger, *The Age of Roosevelt,* 3 vols.

for corporate elites in rationalizing market competition?[8] Is the lesson of American regulatory state development that a pluralist democracy "open to all contending interests" is a hopelessly irrational mechanism of regulatory choice?[9] Or, is a more important lesson learned by situating its development within a broader social dynamic of increasing centralization and bureaucratized forms of control?[10] My purpose here is not to array the full range of interpretative schemes that have been brought to bear on this question. Nor do I mean to imply that such schemes by their nature are mutually exclusive. What I want to suggest is that what is at stake in these different historical readings is our understanding of the nature of political influence in the United States, an understanding with implications for the normative significance of American political development.

Analytic Issues: Social Groups, the New Institutionalism, and Party System Variables

For generations, scholars debating these issues sought their answer through the study of relative group power. Of course, analytic frameworks have shifted with time and predilection. In the process, different historical actors have earned analytic pride of place in the unfolding developmental narrative: small producers and large producers, capital and labor, localists and cosmopolitans, industrial core and agrarian periphery, to name just a few.[11] However, whether the focus has been on interest groups proper, broad social classes, or cross-class, multiinterest social movements, the assumption common to each of these frameworks has remained relatively constant: relative group power is a function of the *resource endowments* of the groups involved – fungible wealth, group size, control over information and expertise, social status and elite

8. Kolko, *The Triumph of Conservatism*; Weinstein, *The Corporate Ideal in the Liberal State, 1900–1916*; Radosh, "The Myth of the New Deal"; Sklar, *Corporate Reconstruction*.
9. Skowronek, *Building a New American State*, ch. 5.
10. Berkhoff, "The Organizational Interpretation of American History: A New Synthesis"; Galambos, "The Emerging Organizational Synthesis in Modern American History"; Galambos, "Technology, Political Economy, and Professionalism: Central Themes of the Organizational Synthesis"; Israel, ed. *Building the Organizational Society*; Archon, *The Invisible Hand of Planning*; Chandler, Jr. "The Large Industrial Corporation and the Making of the Modern American Economy."
11. Wiebe, *Businessmen and Reform*; Hays, "Political Parties and the Community-Society Continuum"; Sanders, "Industrial Concentration, Sectional Competition, and Antitrust Politics in America, 1880–1980."

connections, or, more subtly, authority over the private investment function.[12]

More recently, scholars have investigated the effect of political structure on the character of American regulatory state development. Many of these studies emphasize the effect on policy choice of the fragmented structure of the U.S. state, with its multiple points of access and its decentralized, patronage-oriented political parties. Many more have privileged the role of Congress and its particular institutional arrangements (for example, the committee system; the seniority system) in conjunction with the presence of weak congressional parties. Additionally, the bulk of these studies pivot on the centrality to regulatory choice of Congress's geographical basis of representation, a decentralized incentive system in which the policy choices of reelection-minded legislators are tied to the imperatives of local elections.[13]

My party system account of American regulatory state development takes issue with both group and conventional "new institutionalist" accounts. It is at odds with the former over its reliance on relative group endowments as the principal determinant of policy influence. Against this stance, the party system explanation posits that policy influence derives from the *structure of the political environment in which group action is embedded*, a position that at least so far is consistent with "new institutionalist" accounts of regulatory choice. In each of the three cases we will consider, a group's strategic importance to the building or maintenance of a political party's national coalition was a principal determinant of its policy influence. In turn, it was the institutional and structural features of the party system that enabled these "selected" interests to occupy a pivotal position in the coalition-building process: for example, the competitive balance of national party competition and group

12. Kolko, *The Triumph of Conservatism*; Weinstein, *The Corporate Ideal in the Liberal State, 1900–1916*; Radosh, "The Myth of the New Deal"; Sklar, *Corporate Reconstruction;* Sanders, "Industrial Concentration, Sectional Competition, and Antitrust Politics in America, 1880–1980"; Thompson, *The "Spider Web"*; Miliband, *The State in Capitalist Society*; Domhoff, "How the Power Elite Shapes Social Legislation"; Orren, *Corporate Power and Social Change*; Lindblom, *Politics and Markets*.

13. Lowi, "Party, Policy, and Constitution in America"; Skocpol, "Bringing the State Back In"; Skocpol, "Political Responses to Capitalist Crisis"; Skocpol and Finegold, "Explaining New Deal Labor Policy"; Finegold and Skocpol, "State, Party and Industry"; McDonagh, "Representative Democracy and State Building in the Progressive Era"; Fiorina, "Legislative Choice of Regulatory Forms." Fiorina, "Group Concentration and the Delegation of Legislative Authority"; Fiorina, "Legislator Uncertainty, Legislative Control, and the Delegation of Legislative Power"; Gilligan, Marshall, and Weingast, "Regulation and the Theory of Legislative Choice."

location in states privileged by the operation of the electoral college. Put differently, in all three instances, party-system variables were constitutive elements of relative group influence in the politics of regulatory choice, factors wholly separate from the consideration of relative group resource endowments.

Consider briefly an example drawn from outside the time frame of this book: Harry Truman's decision to desegregate the armed forces by executive order in 1948. Needless to say, the issue here was the deregulation of military race relations and not the regulation of interstate economic activity. Neither did it involve party intervention in the legislative process like the cases that comprise this study. Nevertheless, the basic political forces at work were the same, and the case helps to illustrate more concretely the constitutive nature of party-system factors to the determination of relative group influence.[14] In this instance, strategists for President Truman's 1948 reelection effort were concerned that a third party bid by progressive Democrat Henry A. Wallace might attract a sufficient number of liberal Democratic votes to throw the election to Republican Thomas E. Dewey. The Truman team was confident of holding the 216 electoral votes in the southern and western states carried by Franklin Roosevelt in 1944. This left them in need of 50 electoral votes in the doubtful states of the industrial East and Midwest, where it was estimated that Wallace might attract as much as 5 to 10 percent of the Democratic vote. Campaign strategists like Clark Clifford considered the African-American vote to be crucial to winning these states, and they expected the Wallace forces to enter into a bidding war for these votes. The key to holding the African-American vote, they judged, was for Truman to put forth a vigorous program of civil rights. As one student of the Truman presidency put it, "The Truman strategy board feared Wallace's inroads in the big-city precincts, where the Negro vote is decisive, far more than they feared defections in the South. Regardless of the provocations, they reasoned, the South would retain its historic Democratic solidarity."[15] That Truman's campaign strategists were wrong about the southern response is beside the point. From our perspective, what is significant is that Truman chose to disregard the preferences of a large and powerful party constituency (southern whites) in favor of a group clearly less powerful in terms of its relative resource endowments,

---

14. Of course, the following discussion is meant to be suggestive rather than conclusive. The sources on which this paragraph relies are: Phillips, *The Truman Presidency*; Bernstein, "The Ambiguous Legacy: The Truman Administration and Civil Rights"; Berman, "Civil Rights and Civil Liberties"; Yarnell, *Democrats and Progressives*, ch. 5; Clifford, *Counsel to the President*.
15. Phillips, *The Truman Presidency*, 206.

but, nonetheless, one that had been deemed electorally pivotal (African-Americans). In February 1948, Truman sent a sweeping civil rights message to Congress; and in late July, with the national Democratic convention safely behind him, he issued executive order 9981 deregulating relations between the races in the American armed forces.

As the Truman example indicates, my party system perspective shares basic affinities with the "new institutionalism" in that both approaches insist that political institutions are constitutive elements of group influence. Where my approach parts company is over the "new institutionalism's" typical focus on the policy effects of fragmented institutions and decentralized patronage parties, as well as the causal priority it accords to Congress and its system of elections. Such features, we have learned, create an environment of "competing, narrowly specialized, and weakly disciplined interests,"[16] a setting in which party organizations and party interests hold little sway in the policy-making process. By contrast, the party system perspective spotlights what tentatively might be called the "centripetal" or nationalizing properties of American politics: again, its system of presidential elections and the operation of its national party processes. It also gives causal weight to the strategies and resources of national party leaders to overcome the problems of dispersed political authority afflicting legislative policy deliberations. My conclusions suggest the inadequacy of an image of "party-in-government" in which party leaders are little more than a league of local politicians engaged in the division of patronage, pork, and privilege. As a supplement to this image, I would posit the presence of a party policy logic. Such a logic is not necessarily inconsistent with the patronage orientation of American parties. It merely implies that policy choices sometimes have electoral implications (and, by extension, implications for party control of spoils). Where they did, party leaders had strong political incentives to take sides on policy matters and intervene in the legislative process to secure policy outcomes consistent with national electoral goals.

Two "new institutionalist" accounts of American state development in which political parties and party system dynamics are central are Stephen Skowronek's *Building a New American State* and Theda Skocpol and Kenneth Finegold's work on the origins of the National Labor Relations Act.[17] As well, both studies treat state-building episodes that fall within the period parameters of this book and each shares important commonalities with the party system perspective offered here. Indeed,

---

16. Skocpol, *Protecting Soldiers and Mothers*, 50. The same point is made in Skocpol, "Bringing the State Back In," 25.
17. Skowronek, *Building a New American State*; Finegold and Skocpol, "State, Party and Industry"; Skocpol and Finegold, "Explaining New Deal Labor Policy."

their broadest theoretical formulations appear to preempt the call made here for a separate party system vantage point on American regulatory state development. For this reason we will consider briefly each of these works for the purpose of differentiating their interpretations of regulatory choice from the one proposed here.

Stephen Skowronek's book is in large part a study of party hegemony over the operations of the nineteenth-century American state and its consequences for the development of modern administrative capacities. As his analysis shows, the building of a new American state posed a direct challenge to the well-being of party organizations dependent on the spoils of office for continued electoral good fortune. Every new island of bureaucratic expertise in the American state came at the expense of party control over valuable resources. Skowronek demonstrates that party system dynamics effectively structured governing party responses to the state-building imperatives of the Gilded Age and the Progressive Era. In the former period, tight party competition constrained parties in power to resist significant departures from existing governmental modes of operation. As a result, institutional solutions were largely "patchwork" affairs. Only after the constraints of national party competition loosened in 1896 were American state-builders able to drive a wedge in party government and effectively reconstitute the governing capacities of the U.S. state.[18]

The Interstate Commerce Act (ICA) will receive detailed consideration in Chapter 2. For now, the point to stress is that Skowronek's study of the legislative origins of the ICA – his only analysis of *regulatory* state development – is significant not for its focus on national party structures, but for its similarity to conventional "new institutionalist" accounts of the policy-making process. Skowronek concentrates on the structure of congressional elections and the character of local party politics, presenting a picture of the legislative process driven by the pressures and uncertainties of a highly competitive and highly provincial district politics. To Skowronek, the ICA is a paradigmatic example of the subversion of public policy by pluralist pressures: A coherent and authoritative governmental response to the demand for national railroad regulation was precluded by the existence of a well-organized and fully mobilized democratic system, a system "open to all contending factions."[19] Thus, in this account, bound to district preferences by the threat of electoral defeat and goaded into action by the Supreme Court's gutting of state-level regulation of interstate commerce, Congress responded to the regulatory demands of diverse geographical constituencies with a discretionary commission and a tangle of vague statutory provisions, often working at cross-purposes, to serve as the commission's guide.

18. Skowronek, *Building a New American State*, ch. 5.   19. Ibid., 131.

When we turn to Theda Skocpol and Kenneth Finegold's work on the Wagner Act, we appear to find an even closer approximation to the party-system logic advanced here. In their analysis, party members pursue policy as well as patronage, and party competition and party alignments are central to the process of policy selection. Indeed, the authors effectively steer a parallel course to the approach offered here when they advance the proposition that relative group influence is shaped by the operation of electoral and party processes.

> In liberal democracies with elements of "polyarchy" – rule by many – social groups will receive varying amounts and kinds of attention from elected politicians, depending not so much on their sheer weight in the voting process *as upon their strategic location (or lack of it) in the electoral process*. Different forms of party organization, different party systems, and different historical conjunctures of intraparty influence, for governmental office, and for influence within government, will all affect which groups are attended to or ignored as politicians compete among themselves for authority [emphasis added].[20]

Like Skowronek's account of the ICA, however, the study of the Wagner Act offered by Skocpol and Finegold retains close affinities with dominant "new institutionalist" accounts of regulatory choice. Most notable is their tendency to view party coalitions and party alignments through the lens of Congress and congressional elections. In their analysis, it was the limited planning capacity of the American state that ultimately doomed the National Industrial Recovery Act (NIRA) as an effective strategy for national economic recovery. As a consequence, even before the Supreme Court's *Schechter* decision in May 1935 – in which the NIRA was held to be an unconstitutional delegation of legislative power – the United States was without an effective plan for ending the depression. But of course the structure of the American state cannot in itself explain the decision to supercede the NIRA with the Wagner Act, and Skocpol and Finegold turn to the operation of district-level political factors to supply the logic behind the policy change. Specifically, they look to the congressional redistricting of 1930 and the results of the 1934 midterm elections. The consequence of these district-level events, they argue, was to transform the intraparty balance of power within the congressional Democratic party, to swell the representation of northern urban liberals at the expense of conservative southerners and push congressional policy making far to the left of a politically cautious Executive Branch. The result: an intraparty realignment within the congressional Democratic party, one conducive to the passage of liberal labor legislation like the Wagner Act.

20. Finegold and Skocpol, "State, Party and Industry," 164–5.

The Party System Perspective: A Theoretical Introduction

The preceding discussion of social-group and "new institutionalist" frameworks should not be taken to assert the unimportance of group power, institutional fragmentation, and local electoral dynamics broadly speaking. To the contrary, in many circumstances these pressures can impose the most immediate constraints on national political action. The prevalence of group and district explanations in most accounts of regulatory choice is itself an indication of their importance as explanatory factors. This said, the danger to our understanding of American regulatory state development lies in treating a frequent empirical occurrence as an empirical constant, and thus as an a priori assumption of causality. Such tendencies are pronounced in the social sciences, in disciplines like political science that prize empirical regularities, parsimony, and generalization.

To be sure, such disciplinary values have their advantages. In league with dominant paradigms, they impart order to an otherwise complex political universe and make more tractable the enterprise of scholarly research. On the down side, however, such simplifying schemes necessarily privilege some sets of institutions, processes, actors, and behaviors at the expense of others. The potentially deleterious consequences are of two types. On the one hand, important information can be filtered out of our analytic field of vision. On the other hand, the impulse to universalize key aspects of the historical record is heightened, imparting a mistaken character of sameness to past and present. These discipline-induced side effects subvert the very possibility of development; a consequence of particular concern when empirical "outliers" – properly recognized as such – have the potential to clarify relationships of interest to students of politics: those, for example, involving structure and agency, constraint and opportunity, equilibrium and change.

How then should we understand the relationship between district, group, and party system constraints on the politics of regulatory choice? My research suggests that party system constraints are most likely to impinge on national policy choice where such decisions have immediate and consequential implications for a party's hold on the presidency. Parties expend considerable resources to win and retain the presidency because of its tangible contribution to party power.[21] Indeed, competi-

---

21. The claim that American parties are primarily concerned with winning and retaining power is compatible with different explanations of why parties seek power. It is not necessary to assume that American parties are solely concerned with patronage and the other perks of office. In choosing the parliamentary road to socialism, European socialist and labor parties pragmatically opted to subordinate programmatic purity

tion for the presidency was the impetus behind the emergence of the American two-party system and it remains its principal glue to this day. In the words of historian Richard P. McCormick, himself a student of presidential party politics,

> The Constitutional requirement that the victor must secure an absolute majority of the electoral vote, or risk a contingent election by the House, operate[s] powerfully to restrict the contest to two major candidates, each of whom must seek to create a coalition of supporters that ha[s] the potential of producing the requisite majority. The logic of this basic rule of the game . . . fostered the creation of a two party system.[22]

As in any environment in which actors compete for control of scarce resources, competition in presidential elections operates like a natural-selection mechanism between parties: Any party will survive in office only as long as it is able to out-mobilize its rivals in the struggle for an electoral college majority. In the language of rational choice, such parties are constrained to behave as if they were "single-minded seekers of reelection," to preoccupy themselves on an ongoing basis with putting together and retaining a coalition of groups capable of winning plurality victories in a combination of states equal to an electoral college majority.[23]

This systemic constraint on the policy choices of parties in power is the essence of the Downsian dilemma, and it provides the central departure for the analysis in this book. In the period between the Gilded Age and the New Deal many of the key institutions of the modern American regulatory state were constructed. These state-building initiatives also coincided with the coming to power of the Democratic party. Between the years of the Civil War and the Great Depression, the Republican party was the majority party in American politics. The Democratic party was consigned to the status of out-party, the minority party in presidential politics. The Democratic administrations of Grover Cleveland, Woodrow Wilson, and Franklin Roosevelt came to power through the operation of political or economic factors largely outside their control. Respectively, these were: the defection of New York Mugwumps

to coalition-building and electoral victory, not because they valued office per se, but because the seizure of government power was the precondition to securing working-class gains. On the deleterious consequences for socialism of the parliamentary path to power, see Przeworski and Sprague, *Paper Stones*.

22. McCormick, *The Party Game*, 11.
23. The proposition that rational, maximizing behavior is the product of severe environmental constraints is the subject of Satz and Ferejohn, "Rational Choice and Social Theory." The assumption that legislators are single-minded seekers of reelection is central to Mayhew's seminal *Congress: The Electoral Connection*.

from the Republican party over the issue of civil service reform in 1884, the collapse of the Republican party organization with the formation of the Progressive party in 1912, and the depression era repudiation of the Republican party in 1932. Such circumstances cast considerable doubt on the ability of the Democrats to retain national power in the next round of elections. Of necessity, stabilizing their hold on national political power was a primary objective of Democratic leaders.

It was in this highly unstable electoral context that the Democratic party confronted the governing dilemmas posed by industrial concentration and corporate power. Historically the party of limited government and states rights, Democrats in power presided over major extensions in the reach of the American state. Perhaps most paradoxically, Democrats in the Progressive era were principally an agrarian party with marked animus toward economic concentration and corporate industrial power. Yet these commitments notwithstanding, the Democratic party in power would be intimately involved in laying the legal groundwork for the consolidation of corporate capitalism.

The claim I am making is that one can understand these dramatic reversals of party policy and doctrine as the product of dilemmas involved in the process of building national party coalitions. Democratic victory in presidential elections required an absolute majority in the electoral college, while party competition and the imperatives of majority coalition building gave added weight to interests whose allegiance was tenuous and whose votes were necessary to presidential victory. As I hope to document, such interests held disproportionate influence over the direction of Democratic regulatory policy – even though their preferences clashed with those of traditional party supporters – because of their pivotal position in the building and maintenance of the governing party's majority coalition. On issues ranging from railroad rate-making practices, to business-trading practices, to the economic utility of public utility holding companies, the Democratic party had long been associated with specific regulatory policy prescriptions. Democrats in the Gilded Age and the Progressive Era articulated an antimonopoly producers' vision of the American political economy, stressing the values of competition and decentralized production by small economic units. By contrast, Democrats in the era of the New Deal articulated a more moderate regulatory stance toward public utility holding companies. What these cases have in common is that in each instance, broadly supported regulatory stances would be shunted aside by party leaders to accommodate the demands of groups considered pivotal to the building and maintenance of a new majority party. In the first two cases, party system constraints would push Democratic party leaders to steer clear of the demands of antimonopoly radicals. In the third case the reverse was true, with administration officials singling out the preferences of agrarian anti-monopolists for satisfaction in their bid to consolidate a new majority party. In this way, coalition building imperatives and the competition for pivotal voting blocs shaped the structure of interest representation within the governing Democratic party.[24]

The Electoral College and American Political Development

Perhaps above all else, this book seeks to carve out a theoretical place for the institution of the electoral college in the study of American political development. The electoral college is a highly structured environment, with precise rules, procedures, and norms of strategic behavior adhered to by contestants for the presidential office. The constitutional stipulations are well known. Candidates and their party organizations compete for electoral votes allocated by state in numbers equivalent to the sum of its House and Senate representation. The winning candidate must accumulate an absolute majority of the total electoral votes to avoid throwing the contest into the House of Representatives.

Of course, party candidates do not compete for electoral votes with equal intensity in every state. In practice, the electoral college injects a set of biases into presidential elections that work to advantage some states and certain groups over others in the competition for candidate attention. Much has been written about the distorting effects of the electoral college: for example, its contribution to minority vote dilution, its bias against third parties (or even one of the major parties), and its potential to provoke unpopular choices and constitutional crisis.[25] In addition,

24. The logic of this claim has much in common with arguments developed elsewhere by Adam Przeworski and John Sprague to explain the programmatic and electoral failure of European socialist parties. Their analysis pivots on the existence of a simple electoral dilemma. Historically, the European working class never constituted a majority of the electorate. Consequently, to win elections, parties of the left were forced to dilute their programmatic agenda and mute the ideological salience of class in order to secure cross-class electoral support. The result was to weaken the appeal of leftist parties to workers, which in turn encouraged abstention from the electoral process and defection to more traditional parties. This, in turn, accelerated the electoral decline of socialist parties and, more broadly, of the socialist project itself. See Przeworski and Sprague, *Paper Stones*.

25. Hoffman, "The Illegitimate President"; Berthoud, "The Electoral Lock Thesis"; Berns, "Third Party Candidates Face a High Hurdle in the Electoral College"; McGaughey, "Democracy at Risk"; Amar, "A Constitutional Accident Waiting to Happen"; Ball and Leuthold, "Estimating the Likelihood of an Unpopular Verdict in the Electoral College."

a substantial body of literature has debated the effects of the electoral college on the relative influence of large states and small states in national elections.[26] A sustained treatment of this subject is Brams (1978), who has argued that under specified conditions, states with large, winner-takes-all blocs of electoral votes will attract substantially greater party attention than those with smaller allocations – "even out of proportion to their size."[27]

Like this previous work, this book is also concerned with the mechanisms by which the electoral college injects biases into national politics. In particular, it is interested in the advantages and disadvantages that accrue to certain groups because of their geographic location in the competition for state electoral votes. Specifically, my analysis privileges the practice by which presidential campaign strategists carve up the electoral college map into "sure states" and "doubtful states."[28] Sure states are those in which the election day outcome is known in advance, whether it be "sure for" or "sure against" the party in question. With the outcome conceded up front, party organizations have less incentive to invest scarce resources in sure states. The reason is simple: because the application of additional resources is not expected to alter the electoral outcome, such resources are more profitably allocated to states where a marginal increase may mean the difference between defeat and victory. By similar logic, there is less incentive to fashion major campaign themes and programmatic promises to voters housed in sure states, *at least not when such appeals conflict with the preferences of voting blocs located in electorally doubtful states.*

Doubtful states, as the name implies, are those in which parties are competitive and the outcome of their individual presidential contests is

26. Uslander, "Pivotal States in the Electoral College"; Uslander, "Spatial Models of the Electoral College"; Hinich and Ordeshook, "The Electoral College"; Longley and Dana, "The Biases of the Electoral College in the 1990s."

27. Brams, *The Presidential Election Game*, 84. Brams is able to isolate the effect of state size on resource allocation by utilizing the following simplifying assumptions: 1) parties possess equal resources, 2) parties "match each other's resource expenditures in each state," and 3) the number of uncommitted voters, as a percentage of all voters, is constant across states.

28. Brams's electoral college model does not distinguish between sure and doubtful states. In the first instance, it does not systematically consider the competitiveness of state presidential elections as a variable affecting the strategic allocation of electoral resources by partisan organizations. In addition, the model assumes that the percentage size of the uncommitted bloc of voters is constant across all states (Brams, *The Presidential Election Game*, 106). These two variables – competitive balance and swing group size – are at the heart of our distinction between sure and doubtful states. Their absence allows Brams to concentrate on his more immediate concern, which is the effect of state size on resource allocation in electoral college competition.

uncertain. Among doubtful states is a subset of particular interest, the so-called "swing states." In addition to competitiveness, swing states have the characteristic of being states on which the outcome of the national presidential contest is expected to turn. In a party system where the distribution of electoral votes between the two major parties is relatively close, the actual number of swing states may be several, very few, or theoretically just one. On the other hand, if one party holds a lopsided advantage in the electoral college – such as the Republican party during the stable phases of the so-called System of 1896 (1896–1908, 1920–8) – then the existence of a group of doubtful states may not yield an identifiable set of swing states, a condition that under-scores the contingent character of electoral college effects on American politics.[29]

The central hypothesis of this book states that political competition for the presidency induces political parties to give disproportionate political attention to those states that hold the balance of power in the electoral college. Typically, this means making substantive appeals to disaffected groups either within one's own party, the major-party opposition, or attached to third-party organizations. But historically it has also been a stimulus to the enfranchisement of groups previously excluded from electoral participation or the mobilization of inactive voters into the electoral process. Conversely, parties in power have also sought to alter the competitive balance by demobilizing centers of opposition electoral strength in competitive states through the reform of electoral institutions and/or the regulation of voting practices.[30]

29. The logic of swing-state competition is applicable across a range of electoral contexts. In his recent biography of Abraham Lincoln, the historian David Herbert Donald writes of the calculus by which Lincoln, an Illinois Republican party leader, allocated his appearances in 1858 on behalf of party candidates for the statehouse: "[Lincoln] drew up a careful, detailed list of how the representative and senatorial districts had voted in the previous election and . . . tried to predict how each district would go in 1858. Some, mostly in Southern Illinois, he wrote off as 'desperate' [sic], meaning that there was no use wasting Republican resources there; others, chiefly in the North, he marked as 'we take to ourselves, without question,' so that no campaigning in these counties was needed. He allocated his public appearances accordingly, making only four speeches in the North and only four in the South. The rest of his time he devoted to districts 'we must struggle for,' mainly in the central part of the state, where the Whig (and more recently the Know Nothing) party had been strongest." (Donald, 1995: 212).

30. Shefter, "Party, Bureaucracy, and Political Change in the United States"; Burnham, *Critical Elections and the Mainsprings of American Politics*; Sundquist, *The Dynamics of the Party System*; Kousser, *The Shaping of Southern Politics*; Argersinger, *Structure, Process, and Party*; James and Lawson, "The Political Economy of Voting Rights in America's Gilded Age: Electoral College Competition and the Federal Election Law."

Broadly speaking, we will encounter two forms of "pivotal politics" in this book – that is, two patterns of partisan competition for pivotal groups in the electoral college. The first accords most closely with the description just laid out. Here, "pivotal politics" is associated with presidential contests that are closely contested and in which party competition centers on a small handful of states seen to hold the balance of power in the electoral college. The focus here is on a median bloc of competitive states, and party leaders face the challenge of determining which of those groups located in these states can be appealed to in sufficient numbers to swing the national election to their side. As we will see in our examination of the Interstate Commerce Act (Chapter 2), Gilded Age presidential elections were contested almost exactly along these lines, with national outcomes turning on the relative ability of Republicans and Democrats to eke out electoral victories in such states as New York, New Jersey, Indiana, and Connecticut. Mugwumps, prohibitionists, and organized labor were among the groups located in these states that understood the structural bias of the Gilded Age party system and hoped to work it to their advantage.[31] As suggested in my brief discussion of Harry Truman's decision to desegregate the armed forces, the presidential election of 1948 also falls under this first classification.

The second pattern of presidential politics we will observe in this book differs from the first in that national outcomes do not come down to a mad scramble for a handful of competitive states. Indeed, the pattern of partisan contestation characteristic of the System of 1896 (1896–1928) was generally quite uncompetitive, with Republicans regularly trouncing Democrats in national elections.[32] In this regard, the pivotal politics of this era became a structural possibility only when a group of disaffected voters emerged from within the dominant Republican coalition large in size and dispersed across a sufficient number of states to conceivably throw the election to the Democratic party. In such elections, we do not expect to see party strategists explicitly preoccupied with concerns about swing states. Rather, presidential elections assume a more classically Downsian character – as though parties were competing for the national median voter in the popular vote count rather than the median state in the electoral vote count – but only because a successful appeal to such a group promises to "swing" the outcome in so many state contests simultaneously.

31. See, for example, the *Irish World and Industrial Liberator*, July 26, 1884, 4; Schlesinger, ed. *History of U.S. Political Parties* Vol. 2, 1574.
32. The term "System of 1896" belongs to Walter Dean Burnham. See his "The System of 1896: An Analysis."

This second pattern of pivotal politics provides the backdrop for my case studies of the Federal Trade Commission Act and the Public Utility Holding Company Act. The specific electoral characteristics of these cases will be detailed in Chapters 3 and 4. For now, it suffices to say that in the period between 1900 and 1928, the structure of partisan allegiance produced some of the more consistently lopsided presidential elections in the nation's history. Republican ascendence in presidential politics was disrupted only twice – in 1912 and 1916 – owing largely to the disaffection of midwestern and western Republicans who left their party in droves to support progressive presidential candidates. Democrats in power responded to this structural opportunity in typically Downsian fashion, embracing many of the policy preferences of this national median voting bloc. Similarly, in the presidential election of 1932, Democratic strategists placed enormous emphasis on cultivating what they called "progressivism with a capital *R*," this in the hope of reconstructing Woodrow Wilson's South and West reelection coalition of 1916. Franklin Roosevelt also saw the holding of these progressive Republicans in the Democratic column as vital to his reelection in 1936.

As suggested earlier, the capacity of the electoral college to effect political change is perhaps more contingent than many of the institutional features of American politics. Yet I believe that few of our national institutions have proved more dramatic in their impact. In this book I intend to show that electoral college constraints and national party competition were proximate causes behind a dramatic shift in Democratic commitments of interest and ideology. In particular, they help to explain the transformation of the Democratic party from an organization committed to limited government and states' rights, to one pledged to central state authority and activism. In addition, electoral college incentives help to explain why a largely agrarian and antimonopolistic Democratic party nevertheless presided over the "corporate reconstruction of American capitalism" with the passage of the Federal Trade Commission Act of 1914.

Party Leaders and the State-building Process

In addition to its electoral college focus, an integral aspect of my party system framework is an effort to theorize more adequately the role of party processes in American state development. In particular, my analysis gives pride of place to the semiautonomous activities of party leaders. Over the course of the next three chapters, I will examine the legislative intervention of party leaders to deflect longstanding commitments of interest and ideology in favor of regulatory policies consistent with national party objectives. I hope that this extended consideration of party involvement in the politics of regulatory choice will help to fill several gaps in existing literature. First, at a descriptive level, this book provides a series of analytically focused narratives of the political processes by which these landmark policies were determined. More theoretically, I hope to rethink the role that political parties have played in shaping the content of American regulatory principles and the character of its regulatory institutions. Political parties were not simply the organizational backdrop against which a new American state had to be extorted. Rather, they were the principal medium through which substantive and institutional choices about the American political economy were ultimately made. Finally, I believe that the empirical study of political party processes will shed needed light on the neglected role of party leaders, their distinctive role in the structuring of political choice, and therefore their unique contribution to the historical trajectory of American regulatory state development.

Conceptualizing Significant Party Behavior

In a provocative 1993 article, political scientist Keith Krehbiel has thrown down the gauntlet to scholars insisting on the explanatory importance of American political parties to legislative choice.[33] Krehbiel issues a series of challenges to proponents of party. The most important of these concerns is conceptual. Krehbiel asks, what constitutes *significant* party behavior? His response (a correct one), is that if our interest is in policy-relevant legislative actions, then party behavior is significant when it has an effect on legislative outcomes *independent of individual legislator preferences*. To have theoretical significance, that is, party processes should yield policy-related outputs we would not expect in their absence. Simply to demonstrate that Republicans and Democrats line up on opposite sides on a series of roll-call votes is an insufficient demonstration of party's causal importance. Statistical models of legislative behavior may yield large and significant party coefficients, but the exact meaning of that party behavior remains unresolved. The central question lingers: What motivates a legislator's policy choice? As Krehbiel puts it,

> In casting apparently partisan votes, do individual legislators vote with fellow party members *in spite of their disagreement* about the policy in question, or do they vote with fellow party members *because of their agreement* about the policy in question? In the former case, parties are significant in

33. Krehbiel, "Where's the Party?"

a potentially policy-relevant way. That is, their partisan behavior may well result in a collective choice that differs from that which would occur in the absence of partisan behavior. In the latter case, however, parties as groups are surely less policy-relevant in terms of the difference they make relative to a non-party baseline.[34]

Krehbiel's principal foil is the "conditional party government" (CPG) model of congressional party organization.[35] In the CPG model, strong legislative party organizations emerge when the policy preferences of party members are homogeneous. The more uniform a caucus member-ship's preferences become, the more willing they will be to delegate significant power to party leaders to secure shared goals. Of course one might reasonably wonder, why does a party with a unified set of prefer-ences need a strong party organization at all? Like minds and large numbers would seem to be a sufficient prescription for legislative success. But one of the core insights of contemporary analytic social science is that shared preferences do not translate unproblematically into preferred collective outcomes. In the language of rational choice, collective action and social choice problems may interdict the attainment of common goals. The function of party leaders, in this regard, is to resolve these collective dilemmas and facilitate the translation of shared preferences into preferred outcomes. This is a critical point. In the CPG model, party leaders help members to realize their shared preferences; they do not use their discretionary power to alter, challenge, or in any other way impede the satisfaction of those wants. But, as Krehbiel suggests, the CPG con-ception of parties simply provides a more sophisticated description of the process by which majority party members are finally able to cast votes consistent with their individual preferences. In the end, it remains legislators' policy-relevant preferences that explain legislative choice – not the independent effect of party upon those preferences.

Krehbiel has framed the conceptual debate exactly right. If parties matter in a policy-relevant way, it should be because they generate legislative outcomes different from those that arise in their absence. In an effort to sort through this issue, one prominent body of research has var-iously sought to ascertain whether legislative choices conform more closely to the preference of the median member of jurisdictionally rele-

34. Ibid., 238.
35. See Rohde, *Parties and Leaders in the Postreform House*; Aldrich, *Why Parties?*; Sinclair, *Legislators, Leaders, and Lawmaking*; Aldrich and Rohde, "The Transition to Republican Rule in the House: Implications for Theories of Congressional Politics." A variant on the conditional party government thesis is the party cartel model elabo-rated in Cox and McCubbins, *Legislative Leviathan*.

vant committees, the median chamber legislator, or the majority party's caucus median – with evidence of the latter indicating the presence of a substantial party effect.[36] While this line of analysis has produced a lively debate among scholars, it has yet to yield a common consensus on any particular conclusions. Moreover, even assuming the uncovering of a significant party effect, there are reasons to remain unsatisfied with this particular approach to the study of party. For, in the end, it is an approach that continues to conceptualize organized party behavior as the coordinated action of a like-minded party caucus.

This book lays an empirical basis for a more stringent conception of party organization. In the case chapters that follow, the party behavior we will observe can be regarded as significant not simply because it generates outcomes that diverge from the preferences of committee and chamber medians. More dramatically, party behavior is significant because it yields collective party choices that also diverge from the median preference of the majority party and toward those of party leaders. In the end, it is because chamber parties act both cohesively and contrary to the preferences of a majority of its rank and file, but consistent with known leadership preferences, that I conclude that party organization has mattered substantively to the politics of regulatory choice and the trajectory of American political development.

Both conceptually and empirically, then, the claim that party leaders may redirect the legislative process away from preferred choices of a party majority directs us toward the complex, creative, and discretionary world of these institutional and organizational elites. Several questions immediately arise: From where do leadership policy preferences derive? Under what conditions will party leaders advance policy goals that run orthogonal to those of a caucus majority? By what methods do party leaders attempt to impose their choices on their rank and file? What are the conditions and limits of their success? Existing theories leave us poorly positioned to answer such questions. Indeed, in most rational choice models of legislative parties, the objection is immediately raised: Why would party leaders *ever* pursue legislative outcomes at odds with the preferences of the median caucus member? Party leaders are, after all, selected by their rank and file and periodically stand for reselection by their party caucus to retain leadership positions. This electoral connection in theory should bind leaders closely to the party median and induce them to act as faithful agents of the party caucus.

36. An excellent overview of this debate can be found in Shepsle and Weingast, eds. *Positive Theories of Congressional Institutions.* Also see Schickler, "Institutional Change in the House of Representatives, 1867–1986."

The findings of this book invite us to qualify our conception of party leaders in several particulars, all of which lead back to the conclusion that the responsibilities of party leaders are more complicated and multifaceted than contemporary, agent-based theories of party leadership allow. In the first place, arguably the leaders' primary responsibility is to secure and stabilize their party's hold on the reins of chamber power. Of course, leaders are motivated by more than a selfless concern for party welfare. Their own institutional power, for example, is conditioned by their success or failure in this regard. But regardless of their precise motivation, the critical point is that the responsibility to advance their party's chamber majority status may push party leaders to pursue policies that run orthogonal to the preferences of the caucus median.[37] Secondly, the exercise of effective governing power (as opposed to simple chamber power) implies a concern for the partisan control of institutions outside of one's particular institution. In the context of this book, an external institution of obvious interest to legislative parties is the presidency. Here, concerns over the distribution of patronage, national party reputation and presidential coattails, control over the executive veto, and a say in the local administration of federal law enforcement may each motivate a set of leadership policy preferences that run contrary to the preferences of the party median.[38]

Thirdly, current conceptions of "parties in government" are almost without exception chamber-specific. We have numerous models of House party organization and a few that address party organization in the Senate, but partisan interconnections between governing institutions are rarely elaborated. In particular, the presidency remains poorly integrated in our conceptions of party organization and legislative choice. Presidents and Congress are typically modeled as institutional rivals who inhabit distinct spheres in a world of separated powers, rather than as a network of political actors joined by mutual interest and electoral fate because of their common party ties. Of course, each vantage point captures something essential about the governing process and there is no reason to choose one to the exclusion of the other. But as we will see in

---

37. This point is also explored in Bawn, "Congressional Party Leadership: Utilitarian versus Majoritarian Incentives." Moreover, historically, party leaders have often had career goals that lead them outside the institution they inhabit, ambitions which should lead them to cultivate reputations and constituencies outside of their party caucus.

38. Recent work has begun to recognize the more complicated functions of legislative party leaders, such as the need to build and retain their party's national reputation. But as yet, few have seriously explored the theoretical implications and substantive consequences of such a position. See Cox and McCubbins, *Legislative Leviathan*.

the chapters that follow, while chamber-specific models are helpful for their analytic simplicity and empirical tractability, they distort the rich and theoretically important sets of interconnections that tie party leaders across governing spheres and complicate the set of preferences that chamber-specific party leaders hold in relation to their rank and file. In two of our three case studies (the Federal Trade Commission Act and the "death sentence" for public utility holding companies), the policies that Democrats in Congress would eventually secure originated with presidential party leaders (Wilson and Roosevelt) and ran directly contrary to the revealed preferences of the Democratic majority. And even in the one case in which the president does not play a significant role in the formation of congressional leadership preferences (the Interstate Commerce Act), *the presidency does* play a role, this owing to the simple fact that legislative party leaders placed such a premium on keeping that institution out of the hands of the opposition party.

Democratic Organization and Party Leadership in Three Historical Eras

As we will see in the course of this book, the contours of Democratic party organization and the specific composition of its leadership strata are themselves historically contingent. Each of our studies of regulatory choice tracks a particular configuration of legitimate party authority, even as all three consistently rely upon a set of linkages that tie the presidency and national party incentives to legislative party leaders and congressional policy processes. The evolution of Democratic party organization tracked by this book is itself propelled along by broad changes in the institutional organization of Congress and the functions of the presidency. Party organization changes over time not only because the internal structure of these institutions is constantly changing, but because the precise manner in which Congress and the executive branch articulate with each other in the processes of government is always changing as well. The following discussion is intended to provide readers with a brief overview of each of the three eras of Democratic party organization covered in this book. I have somewhat tentatively labeled these periods "the era of congressional pluralism," "the era of unified party government," and "the era of presidential party leadership."

The Era of Congressional Pluralism: Institutional Rivalry between Traditional and Emergent Sources of Leadership. Our first encounter with Democratic leadership is in some ways the most interesting, both because of the relatively marginal status of the presidency to the Gilded Age policy process and because of the still nascent character of legislative party authority in the 1880s. As we will see in Chapter 2, even though in possession of considerable resources, House party leaders – and in particular, the Speaker of the House – still confronted substantial resistence to their assertion of policy leadership. In only a few years time, under Speakers like Thomas Reed, Charles Crisp, and Joe Cannon, the perfection of Speaker-led party government would reach its apex. The Speaker's authority over committee assignments, the chamber calendar, and floor proceedings would make the holder of that office truly master of the House. But at the time railroad regulation was under consideration, the leadership of the Speaker and his assertion of policy authority were still relatively novel, and hence contested.

In the case of the Interstate Commerce Act, the party process we will observe can be characterized as one of congressional elite pluralism, one in which an emergent party organization is set in opposition to traditional sources of authority and established modes of legislative procedure. Legislative decision making takes on the character of a competitive struggle between institutional rivals for control of the chamber agenda. Democratic party leaders held potent agenda-setting powers through which national party objectives might be pressed: a standing Rules Committee with authority over the flow of House business, control over the allocation of committee assignments, and discretionary control of floor recognition (to be used as a system of reward and punishment). But as we will observe in considerable detail, party leaders looking to pass railroad commission legislation were quickly challenged by party rivals brandishing their own institutional weapons. Committees, and in particular committee chairs, possessed their own privileges and agenda-setting powers, along with substantial party constituencies by which they might resist encroachment upon their traditional prerogatives by these increasingly assertive party leaders.

The Senate will receive only perfunctory attention in this overview. Most importantly, this is because it was in the House of Representatives that Democratic opposition to the independent railroad commission was strongest. But as well, the situation facing Senate Democrats was substantially different because, unlike the House, they were the chamber's minority party. This said, as we will see, the actions of Senate Democratic leaders would prove critical to the passage of the ICA. Moreover, it is in the Senate that we will observe our most tangible connection to national party interests. In particular, national party responsibilities would be carried forward by the new Democratic vice president, Thomas A. Hendricks, acting in his capacity as president of the Senate. Equally important was the leadership of Senator Arthur Pue Gorman, a Democrat and the former chairman of the executive committee of the Democratic National Committee and director of Grover Cleveland's successful 1884 presidential campaign. Through the actions of both of these men, Senate Democrats would assume a prominent role in both the framing and the final passage of the ICA – this despite their party's chamber minority status.

The Era of Unified Party Government.   Democratic party organization would reach its zenith in the Progressive era, dominating its traditional institutional rivals (committees and committee chairs) and subordinating them to the vindication of national party objectives. Broad-scale institutional changes had left their mark on the precise configuration of party authority. In the aftermath of the revolt against Speaker-led party government in 1910, Democrats would institute their own variant of legislative party government through the instrument of the party caucus. As a consequence of the overthrow of Republican leader Joseph G. Cannon, the Speaker was divested of both his place on the Rules Committee and his control over committee appointments. Under Democratic rule, authority shifted away from the Speaker further still and toward the chairman of the Ways and Means Committee, on the one hand, and the Democratic party caucus on the other. Legislation by binding caucus agreement was the hallmark of this brief period of Democratic party government.

But while this form of party organization was highly disciplined, it lacked the directive leadership that had been a hallmark of party government in the era of the great Republican Speakers. That new vital center would be supplied through the office of the presidency, a product of transformations in that office first begun under Theodore Roosevelt and subsequently by Woodrow Wilson. In the process, interbranch party relations were recast, in effect transferring primary responsibility for the management of national party concerns to the most interested institutional actor – the president. The national rise to prominence of the office of the presidency allowed Wilson in particular to exploit the party leadership vacuum left in the wake of the decline of the Speaker's powers. The Democratic president would emerge as the chief engine for igniting the public imagination, framing national debate, and focusing public opinion. As a consequence, he would earn the right to enter into negotiations over the direction of the party policy on a plane of relative equality with legislative party leaders.

In my analysis of the Federal Trade Commission Act (Chapter 3), the change in the relative position of the presidency and Congress is clearly manifest. So too is the alteration in relationship between committee chairs and party authorities, which only a generation earlier had produced an intense rivalry for chamber ascendency in battle over the railroad commission. This will most clearly be seen in the behavior of the chairman of the House Committee on Commerce, William C. Adamson. Adamson had strenuously opposed the creation of a regulatory trade commission, as had a large Democratic majority on his committee. But while Adamson's preferences were by no means ignored by party leaders, once the decision had been made to embrace the FTC as party legislation, Adamson quietly fell into line behind Wilson and the Democratic caucus, declining to explore alternative political avenues in the manner of his Gilded Age committee predecessors. Indeed, in the end, the fusion of presidential leadership with binding caucus action would combine to affect the starkest reversal of party policy we will observe in this book – with virtually no dissenting Democratic votes.

The Era of Presidential Party Leadership. By the time of the New Deal and our final case, the Public Utility Holding Company Act, the institutions of the presidency and the Congress (in particular the House) have once again been dramatically transformed, with new permutations in the configuration of party authority again the product. With the election of Franklin Roosevelt, the presidency clearly emerges as the motor force driving national party leadership. The explanation for this development is twofold. First, the *capacity* for presidential domination of party had been put in place by the continued development of the presidency as an institution, one which had harnessed the now substantial talent and expertise of the executive branch to draft complex legislation, press Congress on behalf of that legislation, and mobilize mass opinion through the use of new forms of technological outreach. With Franklin Roosevelt, we will encounter a president with both the institutional capacity and personal willingness to assert leadership over the Democratic party in Congress, a virtuoso performance that would leave subsequent presidents "in the shadow of FDR."[39]

But secondly, the *need* for presidential party leadership had also grown enormously because of dramatic changes in congressional organization that had taken place since the Progressive Era. In the case of the Public Utility Holding Company Act, the institutionalization of the seniority system and the rise of an autonomous Rules Committee have now placed clear limits on the capacity of traditional institutional leaders – both legislative party leaders and committee chairs – to act on behalf of national

39. Leuchtenburg, *In the Shadow of FDR.*

party objectives. If leadership in this period continues to conform to notions of a party process it is because Roosevelt continued to try to affect policy choice through the Democratic party – at least through his first term – involving committee chairs and legislative party leaders in the planning of Democratic party programs, though in a manner that clearly indicates the subordination of congressional party leaders in the framing of policies bearing on national party goals. In this last case of regulatory choice, we will also begin to observe a palpable tension between presidential and congressional party leaders. With resources and initiative passing to the presidency, a sense of institutional leaders inhabiting distinct and separate spheres is beginning to harden, with rivalries, jealousies, and conflicting electoral incentives compounding the formal constitutional division between these two party wings. In the years after Roosevelt, divided government and the phenomenal growth of the institutional presidency would further complicate the differences between branches, eventuating in definitively contemporary form of presidential leadership by "going public," a coercive strategy that deemphasizes traditional mechanisms of partisan compromise for threats of electoral reprisal through opinion mobilization to legislators who resist presidential initiatives.[40]

Presidential Sources of Party Discipline

We have discussed the era of congressional party government and some of the resources at the disposal of legislative leaders to secure choices consistent with national party objectives. It now remains to consider some of the sources of party discipline that derive from presidential sources. Some are, of course, particular to a historical period. For instance, in the Gilded Age, an era in which parties controlled access to the use of their party label, congressmen might find themselves denied renomination if they were too active in their opposition to national party initiatives. The most dramatic example of this form of party discipline occurred in 1894 and involved the young Congressman William Jennings Bryan of Nebraska. At President Grover Cleveland's insistence, Bryan was denied renomination by the leadership of the Nebraska state Democratic party for his vocal opposition to administration efforts to repeal the Sherman Silver Purchase Act.[41]

More common to all three periods under consideration, national coalition management involved the judicious administration of patronage and policy. Prior to the Civil War, the recipe for Democratic coalition

40. Kernell, *Going Public.*   41. Koenig, *Bryan.*

maintenance was centrally that of giving policy to the South and patronage to the North.[42] In the postbellum era this began to change, especially as the electoral position of the Democrats in the party system required them to cultivate partisan allies outside the solid Democratic South. Nonetheless, regardless of which side of the Civil War divide, patronage was crucial to the maintenance of party discipline. Grants of patronage allowed legislators and their local and state party organizations to consolidate their hold on the locality. The withholding of patronage, on the other hand, increased the vulnerability of the legislator to successful electoral challenge. Senator Robert M. La Follette captured well the disciplinary dimension of patronage on legislative behavior. An outsider to the mainstream of his own Republican party, La Follette wrote as if recalling a painful memory:

> No threat is necessary. No word regarding appointments need be spoken. The recalcitrant legislator will have no difficulty in construing the ominous silence which enshrouds the whole subject of patronage when he attempts to discuss recommendations for appointments which he has filed in due course. He will be sorely tempted to yield to the Executive on legislation for he is harried early and late by the party demand from his state or district for the change in political tenure expected to follow a change in administration.[43]

Despite the advance of civil service, patronage was still a critical instrument of congressional party cohesion in the 1930s. By one count, 50 percent of Franklin Roosevelt's mail upon taking office involved patronage requests. As governor of New York, Roosevelt learned to maximize leverage over his legislative party by administering the patronage as slowly as possible. This technique would serve him well as president in obtaining congressional party support for controversial New Deal legislation.[44]

Beyond the stick of patronage, policy advantages accrue to legislators when a president of their party is in power. Through the use of the veto, opposition presidents can be serious obstacles to congressional policy initiatives. Especially as presidents grew in power and authority over the course of the period in question, and policy initiative shifted from the legislative branch to the executive, influence over the character of the legislative agenda required the installation of a sympathetic leader in the White House, a condition which, all things considered, was more likely to occur when the occupant bore the same party label.

42. Polk, *The Diary of James Knox Polk* Vol. 1, 369.
43. *La Follette's Magazine* 7 (January 1915), 3.
44. Freidel, *FDR and the South*, 47.

Equally important, successful presidents have coattails. Congressmen whose seats are in jeopardy have an incentive to ensure that their party's president is perceived by the electorate as popular and successful. To account for the spectacle of congressional obeisance to Woodrow Wilson's policy preferences, the *Saturday Evening Post* offered an explanation based on a fundamental electoral equation. "The explanation is simple," the periodical observed. "The President stands for success. Everybody in Congress wants votes. It is believed the President can command votes. Hence the deference to him."[45] Similarly, Franklin Roosevelt's popular success in his first two years in office was such as to generate one of the few instances in American political history of a president's party gaining seats in an off-year election. The importance of the popular president as an electoral resource for congressional candidates in 1934 was such that, by one estimation, "nearly two thirds [of the Seventy-fourth Congress] had been elected on their pledge to back the purposes of the New Deal."[46] Coattails were of particular interest to the most electorally vulnerable legislators. In the period covered by this book, insecure Democrats came most frequently from outside the South, legislators who owed their seat to calamities befalling the opposition party (Mugwump defections, the rise of progressive third-party challengers; economic depression). Successful presidential action was not only essential to satisfy pivotal national coalition groups, it was crucial as well to these legislators looking to transform their own fragile victories into secure bases of power.

Finally, the same party system dynamics that subjected Democratic presidential tenure to uncertainty, and that afflicted the status of many congressional Democrats from the Northeast and Midwest, also affected the fortunes of southern Democrats in very tangible ways. As just suggested, Democrats in Congress in the first administrations of Woodrow Wilson and Franklin Roosevelt owed their newfound majority-party status to the same configuration of forces that thrust Democratic candidates into the White House. The breakdown of the Republican party in the Progressive Era and the Great Depression in 1929 brought the Democrats to power in Congress by bringing nonsouthern Democrats to power in traditional Republican strongholds of the Northeast and the Midwest. And because of the seniority system, southern Democrats benefited disproportionately from these circumstances. As New Deal historian Frank Freidel stated the matter, southern Democrats "had long been in the minority; they enjoyed power and wished to retain it through

45. *Saturday Evening Post*, August 1, 1914, 22.
46. Robinson, *The Roosevelt Leadership, 1933–1945*, 163.

continuing in the majority."[47] Like it or not, the maintenance of their newfound institutional power depended on the continued return to Congress of nonsouthern Democrats, fellow partisans whose policy objectives could clash radically with the conservative ideological and policy beliefs of southerners.

Electoral College Incentives, Party Processes, and the Decline of Agrarian Democracy

How did Democratic coalition-building imperatives shape the development of the American regulatory state? Of most consequence, I believe it foreclosed the possibility of a distinctively agrarian Democratic "response to industrialism" during America's transition from proprietary to corporate capitalism. The Democratic party articulated a distinctive response to the "railroad problem" of the 1880s and the "trust question" of the Progressive Era. This approach had its roots in the long-standing Jeffersonian ideal of a producers' republic, one predicated on the maintenance of small economic units, with ownership distributed widely among the citizenry.[48] The Democratic approach also articulated

47. Freidel, *FDR and the South*, 48. Similarly, to congressional Southern Democrats under Wilson, fashioning a Democratic program "that would warrant their re-election and continued congressional leadership was to them an all-important matter." Grantham, "Southern Congressional Leaders and the New Freedom, 1913–1917," 443; see also Link, "The South and the 'New Freedom': An Interpretation" and Abrams, "Woodrow Wilson and the Southern Congressmen, 1913–1916." Abrams writes, "Southern Democrats generally would not cross the one man [Wilson] who had a maximum of national respect and could give them the rewards of national power." (437).

48. Jefferson maintained that the moral and political virtue of a citizenry was premised on the wide ownership of productive property. The concentration of wealth and the spread of wage-labor relationships Jefferson saw as spawning subservience and dependency, conditions corrosive of republican values. See Jefferson, "Manufactures," *Notes on the State of Virginia*, 216–17. See also, McCoy, *The Elusive Republic*, 13–17. The original Jeffersonian vision was primarily agricultural – a republic of small farm holders. But within the Democratic party, the concept became more expansive, adapting to the dramatic socioeconomic changes of the nineteenth century. By the "Age of Jackson," the Jeffersonian ideal of a producers' republic had been broadened to include yeoman farmers, small-business owners, master craftsmen, and skilled artisans. During the Progressive era, agrarian Democrats would continue to speak of the producers' republic, though it increasingly assumed the character of a millennial vision, with Jefferson assuming the role of Christian prophet: "Let every man and woman who loves the democratic kingdom act on the square, . . . Let us love and work and work and love, and Jefferson's dream shall come true, when every man, woman and child shall have an equal chance in the land and the old people die happy and not be starved to death through the oppressors' greed [sic]." *The Commoner*, November 24, 1911, 4. On the antebellum producers' vision and its relationship to the Democratic party, see Hattam, *Labor Visions and State Power*, ch. 3.

a clear stance toward the power of both corporate economic actors and the American national state: It distrusted the intentions of both, and it sought to limit the penetration of each into the fabric of traditional economic and social relations.

Agrarian Democrats confronted the challenge of modern industrial organization with ideas and ideals rooted in traditional antimonopolism. Perhaps the most important manifestation of this ideological commitment was the attachment to a policy of free and unrestricted competition in interstate commerce. This reliance upon the principle of mandatory competition was itself a reflection of the agrarian conviction that trusts and monopolies were the product of unnatural advantages rather than efficient organization and market behavior. In the age of Andrew Jackson, monopolies had been the arbitrary dispensations of state legislatures. The state conferred upon a privileged few the right to unilaterally set prices, regulate output, and exclude competitors from the market. Such monopolies, as those excluded believed, were inimical to the right of citizens to employ their labor as they saw fit. To a majority of agrarians, palpably little had changed since the Jacksonian era. Favoritism and corruption were still thought to explain the disadvantaged market position of the farmer and the small-business owner relative to the large corporation, the combine, and the monopoly. Nor were such explanations without factual basis. However, to the extent that these large businesses owed their position in the market to competitive factors, the agrarian prescription of *still more competition* was at best an ineffective solution to the trust problem. But perhaps worse still, by encouraging mergers and tighter forms of combination, such laws worked to accelerate the forces of concentration in the American economy.[49]

Still, the rule of free and unrestricted competition was no simple backward-looking defense of laissez-faire – with its implications of government noninterference and private-sector voluntarism. Rather, through it agrarians pushed an aggressive regulatory stance, one which would actively employ state coercion to compel business competition in the marketplace. More concretely, agrarian Democratic regulatory proposals would subject corporate actors to a legislatively prescribed code of public behavior: strict and detailed rules intended to subordinate corporate welfare to the welfare of the nation's farmers and small-town dwellers. In the spirit of Democratic antistatism, these agrarian proposals turned away from the various visions of national administrative

---

49. On the role of American antitrust law as an inducement to corporate mergers, see Freyer, *Regulating Big Business*.

power. They were wary of building up the power of the state, apprehensive of new institutions with the capacity to impose their arbitrary will upon a free populace. Instead, they looked to the maintenance of local units of authority. When a national response was needed, agrarian Democrats looked mainly to their representatives in Congress: to statutory prohibitions cast in a moral language so simple and unqualified – the Ten Commandments were often invoked as a model – that the interpretive scope left to sophisticated corporate lawyers and conservative judges would be severely limited. As one prominent agrarian leader put it in criticizing the Interstate Commerce Act,

> Suppose the great Lawgiver had constructed the Ten Commandments with the same uncertainty. Suppose he had said: "Thou shalt not steal; thou shalt not bear false witness; thou shalt not covet – contemporaneously or under substantially similar circumstances and conditions"; or suppose, at the conclusion of the decalogue the following provision had been added: "Provided, however, that upon application to the high priest or ecclesiastical commissioner appointed under the provisions of this act persons so designated may be authorized to cheat, steal, bear false witness, or covet, and said commission may from time to time prescribe the extent to which said persons may be relieved from any or all of said commandments." Under such circumstances would not the world have been without moral law from Moses to Cullom and from Mount Sinai to Pike's Peak?[50]

During the battle for national railroad regulation agrarian Democrats sought to bypass the federal courts altogether, looking instead to enforcement of congressional prohibitions in the more responsive system of state courts.

Supporters of the regulatory commission approached the twin problem of corporate prerogative and state strength from a different angle. To

---

50. Haynes, *James Baird Weaver*, 251. In criticizing Theodore Roosevelt's solution to the "trust question," William Jennings Bryan wrote: "His whole bias is wrong. He is more Hamiltonian than Hamilton himself.... No other president ever felt so rebellious against the restrictions which our forefathers thought it wise to throw about the executive." Bryan summed up the Rooseveltian approach as involving "first the absorption by the general government of much of the power now exercised by the states; second, the absorption by the federal executive of much of the power now exercised by other departments, and; third, a president who will be looked to as the steward of the people." "This is not popular government," Bryan wrote, "it is despotism." During the election of 1912, *The Commoner* called Roosevelt's proposal for a federal regulatory commission "the most dangerous plan ever presented to the American people. 'It is a step toward socialism,' [Bryan] declared, 'and by placing complete power in the hands of a few men it would give the predatory interests still more powerful incentive to enter politics and elect a president.'" *The Commoner*, July 26, 1912, 1; September 27, 1912, 6.

these advocates of national administrative power, neither unquenchable greed nor corporate malevolence were responsible for the problems of industrial capitalism. Rather, the socially destructive aspects of corporate behavior, such as predatory pricing, were inherent in the competitive dynamic of oligopolistic markets. Years of inadequate government supervision, they argued, had culminated in a host of pathological practices that, while perhaps rational from the perspective of the individual corporation, were disruptive of the system as a whole, wreaking havoc on the economic livelihood of hundreds of thousands of Americans in the process. The solution advanced by these institution builders was to harness the untapped authority of the national state, to build up expertise and administrative capacity, and with it to "raise the plane of competitive action" in the marketplace by processes of bureaucratic rulemaking and enforcement.[51]

Twice in the course of this critical developmental debate the Democratic party assumed control of the national government.[52] In each instance, the programmatic goals of antimonopoly agrarianism brushed up against the logic of party coalition-building. And in each case, the rules of electoral college competition, in conjunction with the structure of party competition, were severely at cross purposes with the goals of the Democratic Jeffersonian vision. In the Gilded Age, the structure of presidential elections systematically worked to advantage interests in the pivotal northeastern states, making the Democratic party an inefficacious policy vehicle for interests held by the agrarian base of the party. Indeed, one can see in the rising tide of agrarian revolt, so prevalent in the politics of the 1880s and 1890s, a highly conditioned response to the era's competitive party system and the seemingly inexorable electoral logic that pulled both Democratic and Republican party leaders toward a

51. Adams, "The Relation of the State to Industrial Action." Quoted in Skowronek, *Building a New American State*, 133. In an editorial written for *The Outlook* in 1912, Theodore Roosevelt distinguished the progressive state-builders' approach to the "trust question" from that of Democratic party in this fashion: "The methods proposed by the democratic [sic] party for dealing with great national problems are the methods of individualism, of disintegration, and of states' rights. The democratic party and Mr. [Woodrow] Wilson emphasize the limitations of the power of the nation to deal with these problems, . . . This, too, is the substance of the democratic party's proposal with regard to trusts – not regulation, but dissolution; not control but prosecution, . . . The progressives can not accept the democratic ticket and the democratic platform . . . because they believe that the trust question can not be solved by the slow, laborious methods of civil and criminal law suits, but only by the vigorous exercise of power in the national government through a strong and efficient administrative bureau." Quoted in *The Commoner*, July 26, 1912, 10–11.

52. In order to keep the focus on the cases at hand, I am ignoring the Democratic victory of 1892.

handful of electorally pivotal northeastern states. The formation of the Greenback party and later of the People's party, as well as the growing schism between "gold" and "silver" Democrats – all attest to an increasing frustration among western agrarians with the structure of interest articulation in the "third-party system."

Coalition-building imperatives were no less constraining on Democrats in the Progressive Era. As I will endeavor to show in Chapter 3, the Democratic party of Woodrow Wilson came to power committed to the statutory repeal of the Supreme Court's "rule of reason" decision, to the limitation of corporate size, and to the enumeration of the conditions under which corporations would be allowed to conduct their interstate business, with the application of stiff criminal punishment for corporate violations. Yet, in control of national governing authority, the minority Democratic party found itself forced to confront the Downsian dilemma: to choose between programmatic purity and the necessity of attracting interests outside traditional Democratic constituencies. Interests that, in this case, had shown themselves willing to defect from traditional Republican loyalties to vote for the Progressive party of Theodore Roosevelt.

To conclude this discussion, a credible (though admittedly speculative) case can be made that American regulatory state development might have occurred along a substantially different trajectory had the structure of presidential party competition reinforced, and not retarded, the policy proclivities of the Democratic party in power; that is, had coalition-building constraints operated to bring electorally pivotal regulatory preferences into harmony with agrarian antimonopolists. Needless to say, counterfactual historical claims are intrinsically contentious.[53] For this reason a quick juxtaposition of the case of New Deal utility holding company regulation is at least suggestive. This case contrast throws into relief the developmental possibilities attached to a context in which Democratic antimonopoly goals had been fortified by the party system. In the case of the Public Utility Holding Company Act, coalition-building considerations compelled Franklin Roosevelt to push Democratic policy far to the left of his party's regulatory stance toward the holding company giants. As I will develop in Chapter 4, Roosevelt

---

53. Nonetheless, considerable recent attention has been given to the claim that the developmental path taken by the American political economy in the late nineteenth century and early twentieth century was not foreordained, but rather was historically contingent, the product of political conflict mediated by the peculiar organization of the American state. Most recently, see Gerald Berk's thought-provoking book, *Alternative Tracks: The Constitution of American Industrial Order, 1865–1917*. Also significant in this regard is Ritter, *Goldbugs and Greenbacks*.

marshaled all the resources at his disposal in pursuit of the statutory dissolution of all public utility holding companies, pressing his attack against intransigent eastern and southern Democrats in Congress. In advancing the antimonopoly goals of agrarian radicals with such fervency Roosevelt was endeavoring to hold the allegiance of midwestern Republican "power progressives" whose support he considered vital to the construction of a new Democratic majority coalition. One can imagine the consequences for the evolution of Democratic policy had party leaders in the years of Grover Cleveland and Woodrow Wilson been subject to the same incentives to embrace the agrarian antimonopoly solution to the "railroad problem" and the "trust question." Under such conditions it is not unreasonable to imagine that a significantly different pattern of American regulatory state development might have been forthcoming.

The Structure of Analysis in the Chapters to Come: Political Structure, Party Agency, and Regulatory Choice

Let me conclude this introductory chapter with a brief note on the organization of the analysis to come. Each of the three case chapters in this book is organized to provide the answers to several empirical questions, questions that push the analysis forward from initial party needs to final legislative choice. The first question asks, what was the character of electoral challenge faced by the Democratic party in its attempt to retain control of the presidency? In each case, electoral college incentives and party system features will be specified to clarify the nature of the electoral challenge that threatened the consolidation of Democratic electoral power.

A second set of questions asks, which voting bloc was perceived to hold the balance of power in presidential party politics and what were the structural and organizational factors that contributed to the conferral of swing-group status upon them? In most presidential elections, any number of groups might plausibly claim to represent the balance of power in national politics. Why are some groups ultimately successful in persuading party leaders that their votes are pivotal to sustaining their hold on to governing power?

The third question asks, what were the regulatory policy preferences of swing groups and how did these square with the preferences of the party in power? This is a critical part of the analysis not only because it organized the structure of regulatory choice, but because it also establishes the critical conflict that would pit party leaders against their rank and file.

The fourth question asks, what were the key elements of party organization in the period in question and which organizational actors comprised the relevant set of party leaders? A subsidiary task of this discussion is to relate changes in party organization and leadership composition to historical changes in the organization of Congress and the functions of the presidency. Parties function in part to integrate national governing processes and facilitate the communication of shared interests across formally separate units. Therefore, the precise features of these institutional domains should inform party organization and shape the character of party intervention in any historical period.

The final question asks, what are the specifics of the legislative policy process and of party-leader intervention? Here we will examine the particular strategies adopted by party leaders to advance regulatory options consistent with national party objects and to contain the passage of those that were not.

2

Swing States, Business Mugwumps, and the Interstate Commerce Act of 1887

For more than twelve years past the balance of power in the State of New York has been held by a large unattached vote, which belongs to neither political organization. We have in the State, probably 600,000 voters who will vote for the Democratic party nominee whom you may nominate. We have about 580,000 voters who will vote the Republican ticket under any and all circumstances. Now, outside of both these organizations there are a hundred thousand men in the State of New York who do not care a snap of their finger whether the Republican party or the Democratic party, as such, shall carry the election. They vote in every election according to the issues and the candidates presented. These men absolutely hold the control of the politics of New York in their hands. They are the balance of power. You must have their votes or you cannot win.

> Excerpt from address seconding the nomination of Grover Cleveland for 1884 Democratic presidential nominee[1]

[The contrasting approaches of Samuel S. Cox and Abraham Hewitt on the subject of railroad regulation] disclose the conflicting tendencies at work in the bosom of the Democratic party. Mr. Cox may, we suppose, without disrespect be regarded as representing the unthinking mass of the party. . . . His speeches . . . seem to express . . . the feeling of the rank and file of his party. . . . That feeling is that the railways are grinding monopolies, and that they can be regulated in the minutest particular by Congress. . . .

Mr. Hewitt, on the other hand, ["a business man, familiar not only with the affairs of railways, but with those of the merchants and manufacturers,"] . . . recognizes the responsibility of his party for the use it makes of the power intrusted to it. He knows . . . that there are great evils in the management of the railroads . . . ; but he sees the madness of trying to run the vast, complex, and delicate business of the railways by specific provisions of law. The Democracy was kept out of power by precisely the reckless

1. "Address of Hon. Edgar K. Apgar, of New York." *Official Proceedings of the National Democratic Convention* (1884), 142.

tendency that Mr. Cox represents. It has now gained a popular victory. . . . If it is to reap any lasting fruits of that victory it will have to be careful how it follows the lead of its demagogues.

The New York Times (December 20, 1884)[2]

Introduction

Standard treatments of the Interstate Commerce Act paint the Senate as a legislative graveyard where bills to regulate the railroads went to be buried, with the Republican majority in that chamber (often in league with railroad interests) cast as the principal obstacle to reform. Assuming this characterization generally to be true – and there is no reason to doubt its overall veracity – then something clearly changed in the weeks following the presidential election of 1884. For Senate Republicans suddenly initiated a major push to resolve the railroad problem. It is not difficult to discern what finally prodded Republicans into action. Demand for federal intervention was beginning to crest,[3] and with the first Democratic president of the post–Civil War era only weeks from inauguration, Republicans were forced to decide whether to act now – under the auspices of a Republican government – or cede responsibility for passing an interstate commerce act to the incoming Democratic government. The passage of railroad regulation under the Democrats' watch could bolster the party's reform credentials and demonstrate its capacity for responsible government, helping Democrats finally to shed their reputation as the party of treason and doctrinaire opposition to the expansion of central government functions.

It was an easy call for Republican leaders to make. Arguably, the party's most consistently effective electoral resource had been the simple equation of Democrats with treachery and irresponsibility. Delay on the railroad question would only play into Democratic efforts to rehabilitate the party's tarnished national image. In his third Annual Message (December 4, 1883), President Chester A. Arthur, a Republican, had urged Congress to address the mounting railroad crisis, but with no effect.[4] Now, however, regulatory commission legislation under the sponsorship of Senator Shelby M. Cullom, Republican from Illinois, was released from committee – where it had been bottled up for a year – and onto the chamber floor. When Cullom first introduced his commission bill, he had garnered little support from among his Republican

2. The *Times* was an important source of Mugwump opinion in New York.
3. Purcell, "Ideas and Interests: Businessmen and the Interstate Commerce Act."
4. Richardson, ed. *A Compilation of the Messages and Papers of the Presidents* Vol. 7, 4772.

colleagues. Indeed, Illinois's senior Republican senator reportedly warned the junior Cullom that "he would ruin himself by advocating such a law."[5] Now, however, both senior and junior Republicans pressed hard for its immediate passage.

The actions of Democratic party leaders were just as incongruous. For several years, the Democratic party had been a primary force behind the push for railroad regulation in Congress. Now, however, with the party about to assume the reins of government, Democrats suddenly emerged as champions of caution and delay. In the Senate, Thomas Bayard, Democrat from Delaware, and Augustus Garland, Democrat from Arkansas, led the effort to defer final consideration of the railroad question to the following Congress.[6] Garland began his remarks wryly, commending Cullom for making more rapid progress toward the disposition of an important measure than any senator in recent memory. He then proposed to send the Republican bill back to committee for further deliberation.[7] Bayard likewise requested more time and greater information before passing on a matter "of such far-reaching magnitude."[8] But in the end, despite Democratic protestations and a divided Democratic vote, the Cullom bill easily passed the Republican-dominated Senate.[9]

The politics of delay was more curious still in the Democratic-controlled House of Representatives, because there the conflict seemed to pit Democratic leaders against their own party rank and file. Having successfully guided his own regulatory legislation through the House, Commerce Committee chairman John H. Reagan, Democrat from Texas, sought a conference committee to reconcile differences with Cullom's Senate bill. But with the Forty-eighth Congress (1883–5) set to expire in only a matter of weeks, the move to conference required special action by the Rules Committee, firmly controlled by Democratic party leaders. Special action would allow Reagan to remove his railroad bill from its regular order on the House calendar by simple majority vote; otherwise, it would require unanimous consent. But action by the Democratic leadership to expedite the passage of an interstate commerce act never

5. Neilson, *Shelby M. Cullom*, 89.
6. Bayard was set to become the Secretary of State in the new Democratic Administration; Garland was about to take over the post of Attorney General. It is therefore possible to see these two men as spokesmen for national party interests in this matter.
7. *Congressional Record*, 48th Cong., 2d sess., Vol. 15, pt. 1: 568.
8. Ibid., 515.
9. Republicans were virtually unanimous in their support of the Cullom bill (31 to 1), while Democrats split on the question of passage (11 to 11). Of the 21 Senators who did not cast a vote, 14 were Democrats, further underscoring their cool stance toward resolution of the railroad question in the 48th Congress.

materialized. Twice in a period of roughly three weeks Reagan sought unanimous consent to proceed to conference; twice he failed.[10] In the end, the opportunity to pass historic legislation establishing a federal regulatory presence in interstate commerce died through the inaction of Democratic leaders.

Like the delay tactics of Senate Democrats, the decision of the Rules Committee to let railroad regulation expire with the Forty-eighth Congress indicates the preference of House leaders to defer final disposition of that issue to the next Congress. Structurally, there was little to distinguish the Forty-ninth Congress from its predecessor – except that Grover Cleveland was now safely ensconced in the White House. Once again, a Democratic House would pass the Reagan bill and a Republican Senate would pass commission legislation. Once again, Commerce Chairman Reagan would seek a conference committee. This time around, however, the two chambers would proceed to conference unimpeded by the delay tactics of Democratic party leaders. And on February 4, 1887, the new Democratic president would sign the landmark Interstate Commerce Act into law, ushering in an era of federal regulation of interstate business transactions.

Parties, the Presidency, and the Politics of Regulatory Choice

The purpose of this opening vignette is to motivate the central claim of this chapter: Presidential electoral politics and the maneuvering of political party leaders were central to the legislative evolution of the Interstate Commerce Act (ICA). Stunned by the loss of their first presidential election in a generation, Republicans sought to rehabilitate their tarnished image as a reform party by passing landmark legislation before the new Democratic government could take office. Similarly, Democratic leaders sought to delay the passage of historic legislation until the following Congress in order to reap the lion's share of credit for their own party. The politics of delay divided Democrats. But, as this chapter will document in some detail, the tension between Democratic leaders and their rank and file ultimately extended to much thornier issues than the *timing* of legislative action. A more significant rift would open up over the *substance* of the regulatory choice, a conflict with substantially greater implications for the long-term electoral welfare of the national Democratic party.

---

10. *Congressional Record*, 48th Cong., 2d sess., Vol. 16, pt. 2: 1386; ibid., pt. 3: 2247.

Because the literature on the ICA has seen fit to ignore political party processes, we have in my opinion yet to produce an adequate explanation for the particular substantive and institutional choices made by Congress in 1887. Political parties were a constituent feature of the Gilded Age landscape and it would be surprising if they did not loom large in the unfolding politics of the ICA. Labels like "the party period" and phrases such as "the triumph of organizational politics" and the "full flowering of the American party state" attest to the vibrant partisan life of the late nineteenth century.[11] Moreover, the competitiveness of national elections in this era only served to heighten the partisan stakes involved in the resolution of pressing public problems. As the political scientist Stephen Skowronek wrote:

> The nature of electoral competition in these years further extended the hegemony of party concerns over governmental operations. More than ever before, the calculations of those in power were wedded to the imperatives of maintaining efficiency in state and local political machines and of forging a national coalition from these machines for presidential elections.[12]

Yet studies of the ICA have consistently neglected political parties and national coalition politics as factors in that statute's substantive evolution. Social group analyses have provided us with detailed accounts of the policy preferences and political activities of organized groups – midwestern and southern farmers, Pennsylvania oil producers, mercantile communities, railroad leaders, and businessmen – pressing for national railroad regulation. Accounts of the ICA's legislative evolution, on the other hand, point to the structure of district-level electoral politics to account for the statute's vague and sometimes contradictory provisions.[13] To the extent that presidential electoral politics and national party concerns have received attention in this

11. McCormick, *The Party Period and Public Policy*; Keller, *Affairs of State*; Skowronek, *Building a New American State*.

12. Skowronek, *Building a New American State*, 39.

13. Buck, *The Granger Movement*; Benson, *Merchants, Farmers and Railroads*; Nash, "Origins of the Interstate Commerce Act of 1887"; Kolko, *Railroads and Regulation, 1877–1916*; Purcell, "Ideas and Interests: Businessmen and the Interstate Commerce Act"; Hoogenboom and Hoogenboom, *A History of the ICC*; Sanders, "Industrial Concentration, Sectional Competition, and Antitrust Politics in America, 1880–1980"; Sanders, *Roots of Reform*, 179–216; Gilligan, Marshall, and Weingast, "Regulation and the Theory of Legislative Choice: The Interstate Commerce Act of 1887"; Skowronek, *Building a New American State*, ch. 5; Fiorina, "Legislative Choice of Regulatory Forms: Legal Process or Administrative Process?"; Fiorina, "Group Concentration and the Delegation of Legislative Authority"; Fiorina, "Legislator Uncertainty, Legislative Control, and the Delegation of Legislative Power."

body of literature, it has been to dismiss them for their explanatory irrelevance.[14]

In this chapter I will argue that political parties were central factors in both the passage and legislative evolution of the ICA. In particular, I will document the critical role of electoral college constraints and Democratic party leadership to the unfolding politics of regulatory choice.[15] It is clear, for example, that contemporaneous legislators recognized the influence of presidential elections and national party needs upon the congressional policy process. Consider Representative James B. Weaver's denunciation of House colleagues in 1886 for subordinating district interests to the electoral college concerns of party leaders. Weaver, of Iowa, was a renegade from the two-party politics that dominated the period, an apostate in the eyes of many party loyalists. A member of the Greenback party, Weaver had been elected to Congress in 1879 and again in 1885. He was also the Greenback candidate for president in 1880, and in 1892 he would head the ticket of the People's party. As a congressman, Weaver stood outside the network of dependence and obligation that characterized ties to the major parties. Unfettered, he could freely speak his mind, and he expressed well the frustration of agrarian representatives with party obstruction in the legislative process:

> We are all full of the spirit of reform when we are before the people. In our several districts we are all reformers. . . .
> But . . . when we come into this House these things are all forgotten, and the great reformer in the district, when he gets here, roars like a sucking dove. [Laughter]. Why? Because if he enforces his particular views, some other member in his own party says, "If you carry out that doctrine or pledge you can not carry Pennsylvania or you can not carry New York or some other state. Is that not true?"[16]

This chapter offers an account of the ICA that takes seriously Weaver's indictment of congressional sensitivity to national party interests. It explores the impact of national structures of party competition, mediated by the institution of the electoral college, upon the legislative resolution of the railroad crisis of the 1880s. In particular, we will observe

14. See, for example, Fiorina, "Legislator Uncertainty," 47; and Sanders, "Industrial Concentration," 144.

15. Elsewhere I have documented the pervasiveness of statistically significant party behavior on legislative roll-call votes on railroad regulation. It is not my intention to replicate that analysis here. Instead of examining *whether* parties mattered to the ICA, I am interested in exploring *how* parties mattered to the politics of legislative choice – the process of party leadership intervention. On the subject of party cohesion and legislative roll call votes on the railroad question, see James, "A Party System Perspective on the Interstate Commerce Act of 1887."

16. *Congressional Record*, 49th Cong., 1st sess., 1886, Vol. 17, pt. 3: 2966.

how the competition for swing states and pivotal groups worked to winnow the number of politically acceptable responses to the railroad problem. I will argue that coalitional constraints prompted Democratic party leaders, embroiled in the battle over federal railroad regulation, to consider the implications of regulatory choice for their party's competitive position in presidential elections. Such concerns found their way into the national legislative process and, ultimately, into the substantive character of the final regulatory scheme adopted.

In 1884 the Democrats captured the White House for the first time in almost thirty years. Party success in the electoral college count had been predicated on both the mobilization of traditional Democratic constituencies and a successful appeal to independent Republicans – Mugwumps – in electoral college swing states, most crucially in New York State. Now in power, Democrats found themselves forced by public pressure to address the escalating railroad crisis. In so doing, party leaders were also forced to confront a deep sectional split within their national coalition over the content of interstate railroad regulation.

Agrarians, Mugwumps, and Regulation

Railroad regulation was the federal government's first attempt to exert systematic oversight of the daily decision making of a critical sector of the emerging industrial economy. Indeed, it was a *founding* moment in the development of national regulatory authority in the United States. As such, substantive and institutional choices would give definition to the character of the nascent American regulatory state, and by the weight of precedence and accumulated experience, impart a specific directionality to the trajectory of state–economy relations. As embodied in the Reagan bill and the commission alternative, the choices were starkly posed. The Reagan bill expressed the economic and political grievances of rural and agrarian America suffered at the hands of corporate railroad directors. The agrarian regulatory approach was premised on the belief that the railroads had freed themselves from the competitive discipline of the market, and it would slap heavy criminal and civil penalties for violations of its stringent, statutory rules of acceptable market behavior. Moreover, by its reliance on federal and state courts to enforce conformity to the law, agrarian legislation like the Reagan bill eschewed the creation of new state structures, downplaying the need to augment the administrative capacity of existing political institutions.

On each point, advocates of the regulatory commission differed from their agrarian opponents. To "business Mugwumps" in particular, railroads were not so much above the market as they were the victims of its often perverse logic – as all business persons potentially were. The central problem was not monopolistic greed, but the irrationalities of a competitive market economy. Even more fundamentally, they questioned the competence of popularly elected legislatures to manage the affairs of an intricate national railway system, and fiercely opposed regulation through inflexible and moralistic statutory proscriptions on market-driven behavior. Perhaps above all else, they placed their faith in the creation of new governmental authorities, insulated from partisan political pressures and staffed by experts. They sought the buildup of discretionary state power, with the authority to craft national policy around a rational body of administrative law, to hear cases arising under that law, and to make authoritative rulings backed by the coercive power of the federal government.

In welcoming Mugwumps into their national party coalition, Democratic leaders brought this developmental struggle straight into the heart of their party. In an important sense, the pressures of presidential elections and national coalition building would transform the politics of railroad regulation into a fight to define the direction of the Democratic party, challenging long-standing substantive commitments and core ideological tenets. But commitments made in the context of presidential politics still had to be shepherded through Congress by party leaders. And there, national party commitments naturally competed for primacy with powerful committee chairs espousing their own policy goals, facing their own electoral incentives, and pressing their own institutional advantages.

The analysis in this chapter unfolds over three main sections. The section entitled "Achieving 'Swing Group' Status in the Electoral College" explores the important role played by Mugwumps in the elevation of Grover Cleveland to the presidency in 1884. As we will see, Mugwumps understood the logic of the electoral college and they recognized the contingent opportunity presented to them by the competitive structure of Gilded Age presidential elections. Simply put, that logic stated that groups well-situated and willing to press their advantage could credibly claim to hold the "balance of power" in national politics. In doing so, they might exert considerable leverage over the direction of national party policy. In the case of railroad regulation, partisan calculations involving swing states and pivotal groups would prove decisive. The section entitled "Mugwumps, Agrarians, and the Railroad Problem" is a more explicit effort to link Mugwumps – in particular, a subgroup I have termed *business Mugwumps* – to the agitation for an interstate railroad commission with regulatory power. Because electoral college incentives must be translated into effective legislative behavior and concrete policy options, the section entitled "Democratic Party Leadership and the Politics of Responsible Reform" takes us directly into the legislative process. Here I examine efforts of both House and Senate Democratic leaders to secure party backing for a Mugwump-styled railroad commission in opposition to the revealed preferences of their largely agrarian rank and file. Through an examination of institutional rules, leadership tactics, and roll-call votes, I hope to demonstrate that Democratic leaders acted with purpose to ensure a legislative outcome consistent with their national coalition-building objectives and that, in the end, those efforts were largely successful.

Achieving "Swing Group" Status in the Electoral College: The Structural and Organizational Sources of Mugwump Political Influence

Structure: Electoral College Politics and the Presidential Election of 1884

In the presidential election of 1884, a victory in the electoral college required the winning party to capture a minimum of 201 electoral votes. In that year, as throughout the stable phase of the third-party system (approximately 1876–92), the Democratic party was assured of roughly 150 electoral votes and the Republican party 180 votes in their respective stronghold states. Going over the top required capturing some combination of the electoral votes of the four states in which presidential contests typically were in doubt. All totaled, in 1884 these four swing states accounted for sixty-six electoral votes: New York (thirty-six), Indiana (fifteen), New Jersey (nine), and Connecticut (six).[17] As Table 2.1 depicts, New York held the balance of power in each of the three presidential elections of the 1880s. Moreover, while it was arithmetically possible for Republicans to acquire an electoral college majority without New York, the Democrats required that state's electoral votes for any presidential victory. And presidential contests in New York were particularly close: When Grover Cleveland captured New York in 1884 he took the White House, with an electoral college victory of 219 to 182. But his margin of victory in that state was only 1,143 of the 1,167,175 votes cast, a slim 0.1 percent of the popular vote.[18] In 1880 and 1888

---

17. Some contemporaneous sources identified California as a fifth swing state. See, for example, the New York–based labor newspaper, *Irish World and American Industrial Liberator*, July 26, 1884, 4.
18. Burnham, *Presidential Ballots, 1836–1892*, 249.

Table 2.1. *Electoral College Competition, 1876–1892*

Year	Actual Electoral Vote Count		Counterfactual Electoral Count with New York Reversed		New York State Popular Vote Margin
	Demo	Repub	Demo	Repub	Pct.
1876	184	185	149	220	3.2 (D)
1880	155	214	190	179	1.9 (R)
1884	219	155	183	191	.1 (D)
1888	168	233	204	197	1.1 (R)
1892	277	145	241	181	3.4 (D)

Sources: Walter Dean Burnham, *Presidential Ballots, 1836–1892* (Baltimore: Johns Hopkins University Press, 1955), 249; *Historical Statistics of the United States*, Series Y 79–83 and Y 27–28 (Washington, D.C.: Government Printing Office, 1976), 1073.

the Democrats lost New York (and thereby the election) by 21,033 and 14,343 votes, respectively.

In 1884 independent Republicans bolted their party to support the reform Democrat Grover Cleveland for president.[19] Their defection was less an affirmation of the Democratic party than a rebuke to Republican leaders for their selection of James G. Blaine as the party's standard bearer. Mugwumps rejected Gilded-Age "politics as usual" – a partisan politics based on appeals to increasingly irrelevant Civil War–era issues and identities.[20] With party competition finely balanced and partisan

19. "Mugwump" is an Algonquin Indian word signifying "young chieftain." It was originally applied to liberal Republicans in 1872, as a reference to presumptuous innocents who assumed to know better than their elders. It was first applied derisively to independent Republicans in 1884 by Charles A. Dana, editor of the *New York Sun*, and subsequently picked up by GOP regulars. Eventually it would become an epithet directed at the political independent: a fence-sitter whose "mug" points in one direction and his "wump" in the other.

20. A leading Mugwump periodical wrote: "While the issues upon which Republican and Democratic parties have been long arrayed against each other have in great part ceased to be prominent, it must not be forgotten that a new generation of voters, which has grown to manhood since the war, will appear at the polls this year. Their votes will be very effective in determining the results, but they will not be affected by the considerations which hold old Republicans and Democrats to their party allegiance. These new voters regard chiefly principles and persons." *Harper's Weekly*, May 24, 1884, 326. A discussion of the motivations behind the bolt of New York Mugwumps can be

strategies attuned to the remobilization of increasingly fragile solidarities, Republican leaders feared that the injection of contentious new issues into presidential elections might threaten their precarious majority coalition.[21] Mugwumps, on the other hand, saw themselves as the "advance guard" of a new issue-based politics rooted in the pressing questions of the day. They gambled that the elevation of the minority party to national power with their aid would earn them the leverage to realize some of their more cherished political objectives, most notably in the area of administrative reform.[22]

Mugwumps, then, saw their defection as a test of will with Republican regulars. By withdrawing support and tendering it to an anxious opposition, they hoped to ultimately augment their influence within traditional party counsels.[23] With hindsight, scholars may dispute the empirical importance of the Mugwump vote to Cleveland's national victory, but among contemporaneous observers and participants alike there seemed to be little doubt concerning their decisive role, especially with regard to Cleveland's New York victory.[24] Indeed, Cleveland's

found in Dobson, "George William Curtis and the Election of 1884: The Dilemma of the New York Mugwumps." Curtis was the editor of *Harper's Weekly*, a prominent New York Mugwump periodical.

21. Marcus, *Grand Old Party*, 9–10.
22. On the interrelationship, more generally, between party politics and administrative reform in the late nineteenth century, see Skowronek, *Building a New American State*, ch. 3. Cleveland Democrats were sufficiently responsive to Mugwump demands that by 1892, according to one estimate, roughly 90 percent of the Mugwumps cast their vote for Cleveland, while about 75 percent identified themselves as Democrats. See McFarland, *Mugwumps, Morals, and Politics, 1884–1920*, 74.
23. Mugwump allies within the regular Republican organization, such as Senator George Edmunds of Vermont and Senator George F. Hoar of Massachusetts, disagreed with the utility of the bolters' strategy. McFarland, *Mugwumps, Morals, and Politics*, 16.
24. On the exaggeration of Mugwump influence in the election of 1884, see Benson, "Research Problems in American Political Historiography." More important than the absolute size of the Mugwump faction was their size relative to the margin of electoral victory in key states. More important still were the perceptions of party leaders regarding the relative contribution of Mugwumps to that victory margin. In fact, it is hard to fathom the nomination of Grover Cleveland by the Democratic party *at all* except with reference to the perception that such a move might swing the Mugwump vote and win New York State. Nor was courting Mugwumps anything new to Cleveland. The Mugwump vote had been an important component in Cleveland's meteoric rise to prominence in New York politics. In both his 1880 Buffalo mayoral victory and his gubernatorial win two years later, the Mugwump vote had been judged critical. Cleveland, therefore, was a known quantity with independent Republicans, and that, in turn, was the principal reason they let it be known to Democratic leaders that their support could be won in 1884 if the New York reform governor obtained the party's nomination for president. See Nevins, *Grover Cleveland: A Study in Courage*.

well-honed rhetoric of public service and public morality squared nicely with the Mugwump emphasis on individual character, while his commitment to administrative reform and his decision to stand for reelection on an issue-based campaign for tariff reduction trumpeted key Mugwump concerns and positioned the party to hold this swing constituency in the Democratic column.[25]

Mugwump Organization and Strategy

Of course, in itself electoral college structure could not confer balance of power status on Mugwumps or any group competing for influence within the Democratic party in 1884. It could, however, winnow the set of groups with plausible balance of power claims to those found in swing states. Within the swing states, several groups possessed numbers sufficient to claim the margin of victory in presidential elections – organized labor, antimonopolists, and prohibitionists to name those most frequently identified. But organization, money, tactical skill, and sheer determination were critical to determining which among these structurally advantaged groups would receive sustained consideration from Democratic leaders. In the end, therefore, Mugwump influence within Democratic party policy councils cannot be reduced to either simple vote share or public opinion leadership. In addition, Mugwump political organization, as an adjunct to regular party activities in the swing states, made important contributions to the 1884 Democratic presidential effort. Underfunded and overextended, the Democratic party depended upon the paraparty presence of Mugwumps in the critical states to eke out a victory over Republicans in 1884.

In the months leading up to the 1884 Republican presidential convention, Mugwumps built up an organizational infrastructure with which to press their structural advantage, one which in their words would "establish such communication between Republicans throughout the country, *and especially in the doubtful states*," and enable them "to lay before the Convention, with authority, representations of

---

25. On Cleveland's belief that a commitment to administrative reform was necessary to hold Mugwumps in the Democratic coalition, and on tariff reform as a strategy to attract Mugwump support in 1888, see McFarland, *Mugwumps, Morals, and Politics,* 53, 57. Concerning tariff reform specifically, Mugwump manufacturers were convinced that duties on raw materials placed them at a competitive disadvantage relative to businessmen further west, closer to domestic raw-material sources. Mugwump merchants likewise took offense at the treatment they received at the hands of the Republican-controlled custom house system, "which exacted heavy penalties for minor errors in estimating the value of shipments." Ibid., 49.

Republican sentiment fitted to prevent unwise nominations, or, should such be made, to impose the responsibility for the defeat of such candidates on those who nominate them." Mugwumps reminded Republican leaders that a victory in New York was critical to the party's national electoral success, and they insisted that that state could be carried only if a reform candidate were selected, an individual whose name "will be a warrant, beyond even the pledges of the best party platform, that the cause of administrative reform will be advanced." Making the most of their perceived advantage, Mugwumps insisted that they represented "the controlling force in the Presidential election of this year," and they urged party elites "to take every proper measure to promote the nomination of a Republican candidate who is a satisfactory exponent of the progressive spirit of the party, and who would command the hearty support of independent voters."[26]

When the Republican party nominated the politically tainted James G. Blaine for president, Mugwumps immediately bolted the party. The Blaine candidacy, Mugwumps predicted, would not only "repel the independent voters in New-York and in other doubtful states, but . . . drive out of the party ranks a great body of earnest and life-long Republicans."[27] Railroad expert Charles Francis Adams, Jr., a Massachusetts Mugwump, was one among many to urge the immediate organization of independents in an effort to secure a Democratic reform ticket and derail the Republican party's electoral hopes. "We will at once organize to defeat them," Adams wrote in reference to the party of Blaine.

> Could the Democratic Party be galvanized into that degree of momentary good which would lead it for once to astonish the country and itself by putting forward such a ticket as [New York Governor Grover] Cleveland and [House Speaker John G.] Carlisle, the result in November would not be in doubt for a moment. Experience tells us that the task is desperate, but so is the situation . . . [I]f we will, we can do more than we think to galvanize the Democracy, but to do it, we must act."[28]

With Cleveland's nomination finally secured, Mugwumps representing eleven states immediately met in New York City to organize support for the Democratic presidential bid.[29] The outgrowth of this meeting was the

---

26. *The New York Times*, March 6, 1884, 5; ibid., April 1, 1884, 8; ibid., April 5, 1884, 8; ibid., May 13, 1884, 2.
27. Ibid., June 15, 1884, 14.
28. Ibid., June 8, 1884, 1.
29. The Mugwump conference also coincided with the first post-nomination meeting of the Democratic National Committee, which was scheduled to meet in New York City two days later. Lambert, *Arthur Pue Gorman*, 103.

National Committee of Republicans and Independents (NECRI), a com-mittee of thirty-three chaired by *Harper's Weekly* editor, George William Curtis.[30] The selection of New York City as the site of both the national Mugwump conference and NECRI headquarters underscored New York's preeminence in the upcoming election, as did the dominance of New York Mugwumps on the executive committee.[31] Day-to-day operations were turned over to a committee of sixteen, on which nine New York Mugwumps sat.[32]

The work of the NECRI was threefold: to prepare campaign materi-als for use against Blaine; to put together a communication network to reach persuadable voters, especially "that great body of voters who are beyond the reach of the regular press"; and to facilitate the establish-ment of citizens' groups for Cleveland, and in so doing provide "the moral support so many require to stimulate their individual con-science."[33] By the campaign's end, the committee had published fourteen official documents of which over two million copies had been printed. It also printed over one-half million copies of "special documents for local or specific use," typically in the swing states.[34] The committee also arranged the distribution of campaign literature, organized hundreds of public meetings across several states, and supplied a steady stream of speakers for special events. The range and volume of activities was such that between July, when the work of the committee started in earnest, and election day in November, the staff of the NECRI grew from three persons to over seventy.[35]

---

30. Curtis had been chairman of the New York State delegation to the 1884 Republican National Convention and from 1881 to 1892 he was president of the National Civil Service Reform League.
31. The New York committee members were Curtis, George Waltham Green, George W. Folsom, Theodore Bacon, R. R. Bowker, John H. Cowing, Ethan Allen Doty, Horace E. Deming, Charles P. Miller, and Carl Schurz. For a complete roster of the NECRI, see *Report of the National Executive Committee of Republicans and Independents* (New York: Burr Printing House, 1885), 24.
32. *The New York Times*, June 18, 1884, 1; ibid., June 19, 1884, 8; ibid., June 21, 1884, 5; Fleming, *R. R. Bowker*, 205.
33. *Report of the National Executive Committee of Republicans and Independents*, 4.
34. One circular, for example, made the case to New Jersey independents that "the tariff was not the issue in the presidential campaign," while "cards relating to pensions and the interests of workingmen, [were printed] for use in New York and Indiana." *Report of the National Executive Committee of Republicans and Independents*, 5.
35. *Report of the National Executive Committee of Republicans and Independents*, 5–6. Mugwumps also organized state and local committees to further the Democratic effort. Mugwump organization was most extensive in Massachusetts, where "more than thirty organized bodies were in communication with the central headquarters, and several hundred meetings were held during the course of the fall." In Connecticut, a

The Democratic National Committee (DNC) relied extensively on Mugwump organization in the swing states during the campaign. Ultimately, a separate committee was formed by the NECRI to coordinate activities with Senator Arthur Pue Gorman of Maryland, Cleveland's campaign manager and chairman of the DNC's executive committee. Mugwumps also helped mobilize traditionally Republican businessmen in New York behind Grover Cleveland. With the NECRI's assistance, for example, Oscar S. Straus organized the Cleveland and Hendricks Merchants' and Business Men's Association in New York City, which also coordinated its activities with Gorman and the Democrats. As Straus later recalled, "We organized a parade and marched forty thousand strong from lower Broadway to Thirty-Fourth Street. It was the first time business men [sic] had ever been organized along political lines."[36] In the end, Straus would decline an offer of political office as reward for services rendered, an act that both typified Mugwump propriety and served to differentiate these issue-oriented reformers from mere party hacks.

> When the campaign was over I was told by a member of the National Committee that if there was any political office to which I aspired, the

swing state, efforts were made, partially with the aid of NECRI money, to visit "county fairs where the farmers congregated in good numbers." Public meetings in many of the larger towns were also organized. More important still, the state committee had its own election ballots printed, with the names of state and local Republican candidates and Democratic presidential electors already affixed, and had them "distributed by mail or otherwise, to every Republican voter in the state." Without the availability of pre-split tickets, Mugwump organizers feared that "many independent voters might otherwise be prevented, by political or other pressure, from voting in accordance with their convictions." In New York, local organizations were established in Brooklyn, Buffalo, and Rochester, as well as "in most of the smaller cities, and in very many of the towns." While in New Jersey, where the NECRI was troubled by the apathy of the state Democratic organization, the Mugwump state committee was credited with providing the margin of victory. Here, as in Connecticut, it printed and circulated split party election ballots, "and in Hudson County, particularly, special arrangements were made to keep the polls supplied." In addition, with the support of the NECRI, the local committee hired Pinkerton detectives to help minimize the impact of party corruption at the polling places. Finally, in Indiana the state committee took out an advertising column in the Indianapolis *Evening News* and started up its own weekly publication, *The Freeman*, which proved sufficiently successful that it was continued beyond the election. *Report of the National Executive Committee of Republicans and Independents*, 7–12. Ohio posed its own problem, because the state presidential election was held in October, and political wisdom held that a large majority in that state provided substantial momentum to the victorious party in the November races. For this reason, the NECRI was "compelled . . . against its will" to invest scarce resources in that state (11).

36. Fleming, *R. R. Bowker*, 205; Straus, *Under Four Administrations*, 38.

Committee would be glad to further any ambition I might have; but I replied my only wish was that Cleveland live up to the political principles which had brought him the support of so many "Mugwump" voters and so made possible his election.[37]

Mugwumps, then, made themselves valuable to the Democratic party by their organizational resources and talents as well as by their pivotal voting power. Still, once Cleveland was installed in the White House, Mugwumps could only wait patiently to see whether the Democrats would deliver on their pledge of administrative reform. The question was not simply (or even centrally) one concerning Cleveland's good intentions. Rather, it was the Democratic party's willingness to join in Cleveland's promise of reform. As the NECRI stated the matter: "Independents are scarcely willing to ally themselves definitely with the Democratic party, at least until it is seen whether the admirable sentiments expressed by Mr. Cleveland . . . can be practically carried out by the aid of that party." In December 1884, Mugwump Carl Schurz wrote to President-elect Cleveland, telling him frankly: "The Democrats are not a majority party now."

> The Democratic party won under the banner of reform, aided by the most determined reform-elements coming from the Republican side. . . . The party now come to power must be a reform-party in order to live, for it is certain that the opposition, as long as out of power, will be the most watchful and vociferous advocate of reform ever had. . . . *But [the Democrats] can become a majority party if their policy satisfies those independents and discontented Republicans who have been for some time longing for a new reform-party. . . .* In other words, the Democratic party will have to be, in that sense, the new party itself.[38]

Mugwumps, Agrarians, and the Railroad Problem: The Structure of Regulatory Preferences

Mugwumps and Railroad Regulation?

Mugwump reform commitments in the areas of civil service, the tariff, and currency matters have long been documented. However, the empirical relationship between Mugwumps and the resolution of the railroad problem remains considerably more tenuous. The standard literature leaves us poorly positioned to link these genteel reformers to the gritty

---

37. Straus, *Under Four Administrations*, 40.
38. Emphasis added. Carl Schurz to Grover Cleveland, December 10, 1884. Bancroft, ed. *Speeches, Correspondence and Political Papers of Carl Schurz* Vol. 4, 298–9.

business world from which the demand for railroad regulation emanated. Mugwumps in the traditional frame are principally a sociological category. In Richard Hofstadter's words, Mugwumps were an "old family, college-educated class" with "deep ancestral roots" – upper- and middle-class Yankee Protestants for whom cultural elitism, status deprivation, and a penchant for professionalism put them at odds with the boss-ridden, corruption-filled, democratic world of nineteenth-century American politics.[39] The gap between Mugwumps and railroad regulation grows wider still when we consider that standard historical accounts depict these patrician reformers as adherents of laissez-faire economics and thus as ideological opponents of state economic intervention. To historians such as Sidney Fine and John G. Sproat, the ideological conservatism of these Gilded Age liberal reformers rejected out of hand "all suggestions that the state restrict competition or impose 'unnatural' fetters on the free play of commodity prices and transportation rates."[40] In their renditions, Mugwumps emerge as staunch opponents of a national railroad commission with strong regulatory powers. To be sure, this characterization of Mugwumps is not without a factual basis. Indeed a leading exponent of this view was *The Nation*, a premier Mugwump periodical. *The Nation*'s editor E. L. Godkin had occasion to write that Western Granger legislation was "spoilation as flagrant as any ever proposed by Karl Marx or Ben Butler." Nor did time alter Godkin's views, labeling the Interstate Commerce Act of 1887 "a piece of State socialism."[41]

One need not reject out of hand these traditional accounts of the Mugwumps to take issue with some of their specific conclusions. For example, in *Building a New American State*, Stephen Skowronek offers a more complicated twist on these nineteenth-century reformers, and in doing so, has produced a more nuanced account of Mugwump regulatory thought. Skowronek distinguishes between "political Mugwumps" and "economic Mugwumps." Like the Mugwumps depicted in Sproat and Fine, political Mugwumps "tended to cling dogmatically to laissez-faire doctrines." But economic Mugwumps, Skowronek observes, "would use the state in a positive way to compensate for the market's most manifest deficiencies."[42] Skowronek identifies several prominent

---

39. Hofstadter, *The Age of Reform*, 137. Also representative of this extensive literature are Fine, *Laissez-Faire and the General Welfare State*; Blodgett, *The Gentle Reformers*; Sproat, *The Best Men*; McFarland, "Partisan of Non-Partisanship: Dorman B. Eaton and the Genteel Reform Tradition"; and McFarland, *Mugwumps, Morals and Politics, 1884–1916*.
40. Fine, *Laissez-Faire and the General Welfare State*, 51; Sproat, *The Best Men*, 158.
41. Sproat, *The Best Men*, 163–4.
42. Skowronek, *Building a New American State*, 133.

economic Mugwumps, among them economists Henry Carter Adams and Arthur Twinning Hadley, jurist Thomas M. Cooley, Union Pacific President Charles Francis Adams, Jr., and the lawyer Simon Sterne. From their divergent occupational positions, these men converged on a similar solution to the railroad problem, one that "looked to experts working as administrative authorities in government."

> National administrative regulation under the guidance of enlightened pro-
> fessionals promised to mediate economic conflicts, to stabilize a vital
> industry, and, in the process, to circumvent the unfettered plutocracy and
> the chaotic market competition emerging out of our past economic policy.[43]

In the end, however, Skowronek locates economic Mugwumps at the periphery in the legislative struggle over railroad regulation. In his analysis, state-building Mugwumps are confined to a narrow and nascent circle of social scientists and railroad experts – too little, too late, and too uninfluential – leaving it still to seem unlikely that Mugwump regulatory preferences directly fed into the framing of the Interstate Commerce Act.

My interest is strictly in those individuals who left the Republican party in 1884 and organized politically on behalf of the Democratic presidential candidate Grover Cleveland. And both the identity of these Mugwumps and their attitudes toward railroad regulation can be further refined. Most prominently, there existed a sizeable group of prosperous and pragmatic business Mugwumps who helped feed the demand for a national railroad commission. Drawn from the ranks of commercial wholesalers and larger manufacturers, these individuals were in on the ground floor of the Republican revolt against James G. Blaine in 1884. With similar energy, they joined the debate over economic regulation on the side of state intervention. How large was this business contingent within the Mugwump movement? No one can say for certain. But, as Table 2.2 makes clear, businessmen made up 40 percent of all those attending the National Convention of Republicans and Independents, which met in New York City on July 22, 1884. And among members of the New York delegation, business Mugwumps numbered almost one-half.[44]

Business Mugwumps differed from economic Mugwumps in their occupational profile and, as a consequence, in their relationship to the market and the railroad problem. With few exceptions, economic Mugwumps did not derive their livelihood from the day-to-day operation of ongoing,

---

43. Ibid., 138.
44. McFarland, *Mugwumps, Morals, and Politics*, 24, 25.

Table 2.2. *Mugwump Occupational Profiles*
(1884 Samples)

Occupations	New York City Mugwumps	National Sample Mugwumps
Businessmen	48%	40%
Lawyers	26	28
Educators	3	9
Publishing	8	8
Doctors	9	6
Clergymen	3	5
Other	3	4
(N)	(422)	(660)

Source: Gerald McFarland, *Mugwumps, Morals and Politics, 1884–1920* (Amherst: University of Massachusetts Press, 1975), Appendix B, Table B.2.

nonrailroad business enterprises. Rather, whether by professional training or accumulated experience, these individuals entered the public debate because of their expertise in the field of political economy and their extensive writing on the economics of the railroad problem. Economic Mugwumps often held academic posts, served on state railroad commissions, offered expert testimony in public investigations, and, in some instances, managed individual railroad lines. Casting themselves as above the immediate play of interests, they offered their brand of enlightened expertise to the resolution of the railroad problem. Detached and disinterested, they sought to elucidate the bedrock principles of railroad economics and shape informed public opinion, prescribing alterations in market and governmental behavior consistent with their vision of the public good.

By comparison, business Mugwumps experienced the railroad question as a concrete and immediate business problem. These Mugwumps were heavy consumers of transportation services, directly engaged in the struggle for survival in the intensely competitive Gilded Age marketplace. Freight rate discriminations injected myriad uncertainties into the daily lives of business Mugwumps, affecting everything from pricing and employment decisions to investment and locational choices. In this competitive environment, transportation advantages and disadvantages could mean the difference between business success and business failure. It was above all else the desire to inject greater predictability into their daily business lives that drew business Mugwumps into the public debate on the railroad problem.

Jackson S. Schultz of New York embodied most of the characteristics of the business Mugwump.[45] Schultz was an officer of the American Public Health Association, as well as sanitary commissioner for New York State, and he participated actively in the organized opposition to Blaine in 1884. He was also a prosperous leather-goods manufacturer (with a book on the subject to his credit), an owner of several Pennsylvania lumber mills, and a prominent member of the New York Chamber of Commerce. It was as a representative of the New York Chamber of Commerce that Schultz testified before the Senate Select Committee on Interstate Commerce on May 22, 1885. Before the committee, Schultz spoke at length of the problems facing businessmen and of the need for uniform, orderly, and responsible railroad practices. He described in detail the ways in which the various personal and locational discriminations meted out by the railroads worked hardships on entrepreneurs like himself. Discriminatory short-haul pricing by the Pennsylvania Central Railroad, Schultz calculated, had cost him roughly three-hundred thousand dollars over the course of several years. Schultz told the committee of being forced to pay $600 to $700 to ship pine lumber 400 miles to Philadelphia, while 1,000 miles outside Philadelphia, Michigan producers were paying between $1.00 and $1.50 for an equivalent load.[46]

A property owner himself, Schultz was cautious regarding legislated remedies that might inflict undue hardship on railroad stockholders. In his mind the goal was simply to secure principled railroad behavior and, therefore, uniformity of treatment. Toward this end, Schultz offered numerous recommendations. Among them, Schultz believed the creation of a federal railroad commission to be the most salutary step Congress could take. Such a commission, he suggested, should be armed with ample powers of publicity. More important, it should be required to prosecute all violations of the law, and generally enforce good order on the interstate railway system.[47]

---

45. I have identified Schultz from a master list of New York City Mugwumps listed as part of Appendix A in McFarland, *Mugwumps, Morals, and Politics*, 191.
46. Schultz's testimony can be found in U.S. Congress. Senate. Select Committee on Interstate Commerce. *Report*. 49th Cong., 1st sess. (Washington, D.C.: Government Printing Office, 1886), Vol. 1, 259–67.
47. Schultz further suggested that Congress require the railroads to publish their rates on all freight classifications and, once published, to adhere to them. He was also adamant about the need for a prohibition on the practice of charging more for a short haul than a long haul "under similar circumstances." Again Schultz conceded the need to balance interests, and he reasoned that the goal of uniformity might leave room for

*Mugwumps and Agrarians before the Select Committee on
Interstate Commerce*

Jackson Schultz was only one of several Mugwumps to testify before the
Senate Select Committee on Interstate Commerce. The committee was
organized in the final days of the Forty-eighth Congress (1883–5) to
collect nationwide testimony on the interstate railroad problem and
report back remedial legislation to the Senate. Because economic and
business Mugwumps addressed the committee, the records offer a rare
glimpse into Mugwump regulatory attitudes in the period immediately
after Grover Cleveland's presidential inauguration (March 4, 1885) and
before the deliberations of the Forty-ninth Congress, which would pass
the ICA.

This testimony is important for several reasons. First, it helps to clarify
areas of both convergence and dispute between economic and business
Mugwumps on the question of railroad regulation. At the same time,
it serves to highlight the differences between Mugwump and agrarian
approaches to the railroad problem, as well as politically crucial points
of convergence. To Democratic party leaders looking to reconcile the
policy preferences of their agrarian base with a recently cultivated electoral college ally, reliable information on the regulatory preferences of
each group was valuable.[48] Finally, this testimony is important because
it reveals strong parallels between business Mugwump preferences and
the final policy recommendations of the Senate Select Committee.

The Ontology of the Railroad Problem.   Both economic and business
Mugwumps took a structural view of the railroad problem: for each, the
trouble lay with the perverse incentives arising from the economics of
railroading. The root of the problem lay in the high ratio of fixed-to-
variable costs in the railroad industry and the intense competition for
available traffic. Cost structure and ruinous competition at the terminal

----

the railroads to charge as much for a short haul as for a long haul. The New York
business Mugwump opposed giving a federal commission the authority to set
maximum and minimum rates, nor did he speak to the issue of pooling. On Jackson
S. Schultz, see McFarland, *Mugwumps, Morals, and Politics*, 25, 43.

48. I have used two sources to identify Mugwumps who testified before the Senate Select
Committee on Interstate Commerce. The first is McFarland, *Mugwumps, Morals,
and Politics*, Appendix A. Secondly, I relied upon *The New York Times* coverage of
the Mugwump agitation in 1884, reporting that provided a number of names and their
states of origin. Nevertheless, I am under no illusion that I have been able to identify
every Mugwump who came before the Select Committee to comment on the railroad
problem.

points generated incentives for competing railroads to slash their rates below the immediate cost of moving freight (variable costs) and to compensate for lost revenue by a host of discriminatory tactics and by charging all the market could bear at noncompetitive points. Mugwump businessmen had suffered firsthand from railroad discrimination.[49] Nevertheless, a certain empathy between these antagonists is also apparent in the Select Committee testimony. These Mugwumps expressed understanding of the competitive plight of the railroads, for they too were locked in a competitive struggle for market survival. Additionally, as property holders they were sensitive to the property rights of the railroads and the right of shareholders to a fair return on their investments. For this reason, Mugwumps usually opposed the creation of a railroad commission with the power to set minimum and maximum freight rates. The problem was *relative* price discrimination and the unpredictability of rates over time, not arbitrarily high absolute charges – "extortion" or "systematic oppression" as agrarian supporters of the railroad regulation frequently charged. In fact, as they frequently pointed out, railroad rate levels had fallen continuously since the 1870s, the high tide of western Granger agitation against railroad monopolies. Mugwumps principally sought to curb the pattern of discrimination against persons and locales that inhibited market success by otherwise competitive producers and merchants. In their view the issue was equality of treatment, not a war of retribution on grasping railroad barons.

Agrarian railroad critics were also property owners and they too professed a respect for the rights of those holding railroad securities. But agrarians fundamentally differed from Mugwumps in their understanding of the railroad problem. They expressed the ideological tenets of anti-monopolism. These agrarians were less likely to pin responsibility on the failure of the market than they were on the moral failure of corporate decision makers; they blamed not invisible market forces but railroad arrogance and greed. What enraged these farmers and country proprietors the most was the arbitrary power the railroads seemed to exercise over their daily lives. By fiat these economic barons could destroy individual livelihoods, render particular lines of business unprofitable, oppress entire communities, and infringe upon the natural right of citizens to pursue a calling. As one Nebraska journalist put it, railroads were analogous to the British kings of old, with the power to do great

49. See, for example, the testimony of Francis B. Reeves (a wholesale grocer in Philadelphia) and A. C. Bartlett (a wholesale hardware dealer from Chicago), U.S. Congress. Senate. Select Committee on Interstate Commerce. *Report.* 49th Cong., 1st sess., 1886. S. Rept. 46, pt. 2: 448, 752. See also the testimony of Jackson S. Shultz, cited in footnote 53.

good or great harm, depending merely on royal whimsy.[50] Similarly, a Nebraska farmer warned of "a power growing up in this country that to-day [sic] dominates the sovereignty of the people, and that any such power is inconsistent with the sovereignty of the people."[51] The animosity was such that one Minnesota farmer was prompted to observe:

> There is nothing more dangerous than this sentiment that is springing up about the country against these large corporations. The people are absolutely feeling that their rights are being jeopardized; and there is an idea taking possession of them that unless there are some steps taken to mitigate or regulate the conditions of things in some way a feeling will spring up that will be dangerous at times. If there were a failure of the crops the people might become violent.[52]

In sum, where Mugwumps held impersonal market incentives accountable for the patterns of injustice incurred, agrarians saw a failure of corporate ethics and personal responsibility on the part of railroad decision makers. The concentration of market power in the hands of these corporate actors had allowed them to subvert the moderating effects of competition on railroad pricing policy. Thus shorn of the externally imposed discipline and accountability of the market, the roads were left free to prey on small producers and merchants dependent on cheap transportation for their survival, subject only to the dictates of a flagging moral conscience.

Competition and Cooperation.   Such understandings framed the broad parameters of the regulatory debate and distinguished Mugwumps from agrarian interpretations of the railroad problem. But, economic Mugwumps and business Mugwumps did not agree on all aspects of the railroad problem. Nowhere was this more apparent than in the disagreement that emerged over the beneficial effects of competition in the railroad industry. While most Mugwumps could agree that ruinous competition was disastrous to business interests, a split emerged nevertheless over the issue of railroad pooling, a practice designed to supplant railroad competition with institutionalized forms of cooperation.[53] Economic Mugwumps, like railroad expert and Union Pacific Railroad

---

50. U.S. Congress. Senate. Select Committee on Interstate Commerce. *Report*. 49th Cong., 1st sess., 1886. S. Rept. 46, pt. 2: 1131.
51. Ibid., 1173.
52. Ibid., 1340.
53. In the early 1880s the New York merchant community strongly supported the Reagan bill with its ban on pooling. Time had softened this opposition, but their testimony before the Senate Select Committee reveals a lingering distrust of the practice. On these early demands, see Benson, *Merchants, Farmers, and Railroads*.

President Charles Francis Adams, Jr., associated railroad competition with "the wildest discrimination and utmost individual hardship." Under questioning, Adams elaborated:

> How the business community, under the full working of railroad competition, can carry on its affairs I cannot understand. I had not been able to understand how it could do it before I became president of a railroad, and I do not understand now. The business man never knows what railroad rates are going to be at other places, or at different times. He cannot sit down and say "I can count upon such a transportation rate for such a period of time, and make my arrangements accordingly." He has to say, "I cannot tell to-day [sic] what the transportation rate is going to be to-morrow, either for me or my competitor." This must be just so long as uncontrolled competition exists. It cannot be avoided.[54]

In a similar vein, Yale economist and railroad expert Arthur Twining Hadley insisted that no nation had ever succeeded in eliminating discrimination without at the same time suppressing competition. This was simply "a historic fact," Hadley told the Select Committee in New York City. The question was therefore a simple one: "Shall we have poolings or discriminations?"[55] For both Adams and Hadley the question was easily resolved in favor of legally enforceable pooling contracts.

Business Mugwumps, on the other hand, espoused a more complicated (indeed, almost contradictory) position on railroad competition. At times, these differences pushed business Mugwumps surprisingly close to the agrarian position, which held price competition to be the master regulatory principle. This position was well expressed by the president of the New York Produce Exchange, who was clear in his opposition to extreme forms of market competition. He observed: "We cannot think that anybody, either the carrier or the public, is benefitted by any system which compels a ruinous loss, and the public and the railways equally suffer by the present ruinous war." Yet this business Mugwump was also opposed to the artificial cessation of competition through legalized pooling arrangements. In his words, "[w]e are great believers in the 'survival of the fittest.'"[56] Similarly, a wholesale grocer and Philadelphia Mugwump expressed his commitment to competition and his opposition to railroad combinations. Asked by the Select Committee to clarify his use of the word "combination," this Mugwump replied: "I mean a combination, for example, between the railroad companies to maintain pooling arrangements. I believe in free, open competition." Yet, like

---

54. U.S. Congress. Senate. Select Committee on Interstate Commerce. *Report.* 49th Cong., 1st sess., 1886. S. Rept. 46, pt. 2: 1205.
55. Ibid., 194.   56. Ibid., 216.

many business Mugwumps, the wholesaler's position on competition and combination proved ultimately more ambiguous. This was apparent when he later asserted his interest in preventing only "unjust combination" through national legislation.[57]

Perhaps most illuminating is the testimony of John D. Kernan, the chairman of the New York Railroad Commission. As we will see in more detail, though Kernan was not himself a businessman, his testimony is important because of his strong ties with both the New York business community and President-elect Grover Cleveland. Indeed, some of the credit for swinging New York businessmen behind the regulatory commission idea can be traced to the success of the New York Commission. Before the Senate Select Committee, Kernan voiced his strong opposition to the legalization of railroad pools, even as he conceded their effectiveness in restraining excess competition. The rationale for the commissioner's opposition was clear and politically resonant, and it is worth reproducing at length:

> The "pool" of railroads would determine what are reasonable rates, and what is and what is not unjust discrimination. An impartial observer can concede all that is claimed by the advocates of "pools" and still he cannot shut his eyes to the fact that, as at present constituted, they absolutely, and without appeal to any tribunal, determine what are their duties and what are the transportation rights of the citizen. Every decision made by the "pool" may be right, in fact, compelled, as asserted, by competitive and other considerations, and yet be a wrong upon the citizen, because it is made by an interested party who is engaged in disputing the claim presented. The submission pretended by railroads in debate to the corrective influences of public opinion, the good-will of shippers, &c., is somewhat exaggerated. This is beside the question under present discussion, for whatever the influences are about an arbiter it is a strange anomaly for a contestant to occupy that position.[58]

In sum, there was vocal opposition to railroad pooling practices within the business Mugwump community. As we will see, opposition to pooling was an important point of commonality between New York Mugwumps and agrarian Democrats, one that could be used to advantage by party leaders looking to reconcile the demands of the agrarian wing with the push for a national regulatory commission.

Long Haul–Short Haul Discriminations. The practice of charging shippers more to move their freight a short distance than a long distance engendered as acrimonious a conflict as any to flair up around the rail-

57. Ibid., 450, 455.   58. Ibid., Appendix. "John D. Kernan's Statement," 17–18.

road problem. As the railroads explained it, the trouble was excessive competition at the terminal points. Fierce competition for customers at these urban centers resulted in the frantic slashing of freight rates, often below the actual cost of doing business. In order to make up for the revenue lost to cutthroat competition, railroads compensated by raising prices over those portions of their lines where they faced no competition. To the railroads, long haul–short haul discriminations injected a needed flexibility into the system, and its maintenance was critical to continued financial solvency. To agrarians, on the other hand, it epitomized the ruthless character of railroad monopolies. It was oppression pure and simple. Long haul–short haul discrimination raised the cost of doing business for the "little guy," who could least afford it, and spread financial ruin throughout rural and small-town America. Farmers and small businessmen demanded an immediate and unconditional end to the practice.

Business Mugwumps were also more likely than economic Mugwumps to support a long haul–short haul law, though one with provisions limited in scope and flexible in application, not absolute or ironclad like the stringent agrarian proposals. As one business Mugwump put it, a long haul–short haul rule should not be "made inflexible and applicable to all points . . . ; that is, not making it compulsory by legislation."[59] In his judgment, it was unwise "to make that an unyielding and invariable rule," because cheap through rates allowed businessmen access to distant product and consumer markets that would cease to be profitable if railroads were prohibited from subsidizing low terminal rates with higher charges on the noncompetitive points.

Asserting a desire to balance railroad interests against their own, business Mugwumps suggested that a ban against charging more for a short haul than a long haul need not preclude *equivalent* charges for the two. Here lay an important difference between business Mugwumps and agrarian reformers. Business Mugwumps were more likely to be larger and more efficient producers or merchants. They had confidence in their ability to successfully compete in the market if transportation costs could only be equalized (and therefore neutralized as a competitive factor). Sometimes these businessmen moved their operations (or sought to move them) just outside a terminal city in order to exploit locational advantages like cheap power sources or a fresh labor supply. But under existing railroad pricing policies, such a decision subjected them to steep short-haul rates and priced them out of their market.

By contrast, agrarians generally advocated *pro rata* transportation

59. Ibid., 455.

charges – rates calculated on the basis of distance traveled. As such, they insisted that a prohibition on long haul–short haul discrimination include a ban on the charging of equal rates for unequal distances. As agrarians were more often than not small producers and merchants, such restrictions would allow them to compete more effectively with large competitors shipping from distant markets. To Mugwumps, on the other hand, the agrarian long haul–short haul proposal was little more than an effort to subsidize small, uncompetitive producers at the expense of the large and efficient enterprise, while to railroads it spelled bankruptcy, pure and simple.[60]

A National Railroad Commission. Both economic and business Mugwumps agreed on the need for a national railroad commission. However, they frequently differed over the scope of its authority and power. All could agree that a commission with information-gathering and publicity functions was in the public interest. But before the Select Committee, economic Mugwumps were inclined to limit the powers of a national commission to these basic "sunshine" functions, modeling their proposals on the New York, Massachusetts, and Iowa commissions.[61] Economic Mugwumps like Arthur T. Hadley and Charles Francis Adams, Jr., were the most prominent supporters of a national commission with vigorous information-gathering powers, but without the power to enforce its judgments. Adams, in particular, was pessimistic about the good that could be accomplished by a commission with regulatory powers. Rather, he preferred "a commission of men . . . whose business it would be to observe this question much as a physician would observe

60. Benson finds that the division over pro-rata rates effectively ended the antimonopoly alliance for railroad regulation between New York merchants and upstate farmers. See Benson, *Merchants, Farmers and Railroad Regulation*, 198. Business Mugwumps were also more likely to be involved in moving large quantities of goods in a single shipment, which typically brought preferential rates. For this reason, they were also opposed to any law that banned volume discounts as an unjust discrimination.

61. The New York railroad expert and economic Mugwump Simon Sterne was a notable exception. Sterne strongly argued before the Select Committee for a national railroad commission with the power to adjudicate rate disputes and enforce its decisions in court. Sterne's position might be explained by his long-standing relationship with the New York business community. For many years Sterne had acted as attorney for the New York Board of Trade and Transportation. Thus, Sterne's views represent a hybrid of those held by both business and economic Mugwumps. Evidence of this is the fact that Sterne broke with business Mugwumps on the question of pooling, a practice he strongly endorsed. U.S. Congress. Senate. Select Committee on Interstate Commerce. *Report.* 49th Cong., 1st sess., 1886. S. Rept. 46, pt. 2: 52–89. On the rationale and operation of the sunshine commission, see McCraw, *Prophets of Regulation*, ch. 1.

the progress of disease."[62] Similarly, Hadley judged the granting of judicial and executive powers to a national commission "a somewhat hazardous experiment." Such power, the railroad expert suggested, would only impede frank communication between the roads and the commission, with railroad officials fearing that sensitive information offered in good faith might be used against them in court. Still, unlike Adams, Hadley ultimately conceded the possibility that a stronger, regulatory commission might be required. "I should not say that I disbelieved in it[,]" Hadley cautiously admitted. "It might be worth trying."[63]

Business Mugwumps were quicker than economic Mugwumps to confer regulatory power upon the commission. While no Mugwump testifying before the committee advocated a commission with rate-fixing powers, a number of business Mugwumps argued that an effective commission required the authority to resolve rate disputes, to enforce its rulings in court, and to have its findings constitute *prima facie* evidence in judicial proceedings.[64] Along these lines, one Chicago business Mugwump was convinced that "a commission could [not] be of any great service unless it had considerable power," lending his support to a commission with adjudicatory powers.[65] A New York business Mugwump, on the other hand, insisted that a national commission be granted the authority to initiate prosecutions.[66] In sum, the proposals of business Mugwumps would draw the commission more deeply in the determination of just rates, transfer the onus of prosecutorial initiative and its related costs from shippers and producers to the commission, and place the burden of proof on railroads to justify their rates in court –

62. U.S. Congress. Senate. Select Committee on Interstate Commerce. *Report.* 49th Cong., 1st sess., 1886. S. Rept. 46, pt. 2: 1208.

63. Ibid., 1205.

64. The University of Pennsylvania political economist Edmund J. James seems to have been alone among Mugwumps in suggesting that commission rulings be final, without the possibility of appeal. The Select Committee appears to have quickly rejected such a possibility, worried about the constitutionality of the proposal. Indeed, on a number of issues James was the most radical Mugwump to testify before the committee. U.S. Congress. Senate. Select Committee on Interstate Commerce. *Report.* 49th Cong., 1st sess., 1886. S. Rept. 46, pt. 2: 493–506, 500.

65. Ibid., 755.

66. Ibid., 266–7. A tension in the minds of some business Mugwumps was apparent, between the desire to limit the powers of a national commission and the desire to solve the railroad problem. Thus the Mugwump businessman Francis B. Reeves of Philadelphia preferred an information-gathering commission to a regulatory commission, while also supporting a flexible long haul–short haul law. The inconsistency in Reeves's thinking is clear, as the allowance for exceptions to the long haul–short haul rule presumed some ongoing authority with the power to identify those exceptions.

elements that became the mainstay of the legislation drawn up by the Select Committee as well as the final Interstate Commerce Act.

While differences can be found among agrarians, these reformers typically opposed the creation of a national railroad commission. State commissions, they believed, had worked to the benefit of the railroads, whose power and influence allowed them to dominate commission actions. What was needed, agrarians believed, was simple and unambiguous legislation stating the rights of shippers and producers and prohibiting in no uncertain terms the worst abuses of the railroads. Asked by the Select Committee whether he endorsed regulation by commission or by legislation, a Nebraska farmer recently turned banker replied:

> I will say by legislation, *plain* and *direct*. As the commission system was rejected by the people of this state at the polls last fall, for the reason that it does not work to the advantage of the producers, and as it has proved itself a jug-handle system, all on one side, and that side the corporations, I am firm in the opinion that other legislation should be tried.[67]

M. A. Fulton, a representative of the National Grange and country merchant from Hudson, Wisconsin, reiterated this point in the following exchange:

> MR. FULTON: We want an absolute law, if you can consistently give it to us, and we do not want our justice strained through a commission, because our experience with a commission . . . is that they are not only worthless, but worse than worthless.
> THE CHAIRMAN: You consider them an absolute obstruction?
> MR. FULTON: Yes, sir; we consider them an absolute obstruction. We want it enforced by the ordinary courts and juries of the country. Give us a plain law, and fix it so that the local courts and juries can understand it.[68]

As these passages make clear, agrarians demanded an "absolute law," and typically opposed statutory language qualifying railroad obligations – for example, the prohibition of discriminations against persons and locales "under substantially similar circumstances and conditions." Even if warranted on policy grounds, such qualifications injected interpretative and technical ambiguities in the heart of the law that allowed talented and well-financed corporation lawyers to subvert the statute's intent and control the construction of its legal meaning in court. The resulting time, money, and expertise required to rebut railroad counsels in court would virtually nullify the legal remedies ostensibly gained by

---

67. U.S. Congress. Senate. Select Committee on Interstate Commerce. *Report.* 49th Cong., 1st sess., 1886. S. Rept. 46, pt. 2: 1107.
68. Ibid., 1284.

agrarians. For this reason they demanded unqualified or ironclad statutory language in the crafting of legislative rules governing railroad behavior, such as that contained in the agrarian-styled Reagan bill.

New York Mugwump Model Legislation and the Recommendations of the Select Committee on Interstate Commerce

The Senate Select Committee on Interstate Commerce held its last hearing in Atlanta, Georgia, on November 18, 1885. With the start of the Forty-ninth Congress less than a month away, the Select Committee set about preparing its final report and drafting statutory recommendations. For the purposes of this book, what is perhaps most notable about these recommendations is their conformity to model legislation earlier submitted to the committee by New York Railroad Commission chairman John D. Kernan. Both Kernan's presence before the committee and his model bill are significant for several reasons. First, Kernan's commission oversaw railroad activity in the most important state in electoral college politics, and in its short existence its actions had done much to swing business support behind commission-style regulation. Indeed, prior to his appointment as commission chairman, Kernan had served as legal counselor for the Merchants, Manufacturers and Farmers' Union, an organization opposed to the creation of the New York commission. Now, however, Kernan urged the Senate committee to adopt a national commission more powerful than his own. The New York commission possessed only sunshine powers, and Kernan's judgment that such powers were inadequate to solve the interstate railroad problem paralleled the judgment of the business Mugwumps who testified before the committee. Secondly, Kernan had been appointed to head the New York commission by then-governor Grover Cleveland. Kernan had been Cleveland's choice for the Democratic slot of the bipartisan institution, an appointment that met with Mugwump approval both because Kernan was not a career politician (though he was active in local party politics) and because his appointment had been opposed by antimonopolists.[69] Finally, in at least some quarters, President Cleveland was rumored to have qualms regarding the constitutionality of a national regulatory

69. Benson, *Merchants, Farmers and Railroads,* 188–9; Nevins, *Grover Cleveland: A Study in Courage,* 114; and *New York Times,* January 11, 1883, 4, 10. Nevins notes that Kernan and Republican Cleveland appointee W. E. Rogers "were known only for their technical qualifications." Kernan was also a New York delegate to the 1884 Democratic convention in Chicago, where he actively worked on behalf of Cleveland's candidacy. Lynch, *Grover Cleveland: A Man Four-Squared,* 173.

commission.[70] Thus, legislation bearing the mark of his own commission appointee might stand a better chance of obtaining final executive approval.

Because the Interstate Commerce Act would draw so heavily from the Senate Select Committee bill, the close correspondence between the latter and the provisions of the Kernan bill presents our first tangible linkage between New York Mugwumps and the creation of the ICC. A side-by-side comparison of the Kernan bill and the Select Committee bill is provided in Table 2.3. It details the direct parallels between these two regulatory proposals. Here I will simply summarize the provisions of the Kernan bill, which de facto will also serve as an introduction to the Select Committee legislation introduced at the start of the Forty-ninth Congress. It will also help begin to lay the groundwork for the analysis of legislative politics provided in the next section.

Kernan's recommendations tracked the Select Committee bill on most of its essential points. It would subject all railroad charges to the common law requirement that they be just and reasonable, with no undue preference or advantage afforded an individual, firm or corporation, or locality. Rebates, drawbacks, and other direct or indirect forms of personal discrimination were to be made illegal, subject to a maximum fine of $1,000. In addition, all railroad schedules detailing freight classifications, destinations, rates, and shipment regulations were required to be posted at least five days before going into effect. They would remain in effect until such time as they were superseded by a new schedule, posted according to the same rules. Kernan's model legislation also provided for a five-member Board of Interstate Commerce Commissioners with the power to conduct investigations; issue subpoenas and examine subpoenaed witnesses; examine books, records, and agreements of the railroads; and punish for contempt in proceedings before it. The failure to comply with commission requests was punishable by a maximum $5,000 fine and/or one year in prison.

But Kernan's commission was no mere sunshine agency. Upon complaint, the commission was required to conduct investigations,

70. Illustrative of this is the letter from *Chicago Tribune* editor Joseph Medill to Senator Shelby M. Cullom, chairman of the Select Committee on Interstate Commerce, immediately upon President Cleveland's signing of the Interstate Commerce Act. Medill's comments imply that neither the President's personal nor constitutional predilections alone could account for his embrace of a federal regulatory commission. Rather, he believed a more decidedly political calculus underlay Cleveland's acquiescence to expanded federal power. To the Chicago editor the interpretation was quite clear: "His signing it shows that he is a candidate for a second term. That was the test." Joseph E. Medill to Shelby Cullom (February 6, 1887). In Cullom, *Fifty Years of Public Service*, 440.

Table 2.3. *Comparison of the Bill of the Senate Select Committee on Interstate Commerce with the Kernan Model Commission Bill*

The Select Committee Bill	The Kernan Bill
SEC. 1. . . . All charges made for any service rendered or to be rendered in the transportation of passengers or property as aforesaid, or in connection therewith, or for the receiving, delivering, storage, or handling of such property, shall be reasonable and just.	SEC. 19. All charges by common carrier shall be reasonable.
SEC. 2. That if any common carrier shall, directly or indirectly, by any special rate, rebate, drawback, or other device, charge, demand, collect, or receive from any person or persons a greater or lesser compensation for any service rendered, or to be rendered, in the transportation of passengers or property, subject to the provisions of this act, than it charges, demands, collects, or receives from any other person or persons for doing for him or them a like and contemporaneous service in the transportation of a like kind of traffic under substantially similar circumstances and conditions, such common carrier shall be deemed guilty of unjust discrimination, which is hereby declared to be unlawful; and any common carrier who shall violate the provisions of this section as aforesaid shall be liable to all persons who have been charged a higher rate than was charged any other person or persons for the difference between such higher rate and the lowest rate charged upon like shipments during the same period;	SEC. 20. And it shall be unlawful for any such common carrier . . . to charge or receive, directly or indirectly, or by means of rebates, drawbacks, or otherwise, more or less compensation . . . than shall be specified in such schedule as may at the time be in force, except that special contracts for such service may be made at lower rates than stated in such schedules. . . . Any common carrier who shall fail to comply with the provisions of this section shall be liable to a penalty not exceeding $1,000 and not exceeding $50 for each day that such violation shall continue.
SEC. 3. That it shall be unlawful for any common carrier subject to the provisions of this act, to make or give any undue or unreasonable	SEC. 19. No such carrier shall make or give any undue or unreasonable preference or advantage to any particular person, company, firm,

Table 2.3. *(cont.)*

The Select Committee Bill	The Kernan Bill
preference or advantage to any particular person, company, firm, corporation, or locality, or any particular description of traffic, in any respect whatsoever, or to subject any particular person, company, firm, corporation, or locality, or any particular description of traffic, to any undue or unreasonable prejudice or disadvantage in any respect whatsoever.	corporation, locality, or any particular description of traffic, in any respect whatsoever; nor shall any such carrier subject any particular person, company, firm, corporation, locality, or any particular description of traffic to any undue or unreasonable prejudice or disadvantage in any respect whatsoever; and every such common carrier having or operating a part of a continuous line of communication, or which has the terminus or station of the one at or near the terminus or station of the other, shall afford all due and reasonable facilities for receiving andforwarding all the traffic arriving by one of such common carriers by the other without any unreasonable delay, and without any such preference or advantage or prejudice or disadvantage as aforesaid.
Every common carrier subject to the provisions of this act shall, according to their respective powers, afford all reasonable and proper facilities for the interchange of traffic between their respective lines, and for the receiving, forwarding, and delivering of passengers and property to and from their several lines and those connecting therewith; but no such common carrier shall be required to give the use of its tracks or terminal facilities to another carrier engaged in like business. Any common carrier who shall willfully violate the provisions of this section of this act shall be liable to the person or persons injured thereby for all damages occasions by such violation.	
SEC. 5. That every common carrier subject to the provisions of this act shall, within sixty days after this act shall take effect, file with the Commission appointed under the provisions of this act copies of its tariffs of rates and fares and charges relating to all classes of traffic affected by the provisions of this act, including classifications and terminal charges which in any wise change,	SEC. 20. Each common carrier covered by the provisions of this act shall by schedules to be adopted and kept posted as hereinafter stated, prescribe –

FIRST. The different kinds and classes of property to be carried.
SECOND. The different places between which such property shall be carried. |

Table 2.3. *(cont.)*

The Select Committee Bill	The Kernan Bill
affect, or determine any part of the aggregate of such rates and fares and charges, and from time to time all changes made in the same. Such rates, fares, charges, and classifications shall be made public by such common carriers so far as may, in the judgement of the Commission, be deemed practicable; and said Commission shall from time to time prescribe the measure of publicity which shall be given to such rates, fares, charges, and classifications, or to such part of them as it may deem it practicable for such common carriers to publish, and the manner, extent, and localities to which they shall apply and in which they shall be published. And when any common carrier shall have established and published its rates, fares, and classification, or any part of the same, in compliance with the provisions of this section, it shall be unlawful for such common carrier to charge, demand, collect, or receive from any person or persons a greater or lesser compensation than is set forth and specified in such published rates, fares, charges, and classifications, until the same shall have been changed as herein provided. No advance in such published rates, fares, charges, and classifications shall be made except after ten days public notice, but reductions in the same may be made without public notice; and the Commission shall prescribe the manner in which notice of changes, advances, and reductions in such published rates, fares, charges, and classifications shall be given.	THIRD. The rates of freight and charges for all services connected with the receiving, transporting, delivering, loading, unloading, storing, and handling of the same. FOURTH. The conditions, rules, and regulations with respect to the receiving, transporting, delivering, loading, unloading, storing, and handling of the same, provided that any such condition, rule, or regulation shall cease to be valid, or further permitted, whether assented to by the shipper or not, if upon compliant to the said commission the same shall be found by the commission, and adjudged by the court, to be unjust and unreasonable. Copies of such schedules . . . shall be posted, as above provided, at least five days before the same shall go into effect; and each schedule shall remain in force until another schedule shall, as aforesaid, be substituted. A copy of each of said schedules shall, as soon as posted as aforesaid, be filed in the office of said board.

Table 2.3. *(cont.)*

The Select Committee Bill	The Kernan Bill
SEC. 6. . . . That it shall be unlawful for any common carrier subject to the provisions of this act to enter into any combination, contract, or agreement, expressed or implied, to prevent, by change of time schedule, carriage of freights from being continuous from the place of shipment to the place of destination; and no break of bulk, stoppage, or interruption made by such common carrier shall prevent the carriage of freights from being and being treating as one continuous carriage from the place of shipment to the place of destination, unless such break, stoppage, or interruption was made in good faith for some necessary purpose, and without any intent to avoid or unnecessarily interrupt such continuous carriage or to evade any of the provisions of this act.	SEC. 19. . . . and so that no obstruction may be offered to the public desirous of using such common carrier as aforesaid as a continuous line of communication, and so that all reasonable accommodation may by means of such carrier be at all times afforded to the public. No breakage, stoppage, or interruption, or any contract agreement, or understanding shall be made to prevent the carriage of any property from being and being considered as one continuous carriage in the meaning of this act from the place of shipment to the place of destination, unless such stoppage, interruption, contract, agreement, or understanding was made in good faith for some practical and necessary or interrupt such continuous purpose, without any intent to avoid carriage or to evade any of the provisions of this act.
SEC. 9. That the Commission hereby created shall have authority to inquire into the management of the business of all common carriers subject to this act, and shall keep itself informed as to the manner and method in which the same is conducted, and shall have the right to obtain from such common carriers full and complete information necessary to enable the Commission to perform the duties and carry out the objects for which it was created.	SEC. 10. The said board shall have general supervision over all common carriers engaged in interstate commerce, and shall keep themselves informed in relation thereto and in regard to the manner and method in which the same is conducted, and as to the rates thereon, and the rules, regulations, contracts, and conditions made in connection therewith, and shall have the right to obtain from such common carriers full and complete information in regard thereto, and to conduct or to direct, before one or more of its members, examinations and investigations in relation thereto at any time or place within the United States.

Table 2.3. *(cont.)*

The Select Committee Bill	The Kernan Bill

SEC. 9. . . . and for the purposes of this act the Commission shall have power to require the attendance of witnesses and the production of all books, papers, tariffs, contracts, agreements, and documents relating to any matter under investigation, and to that end may invoke the aid of any court of the United States in requiring the attendance of witnesses and the production of books, papers, and documents under the provisions of this section.

And any of the circuit courts of the United States within the jurisdiction of which such inquiry is carried on shall, in case of contumacy or refusal to obey a subpoena issued to a common carrier subject to the provisions of this act, or, when such common carrier is a corporation, to an officer or agent thereof, or to any person connected therewith, if proceedings are instituted in the name of such Commissioners as plaintiffs, issue an order requiring such common carrier, officer, agent, or person to show cause why such contumacy or refusal shall not be punished as and for a contempt; and if, upon the hearing, the court finds that the inquiry is within the jurisdiction of the Commission, and that such contumacy or refusal is willful, and the same is persisted in, such contumacy or refusal shall be punished as though the same had take place in an action pending in said circuit court of the United States.

SEC. 11. To the end of carrying out the purposes of this act, said board shall have full power to subpoena and examine witnesses upon subpoenas to be signed by the chairman of the board, or by its secretary under its direction. Such witnesses shall be paid the same fees as in the United States district courts, the same to be approved by the board and to be audited by the Secretary of the Interior. Officers, directors, principals, and employees of such common carriers shall not be paid any fees unless the same are specially allowed by the board. Such board shall also have the right to examine the books, records, and agreements of any such common carrier and to require the production thereof at the place where the principal office of said common carrier may be situated, or to require sworn copies thereof to be furnished to it at any time or place. For the purpose of compelling the attendance and examination of witnesses and the production of books, documents, and agreements, or the furnishing of sworn copies thereof, and for the purpose of preserving order and punishing contempt in proceedings before it, said board shall have the same powers as are exercised by the United States district courts, and the action of the board thereon shall be subject to review in like manner.

SEC. 12. Every principal, officer, agent, or employee of any such common carrier as aforesaid, who shall refuse or neglect to make or

Table 2.3. *(cont.)*

The Select Committee Bill	The Kernan Bill
	furnish any statement, report, or information required by said board under the provisions of this act, or who shall willfully hinder, delay, or obstruct said commission in the discharge of its duties, shall be guilty of a misdemeanor, punishable by fine not exceeding $5,000, or by imprisonment not exceeding one year, or by both said fine and imprisonment.
SEC. 10. That any person, firm, corporation, or association, or any mercantile, agricultural, or manufacturing society, or any body politic or municipal organization complaining of anything done or omitted to be done by any common carrier subject to the provisions of this act in contravention of the provisions thereof, may apply to said Commission by petition, which shall briefly state the facts; whereupon a statement of the charges thus made shall be forwarded by the Commission to such common carrier, who shall be called upon to satisfy the complaint or to answer the same in writing within a reasonable time, to be specified by the Commission. . . . If such carrier shall not satisfy the complaint within the time specified, or there shall appear to be any reasonable ground for investigating said complaint, it shall be the duty of the Commission to investigate the matters complained of in such manner and by such means as it shall deem proper. . . . No complaint shall at any time be dismissed because of the absence of direct damage to the complainant.	SEC. 21. That any person, firm, corporation, or association, complaining of anything done or omitted to be done by any common carrier covered by the provisions of this act in contravention of the provisions thereof, may apply to said board by petition in writing, which shall briefly state the facts. If the petition is signed by any board of trade or commercial body, or, when signed by an individual, if it bears the certificate of any district attorney of the United States, or any district or country attorney or officer corresponding thereto of any State or Territory, that he has examined the facts, and in his opinion the complaint is well-founded, the board is hereby required to entertain and investigate the same. In all other cases, the board shall decide whether or not the petition ought to be proceeded with. . . .

Table 2.3. *(cont.)*

The Select Committee Bill	The Kernan Bill

SEC. 11. That whenever an investigation shall be made by said Commission, it shall be its duty to make a report in writing in respect thereto, which shall include the findings of fact upon which the conclusions of the Commission are based, together with its recommendation as to what reparation, if any, should be made by the common carrier to any party or parties who may be found to have been injured; and such findings so made shall thereafter, in all judicial proceedings, be deemed *prima facie* evidence as to each and every fact found.

All reports of investigations made by the Commission shall be entered of record, and a copy thereof shall be furnished to the party who may have complained, and to any common carrier that may have been complained of.

SEC. 12. That if in any case in which an investigation shall be made by said commission it shall be made to appear to the satisfaction of the Commission, either by the testimony of witnesses or other evidence, that anything has been done in violation of the provisions of this act, or of any law cognizable by said Commission, by any common carrier,

SEC. 21. If in any case in which an investigation shall be made by said commission it shall be made to appear to the satisfaction of the commission, either by the testimony of witnesses or other evidence adduced before it, or by the report of any person to whom the commission may have referred the inquiry or any part thereof, that anything has been done or omitted to be done in violation of the provisions of this act by any such common carrier, it shall be the duty of such commission to make its report in writing in respect thereto, which report shall include the findings of fact upon which the conclusions of the commission are based, and which findings so made shall thereafter be deemed *prima facie* evidence as to each and every fact found in all courts and places. Within a reasonable time, not to exceed twenty days, after such report is made by said commission it shall cause a copy thereof to be served upon or delivered to the said common carrier so found to have violated the provision of the act, together with a notice to said common carrier forthwith to cease and desist from such violation.

SEC. 22. Unless said common carrier shall within twenty days after service upon it of said report and notice . . . cease and desist from such violation, it shall be the duty of the district attorney of the United States for the district in which the violation occurred, to apply by petition, in the name of the complainant before said board, or of the party aggrieved,

Table 2.3. *(cont.)*

The Select Committee Bill	The Kernan Bill
or that any injury or damage has been sustained by the party or parties complaining, or by other parties aggrieved in consequence of any such violation, it shall be the duty of the Commission to forthwith cause a copy of its report in respect thereto to be delivered to such common carrier, together with a notice to said common carrier to cease and desist from such violation, or to make reparation for the injury so found to have been done, or both, within a reasonable time, to be specified by the Commission; and . . . if said common carrier shall neglect or refuse, within the time specified, to desist from such violation of the law or to make reparation for the injury done, in compliance with the report and notice of the Commission as aforesaid, it shall be the duty of the Commission to forthwith certify the fact of such neglect or refusal, and forward a copy of its report and such certificate to the district attorney of the United States for the judicial district in which such violation of law occurred, for redress and punishment as in this act provided.	to the circuit court of the United States for such district, for, and it shall be the duty of such court to grant, an order for such common carrier to show cause why it should not be enjoined and restrained against the continuance of such violation, and for such other order and relief in the premises as may be just and proper. Upon the service and return of such order to show cause, and notice to such parties as may be deemed necessary said court shall proceed as speedily and summarily as possible to hear and determine the matters in controversy; and whenever said court shall be of opinion that such common carrier has done as aforesaid, or is doing any act in violation of the provisions of this act as in said report set forth, it shall then be the duty of said court forthwith to issue a writ of injunction requiring such common carrier to desist and cease from such violation of the provisions of this act. Such court may enforce obedience to any such injunction, order, or decree by any such common carrier, or any officer, agent, or employee thereof, by fine, proceedings for contempt, and all other means within its lawful jurisdiction, sitting as a court of equity. . . . Such court may, in its discretion, award or deny costs to any party to such proceedings. In any case where the court shall adjudge that the violation of the provisions of this act by any such common carrier has been willfully continued after the expiration of said twenty days, or after the expiration of the time fixed as aforesaid by said board, the court may award to any

Table 2.3. *(cont.)*

The Select Committee Bill	The Kernan Bill
	party injured such a gross sum, by way of costs, as will reimburse all his costs, charges, expenses, counsel fees, and disbursements to be paid by such carrier, and shall also impose a penalty not exceeding $5,000, and not exceeding $100 per day for each day that such violation shall continue after the expiration of the time aforesaid.
SEC. 13. That it shall be the duty of any district attorney to whom said Commission may forward its report and certificate . . . to forthwith bring suit, in the circuit court of the United States in the judicial district wherein such violation occurred, on behalf and in the name of the person or persons injured, against such common carrier, for the recovery of damages for such injury as may have been sustained by the injured party; and if on the trial of said cause judgment shall be rendered against said common carrier, the court may allow a reasonable attorney's fee to the district attorney for prosecuting said cause, to be taxed as part of the costs; and in case of failure to recover, the United States shall pay the necessary costs of suit.	SEC. 18. The district attorneys of the United States in their respective districts shall at the request of said commission act for and represent it in all suits and proceedings before the courts of the United States.

call witnesses, take evidence, and enter judgments concerning alleged violations of the law. The commission was further empowered to issue cease-and-desist orders where a railroad failed to conform to the commission's ruling and to institute court proceedings through the U.S. district attorneys to bring railroad behavior into line with the law. The objections to these regulatory powers, Kernan insisted, were "futile."[71] Courts and juries were incompetent to sift through and weigh the numerous and intricate facts of a railroad rate dispute. Moreover, shippers and producers would be spared the burden of information gathering (most of which was in the possession of the railroads) as well as prohibitive legal fees. Finally, in all court proceedings, the commission's findings were to constitute *prima facie* evidence "as to each and every fact found in all courts and places." "It seems idle," Kernan told the Select Committee, "for a commission to spend weeks in accumulating evidence in order to ascertain facts and then to have its findings of no avail to any one [sic] in court."[72]

The only significant difference between the Kernan bill and the bill of the Select Committee was the latter's inclusion of a long haul–short haul provision (neither included a prohibition on pooling). Even this provision, however, conformed to recommendations made by the New York commission chairman before the Select Committee. In his testimony, Kernan had advocated a long haul–short haul law modeled on the conservative Massachusetts law, one which would prohibit charging more "from one station to another a higher rate than it charges at the same time from that same original point of departure to a station at a greater distance in the same direction."[73] Like Kernan's recommendation and Massachusetts law, Section 4 of the Select Committee bill read:

> That it shall be unlawful for any common carrier to charge or receive any greater compensation in the aggregate for the transportation of passengers or property subject to the provisions of this act for a shorter than for a longer distance over the same line, in the same direction, and from the same original point of departure.

Under both the Select Committee bill and Kernan's recommendations, the railroad commission was empowered to make exceptions to this rule. Kernan opposed an absolute ban on the practice of subsidizing long-haul shipments through higher charges on local freight – an ironclad prohibition found in the House Reagan bill. In his judgment, "To pass a statute saying that they shall not charge more for a short than a long distance on any railroad would be an utter failure and would work vast injustice."

With the introduction of the Select Committee's bill into the Senate,

---

71. U.S. Congress. Senate. Select Committee on Interstate Commerce. *Report.* 49th Cong., 1st sess., 1886. S. Rept. 46, pt. 1, appendix, 23.
72. Ibid.
73. Ibid., pt. 2: 17.

business Mugwump regulatory preferences became a constituent part of legislative deliberation on the railroad problem, vying for political supremacy with popular agrarian legislation sponsored in the House of Representatives by Texas Democrat John H. Reagan. It was a clash of regulatory prescriptions that would pit Democratic party leaders in both chambers against their rank and file. Democratic leaders took an active role in moving the commission legislation through Congress. As will be argued in the next section, in so doing they hoped to demonstrate to their new and pivotal Mugwump allies the capacity of the Democratic party for responsible reform. In a legislative environment that afforded leaders only limited leverage over committee chairs and an assertive rank and file, the success of party leaders was far from certain.

Democratic Party Leadership and the Politics of Responsible Reform: Toward an Independent Regulatory Commission

Railroad Regulation and the Structure of Legislative Preferences

With this section my analysis moves sharply from the demand side of the politics of railroad regulation to its supply side: from the world of railroads, farmers, and Mugwumps to that of rank-and-file legislators and congressional party elites. The regulatory preferences of agrarians and business Mugwumps, as expressed before hearings of the Select Committee on Interstate Commerce, found their legislative expression in rival congressional bills. In the House, the agrarian railroad solution was pressed forward by John H. Reagan, chairman of the House Committee on Commerce, and backed broadly by rank-and-file members of the congressional Democratic party. The Reagan bill articulated clear antimonopoly principles: a moral code of railroad conduct to help level the economic playing field for farmers and small-town dwellers whose business survival was threatened by railroads' monopoly power at points in between the terminal centers. In unqualified language, the Reagan bill forbade a host of personal discriminations, including rebates and drawbacks. Similarly, it prohibited discrimination between places – the charging of a higher freight rate for a short haul than a long haul. Most threatening from the railroad's point of view, it also banned the practice of pooling freight and revenue, the most effective way yet found by railroad managers to stabilize prices and lessen competitive pressures. Finally, reflecting the traditional antistatism of the Democratic party, the Reagan bill avoided the creation of new federal institutions and the

expansion of administrative power. Rather, upon complaint, it would fall
to the existing system of courts – and ideally the more responsive state
courts – to enforce the statutory will of the people's representatives.

By comparison, the Mugwump commission solution found its champion in the Senate Select Committee on Interstate Commerce and, more
generally, among Republican legislators in both houses of Congress. The
Select Committee bill dismissed the agrarian interpretation of the railroad problem. In their eyes, the issue was neither monopolistic greed nor
corporate malevolence. Rather, as business Mugwumps had themselves
maintained, the problem was the competitive structure of a poorly regulated market for transportation services. Like the Reagan bill, the Select
Committee legislation banned both person and place discrimination. But
the Select Committee bill differed from the Reagan bill in several particulars. First, it lacked an antipooling provision, arguably the central
antimonopoly provision in the Reagan bill. Second, it contained a much
more narrowly drawn long haul–short haul provision, a subject we will
consider in detail later in the analysis. Finally, and most critically, it
created an independent body of experts, the Interstate Commerce Commission, with the authority to exempt the railroads from congressionally
proscribed behavior and craft a body of administrative law based solely
on the judgments of the commissioners.

It was *The New York Times*, a preeminent Mugwump newspaper, that
most closely drew the connection between responsible governing, the resolution of the railroad problem, and continued Democratic electoral
success.[74] As we saw at the opening of this chapter, in the weeks immediately following the 1884 election, action in the House of Representatives quickened on the railroad question and the prospects for the
passage of the agrarian Reagan bill appeared to brighten. Floor activity
on this legislation provided the occasion for the *Times* to clarify
Mugwump expectations regarding Democratic leadership and the railroad problem. The paper identified what it termed two "conflicting tendencies at work within the bosom of the Democratic party." The first
tendency was characteristic of the party's rank and file – supporters of
the Reagan bill – the "unthinking mass of the party" as it derisively
labeled the Democratic base. This element represented the antimonopolist and antistatist element of the party.[75] They believed that "railroads

74. *The New York Times*, December 20, 1884, 4.
75. Indeed Reagan was so popular with antimonopolists that he was queried about his
    availability to be the Antimonopoly party's vice-presidential candidate in 1884. He
    declined, citing his commitment to working for reform from within the Democratic
    party. Gerald Nash, ed. "Selections from the Reagan Papers: The Butler-Reagan Ticket
    of 1884."

were grinding monopolies" and "could be regulated in the minutest particulars by Congress." They also believed in "the unconstitutionality of commissions."[76]

The second tendency was embodied in Democrats like Representative Abram Hewitt of Brooklyn. Like Cleveland, Hewitt was a native New Yorker and popular among Mugwumps for his uncompromising stances on civil service reform, free trade, and the gold standard. He was also a businessman and a manufacturer who "recognize[d] the responsibility of his party for the use it makes of its power." And like the *Times*, Hewitt was a vocal opponent of the Reagan bill, decrying "the madness of trying to run the vast, complex, and delicate business of the railways by specific provisions of law." The Mugwump paper acknowledged the injustices that shippers and producers experienced at the hands of the railroads, but it was adamant that the Reagan bill was bad law and would only create additional difficulties if enacted. The paper concluded by observing that it was "precisely the reckless tendency" of the antimonopolist wing of the party that "for years kept [the Democratic party] out of power[.]" That party now found itself with a mandate to govern. If it was "to reap any lasting fruits of that victory," it counseled, "it [would] have to be very careful how it follows the lead of its demagogues."[77]

As my discussion of the Public Utility Holding Company Act in Chapter 4 will show, where electoral incentives favored the pursuit of agrarian antimonopoly values, Democratic party leaders have acted aggressively on their behalf, even at the risk of incurring the wrath of large economic actors and a sizeable portion of their own party base. For Gilded Age Democrats, however, national electoral incentives pulled party leaders in an altogether different direction, effectively foreclosing on the possibility that party leaders might see in the agrarian Reagan plan a politically feasible solution to the country's developmental problems. Those same electoral incentives simultaneously enhanced the political acceptability of the regulatory commission scheme among Democratic leaders, given its strong base of support among an important swing constituency in the competitive states of the industrial Northeast. As noted earlier, the Democratic party was consigned to out-party status in presidential politics except as it could incorporate the voters of the industrial Northeast – and especially New York state – into its national coalition. These national electoral incentives operated effectively to limit the political appeal of the Reagan alternative to party leaders with one eye on the next presidential campaign. And on crucial questions – commissions versus courts, competition versus cooperation,

76. *The New York Times*, December 20, 1884, 4.   77. Ibid.

delegation or retention of legislative power – swing-state business Mugwumps brought to the Democratic party preferences very much at odds with those of the party's agrarian base.

The Sources of Party Leadership on the Railroad Question

Perhaps the most striking aspect of this first case study of party leadership and regulatory choice is the absence of any discernable role played by Grover Cleveland, the incumbent Democratic president. In the politics of railroad regulation, presidential coalitional interests would be attended to almost exclusively by congressional party leaders. In large part, this political context reflected the centrality of both party and legislature to the basic functioning of national governance in the Gilded Age. Indeed, the publication of Woodrow Wilson's *Congressional Government* in 1885 and Lord James Bryce's *The American Commonwealth* in 1888 virtually bookend the first administration of Grover Cleveland.[78] Together, these classic studies of nineteenth-century American government depict a legislative process dominated by congressional committees and a presidential office sapped of talent and energy by the electoral needs of vibrant national party organizations. But while capturing essential aspects of Gilded Age governing institutions, these two books are wide of the mark in certain crucial respects. Most important to the analysis that follows, Wilson's description of Congress understated the growing influence of party leaders – especially the Speaker – as a counterpoise to congressional committees and as bearers of national party interests. Similarly, though of less importance to my argument, Bryce missed the latent capacity for policy leadership in the Gilded Age presidency. In addition to general tendencies of the period, the president's marginal role in the politics of the ICA also reflected the fledgling status of the Cleveland administration at the time railroad regulation was under consideration, not to mention Cleveland's surprising lack of prior experience as a political leader.[79] But while Cleveland may have been peripheral to the politics of the ICA, we will nonetheless observe important linkages connecting the presidency and national party interests to congressional party elites. The point to be made in these opening remarks is simply that the expenditure of political energy to retain the presidency

---

78. Wilson, *Congressional Government*; Bryce, *The American Commonwealth*.
79. Indicative of this is the fact that the Democratic executive would assume a more prominent place in the politics of tariff reform toward the end of his first administration, while Cleveland's role during his second administration in orchestrating the repeal of the Sherman Silver Purchase Act in 1893 would help open the eyes of the academic Woodrow Wilson to the potentialities of vigorous presidential leadership.

came first and foremost from congressional party leaders, not from reelection-minded presidents.

Democratic leaders faced their biggest hurdle to the passage of commission legislation in the House of Representatives. For even though Democrats controlled the chamber in the Forty-ninth Congress (1885–7), antimonopoly agrarianism was ascendant within the party, at least on the issue of railroad reform. Democrat John H. Reagan remained the chairman of the House Commerce Committee and his agrarian-styled regulatory bill continued to command rank-and-file majority support on the chamber floor. Senate Democratic leaders faced a challenge substantially less daunting than that which confronted House party leaders. Republicans in the Forty-ninth Congress once again controlled the upper chamber and, as we saw at the outset of this chapter, the GOP was now on record supporting the commission approach to railroad regulation. Still, Mugwumps' emphasis on character and integrity and their circumscribed notions of responsible reform meant that the conduct of the Democratic party *as a party* would be scrutinized along with the chamber's regulatory output. And because the Senate is a more individualistic institution than the House, it provided agrarian Democrats with substantial opportunities to embarrass or otherwise stymie commission legislation from the floor. For this reason it was imperative that Democratic leaders signal their interest in commission legislation early on and use their influence to contain agrarian floor activity as the Senate took up the Select Committee's regulatory proposals.

The remainder of this section analyzes Democratic party leadership – first in the House and then in the Senate – against agrarian railroad measures and on behalf of an independent railroad commission. The following analysis seeks to organize a large quantity of information, with material spanning two Congresses, both House and Senate chambers, and a number of roll-call votes. Because the analysis is organized analytically rather than chronologically, Table 2.4 assembles information for quick reference, so that readers may refer back to it as needed.

Party Leadership in the House of Representatives

The Democratic party in the Forty-ninth Congress was predominately a party of the South and the West, regions of the country where antimonopoly agrarianism thrived. A little over 60 percent of House Democrats elected in 1884 came from districts located in the southern, Great Plains, and far-western states (for Republicans the corresponding figure was 30 percent). By contrast, only 19 percent of House Democrats hailed from districts located in the industrial Northeast (the Republican figure

Table 2.4. *Information on Congressional Dates in Session, Chamber Majority Party in House and Senate, and Votes Used in Analysis (Forty-eighth and Forty-ninth Congresses)*

Congress	Session	Dates in Session	Senate Majority	House Majority
48th	1st	Dec. 3, 1883–Jul. 7, 1884	Republican	Democrat
	2d	Dec. 1, 1884–Mar. 3, 1885		
49th	1st	Dec. 7, 1885–Aug. 5, 1886	Republican	Democrat
	2d	Dec. 6, 1886–Mar. 3, 1887		

Votes Used in Chapter Analysis

	Date	Vote	Democrat	Republican
48th Congress (Senate)				
1. Substitute Cullom Bill for Reagan Bill	Fed. 3, 1885	35-18	7-15	26-3
2. Pass Cullom Bill	Feb. 4, 1885	43-12	11-11	31-1
48th Congress (House)				
1. Substitute Reagan Bill for Committee Bill	Dec. 16, 1884	142-98	124-27	16-70
2. Delete Reagan Bill's Long Haul–Short Haul Provision	Jan. 7, 1885	90-120	24-113	64-14
3. Prohibit Removal of Cause from State to Federal Court	Jan. 7, 1885	125-88	118-12	6-73
4. Create a Railroad Commission	Jan. 7, 1885	97-125	23-113	72-10
5. Allow Exceptions to Regan Bill's Antirebate Provision	Jan. 7, 1885	73-130	10-115	62-14
6. Pass Reagan Bill	Jan. 8, 1885	161-75	122-26	37-37

49th Congress (Senate)				
1. 2d Camden Amendment to Expand Sec. 4 (Long Haul–Short Haul)	May 5, 1886	29-24	24-2	3-22
2. McPherson Amendment to Delete Sec. 4 (Long Haul–Short Haul)	May 12, 1886	20-29	2-21	18-8
3. Recommit ICA	Jan. 14, 1887	25-36	5-21	19-15
4. Pass ICA	Jan. 14, 1887	43-15	20-3	23-11
49th Congress (House)				
1. Hiscock Amendment	Jul. 27, 1886	102-126	10-118	92-6
2. Reagan Substitute	Jul. 30, 1886	134-104	119-18	13-86
3. Recommit Reagan Bill	Jul. 30, 1886	70-158	6-127	64-29
4. Pass Reagan Bill	Jul. 30, 1886	192-41	125-6	66-35
5. Pass ICA	Jan. 21, 1887	219-41	128-15	90-24

Note: Because of third-party exclusions, partisan vote totals do not sum to aggregate vote.

Source: American Leaders, 1789–1987: A Biographical Summary (Washington, D.C.: Congressional Quarterly Inc., 1987), Appendix; *Congressional Record.*

was 44 percent). Given a choice between the Reagan bill and commission regulation, the agrarian Democratic majority on the floor invariably chose the former, as evidenced by their roll-call voting behavior. But the precarious position of commission legislation in the House was the result of factors in addition to agrarian floor power. House organization lodged considerable agenda-setting power with committees and their chairs, and agrarian Democrat John Reagan of Texas remained the chairman of the House Commerce Committee. It was this combination of Reagan's institutional advantages and the bloc voting strength of agrarian Democrats on the floor that framed the challenge to party leaders intent on securing commission regulation.

While committees and committee chairs constituted a formidable organization of power in the House, the years since 1880 had also seen the rise of a countervailing power lodged with party leaders, particularly with the Speaker of the House. By the mid-1880s, the Speaker securely controlled the distribution of committee assignments – a tremendous source of agenda power – while his discretionary power of recognition made a potent tool for both managing floor deliberations and fostering relationships of obligation and dependence with rank-and-file members. Moreover, major rule changes in 1880 had created a powerful standing Rules Committee, chaired by the Speaker, with formidable agenda-setting powers of its own. These partisan leadership structures grew up alongside and challenged the traditional authority of committee chairs. By the era of Republican Speakers Thomas Brackett Reed (1889–91, 1895–9) and Joseph G. Cannon (1903–11), party leaders would dominate the organization of power in the House. But in the mid-1880s, the relative authority of committee chairs and party leaders still remained to be sorted out. As we will shortly see, much of the strategic maneuvering in the House on the railroad question involved efforts by party leaders to circumvent the potent alliance maintained between Commerce Chairman Reagan and agrarian Democrats on the floor.

Particularly challenging for this analysis is the relative absence of direct evidence to either substantiate or refute the claim that House party leaders sought to block the Reagan bill and advance commission legislation. There is no "smoking gun" in the historical record; Democratic Speaker John G. Carlisle left behind no definitive statements of either his personal attitudes toward the various regulatory proposals or of any steps undertaken as Speaker on behalf of any particular plan.[80] For this

---

80. Nineteenth-century party leaders generally appear to have avoided a paper trail. For example, years after his retirement from the Senate, former Democratic Majority Leader Arthur Pue Gorman told one historian who sought access to his personal papers, "I burn all my important political papers." And railroad regulation was one

reason, I will undertake a broad investigation of leadership actions – covering both the Forty-eighth and Forty-ninth Congresses. My aim is to uncover patterns of behavior consistent with the claim that party leaders consciously took steps to contain the Reagan bill and promote its commission rival. In the course of this analysis, evidence will be culled from several sources, the sum of which I believe warrants the conclusion that Democratic party leaders actively intervened to press the interests of the national party against the longstanding policy commitments of their agrarian rank and file on the railroad problem.

The Programmatic Use of Committee Assignments. An effective place to start our analysis of House Democratic leadership is with the congressional committee assignment process. Scholars have described the assignment of committees in the modern Congress as essentially a process of self-selection, while adherence to the seniority system is typically invoked to explain the relative ranking of committee members within party delegations. While such concepts have definite application to the Gilded Age House, they nonetheless leave us underprepared for the degree to which committee appointments were employed as instruments of party policy leadership.[81] Indeed, the literature on Congress' historical development depicts the Democratic Speaker John G. Carlisle (1883–9) as an institutional innovator in this regard. According to one student of the House Speakership, Carlisle believed that the Speaker's appointment power should not be used

> in a spirit of balancing favors to the majority and minority, not even in a spirit of obedience to the dictates of the majority, but in accordance with the Speaker's individual judgment. He considered it the Speaker's duty to be the leader of Congress, to have a definite legislative policy, and to secure the accomplishment of that policy.[82]

According to another source, Speaker Carlisle "used his power to appoint committees to compose them in such a way that they reflected his views more closely than anyone else's."[83] While in the words of one

of the most contentious problems to arise in the 1880s House. Indicative of this fact – and of the strategic ambiguity that probably facilitated his rise in the party ranks – Carlisle managed to avoid ever casting a vote on railroad regulation in the years prior to his tenure as Speaker, even though it had come before the House in one form or another in 1878, 1882, and 1883.

81. For a critical discussion of the self-selection thesis, see Cox and McCubbins, *Legislative Leviathan.* On the growth of the seniority system, see Polsby, Gallagher, and Rundquist, "The Growth of the Seniority System in the House of Representatives."

82. Follett, *The Speaker of the House of Representatives,* 115.

83. U.S. Congress. House. *History of the United States House of Representatives, 1789–1994,* 104.

final authority, Carlisle "clearly advocated a party program and . . . vigorously supported it."[84]

In the Forty-eighth Congress (1883–5), the House Commerce Committee revolted against the Reagan bill and the committee's chairman, John H. Reagan. A committee majority refused to support the chairman's agrarian-styled legislation and instead reported out a commission bill drafted by committeeman Edward W. Seymour, Democrat from Connecticut. The manifest hostility of the Commerce Committee to Chairman Reagan's regulatory bill makes this episode a good place to begin our discussion of committee assignments. For here, Carlisle's appointments were directly responsible for the formation of an anti-Reagan coalition in committee – a situation that Reagan believed had been intentionally foisted upon him by party leaders. On the floor of the House, Reagan complained of the leadership's efforts to stack the Commerce Committee against his railroad bill. His frustration is well captured in the remarks of Minority Leader Joseph Warren Keifer, Republican from Ohio, a supporter of commission legislation, who remarked: "I know the distinguished gentleman in charge of this measure has seen fit to say that the Commerce Committee was packed in favor of a particular bill, and that this same statement has been made more than once on the floor."[85]

Reagan believed that party leaders were stacking the deck against his agrarian regulatory bill, but are his accusations supported by more systematic evidence? The claim that Speaker Carlisle foisted an anti-Reagan majority on the Commerce Committee chairman is not apparent using conventional measures of committee bias. Most obviously, Reagan enjoyed a 9 to 6 advantage of Democrats over Republicans in committee, reflecting the partisan seat ratio in the full House. This partisan advantage, in conjunction with the fact that the vast majority of House Democrats backed Reagan's regulatory position, should have boded well for the chairman's ability to retain control of the committee's legislative agenda. Nor does the economic and demographic composition of the Commerce Committee suggest that Carlisle had stacked the committee with "preference outliers" – that is, committee members with policy preferences out of step with the Democratic floor majority.[86] In its economic

84. Peters, *The American Speakership*, 62.
85. *Congressional Record*, 48th Cong., 2d sess., Vol. 16, pt. 1: 528.
86. The classic statement of committees as preference outliers is Weingast and Marshall, "The Industrial Organization of Congress." A classic critique is Krehbiel, "Are Congressional Committees Composed of Preference Outliers?" A more extended treatment is Krehbiel, *Information and Legislative Organization*. Another critique can be found in Cox and McCubbins, *Legislative Leviathan*.

Table 2.5. *Comparison of Commerce Committee and Floor Characteristics (Forty-eighth Congress, 1883–1885)*

	1. Commerce Committee Median		2. Floor Median	
A. Improved Farm Acreage (*per capita*)	5.9		5.4	
B. Value of Manufacturing Product (*per capita*)	58.3		58.6	
	Democrat Median	Republican Median	Democrat Median	Republican Median
A. Improved Farm Acreage (*per capita*)	5.2	8.1	5.7	5.3
B. Value of Manufacturing Product (*per capita*)	57.6	77.5	41.6	78.7
Committee Members from districts with competitive points (N = 15)	20.0%			
All House members from districts with competitive points (N = 323)	19.1%			

characteristics, the Commerce Committee virtually mirrored the composition of the full House. As reported in Table 2.5, whether measured in terms of district-level agricultural or manufacturing activity, the median characteristics of the committee closely tracked those of the floor. This pattern continues to hold when we compare each party's median characteristics in committee with those found on the floor. Table 2.5 also shows that the percentage of committee members from districts with competitive terminal points (where opposition to the Reagan bill was strong) roughly paralleled the chamber percentage. Finally, Table 2.6 also suggests that Carlisle took additional pains to assure regional balance on the committee in rough proportion to the regional makeup of each party's coalition.

Committee profiles convey important political information to interested observers. In this context, the observable characteristics of the Commerce Committee clearly suggest that Speaker Carlisle sought to

Table 2.6. *Comparison of Regional*
Representation on Commerce Committee and
the House Floor (Forty-eighth Congress)

Region	Floor	Committee
New England	8.0	13.3
Mid-Atlantic	21.4	20.0
East-North-Central	22.9	13.3
West-North-Central	12.4	20.0
South	26.3	20.0
Border	6.2	6.7
Mountain	0.6	0.0
Pacific	2.2	6.7

communicate a posture of equal treatment and fair representation to each of the parties and most of the factional elements within each party. This seemingly nonpartisan handling of committee assignments is likely one of the reasons that Mugwumps looked upon Carlisle with considerable favor.[87] The real issue, however, is whether the necessity of attending to the representational and symbolic aspects of the assignment process impeded the Speaker's ability to introduce a substantive bias into the Commerce Committee. And here the empirical evidence suggests – as Reagan maintained – that party leaders had indeed taken steps to assure a committee hostile to the agrarian railroad measure.

On the floor vote to substitute the Reagan bill for the Commerce Committee's own commission bill (Forty-eighth Congress, Dec. 16, 1884), 81 percent of all Republicans voting opposed Reagan's measure (16–70). It might therefore be argued that Republican Reagan supporters were simply too few in number to fill up the committee without upsetting the political balance Carlisle sought to craft. However, the evidence suggests that Republicans could in fact be found across a range of different economic and demographic profiles. Utilizing the per capita value of manufacturing production as one measure of the agrarian/industrial character of a district, Republican supporters of the Reagan bill existed

87. Recall the remarks earlier cited of Massachusetts Mugwump and railroad expert Charles Francis Adams, Jr., on the desirability of a Cleveland-Carlisle team in 1884. In the second Cleveland Administration (1893–7) Carlisle would be appointed secretary of the treasury, much to the satisfaction of Mugwumps, for whom the defense of the gold standard against free silver heretics was one of the overriding issues of the 1890s.

in almost equal proportion on both sides of the party floor median (nine members below the median and seven above). These sixteen Republicans were also regionally well-distributed: six from the mid-Atlantic states, two from east-north-central states, three from west-north-central states, and five from the south or border states. This distribution suggests that had Carlisle desired to use his minority-party appointments to smuggle additional friends of the Reagan bill onto the committee, he could have done so without sacrificing the principle of equal representation for the different economic and demographic groupings. Instead, as we will see shortly, Carlisle's appointments yielded a Republican minority even *more* uniformly hostile to the Reagan bill than Republicans on the floor, as measured by the floor vote to substitute the Reagan measure for the committee's commission bill.

Because of the anti-Reagan orientation of Carlisle's Republican appointments in the Forty-eighth Congress, the Commerce Committee's disposition of the railroad question necessarily turned on the preferences of its Democratic majority. Faced with unified Republican committee opposition, it required only two Democratic defections to produce an 8 to 7 anti-Reagan working majority. This need not have been problematic. Had Carlisle been intent on supporting the Reagan bill, he could have easily populated the committee with Democratic Reagan supporters without sacrificing economic or demographic representation, for the vast majority of Democrats supported the Reagan bill.[88] While it is empirically true that Democratic opposition to the Reagan bill increased with the size of a district's manufacturing base, it remains the case that forty-six Democrats from districts above the median party value for manufacturing activity supported the Reagan bill on the floor vote to substitute.[89] Democratic supporters of the Reagan bill could likewise be found in every region of the country. Here, then, Carlisle's choices are particularly revealing, for in the end his Democratic appointments worked to create a 2 to 1 committee majority opposed to Reagan, as again measured by its 5 to 10 vote to oppose the Reagan substitute on the House floor (see Table 2.7).

More systematic evidence of the anti-Reagan bias on the Commerce Committee is presented in Table 2.8 and Table 2.9, which report several LOGISTIC REGRESSION equations estimating House voting behavior on a series of proposed amendments to the Reagan bill. The equations include

---

88. On the vote to substitute the Reagan bill for the committee bill, 85 percent of Democrats voting supported Reagan.
89. In all, Democrats below the party median voted for the Reagan substitute 78 to 4, with 18 not voting. Democrats above the party median voted 46 to 23 in support of Reagan, with 30 not voting.

Table 2.7. *Regulatory Preferences of House Commerce Committee Members as Shown on Two Floor Votes*

	Democrats			Republicans		
	Yes	No	No Vote	Yes	No	No Vote
A. Substitute Reagan Bill	5	4	0	0	6	0
B. Pass Reagan Bill	5	3	1	1	3	2

Table 2.8. *Logit Estimation of Four Key Amendments to the 1885 Reagan Bill (Forty-eighth Congress, Second Session)*

Variables	Delete Long Haul– Short Haul	Include State Courts	Include Commission	Allow Exceptions to Antirebate Section
Party	−3.32**	7.44**	−3.68**	−4.23**
	(.49)	(1.24)	(.49)	(.58)
New York	3.78**	−1.78	2.67**	0.17
	(1.10)	(1.72)	(1.03)	(1.08)
Commerce	1.60*	−3.33**	0.55	1.81*
Committee	(.84)	(1.24)	(.97)	(.93)
Farmers	0.40	2.93**	−0.94	−2.13**
	(.58)	(1.13)	(.66)	(.79)
Railroad Capital	−3.47**	0.21	−0.34	0.67
	(.77)	(1.86)	(1.15)	(1.22)
ROI	0.13**	−0.22**	0.11*	0.02
	(.05)	(.07)	(.05)	(.05)
Terminal Centers	1.04	0.27	−1.11	−0.81
	(.60)	(.93)	(.74)	(.82)
West	0.74	0.49	2.49**	1.31
	(.82)	(.96)	(.82)	(.85)
Constant	0.14	−3.13	1.16	2.60**
	(.83)	(1.67)	(.88)	(1.11)
−2 Log Likelihood	162.25	74.51	153.41	120.63
% Correctly Predicted	83.7	93.9	86.5	90.0
Observations	202	195	207	189

Note: Asymptotic standard errors in parentheses.
* = p < .05; ** = p < .01.

Table 2.9. *Logit Estimation of Three Key Votes on
the 1885 Reagan Bill (Forty-eighth Congress, Second Session)*

Variables	Substitute Reagan Bill	Vote to Recommit Reagan Bill	Final Vote on Reagan Bill
Party	2.86**	−4.89**	2.45**
	(.42)	(.67)	(.42)
New York	−0.75	3.34**	−2.97**
	(.86)	(1.30)	(.96)
Commerce Committee	−1.79*	0.72	−2.00**
	(.84)	(1.04)	(.82)
Farmers	1.04	−1.49*	0.50
	(.60)	(.78)	(.56)
Railroad Capital	−0.43	−2.76*	(2.88)**
	(1.01)	(1.40)	(1.13)
ROI	−0.16**	0.16**	−0.16**
	(.05)	(.06)	(.04)
Terminal Centers	−0.15	−1.02	−0.61
	(.63)	(.82)	(.57)
West	−1.94**	1.70	0.92
	(.66)	(.90)	(.72)
Constant	0.41	2.45*	0.56
	(.82)	(1.12)	(.76)
−2 Log Likelihood	178.20	127.84	272.08
% Correctly predicted	81.7	88.9	80.9
Observations	224	208	219

Note: Asymptotic standard errors in parentheses.
* = $p < .05$; ** = $p < .01$.

both variables of theoretical importance to this analysis and a set of control variables. An appendix at the end of this chapter offers a full description of all variables used in regression analyses for this chapter. Taken together, these results document the persistent, *negative* relationship between the regulatory preferences of the Commerce Committee and those of floor Democrats, underscoring the extent to which the latter was at odds with the committee party leaders had constituted. Looking simply at the direction of each HCC (House Commerce Committee) coefficient in Table 2.8, we see that Democratic leaders had effectively organized a committee hostile to the Reagan bill's absolute ban on long haul–short haul discriminations, its rigid antirebate provision, and its failure to provide for a railroad commission (though in this latter case, the coefficient is not statistically significant). In addition, the committee also opposed a provision to prohibit the removal of railroad rate disputes from state to federal courts, expressing its intolerance of the states' rights ideology of the Democratic party. Turning to Table 2.9, we see that members of the Commerce Committee broke with the Democratic floor majority both on the vote to substitute the Reagan bill for the committee's commission bill and on the Reagan measure's vote of final passage, in each instance voting to kill agrarian legislation.

In addition to committee/floor differences, these tables further document the persistent opposition of New York legislators to the preferences of the Democratic floor majority on many of these same substantive questions, and their equally persistent conformity with the voting direction of the Commerce Committee. These patterns are important because they are consistent with the claim that Democratic leaders not only organized the Commerce Committee to be hostile to the Reagan bill, but also to be one that would advance the preferences of New York business Mugwumps. Vote probability statistics can be calculated from the equations reported in Table 2.8 and Table 2.9. When this is done, we find that the likelihood of a Democrat opposing the Reagan position on any given vote increased from 50 to 70 percentage points if that representative also came from New York State. Republican opposition to the Reagan bill was generally strong. Still, the likelihood of a Republican opposing the Reagan position increased an additional 17 to 40 percentage points if that representative was also from New York. New York representatives strongly supported both the deletion of Reagan's long haul–short haul section and the addition of a railroad commission. Most telling, on the final vote to pass the Reagan bill – or, put differently, faced with the choice of the agrarian measure or no regulation – the probability of a Democrat voting to pass the Reagan bill dropped by more than 50 percentage points if that representative was also from New York. Even for a New York Republican, the drop was just under 50 percentage points.

Finally, additional evidence buttressing the claim that House leaders intentionally composed a Commerce Committee opposed to agrarian railroad legislation is suggested by the subsequent appointment history of Edward Seymour, Democrat from Connecticut, the Commerce Committee member who drafted the committee's commission bill in the Forty-eighth Congress. Seymour was also a member of the Forty-ninth Congress. There, had he chosen to do so, Speaker Carlisle might have disciplined this relatively junior representative (it was only his second term) by banishing him to insignificant committee posts. Instead, Carlisle placed Seymour on one of the most important and politically charged committees in the House, the Committee on Coinage, with jurisdiction over currency legislation. Subsequent events on the Coinage Committee would replicate in eerily similar ways what had transpired on the Commerce Committee in the previous Congress. Like the revolt against Reagan, a majority of the Coinage Committee would align themselves against the longstanding preference of the agrarian committee chair, Richard Bland of Missouri. In this case this meant that a committee majority would report adversely on a bill for the free coinage of silver (with Seymour again among the Democrats whose defections made the committee majority possible). Moreover, Bland (like Reagan) would use the chairman's power of recognition to nevertheless secure floor consideration of the free coinage measure, eventually securing a vote on the bill (also like Reagan).

What makes the Coinage Committee example particularly revealing is that, like the case of railroad regulation, Mugwumps had staked out clear and strong opposition to the policy preference of the committee chair (free coinage/the Reagan bill). Mugwumps were ardent proponents of the gold standard. In the case of free coinage, Democratic leaders understood that the passage of silver legislation under their watch might sound the death knell for their fledgling reform coalition. Additionally, the Coinage Committee episode underscores the more general leadership practice of using committee chairmanships to accord representation and party recognition to factional leaders but, where necessary for broader party goals, stacking the rest of the committee with bipartisan majorities that more faithfully reflected the preferences of the party leadership. It also indicates once again the limits of such a strategy, as committee chairs had advantages on the floor which could successfully be wielded against both their committee and the party leadership, assuming the preferences of the chamber majority were closer to those of the chair than to either of these other actors.

Institutional Context and Agenda Control: The Conference Committee and Party Leadership. Reagan, like the agrarian Bland, was ultimately able to work around the opposition of his committee by utilizing the chairman's right of floor recognition and harnessing floor Democratic support behind the Reagan bill, which passed the House in the Forty-eighth Congress on January 8, 1885. As we saw at the outset of this chapter, a final resolution to the railroad problem was in the end stymied only because Democratic leaders engaged in a politics of delay, failing to take the steps needed to organize a conference committee before the final session of Congress expired (on March 3, 1885).

The historical record is silent on the conclusions Democratic leaders drew from Reagan's tactical victories in the Forty-eighth Congress and the adjustments needed to facilitate the movement of commission legislation in the following Congress. But indirect evidence allows us to make certain inferences about the alterations they undertook and the rationale behind them. And that evidence suggests that Democratic leaders were intent to avoid another floor fight on the details of railroad regulation. They had good reason to do so. Over the course of an extended floor amending process in the Forty-eighth Congress, efforts to add a commission, weaken Reagan's stringent long haul–short haul and antirebate provisions, and delete its antipooling section had all gone down to defeat (the latter without a roll-call vote).[90] Particularly revealing was the amendment vote to add a commission to the Reagan bill. The commission amendment went down to defeat on a chamber vote of 97 to 125. Indicative of the rank-and-file stance on this subject, 83 percent of all Democrats voting had opposed the addition of a commission (23 to 113). But significantly, only five of the twenty-one Democrats representing New York had opposed the commission (while six had voted "aye" and another ten [almost 50 percent] had not cast a vote). Thus, if party leaders wanted to contain agrarian legislation and advance the preferences of business Mugwumps, they had every reason to avoid another open amendment process on the floor, where party support had shown itself to be weak. Faced with this predicament, there is evidence to suggest that a caucus agreement was subsequently worked out between party leaders and rank-and-file Democrats in the Forty-ninth Congress, to move the Reagan bill out of committee, through the chamber unamended, and from there to a conference committee, where Democratic leaders might play a more prominent role in reconciling local and national party interests.

Before we turn to the evidence, a question naturally arises: Why would agrarian Democrats willingly relinquish their floor power to party leaders working behind closed doors in conference? We are not without certain guides in making our hypotheses. Perhaps most important, the Forty-ninth Congress was the first post–Civil War Congress to be conducted under the auspices of a Democratic president, and all eyes were upon the party of "rum, Romanism, and rebellion" to see whether it was up to the challenge of governing. While all Democrats had a collective stake in the success of the new Cleveland administration – whether it be for patronage, presidential coattails, or control of the executive veto and instruments of federal law enforcement – each Democrat faced strong

90. See Table 2.4 for breakdown of raw vote totals.

individual incentives to press the interests of their district on the floor and leave it to others to shoulder the burden of advancing shared party interests. Removing the site of negotiation over the substance of regulation from the floor to conference, therefore, would allow party leaders greater leeway in resolving this collective action problem and resolving tensions between conflicting party needs.

Moreover, by the early 1880s the conference committee was well developed as an "instrument of control by party leaders."[91] To enhance leadership's control over the substance of conference legislation, the practice of "amending by substitute" had achieved wide currency. By this procedure, according to one prominent scholar of the nineteenth-century Congress, "one House strikes out all of a bill from the other House except the enacting clause and substitutes a bill of its own."[92] Because the deliberations of conference managers are confined to the points of difference between the chambers, this action afforded Gilded Age party leaders maximum latitude to negotiate the final content of legislation.[93] Moreover, because conference reports are privileged and conference bills are not subject to amendment – only to an up or down vote – the agenda control of party leaders was considerably enhanced once back on the floor. The chamber was in essence given a single choice: to accept the conference legislation or retain the status quo. As we will see at several points in this analysis, any bill paired against the status quo was likely to meet with chamber approval as members were loathe to appear as though they were opposed to railroad regulation per se.

There are several indications that party leaders sought to shift the institutional context to their advantage by recourse to the conference committee. First, in April, 1886, the House Commerce Committee reported out the commission bill of the Senate Select Committee on Interstate Commerce, which had passed the upper chamber in only slightly amended form. Following the procedure sketched above, the Senate legislation was accompanied by the Reagan bill, to be offered as an "amendment in the nature of a substitute."[94] Given the wide differences in the provisions of these bills, the passage of the Reagan bill in the House guaranteed that the final substance of railroad regulation would be written in conference. As we will see, with public opinion demanding railroad

---

91. McCown, *The Congressional Conference Committee*, 104.
92. Ibid., 74.
93. Republican leaders relied on this technique to great effect in 1883, using the conference committee to write higher tariff schedules into law than could be obtained on the floor of either chamber.
94. U.S. Congress. House. Committee on Commerce. *Report*. 49th Cong., 1st sess., 1886, no. 2554.

regulation, legislators on the House floor would be hard pressed to reject a regulatory commission bill returned from conference.

Equally important, in constituting the Commerce Committee for the Forty-ninth Congress, Speaker Carlisle appears to have been anticipating the appointment of a conference committee on railroad regulation. Here Carlisle pushed aside considerations of seniority in filling the second-ranking majority seat behind Reagan. Specifically, Carlisle passed over third-ranking Democrat Martin Clardy of Missouri – one of the few committee holdovers from the Forty-eighth Congress – in favor of Charles Crisp, a second-term congressman from Georgia.[95] Considerations of subject-matter expertise could not have been at issue in Carlisle's decision to violate seniority. Clardy had six years experience on the Commerce Committee, more than any Democrat with the exception of Reagan. Indeed, Carlisle would appoint Clardy to chair the Commerce Committee in the Fiftieth Congress (1887–9), in the wake of Reagan's elevation to the Senate. So why did Carlisle bypass Clardy for Crisp in this instance? Though junior and inexperienced in railroad affairs, Crisp was already a presence within the House party leadership, having quickly distinguished himself as a favorite of Speaker Carlisle.[96] In Carlisle's absence, Crisp filled the role of Speaker *pro tempore* in the Forty-ninth Congress, and he would assume the Speakership in his own right in the Fifty-second Congress (1891–3).[97] Crisp's appointment was critical because it gave party leaders direct representation on the Commerce Committee. Moreover, as the committee's second-ranking majority member Crisp would accompany Reagan to the six-person conference committee in which the final ICA was written, assuring House party leaders the crucial swing vote in these final negotiations (assuming that the Senate delegation was unanimous behind the commission). Crisp would also assume the difficult responsibility of managing the ICA on the House floor – as a result of Reagan's timely absence from the chamber – a duty that would include the onerous task of defending its provisions against angry agrarian critics.

While Crisp's Commerce Committee appointment is critical, it is the roll-call behavior of Reagan's traditional Democratic opponents *in support of* the Reagan bill that is the best indication we have of a caucus action to move consideration of railroad regulation into conference. And among the several votes leading up to the final passage of the Reagan

95. Preston, "The Political Career of Charles Frederick Crisp," 19.
96. Ibid., 38.
97. Luce, *Legislative Procedure: Parliamentary Practice and the Course of Business in the Framing of Statutes*, 479.

bill, the vote on the Hiscock substitute is perhaps the best measure we have of this *party* agreement. The substitute was introduced by New York Republican Frank Hiscock, a member of the distinguished Republican minority leadership that included Thomas Brackett Reed and William McKinley. Technically, Hiscock's amendment was itself a substitute for Reagan's own substitute to the Senate-passed commission bill. Substantively, it proposed to strike out everything after the enabling clause of the Reagan bill and reinsert the provisions of the Senate commission bill.[98] In essence then, the Hiscock vote was one to concur in the Senate bill. This point is crucial. A victory for the Hiscock amendment would have obviated the need for a conference, which was vitally important to Democratic leaders hoping to reconcile the Mugwump-backed regulatory commission plan with the substantive concerns of agrarian House Democrats. Put differently, by supporting the Hiscock amendment, Democratic opponents of the Reagan bill (with Republican support) could immediately enact the provisions of the Senate commission bill and thereby avoid the uncertainty of a conference committee with its potentially crippling agrarian concessions.

The vote on the Hiscock substitute was the first vote taken on the railroad question in the Forty-ninth Congress. It was therefore also the most critical test of relative support for the Reagan bill and the Senate commission bill. First votes on controversial legislation are often acknowledged to be "test votes" because they gauge the relative support for a measure on the floor. This had been the case on the vote to substitute the Reagan bill for the House Commerce Committee's own commission bill in the Forty-eighth Congress.[99] A test vote conveyed essential information about the relative prospects for passage of important legislation. Given the opportunity presented by Hiscock's motion, Reagan's Democratic opponents had every reason to support his amendment. For in combination with the Republican minority these Democrats might claim a floor majority for the Senate bill. Therefore, absent caucus constraints, it is reasonable to expect Democratic voting patterns to have resembled the patterns we observed in the Forty-eighth Congress, with defections modest in number, but in conjunction with a disciplined Republican minority, large enough to swing the outcome to the

---

98. Technically, the Senate bill could not be offered as an amendment to the Reagan bill, since it was itself the subject of a move to amend. To meet this objection, Hiscock altered the date at which the Interstate Commerce Commission would commence its activities. Aside from this change, it remained the bill of the Senate.

99. *Congressional Record*, 48th Cong., 2d sess., Vol. 16, pt. 2: 1386; ibid., pt. 3: 2247. It was also the case with free-coinage legislation in the 49th Congress, to cite another instance.

commission bill.[100] Instead, roll-call data indicate that Democrats responded to the Hiscock amendment with a level of partisan unity unmatched in any previous vote on the railroad question. The Hiscock substitute ultimately went down to defeat, but the vote was close, 102 to 126 (with 94 not voting). Democrats voted 10 to 118 against Hiscock, while Republicans voted 92 to 6 for the amendment. A switch of only 13 Democratic votes would have resulted in House concurrence and the enactment of the Senate bill into law. Thus, it is all the more remarkable that traditional Democratic opponents of the Reagan bill stood firm against Hiscock, agreeing de facto to take their chances in a reconciliation process where important concessions to the Reagan forces might be forthcoming.

Table 2.10 presents the results of a multivariate estimate of the Hiscock vote using LOGISTIC REGRESSION. The equation in Table 2.10 confirms systematically what the raw-vote scores clearly suggest: Little else mattered to the determination of the vote but a legislator's party identification. In addition to this party effect, however, several aspects of the Hiscock vote seem difficult to explain outside the caucus thesis. First, Democrats who had previously served on the Commerce Committee in the Forty-eighth Congress and had voted against the Reagan bill, now threw their support on balance behind the agrarian measure (2 to 1). So too did current Democratic members of the Commerce Committee (7 to 1), despite constituency profiles that made them more likely opponents of Reagan.[101] Most striking of all, New York Democrats, who as we will see registered the most vigorous dissent against the Reagan bill in *sub-*

---

100. Recall that in the 48th Congress, 27 Democrats had broken ranks to support the Commerce Committee's commission bill over the Reagan substitute.

101. With the installation of Grover Cleveland in the White House, Carlisle appears to have shifted the mix of signals in his appointments to the Commerce Committee. The committee was substantially reorganized. To begin with, only three of the fifteen Commerce Committee members from the 48th Congress retained their committee seats in the new Congress, the most important being chairman Reagan and the ranking Republican, Charles O'Neill of Pennsylvania. Unlike the 48th Congress, the new committee was packed with legislators representing constituencies strongly opposed to the Reagan bill. One measure of this change was the precipitous decline in the agrarian character of the committee. This was especially pronounced among members of the Republican minority, which was heavily representative of urban commercial and manufacturing interests. In addition, a working majority on the Commerce Committee members now came from districts in which a competitive terminal point was located, significant because groups situated in these terminal cities were typically loud opponents of the Reagan bill's rigid ban on person and place discrimination. Thus, given its composition, the likelihood of this committee reporting out the Reagan bill without outside intervention of some sort would have been very unlikely.

Table 2.10. *Logit Estimation of Three Votes on the Reagan Bill*
(Forty-ninth Congress First Session)

Variables	Hiscock Amendment	Substitute Reagan Bill for Senate Bill	Final Vote on Reagan Bill
Party	−5.53**	6.44**	2.81**
	(.70)	(.95)	(.77)
New York	0.80	5.80**	−7.35**
	(1.49)	(1.55)	(1.67)
Commerce Committee	−0.55	3.12	−0.81
	(1.60)	(2.53)	(1.32)
Farmers	−1.50	1.89	0.41
	(1.11)	(1.09)	(.98)
Railroad Capital	1.57	2.17	5.67**
	(1.73)	(1.69)	(2.12)
ROI	0.10	−0.27**	−0.30**
	(.07)	(.07)	(.08)
Terminal Centers	−0.19	−1.81	−2.08
	(1.21)	(1.13)	(1.07)
West	0.38	0.96	−0.58
	(1.02)	(.82)	(1.00)
Constant	2.17	−1.31*	4.24**
	(1.37)	(1.37)	(1.53)
−2 Log Likelihood	100.36	121.23	176.31
% Correctly predicted	92.9	91.9	91.8
Observations	235	235	231

Note: Asymptotic standard errors in parentheses.
* = p < .05; ** = p < .01.

sequent votes, substantially failed to cross party lines when it mattered – to support Hiscock. Of the sixteen Democrats representing New York state in the Forty-ninth Congress, only three sided with Hiscock on this critical vote. Among the remaining thirteen, seven opposed the commission substitute and six did not vote. It is also worth observing that the thirteen New York Democrats who either voted "nay" or abstained alone comprised a bloc of votes just large enough to have swung the outcome to Hiscock.

In subsequent floor actions, party remained the single best predictor of a legislator's vote. However, with the relative balance of power on the

Table 2.11. *Probability of Voting "Aye" on Vote to Substitute Reagan Bill and on Final Vote of Passage (Forty-ninth Congress, 1885–1887)*

	Democrats		Republicans	
	Floor	New York	Floor	New York
Vote to Substitute Reagan Bill for Senate Bill	.98	.20	.11	.01
If Terminal Point Also in N.Y. District		.04		.00
Vote to Pass Reagan Bill	.10	.63	.82	.99
If Terminal Point Also in N.Y. District		.04		.00

floor now known, the pull of party grew weaker with each succeeding vote, revealing the deep structure of constituent preferences that underlay earlier caucus unity. The next vote was on the motion to substitute the Reagan bill for the Senate commission bill, which passed on a vote of 134 to 104 (with 84 legislators not voting). Democrats supported the Reagan substitute 119 to 18, with Republicans voting 13 to 86 against it. Despite the persistence of partisanship, LOGISTIC REGRESSION results also reported in Table 2.10 now reveal the antagonism of New York representatives toward the agrarian railroad bill. Selected vote probability scores are reported in Table 2.11. They indicate that the likelihood of a Democrat supporting the motion to substitute the Reagan bill for the Senate commission bill plummeted – from .98 to .20 – if that representative was also from New York State.[102] If, in addition, that New York Democrat came from a district with a competitive terminal point, the probability of supporting Reagan fell to .04. Among Republicans, the probability of supporting the Reagan substitute was already low (.11). When that representative was also from New York, the probability of voting "aye" dropped virtually to zero, even before factoring in terminal point status.

Opposition to the Reagan bill finally collapsed altogether on its final

102. In discussions involving probabilities attached to roll call voting behavior, all Republican or Democratic legislators referred to are ideal-types constructed by setting all continuous variables equal to their mean value and all dummy variables equal to "0" (absence). Unless otherwise stated, the only variables manipulated for comparison are PARTY, COMMITTEE, and NEW YORK. Manipulating the value of the other variables does not substantively alter the conclusions reached.

vote of passage, with legislators voting 192 to 41 (with 89 not voting). This vote is most significant for what it reveals about the opportunity forsaken by Democratic friends of the Senate commission bill to secure its undiluted, final passage by withholding support for the Hiscock amendment. Faced with a choice of the Senate bill or the status quo, a large Democratic contingent would likely have accepted the Senate commission legislation to avoid being labeled obstructionists. This is made clear by the way anxious Republicans, who had previously opposed the Reagan bill, now ran for political cover to make sure that *they* were not caught appearing to oppose regulation per se. Democrats still overwhelmingly voted to pass the bill, 126 to 6. But now, by a margin of almost 2 to 1, Republicans also supported the Reagan bill – 66 "aye" to 35 "nay" (see Table 2.10 for LOGISTIC REGRESSION estimates of this vote).

Despite this more overtly bipartisan atmosphere, however, New York representatives continued to resist the pressure to pass the Reagan bill, underscoring the depth of opposition to the Reagan bill to be found in this crucial electoral college state. Once again the probability of a Democrat supporting the Reagan bill fell precipitously if that legislator was also a representative of New York: from .98 to .20 – and again to .04, if he also hailed a competitive terminal district. Likewise, even as constituent pressures drove large numbers of Republicans into an opportunistic embrace of the agrarian legislation, New York Republicans continued to maintain their opposition. Thus the likelihood of a Republican voting to pass the Reagan bill fell from .76 to .06 if that legislator also represented a district in New York State.

The Restructuring of Legislative Choice and the Agrarian Response to the Interstate Commerce Act. The substitution of the Reagan bill and its subsequent passage on July 30, 1886, meant that the final substance of interstate railroad regulation would be written in conference. The House delegation to the conference committee was comprised of ranking Commerce Committee Democrats Reagan and Crisp, along with commerce Republican Archibald J. Weaver of Nebraska. The conferees met throughout the summer and fall of 1886, and they would be ready to report their compromise bill (the ICA) at the start of the second session of Congress that December.

Introduction of the ICA into the House recast the structure of collective choice in that chamber. Agrarian Democrats no longer faced a familiar two-stage voting sequence: an initial choice pitting the Reagan bill against a commission bill (resolved in Reagan's favor), and a second placing the Reagan bill in a final pairing with the *status quo ante*, resolved once more to Reagan's advantage. The move to the conference committee had upset this traditional frame. Legislators faced a new context of collective choice, one that would force Democrats to choose between an independent railroad commission with regulatory power or the status quo of no regulation. As we have just seen, nervous congressmen were more likely to support almost any regulatory strategy when paired with the alternative of no regulation. Indeed, the pressure to pass some kind of regulatory legislation had ratcheted upward with a Supreme Court decision in October 1886 striking down as unconstitutional all state-level regulation of interstate commerce.[103] Any regulatory legislation presented to the floor by the conference committee would have a momentum that would be hard for legislators to resist.

Substantively, the conference bill was a victory for national Democratic party objectives. As Senate conferee Shelby Cullom would later recall, aside from the provision outlawing the pooling of railroad freight and revenue, "Reagan had yielded on nearly everything else."[104] And while Cullom's recollection is doubtless somewhat self-serving – as we will see, Senate Republicans were not as pleased with the compromise – his assessment is generally more right than wrong. On the majority of significant points, Reagan was unexpectedly conciliatory. Perhaps most surprising of all was Reagan's agreement to accept the railroad commission. What makes this concession so significant is that Reagan did not simply compromise his own preferred position. Rather, the Texas Democrat sacrificed a core agrarian conviction that relief from railroad abuses was best administered through institutions of local government such as the state courts.

Agrarian Democrats passionately echoed this criticism throughout the floor debates on the ICA. Congressman Andrew Caldwell, Democrat from Tennessee, otherwise in agreement with the "common law principle" embodied in each substantive provision of the ICA, adamantly opposed the "interposition of a commission . . . between the people and the courts," fearing it might turn out to be "a Trojan horse and a deception to close the courts against [rural shippers]."[105] Similarly, Charles O'Ferrall, Democrat from Virginia, a member of the Commerce Committee, was almost shrill in his denunciation of commissions, insisting: "I want no commission. The Congress of the United States is the commission created by the people for the enactment of laws, and the courts of the country the tribunals for their enforcement."[106] As these state-

---

103. *Wabash St. Louis & Pacific Railway Co. v Illinois*, 118 U.S. 557 (1886).
104. Cullom, *Fifty Years of Public Service*, 321–2.
105. *Congressional Record*, 49th Cong., 1st sess., Vol. 17, pt. 7: 7292–3.
106. Ibid., 7296.

ments suggest, when Reagan acquiesced to the creation of an interstate commerce commission, he reneged on much more than a personal commitment to avoiding a particular institutional form. Rather, a well-articulated and deeply felt agrarian aversion to railroad commissions was also jettisoned.

Reagan's acceptance of the railroad commission was also devastating because it necessitated a further gutting of the agrarian regulatory scheme. To open up greater scope for the discretionary judgment of the new commission, unequivocal prohibitions, such as those found in Reagan's antirebating and long haul–short haul sections, also had to be abandoned. Conferees did so by adopting the purposely vague phraseology of the Senate legislation. The inclusion of phrases such as "for . . . like and contemporaneous service" and "under substantially similar circumstances and conditions," allowed legislative draftsmen to shift interpretative responsibility, and thus policy power, away from Congress and toward the new interstate commerce commissioners. Democratic conferee George F. Crisp, who managed the final legislation bill on the floor in Reagan's absence, tried to soften the blow to House agrarians by arguing that the word "substantially" had been incorporated into the provisions of the legislation "in the interest of the people," to avoid their narrow application to strictly similar circumstances and conditions. In response, an indignant Iowa Greenbacker, James B. Weaver, a long-time supporter of the Reagan bill, insisted that if House conferees had intended to be faithful to the people's interest, then the entire phrase would have been deleted from such provisions.[107]

Weaver professed his dismay at the retreat of the House conferees from unequivocal statutory prohibitions, in particular questioning the motives of the now-absent Reagan. During a discussion of Section 2 – the antidiscrimination provision – Weaver puzzled aloud: "It is a very strange thing, Mr. Speaker, that the gentleman from Texas approved that section at the insistence of the author of the Senate bill, and approved it in this conference committee, although he had never approved it before at any time in the long history of this controversy."[108]

The historical record does not provide a certain guide to the motivations that compelled Reagan's acceptance of the commission plan. Nor is it possible to discern with confidence the forces that Weaver insinuated lay behind Reagan's capitulation. It will be recalled, however, that we began this chapter with the Greenbacker's denunciation of the major congressional parties for subverting agrarian reform and constituency

107. Ibid., 2d sess., Vol. 18, pt. 1: 818.
108. Ibid.

Table 2.12. *Percentage of House Membership*
Voting Against the Reagan Bill and
the Interstate Commerce Act

	Reagan Bill	ICA
Republican Strongholds	56%	66%
Democratic Strongholds	02%	22%
Swing States	41%	12%

interests to the demands of electoral college politics. Whether this is what Weaver had in mind as he impugned Reagan's motives, it is difficult to say. What is clear is that the concessions extracted from Reagan were consistent with those needed to relieve the immediate coalitional pressures facing the national Democratic party.

This can be shown by comparing the structure of roll-call opposition to the final ICA, with that found on the earlier vote to pass the agrarian Reagan bill. The ICA passed the House on January 21, 1887, by a vote of 219 to 41 (with 58 not voting). Overall, support was strongly bipartisan, with Democrats voting 128 to 15 and Republicans 90 to 24. Table 2.12 compares the electoral college status of those congressmen who voted against the Reagan bill on July 30, 1886 (on its final vote of passage), with those who opposed the passage of the ICA. Overall, the table shows that opposition to the passage of an interstate commerce bill dramatically shrank among swing-state representatives and increased in both Democratic and Republican stronghold states. While 41 percent of all opposition to the Reagan bill came from swing-state representatives, only 12 percent of all opposition to the ICA came from these same states. Likewise, 2 percent of all opposition to the Reagan bill came from Democratic strongholds and 56 percent of all opposition from Republican strongholds, while 22 percent of all opposition to the ICA came from Democratic stronghold states and 66 percent from Republican strongholds. In sum, as the party system framework would predict, opposition to a national regulatory law shrank most notably among those states where Democrats were locked in vigorous competition for electoral college support. Conversely, opposition rose among states where Democratic leaders had reason to be most confident of future electoral outcomes.

More systematically, Table 2.13 reports the estimates of a model measuring the change in support levels for railroad regulation from the final

Table 2.13. *Ordered Logit Estimation of*
Change in Support for Railroad Regulation from
Final Vote on 1886 Reagan Bill to the ICA
(Forty-ninth Congress)

Variables	Shift in Support
Party	−0.718**
	(.252)
New York	1.561**
	(.581)
Commerce Committee	−0.605
	(.521)
Farmers	−0.561
	(.409)
Railroad Capital	−0.424
	(.603)
ROI	0.050
	(.028)
Terminal Centers	−0.559
	(.387)
West	−0.444
	(.450)
(N)	(311)
Log Likelihood	−347.52
chi2 (8)	28.26

** $p < .01$.

vote on the Reagan bill (July 30, 1886) to the vote on the ICA. The statistical technique used here is ORDERED LOGIT, a maximum likelihood model useful where the dependent variable is made up of more than two ordinal categories. The model's independent variables are specified in a fashion identical to the other multivariate analyses in this chapter (again, see the appendix to this chapter for a discussion of variable construction). However, the dependent variable used in this analysis requires some elaboration. While LOGISTIC REGRESSION models of the legislative vote exclude nonvoters from their estimations, the ORDERED LOGIT model utilized here retains this information. In essence, it assumes that abstention from voting is a strategic choice made by legislators, with a level of utility for the act midway between voting "aye" and voting "nay." The construction of the dependent variable (SHIFT IN SUPPORT) is described more fully in the following footnote.[109] Here, suffice to say that SHIFT IN SUPPORT is an ordinal 5-point scale (scored from −2 to +2), similar to a thermometer scale, and it measures changes in the intensity of support for railroad regulation as a result of alterations made by the conference committee. A positive coefficient will indicate increased support for regulation, while a negative coefficient will indicate decreased support.

As the results in Table 2.13 show, the positive and statistically significant NEW YORK coefficient supports the claim that the changes made in conference had a special appeal to interests located in the critical electoral college state of New York. With the adoption of the commission form and the delegation of discretionary regulatory power to that new body, New York representatives shed their opposition to an interstate commerce law. Equally striking is the absence of any statistically significant fall in agrarian support for the final law; indeed, in raw votes, final Democratic support for railroad regulation actually slightly increased. Democrats voted 122 to 26 to pass the 1886 Reagan bill; they voted 128 to 15 to pass the ICA. The high level of Democratic unity, juxtaposed against the accusations of betrayal leveled by agrarians on the floor, offers us one clear measure of the success of Democratic party leaders in holding their party in line behind the Mugwump commission. Finally, the negative party coefficient captures the increased level of Republican support for regulation, most likely the result of the move from the agrarian to a commission-based approach.

Democratic Party Leadership in the Senate

Vice-Presidential Power: The President of the Senate and Appointment of the Select Committee on Interstate Commerce. The analysis of Senate Democratic leadership on behalf of the business Mugwump-styled regulatory approach rightfully begins with the formation of the Senate Select Committee on Interstate Commerce (SCIC). It will be recalled from our previous discussion that the SCIC was organized in the last days of the Forty-eighth Congress (1883–5). Its mandate was to travel the country and collect testimony on the railroad problem. It was further

---

109. The dependent variables for the Reagan and ICA votes are coded identically – 1 'no,' 0 'no vote,' and 1 'yes.' SHIFT IN SUPPORT measures the change in an individual legislator's preference for regulation. It is calculated as follows: (ICA vote) minus (Reagan Bill vote). This calculation yields the following five categories of the dependent variable: −2 'yes to no,' −1 'no vote to no,' 0 'no change,' 1 'no vote to yes,' 2 'no to yes.'

required to report back its findings to the Senate, along with legislative recommendations, in time for the start of the Forty-ninth Congress. As documented earlier in Table 2.3, the SCIC regulatory proposals conformed closely to the recommendations of John Kernan, the Democratic chairman of the New York Railroad Commission, which in turn conformed to principles articulated by business Mugwumps before the SCIC. Indeed, it is this substantive linkage between Mugwump preferences and the Select Committee bill that makes the appointment of the SCIC a useful starting point for this analysis.

It will seem odd to assert that Democratic leadership was important to the constitution of the SCIC. After all, the Democrats were the Senate's minority party in the Forty-ninth Congress. But as we will see, upon the transfer of the presidency to the Democrats, control over the select committee appointment process in that chamber passed to the president's party. As a consequence, Democratic leaders were able to signal their strong backing of commission legislation early on and assume a more prominent leadership role in the constitution of the SCIC.

The presidential inauguration of Grover Cleveland on March 4, 1885, provided Senate Democratic leaders with a fresh opportunity to assume the initiative on behalf of Mugwump-sanctioned regulatory principles. With Cleveland installed in the White House, the new presiding officer in the Republican Senate became the Democratic vice president, Thomas A. Hendricks of Indiana. Historically, the presiding officer's extra-institutional loyalties have rendered the position of president of the Senate a less effectual instrument of party leadership than the House Speakership. Still, the office is not without influence, and in this particular instance its duties conferred strategic opportunities that Democrats could quickly utilize. On the matter of railroad regulation, the opportunity presented to Democrats involved Hendricks's responsibility to appoint select committees. Thus, it fell to the Democratic vice president, and not the Republican president *pro tempore*, to appoint members to the Select Committee on Interstate Commerce (SCIC).[110]

To be sure, there were important constraints operating on Hendricks's discretion in the appointment of the SCIC. Because the Republicans were

---

110. Neilson, *Shelby M. Cullom*, 95; *Congressional Record*, 49th Cong., 1st sess., Vol. 17, pt. 1: 71–2, 309–10. The Republican President *pro tempore* was Senator George F. Edmunds from Vermont. This will not be the last time we observe the exercise of discretionary vice-presidential authority on behalf of national party interests. In Chapter 4, we will see Franklin Roosevelt's vice president, John Nance Garner, exploit his authority over the appointment of conference committees to stack the Senate delegation with members sympathetic to the "death sentence" for public utility holding companies.

the chamber majority party, the select committee would be chaired by a Republican and Republicans would hold a majority of the committee's five seats. In addition, institutional norms favored the appointment of Republican Shelby M. Cullom to chair the committee, having authored the resolution to create the select committee. Beyond this, however, Hendricks possessed substantial latitude to influence the composition of the committee in the direction of either agrarian or Mugwump preferences.

As we observed in the case of Speaker Carlisle and the House Commerce Committee, the composition of the SCIC would go far toward shaping its attitudes toward appropriate reform, Hendricks's selections are particularly noteworthy in two respects. First, and most important, the vice president excluded diehard Reagan bill supporters from positions on the ad hoc body. In itself, this made it unlikely that the Select Committee would report agrarian-styled legislation to the Senate. Second, Hendricks's choices suggest a clear concern for presidential coalition politics, filling Republican seats with commission supporters drawn from northeastern reform circles and Democratic seats with party leaders.

On the Democratic side, Hendricks turned to Arthur Pue Gorman of Maryland. Gorman's appointment to the Select Committee was critical. It sent a clear signal to Democrats in both houses of Congress of the importance national party leaders placed on the select committee's activities. Gorman was arguably the most influential Democrat in Congress in 1885. The Maryland senator had been instrumental to Cleveland's electoral victory in 1884, having chaired the executive committee of the Democratic National Committee. As Cleveland's campaign manager, Gorman had worked closely with Mugwumps through the election-related activities of the NECRI. He also chaired the Democratic Congressional Committee's executive committee, and with the departure of Thomas Bayard to Cleveland's cabinet, had emerged as a ranking member of the Senate Democratic leadership. At a time when public norms encouraged presidential restraint in the realm of legislative leadership, Gorman played an active part in the promotion of national party concerns both within Congress and among Democratic leaders generally.[111] Gorman would keep President Cleveland "informed of the

111. One such case occurred early in the summer of 1888, when the Mills tariff bill – an administration bill – became stalled in Congress, ensuring that the tariff would be a central issue in the upcoming presidential election. In this instance, Cleveland dispatched Gorman to the Democratic national convention at St. Louis in order to reign in free-trade zealots threatening to saddle the party with a tariff plank that Cleveland feared would jeopardize his reelection. At the convention Gorman argued for

[select] committee's work during the preparation of the [regulatory] bill[,]" and he is also credited with securing "a benign presidential interest" in its passage.[112]

Hendricks's other Democratic selection to the SCIC was Isham G. Harris of Tennessee. Harris was a member of the Senate Rules Committee and widely considered one of the Democrats' most able parliamentarians.[113] On several occasions during his Senate career, Harris would serve as Gorman's ally on important floor battles, such as the one soon to develop over the select committee's narrowly drawn long haul–short haul provision.[114] Harris was also the only southerner on the committee, and in this regard his appointment is significant because he lacked the antimonopolist fire that characterized so many southern Democrats on the railroad question. On the vote to substitute the Cullom commission bill for the House Reagan bill in the Forty-eighth Congress, Harris had cast his support for the latter. But he was also one of only eleven Democrats to vote with the Republican majority to pass the Cullom commission bill, a measure of his pragmatism on the railroad question.[115]

Hendricks's initial Republican choices hailed from New York and Massachusetts, the two strongholds of the Mugwump movement. From the former, Hendricks selected Warner Miller. While Miller did not bolt the Republican party in 1884, he had long allied himself with the reform wing of the party in the cause of administrative reform. For example, Miller had incurred the lasting enmity of the New York state Republican machine by his support of President Rutherford B. Hayes's efforts to reform the operation of the New York Customs House.[116] Similarly,

moderation "on the grounds of expediency, for, he declared, a positive declaration in favor of free trade would turn New York, Connecticut, and Indiana over to the Republicans." Lambert, *Arthur Pue Gorman*, 131.

112. Ibid.; Neilson, *Shelby M. Cullom*, 111. One measure of New York Mugwump sway over Democratic leaders on the railroad question is Gorman's judgment that of the dozen Select Committee hearings held across the country, only the first, which was held in New York City, was important enough to attend.

113. Nevins, *Grover Cleveland: A Study in Courage*, 576. Nevins observes that Harris lacked a capacity for political management. As this was Gorman's peculiar talent, the two men made a particularly able pair.

114. Lambert, *Arthur Pue Gorman*, 130; Neilson, *Shelby M. Cullom*, 111; *Congressional Record*, 49th Cong., 1st sess., Vol. 17, pt. 4: 3728, 3870–1.

115. Watters, "Isham Green Harris, Civil War Governor and Senator from Tennessee, 1818–97," 165.

116. The New York Custom House was the jewel in the crown of party patronage, requiring over one thousand appointments to fill its administrative slots. The custom house was also the cornerstone of the Republican party machine in New York State,

the New York senator had thrown his support behind the efforts of President James A. Garfield to appoint an administrative reformer as collector of the port of New York.[117] Though Miller's specific regulatory preferences prior to his appointment to the Select Committee are difficult to trace, his roll-call record in the Forty-eighth Congress indicates support for commission-styled regulation.

For the last Republican slot, Hendricks first turned to George Frisbee Hoar of Massachusetts. In terms of social background and reformist outlook, Hoar shared much in common with Massachusetts Mugwumps, and though he remained aloof from the Mugwump revolt, he did actively participate in the effort to block the Republican nomination of James G. Blaine in favor of the reform candidate Senator George P. Edmunds of Vermont. Hoar was also an intimate of Charles Francis Adams, Jr., and in the course of their friendship he had been won over to Adams's views on the railroad problem and its solution.[118] Hoar would eventually decline the Select Committee appointment, upon which Hendricks turned to Orville H. Platt of Connecticut. In addition to representing a swing state, Platt was a friend of Yale economist and railway expert Arthur T. Hadley. Like Hadley – as well as Hoar and Adams – Platt was a supporter of the Massachusetts "sunshine" system of regulation and an ardent advocate of legalized pooling.[119]

and its leaders, most prominently Senator Roscoe Conkling, resisted the efforts of reformers to reorganize its operations. See Skowronek, *Building a New American State,* 59–63.

117. Miller's 1881 victory over Republican-machine incumbent Thomas Platt for the latter's Senate seat was also hailed as a reform victory. Miller's ostracism among many regular Republicans heightened his dependence on the New York Mugwump movement. In the 1890s, having suffered defeat in his bid for reelection, Miller would reemerge, fully reborn, as an ardent antimachine independent and a champion of reform causes from primary election laws, to civil service reform, to the Sunday closing of saloons. See Flick, ed. *History of the State of New York,* 162–8; and McCormick, *From Realignment to Reform,* 111–14.

118. Welch, *George Frisbie Hoar and the Half-Breed Republicans,* 50.

119. Before the Select Committee on Interstate Commerce, Hadley advocated the creation of a "national commission of inquiry," one with the power to publicize railroad wrongdoing, but which lacked judicial powers and the authority to set rates. See U.S. Congress. Senate. Select Committee on Interstate Commerce. *Report.* 49th Cong., 1st sess., Vol. 46, pt. 2: 200. Speaking in 1905, Hadley praised Platt's contributions to the debate surrounding the ICA, noting: "His speeches in opposition to certain sections of the Interstate Commerce act [sic] which he believed to be ill-judged are without doubt the ablest presentation of the subject ever made by any man in the United States Congress. Had Mr. Platt's advice been taken at the time many of the difficulties under which we have suffered both financially and industrially in the matter of railroad policy would have been much mitigated." Hadley is quoted in Coolidge, *An Old-Fashioned Senator: Orville H. Platt of Connecticut,* 456, fn. 1.

In sum, the SCIC was well constituted to give a sympathetic hearing to the concerns of business Mugwumps and their allies as it moved about the country in the spring and summer of 1885 collecting testimony on the railroad problem. Nor could it have come as much of a surprise to the full Senate when the committee reported back its recommendations for a discretionary railroad commission. But it remained for Democratic leaders to mobilize their party rank and file behind the Select Committee bill as it moved through the chamber.

Democratic Leadership on the Senate Floor (I): Preserving the Long Haul–Short Haul Provision.   Significant conflict over the shape of the SCIC bill erupted only twice in the Senate, once over Section 4 (the Select Committee's long haul–short haul provision), and the other over the substance of the compromise railroad bill worked out by the conference committee. In each instance Gorman assumed a crucial leadership role, balancing agrarian Democratic preferences and national party goals, and mobilizing party power behind acceptable compromises.

Let us turn first to the long haul–short haul controversy. The purpose of Section 4 was to rein in freight rate discrimination between locales situated in between the major terminus points. The committee provision read:

> That it shall be unlawful for any common carrier to charge or receive any greater compensation in the aggregate for the transportation of passengers or property subject to the provisions of this act for a shorter than for a longer distance over the same line, in the same direction, and from the same original point of departure.

The provision had been narrowly drawn – copied from similar statutes in New York and Massachusetts – and its reach was intentionally limited. As written, the committee provision would make it illegal for a railroad to charge more for a short haul than a long haul only where the discrimination in question occurred "over the same line, in the same direction, and from the same original point of departure." Moreover, agrarian Democrats were doubly incensed over language granting the ICC the authority to make exceptions to the section's already limited antidiscrimination rule, where doing so served the dictates of equity and sound public policy.

Agrarian Democrats rejected the provisions of Section 4 as written by the Select Committee, and on the Senate floor they moved both to broaden its prohibitions and contain the commission's discretionary power. Following the lead of Democrat Johnson Camden of West

Virginia, agrarians proposed to substitute the Reagan bill's long haul–short haul provision for the SCIC provision. That amendment read:

> That it shall be unlawful for any common carrier ... to charge or receive any greater compensation, for a similar amount and kind of property, for carrying, receiving, storing, forwarding or handling the same, for a shorter than for a longer distance, *which includes the shorter distance*, on any one railroad.[120]

The Camden amendment was a direct assault on the Select Committee's conservatively drawn provision. Not only did it dramatically expand the reach of the section's prohibitions, but the discretionary power of the new commission to make exceptions was also withdrawn.

No chamber vote was ever taken on the Camden amendment; indeed, only days later Camden introduced a substitute for his own amendment. The senator from West Virginia insisted that the new amendment would accomplish the same ends as his original, but the provisions of the two amendments belie his protestations. In the first place, Camden's substitute amendment represented a significant retreat from the all-encompassing language of the first amendment, though to be sure it still represented a broadening of the Select Committee's original provision. Camden's new substitute would merely delete the phrase "and from the same original point of departure" from the Select Committee bill, leaving the provision to read:

> It shall be unlawful for any common carrier to charge or receive any greater compensation in the aggregate for the transportation of passengers or property ... for a shorter than for a longer distance over the same line, in the same direction.

Secondly, and a more significant retreat in the eyes of most agrarians, Camden's substitute reinstated the discretionary authority of the commission to grant exceptions to Section 4.

Gorman and Harris led the effort to defend Section 4 against excessive agrarian revisionism, mobilizing Democratic support behind their effort.[121] That the two leaders were implicated in the withdrawal of Camden's first amendment and the introduction of its substitute is suggested by the vocal support they offered Camden upon the introduction of the latter. Indeed, Gorman went so far as to imply paternity of the substitute, asserting from the floor: "The Senator from Tennessee and myself, the minority of the [select] committee, had intended to introduce the identical amendment offered by the Senator from West Virginia."

---

120. *Congressional Record*, 49th Cong., 1st sess., Vol. 17, pt. 4: 3824. (Emphasis added).
121. Neilson, *Shelby M. Cullom*, 111.

Gorman proceeded to defend the reasonableness of the Camden substitute by arguing that it conformed to recommendations made before the Select Committee by Chairman Kernan of the New York State Railroad Commission.[122] In Gorman's judgment, the adoption of the Camden substitute amendment would leave Section 4 "precisely within the rule laid down by the commission of New York."[123] Republican Select Committee member Warner Miller of New York was also amenable to the substitute, arguing that the retention of the commission proviso would provide for a flexible long haul–short haul policy. Indeed, Miller maintained that no great harm could come even from the adoption of Camden's *original* amendment as long as the provision for commission exceptions remained intact, a prescient remark because the long haul–short haul provision of the final ICA would merge the broad language of the House Reagan bill (and Camden's original amendment) with a provision for commission exceptions.[124]

Gorman had successfully staved off the Reaganesque provisions of Camden's first proposal and swung his party behind his substitute, with its modestly more expansive language and its retention of commission exceptions. The final vote on the Camden substitute was close, passing 29 to 24 (with 23 not voting). Final action broke almost strictly along party lines, with Democrats voting 24 to 2 for the substitute and Republicans 22 to 3 against it.[125] Table 2.14 reports multivariate estimates of the Camden vote using LOGISTIC REGRESSION. It confirms the importance of senators' partisan affiliation to the direction of their vote, even after controlling for a range of alternative predictors.[126] In addition, it documents the opposition of western senators who likely feared the effects of a stronger long haul–short haul law on the ability of their states to ship commodities competitively to eastern and overseas markets.

Several more amendments to Section 4 were offered in the course of Senate deliberations, variously narrowing and expanding the scope of its provisions. Each vote was close and determined largely by party line vote.[127] Toward the end, however, New Jersey Republican John R.

---

122. Lambert, *Arthur Pue Gorman*, 130; Neilson, *Shelby M. Cullom*, 111; *Congressional Record*, 49th Cong., 1st sess., Vol. 17, pt. 4: 3728, 3870–1.
123. *Congressional Record*, 49th Cong., 1st sess., Vol. 17, pt. 4: 3871.
124. Ibid., 3728.
125. In this and all subsequent discussions of Senate votes, the two Virginia Readjusters are included in the aggregate chamber vote, but excluded from the partisan breakdown. For this reason, summing the party votes in the text never yields the chamber vote.
126. A full description of the independent variables used in Table 2.14 and all other multivariate equations in Chapter 2 can be found in the appendix to this chapter.
127. *Congressional Record*, 49th Cong., 1st sess., Vol. 17, pt. 4: 4414, 4415.

Table 2.14. *Logit Estimates for Senate Votes on Section 4, the Long Haul–Short Haul Provision (Forty-ninth Congress)*

Variables	Camden Amendment	McPherson Amendment
Party	4.154**	−6.108**
	(1.605)	(2.281)
Select Committee	0.866	−10.369*
	(1.979)	(4.704)
Farmers	0.069	−0.152*
	(.058)	(.071)
Railroad Capital	1.633	−3.842
	(3.794)	(4.439)
ROI	−0.414	0.178
	(.300)	(.197)
Terminal Centers	−0.341	0.823
	(.441)	(.443)
West	−5.388*	0.659
	(2.638)	(1.583)
Constant	0.289	7.434
	(4.128)	(4.532)
N	51	49
−2 Log Likelihood	22.97	24.02
% Correctly Predicted	90.2	91.8

* $p < .05$; ** $p < .01$.

McPherson dramatically altered the tenor of debate when he introduced an amendment to delete Section 4 in its entirety from the Select Committee bill. McPherson's amendment was potentially devastating to Democratic leaders, for the inclusion of a long haul–short haul prohibition, in some form, was essential to continued agrarian support. The amendment was finally defeated on a vote of 20 to 29 (with 27 not voting). But a sizable Republican majority had supported the deletion of Section 4 (18 to 8), a move that was only turned back because of cohesive Democratic opposition (2 to 21). Once again, estimates using LOGISTIC REGRESSION confirm the statistically significant effect of party on senators' response to the McPherson amendment (Table 2.14), further revealing the firm support of both agrarian senators and SCIC members for the retention of a long haul–short haul provision. In the end, the Senate passed the amended Senate bill and sent it to the House. A large bipartisan majority supported the commission bill, 47 to 4. Republicans

voted unanimously for the bill (26 to 0), with Democrats also supporting passage by a vote of 21 to 4.

**Democratic Leadership on the Senate Floor (II): Passing the Interstate
Commerce Act.** The second instance of significant Senate conflict over
the shape of railroad regulation erupted with the introduction of the
compromise ICA worked out by the conference committee. Once again,
Gorman's leadership was critical, though this time not simply to holding
his party in line behind the construction of a specific provision, but to
blocking Republican efforts to kill the final conference bill. In the end,
although the chamber minority party, Democrats would employ their
voting power to ensure the passage of the ICA. Like their party allies in
the House, Senate Democrats could justly take responsibility for the substance of the final regulatory bill signed into law in 1887.

The Senate conference committee delegation had included Select Committee members Cullom, Harris, and Platt, and the plan they reported
back embraced almost all of the particulars of the Senate bill, with two
crucial exceptions.[128] The most important change was the addition of the
Reagan bill's antipooling section, a provision that would make it illegal
for competing railroads to set rates jointly through privately negotiated
freight- or revenue-sharing agreements. The conference committee's
second change was to the long haul–short haul provision. In place of the
Senate's restrictive phrasing – "and from the same original point of
departure or to the same point of arrival" – conferees had substituted
the more expansive Reagan language, "the shorter being included within
the longer distance." In addition, although the conferees had kept the
proviso for making commission exceptions, its authority to make general
rules of exception had been curtailed. In giving relief from Section 4, the
Interstate Commerce Commission would have to proceed on a case-by-
case basis.[129]

---

128. At first glance it might seem odd that Harris, rather than Gorman, obtained the berth
as Democratic conferee. However, the choice politically made sense. Harris and
Reagan had strong common ties. Both men were Southerners and each had held high
office under the Confederacy – Harris as wartime governor of Tennessee and Reagan
as Postmaster General of the Confederacy. But additionally, Reagan had no stomach
for Gorman, considering him a "monopolist." In this light, Gorman's presence on
the conference committee might have made concessions by the House managers more
difficult. For a glimpse of Reagan's hostility toward Gorman, see his letter to Grover
Cleveland dated July 7, 1888. In the *Grover Cleveland Papers*, microfilm, reel 61.
129. The Senate bill had allowed the commission to "make general rules exempting such
designated common carriers in such special cases from the operation of this section
of the act; and when such exemptions shall have been made, they shall, until changed
by the commission or by law, have like force and effect as though the same had been

On the Senate floor, Cullom tried to persuade his Republican colleagues that "while it is not exactly the bill of the Senate, yet except as to the provision in regard to pooling it is practically the Senate bill."[130] But for a large number of Republicans the changes simply went too far in the direction of agrarian accommodation. The incorporation of the antipooling provision was particularly devastating. To many it seemed to undermine the entire rationale for federal regulatory intervention by mandating a government policy of enforced competition in the railroad industry. Among those who endorsed the views of economic Mugwumps like Arthur T. Hadley and Charles Francis Adams, excess competition was the driving reason behind the railroad problem and legalized pooling was the centerpiece of any rational solution. From this vantage point, the antipooling provision rendered the conference bill incoherent as national policy: It would end discriminatory practices arising from the competitive pressures of the railroad industry by mandating *still more* railroad competition.

On policy grounds, it may be that Republicans had the better argument. But Democratic support for the conference changes was grounded in sound party politics, as the legislation squared well with their peculiar coalition needs. As detailed earlier in this chapter, the tensions contained in the Interstate Commerce Act were also clearly manifest in business-Mugwump thinking on the railroad problem. Like Arthur Hadley and Charles Francis Adams, Jr., business Mugwumps recognized the negative effects of competition upon railroad pricing practices. But unlike economic Mugwumps, they retained a much more ambivalent stance toward the practice of pooling, a contradiction in their thinking not fully resolved in the 1880s. This inconsistency allowed Democrats to address what had become key sticking points in conference – Reagan's insistence that regulatory legislation strike at railroad monopolies and his related commitment to an antipooling law – while remaining within parameters set by electoral college considerations.

Senate Republicans strongly opposed the conference settlement. Massachusetts Senator George Hoar, for one, labeled the bill in part "a new scheme," while Nelson Aldrich of Rhode Island objected that its provisions were either "such as the Senate has refused to accede to, or they are propositions which have never been discussed in the Senate at all." Likewise, Kansas Senator J. J. Ingalls insisted that "several of the

specified in this section." The conference bill, on the other hand, only gave the commission the authority to "[p]rescribe the extent to which such designated carriers may be relieved from the operation of this section of the act," which had the effect of limiting exemptions to single cases.

130. *Congressional Record*, 49th Cong., 2d sess., Vol. 18, pt. 1: 171.

positions that were taken by the Senate, after protracted debate, have been abandoned by the report of the committee of conference," suggesting that "the action of the committee on conference . . . has been . . . in opposition to the expressed determination of the Senate upon some very important points." Perhaps most significantly, Orville Platt of Connecticut, a member of both the conference committee and the SCIC, condemned the inclusion of the antipooling provision for setting federal regulatory policy at war with itself and led the opposition to the ICA on the Senate floor.[131]

In his memoirs, select committee chairman Shelby M. Cullom credits Gorman's efforts as essential to mobilizing Democrats behind the compromise bill and securing its final passage. With only a few weeks left before the end of the short second session, Republicans moved to recommit the bill back to conference, a procedural maneuver that would have effectively killed the passage of railroad regulation in the Forty-ninth Congress. The exact methods employed by Gorman are obscure, but the subsequent vote to recommit indicates why the Democrat's leadership was critical. Republicans on balance rejected the conference bill, voting 19 to 15 for recommittal, a vote that split the party along sectional lines. Republicans from the New England and mid-Atlantic states voted almost unanimously to recommit the Interstate Commerce Act, 14 to 1. Republicans from the midwestern and western states opposed recommittal 5 to 14. By contrast, Democrats threw their support behind the ICA, opposing recommittal 5 to 21. When all the votes were tallied, Democratic votes had made the difference, swinging the balance of the chamber against the motion to recommit, 25 to 36 (with 14 not voting). Estimates presented in Table 2.15 offer a more systematic breakdown of the vote to recommit the ICA. It shows once again the pull of party upon a senator's decision to accept or reject the conference committee's handiwork. The ICA subsequently passed the Senate by a large bipartisan majority, 43 to 15 (with 17 not voting).

From the composition of the SCIC, to the containment of agrarian radicalism on Section 4, to the disciplined effort to block Republican recommittal efforts, Democratic leadership was both visible and effective in its effort to place party power behind an effective compromise that could secure Mugwump commission legislation without alienating their agrarian Democratic base. In addition, as a result of Gorman's efforts, the Senate Democratic minority could plausibly claim to share credit with House Democrats for the passage of the ICA in its final form.

131. Ibid., 169, 171, 173–4.

Table 2.15. *Logit Estimate for Senate Vote to
Recommit the Interstate Commerce Act
(Forty-ninth Congress)*

Variables	Recommit ICA
Party	−1.721*
	(.837)
Select Committee	−3.224
	(2.049)
Farmers	−0.023
	(.028)
Railroad Capital	0.286
	(2.739)
ROI	0.223
	(.141)
Terminal Centers	0.188
	(.310)
West	−1.221
	(1.098)
Constant	−0.988
	(2.227)
N	60
−2 Log Likelihood	52.69
% Correctly Predicted	78.3

* $p < .05$; ** $p < .01$.

Conclusion

The actions and preferences of Democratic party leaders were central to the legislative evolution of the ICA. As I have endeavored to show, their fingerprints are all over the final product. Yet if there is a greater historical irony to this developmental episode, it is that the institutional legacy of this partisan effort, the Interstate Commerce Commission (ICC), would quickly become assimilated as part of the broad political inheritance of the Republican party. And of course there is substantial justice in this. The Republican party was, after all, the period's state-building party and, as such, it was the natural home of the independent regulatory commission idea. Moreover, in subsequent years the perfection of the ICC's statutory authority and institutional power would come about largely through the leadership of Republican presidents and legislators.

But in neglecting the Democrats' role in the framing of the ICA, we overlook potentially important lessons regarding the party's halting programmatic transformation, its eventual embrace of the state-building impulse and its accommodation to uses of discretionary central state power. As subsequent history bears out, the lasting impact of this first state-building effort on Democratic party development was negligible. Indeed, if we learn anything from the politics of railroad regulation, it is that we caricature American political parties if we depict them as programmatically empty vessels, mere seekers of office and its attendant perks. Longstanding commitments of party ideology and interest, it would seem, do not die easily. As the legislative reactions cited earlier make clear, agrarian Democrats who otherwise held their noses and cast their votes for the ICA were nevertheless vocally hostile toward what their party leaders had wrought. But in the end, the consolidation of party-governing power superceded other considerations; retaining the reins of power was the keystone to anything else Democrats might hope to accomplish. And because the electoral basis of their power was historically precarious, Democrats could be induced to make programmatic choices that otherwise remain incomprehensible; choices tied to the dictates of short-term electoral needs.

Still, as events following the passage of the ICA make clear, choices made under electoral duress are not readily incorporated into either the contemporaneous repertoire of programmatic party solutions or the selective memory of celebrated party accomplishments, unless reinforced by similar, subsequent choices. The independent regulatory commission was an institution foreign to the ideology of the Gilded Age Democratic party, and as we will see in Chapter 3, it would remain that way for a number of years to come.

Subsequent events would contribute further to the Democrats' orphaning of the independent regulatory commission idea. Years of declining agricultural prices, coupled with the onset of general economic collapse in 1893, ultimately produced a political backlash within the ranks of agrarian Democrats, and they turned their wrath against the electoral straightjacket that had been manufactured for them by national party leaders. Indeed, one can see in the rising tide of agrarian revolt, so prominent in the politics of the 1880s and 1890s, a highly conditioned response to the era's competitive party system and the seemingly inexorable electoral logic that continually drew both Democratic and Republican party leaders back to a handful of electorally pivotal northeastern states for both candidates and programmatic positions. The formation of the Greenback party and later of the People's party, as well as the growing schism between "gold" and "silver" Democrats – all attest to an increasing agrarian frustration with the politics of interest representation in the third-party system. Growing Democratic factionalism and the outbreak of intraparty warfare would finally result in the starkly sectional realignment of the party system in 1896.

The realignment of 1896 finally purged Mugwumps from the Democratic party – indeed it decimated the party's electoral base in the states of the industrial Northeast for more than a generation. The new party system that rapidly emerged was itself set in motion by the insurgent agrarian radicalism within the Democratic party, an impulse well personified in the political character of William Jennings Bryan, titular head of the new Democratic party. With its agrarian base ascendent and seemingly freed from the shackles of old party strategies, the vestiges of earlier commitments to the buildup of central state authority and institutions were mostly purged as well.

This can be seen in the years in between the passage of the ICA and the election of Woodrow Wilson in 1912, when questions involving corporate power and industrial concentration moved foursquare onto the center stage of American politics. Rival solutions would again compete for political ascendency, and within this great national debate agrarian Democrats – once again from the periphery of power – would intensify their antimonopoly and antistatist vision of the American political economy and make it the centerpiece of their program for national renewal. It is for this reason that the presidential election of 1912 represented a potentially critical crossroads in the development of the American state. For in that year, the organizational rupture of the Republican party into conservative and progressive halves raised the minority Democratic party to national power. The Democratic party of Woodrow Wilson would face an electoral challenge eerily similar to that of its Gilded Age predecessor. On the one hand, Democrats desired strongly to follow through on their commitment to agrarian antitrust goals. On the other hand, the party once more needed to reach out beyond its traditional base to new political interests, to construct for itself a new majority coalition for the consolidation of national political power. The tension between these programmatic and electoral impulses would run like a fault line through the politics of the Federal Trade Commission Act, the subject of the next chapter.

Appendix: Definition and Operationalization of Variables Used in Multivariate Analyses

Two sets of variables are employed in the multivariate analyses for this chapter. The first is a set of control variables: ROI, CAPITAL, FARMERS,

WEST, and CENTER. The second is a set of explanatory variables: PARTY, NEW YORK, COMMERCE COMMITTEE, and SELECT COMMITTEE. Among the control variables, ROI, CAPITAL, and WEST have been constructed based on the discussion obtained in Thomas G. Gilligan, William J. Marshall, and Barry R. Weingast, "Regulation and the Theory of Legislative Choice: The Interstate Commerce Act of 1887," *Journal of Law and Economics* 32 (April 1989): 35–61. CAPITAL and ROI are proxies for railroad interest, and are based on state-level data found in the Census Bureau's *Statistical Abstract* of the United States (1886). Districts within a state are assigned identical values of these two variables. CAPITAL is based on the value at cost of railroad property, plant, and equipment and is intended to measure the economic (and hence political) presence of the railroads in the various congressional districts. ROI is computed as annual revenue per dollar of railroad capital investment and, holding constant for CAPITAL, is intended to measure the economic stake of the railroads in a particular district. CAPITAL and ROI are scaled in units of one billion dollars. WEST takes a value of 1 for all districts north and west of Chicago and 0 for all others. FARMERS is a variable representing agrarian interests and is derived from data on the value of agricultural production by county and aggregated by district. This data can be found in Parsons et al. FARMERS is scaled in units of $10 million. Finally, CENTER is a variable representing the major overland and overseas shipping centers of the country, and takes the value of 1 for districts containing major shipping centers and 0 for those without. Data for this variable is obtained from two sources. Information on major port cities can be found in the *Statistical Abstract* (1886). Figures collected by the Census Bureau (1890) on the assessed valuation of total property taxed in the country's urban areas were used to determine major overland shipping centers. This seemed a reasonable procedure for two reasons. First, the major overland shipping arteries of the country are also the country's principle urban and commercial centers. Second, the assessed property values could be used to distinguish larger and smaller commercial areas. Three different cutoff points – $100 million, $75 million, and $50 million – were tested in order to minimize the problem of arbitrariness in the selection of a cutoff point. While there was some variation in the magnitude of the coefficient, the statistical significance of the coefficients varied uniformly. In this chapter, the $50 million cutoff point is employed.

PARTY, NEW YORK, COMMERCE COMMITTEE, and SELECT COMMITTEE are dummy variables. PARTY takes the value of 1 for Democrats and 0 for Republicans. NEW YORK takes the value of 1 for all districts found in the state of New York and 0 for all other states. It is used specifically to examine the regulatory preferences of these critical swing-state representatives and the Democratic party's sensitivity to those preferences. Finally, COMMERCE COMMITTEE and SELECT COMMITTEE represent the House Commerce Committee and the Senate Select Committee on Interstate Commerce, respectively. Each takes a value of 1 if a legislator was a member of the committee in question and 0 if not. These variables measure the preferences of committee members for the various regulatory proposals put before their parent chamber, as well as allowing us to gauge the relationship of committee preferences to floor preferences (in particular, floor Democratic preferences).

3

The Progressive Party Vote and the Federal Trade Commission Act of 1914

A politician, a man engaged in party contests, must be an opportunist. . . . If you want to win in party action, I take it for granted you want to lure the majority to your side. I never heard of any man in his senses who was fishing for a minority. . . . You have got to take the opportunity as you find it, and work on that, and that is opportunism, that is politics, and it is perfectly legitimate.

Woodrow Wilson[1]

The Trade Commission act represents a totally different approach [from the Sherman Act], a spirit strangely contradictory to the campaign theories of the President. . . . It is not the attitude anyone could have expected to see emerge from the tradition of the Democratic party. But nevertheless it did. . . .

In this Trade Commission act is contained the possibility of a radical reversal of many American notions about trusts, legislative power, and legal procedure. It may amount to historic political and constitutional reform. It seems to contradict every principle of the party which enacted it

Herbert Croly[2]

Introduction

On 30 May 1914, Theodore Roosevelt fired the opening shots of the midterm elections against the party of Woodrow Wilson. Roosevelt framed the off-year elections as a referendum on the failures of the New Freedom, the Democrats' three-pronged program to curb the power of

---

1. "The Ideals of Public Life": An Address to the Annual Dinner of the Cleveland Chamber of Commerce, November 16, 1907. In Link, ed. *The Papers of Woodrow Wilson* Vol. 17, 500.
2. Croly, "An Unseen Reversal."

the trusts. Rather than bringing monopolies to heel, the former president asserted, Democratic policies had simply driven the economy into recession.[3] "[T]he Democratic party," Roosevelt explained on a separate occasion, "has been engaged in what is fundamentally an effort to restore the unlimited competition of two generations back and to subject this to only an ineffective and weak governmental control."[4] To all, Roosevelt's counsel was constant: The prudent course for citizens that fall was to register a vote for social and industrial progress, to support the Progressive party candidate for Congress.[5]

Woodrow Wilson also sought to make the off-year elections a referendum on Democratic party governance. The existence of a Democratic majority in Congress, like Wilson's presidential victory itself, had been predicated on the rupture of the Republican party and the formation of the Progressive party. Prospects for the organizational longevity of the new party were dim, and a reunited Republican party threatened the Democrats with a return to out-party status. Constructing a stable Democratic majority in this unsettled electoral environment required the active solicitation of traditionally non-Democratic votes. Wilson hoped to contain the erosion of his artificially inflated congressional majority with an explicit appeal to Progressives and progressive Republicans. By tying congressional Democrats to the coattails of a popular president, and by persuading progressives that the Democratic party had in two short years made good on its reform promises, party leaders hoped to salvage a Democratic congressional majority for the second half of Wilson's administration and lay the foundation for the president's own reelection bid in 1916.

The "trust question" had been the most conspicuous issue of the presidential campaign of 1912, and Wilson moved with purpose to redeem his party's pledges and capture the mantel of reform, even in the face of a deepening recession. The omnibus Clayton bill – the centerpiece of Democratic trust policy at midyear 1914 – would impose strict legislative prohibitions on a list of unfair business practices, along with criminal penalties for their violation. It would also strengthen court

---

3. *The New York Times*, May 31, 1914, 1.
4. Theodore Roosevelt to Edward Prentiss Costigan, August 15, 1914. In Morison, ed. *The Letters of Theodore Roosevelt* Vol. 7, 808.
5. In private, Roosevelt insisted that "the course pursued by the Administration has meant the abandonment of every sane effort to secure the abatement of social and industrial evils." In public, Roosevelt condemned the New Freedom as "merely the exceedingly old freedom which permits each man to cut his neighbor's throat." Theodore Roosevelt to Lyman Abbott, June 29, 1914. In Morison, ed., *The Letters of Theodore Roosevelt* Vol. 7, 768; *The New York Times*, July 1, 1914, 1.

enforcement of the antitrust laws. Supplemental legislation, the Covington bill, would create an interstate trade commission with information-gathering powers to publicize business wrongdoing. It would also aid the attorney general and the courts in the drawing and implementing of dissolution decrees under the Sherman Act.

For months, progressives close to Wilson had pressed the president to abandon his party's antitrust program, and to embrace the regulatory commission bill sponsored in the House by Representative Raymond Stevens, a freshman Democrat from New Hampshire. This little-noticed bill would create a discretionary board of experts with the power to define unfair competition and police the trading practices of business. However, Wilson kept his progressive supporters at bay, unsure of his political footing and hesitant to embrace such a clear departure from party policy and doctrine. Yet by May 1914, with the economy sliding toward depression and their antitrust program under fire from progressives and businessmen alike, Democrats found themselves on the political defensive. With an individual of Roosevelt's stature and progressive credentials bearing down on the party in power, the Progressive party message threatened to obscure Democratic achievements and erode the potential base of support that Democrats had targeted for inclusion in a new majority coalition.

But in revealing his hand, Roosevelt inspired Wilson to act: to initiate the necessary changes in his party's program to preempt the disruptive electoral impact of the Progressive leader's criticisms. As a result, Sections 10 to 12 of the Stevens bill – declaring unfair competition unlawful and empowering a federal trade commission to define and restrain unfair trade practices – were incorporated as Section 5 of the Democrats' new regulatory commission bill (Section 4 in the final version). More ingenious still was the strategic significance of Wilson's action. For the provisions of the Stevens bill, the centerpiece of the Democrats' new Federal Trade Commission bill, had themselves been lifted in wholesale fashion from Sections 1, 2, 5, and 6 of Roosevelt's own regulatory commission bill, a bill introduced several months earlier by the House leadership of the Progressive party.

It was a Faustian bargain of sorts. Democrats had coopted the centerpiece of the Progressive party's trust program by seizing the regulatory trade commission idea. They had acted with "opportunism" – as, Wilson believed, skilled politicians must – "to win at party action."[6] But, in taking steps to consolidate their hold on national power, Democrats simultaneously jettisoned long-standing commitments on the trust ques-

6. "The Ideals of Public Life." In Link, ed. *The Papers of Woodrow Wilson*, 500.

tion, sublimating an historic antipathy toward industrial concentration and corporate power to the dictates of national party supremacy. The passage of the Federal Trade Commission Act (FTCA), as the historian Martin J. Sklar has most recently argued, was essential to "the corporate reconstruction of American capitalism."[7] The historical irony is that this watershed legislation passed at the hands of overwhelming Democratic majorities.

The Corporate Liberal Synthesis in Federal Trade Commission Historiography

The FTCA, along with its companion piece the Clayton Act, inaugurated an era of sustained federal supervision over the interstate trading practices of American business. Of deeper historical significance, these statutes affirmed the legitimacy of the modern corporation and the role of industrial concentration in the American political economy. The institutional centerpiece of this settlement was the independent trade commission, an expert body authorized, subject to judicial review, to delineate unfair business practices and issue cease-and-desist orders to businesses engaged in interstate commerce. As passed, the Clayton Act was subordinate to the FTCA. It made specific business practices – price discrimination, tying contracts, and particular forms of interlocking directorates and intercorporate stockholding – illegal, though in language so qualified as to grant the Federal Trade Commission considerable discretion in determining the scope of its application.[8]

Unlike the other cases in this book, the historiography on the FTCA is strongly bound up with a particular interpretative framework, the so-called corporate-liberal synthesis. Corporate-liberal accounts occupy such a prominent place in this historiography that I have deemed it important to address these arguments directly, as part of the process of building my case for a party system explanation of regulatory choice. The purpose of this section is to begin that dialogue: to briefly review the arguments put forth by corporate liberal scholars, in particular those of Martin J. Sklar, and to clarify the interpretive differences that guide the empirical analysis in this chapter.

An earlier generation of corporate-liberal theorists detailed the class-conscious actions of big business to win state support for their efforts

---

7. Sklar, *Corporate Reconstruction*.
8. The Clayton Act also reaffirmed labor's right to organize and placed certain restrictions on the use of court injunctions in labor disputes.

to rationalize market competition, facilitate the process of corporate concentration, and adjust the tenets of liberal ideology to justify corporate power.[9] More recently, Sklar has recast this interpretation, and in doing so he has significantly advanced our historical understanding of America's transition from proprietary to corporate forms of capitalist organization.[10] Sklar presents the FTCA as the capstone of a decades-long social movement involving big business and various nonbusiness allies, dedicated to the adaptation of law, economic theory, and social relations to the requirements of a newly emergent corporate economy. As Sklar reminds us, the trust question dominated public debate for almost a generation – from roughly 1890 to 1914 – "because, in essence, [it was] about the passage of American society from the proprietary-competitive stage to the corporate-administered stage of capitalism – whether the passage should be allowed, and if so, on what terms."[11] On the first question – shall the passage be allowed? – Sklar identifies the existence of a cross-class, cross-party consensus by 1912, one that accepted the burgeoning corporate sector as natural, historically inevitable, and progressive, one that treated the private administration of corporate-dominated markets as legitimate. Within that consensus, there remained important subsidiary issues for the party system to resolve, the most important concerning what form corporate-liberal business regulation should take. But in this interpretation, differences between parties are less significant than their commonalities.

Sklar identifies three competing corporate-liberal regulatory forms, each associated with one of the three presidential candidates of 1912. The first, associated with Theodore Roosevelt, Sklar characterizes as a "statist tending corporate liberalism on the left." This would be an administrative agency with powers similar to those enjoyed by the Interstate Commerce Commission. But this commission would not simply police interstate business transactions for unfair trading practices, it would administer a federal license-registration system. Armed with the power to exclude corporations for interstate commerce, this licensing mechanism would provide Roosevelt's trade commission with the leverage to influence corporate decision making over prices, wages, and capitalization levels. It would put in place the institutional framework for state direction of the corporate economy: a "public-service capitalism" with the capacity to order "the economy to accord with social policy"

---

9. Kolko, *The Triumph of Conservatism*; Weinstein, *The Corporate Ideal in the Liberal State, 1900–1918*; Lustig, *Corporate Liberalism*.
10. Sklar, *Corporate Reconstruction*.   11. Ibid., 33.

– indeed, with the potential to transcend the confines of corporate liberalism itself.[12]

The second alternative, associated with Woodrow Wilson, Sklar characterizes as an interstate trade commission with regulatory powers to define and police unfair business practices, subject to court review. This alternative dropped the license-registration component of Roosevelt's plan, and thereby withdrew the state from active direction over the corporate economy. The market would remain primarily corporate-administered. Price, wage, and capitalization questions would largely be privately determined, without significant public direction.

The third alternative, associated with William Howard Taft, principally relied upon judicial enforcement of the Sherman Act as interpreted by the rule of reason, eschewing even the weaker Wilsonian variant of administrative regulation.[13]

For purposes of my argument, what is critical about the alternatives sketched above is that each presumed the practice of reasonable restraint and the legitimacy of corporate-administered markets. In Sklar's reading, the remedies advanced by the three major presidential candidates of 1912 were all directed against the abuse of corporate market power, not against corporate market power per se. "Small producer anti-corporate partisans," we learn, "although articulate and influential in party politics, were able to criticize and peripherally modify, *but not define*, the actionable alternatives, as to both kind and mode."[14] The nuanced cross-candidate comparisons offered by Sklar – involving Roosevelt, Wilson, and Taft – are presented as evidence of the cross-party corporate liberal consensus said to have solidified by 1912.

If Sklar's interpretation is correct, the party system interpretation offered here loses its explanatory relevance. Where the latter sees an abrupt shift in the Democratic stance toward reasonable restraint, corporate-administered markets, and the regulatory commission, the former sees continuity along each of these dimensions. I will argue that Sklar's depiction of the antitrust debate on the eve of Woodrow Wilson's inauguration is mischaracterized. In particular, by tying his analysis to the ideas and public statements of these three Progressive Era presidents, Sklar overlooks the more critical regulatory views of the political parties

12. Ibid., 347.
13. On the distinctions between Roosevelt, Wilson, and Taft, see Sklar, *Corporate Reconstruction*, 35–40, 324–5 and, more generally, chs. 5–6. The rule of reason decisions are *United States v Standard Oil* (221 U.S. 1) and *United States v American Tobacco* (221 U.S. 106).
14. Sklar, *Corporate Reconstruction*, 324. Emphasis added.

to which each of these men belonged, organizations with constituencies, ideologies, and programmatic commitments that cannot be reduced to preferences of their presidential candidate. As a proposition, this statement is truest with respect to Wilson and the Democratic party. But it nonetheless applies also to Roosevelt and the fledgling Progressive party. By discounting the substance of *party* positions on the trust question, Sklar overestimates the extent of corporate-liberal consensus in place in 1912, or for that matter in early 1914, when Democrats in power first unveiled their antitrust program to the nation. Because it overlooks the programmatic commitments of party programs on the trust question, Sklar's analysis of the politics of the FTCA is substantially miscast.

The following analysis offers a reassessment of the Democratic party's political accommodation to corporate-liberalism and the practice of reasonable restraint. I will attempt to show that as late as early 1914 – well into the first administration of Woodrow Wilson – the Democrats continued to reject corporate concentration and privately administered markets as legitimate and inevitable features of the American political economy. As I will document, considerable Democratic energy was expended in an effort to undermine the legal protection extended reasonable restraint by the Supreme Court in 1911 and to restore by legislation the Court's earlier, more literal reading of the Sherman Act, first enunciated in 1897 in *United States v Trans-Missouri Freight Association*.[15] Here, the Court held the federal antitrust law to outlaw *every* restraint of trade whether reasonable or unreasonable – an interpretation that announced the rule of "free and unrestricted competition" in interstate commerce. As Sklar observes, the *Trans-Missouri* decision "placed the corporate reorganization of industry in jeopardy" of "a menacing counterattack of the small-producer and anti-corporate populist forces against the corporate regulation of the market."[16] Thus, through their effort to legislate the rule of free and unrestricted competition back into the Sherman Act, Democrats signaled their unabated opposition to reasonable restraint and the consolidation of corporate capitalism and their commitment to jump-start through supplemental legislation the regime of competitive, proprietary capitalism.

All this is not to say that business power played an insignificant role in the legislative evolution of the FTCA. It did not. But its influence was

15. *United States v Trans-Missouri Freight Association* (1897) 166 U.S. 290.
16. Sklar, *Corporate Reconstruction*, 166.

considerably more indirect. As already noted, antitrust politics in the Sixty-third Congress (1913–15) was played out against the backdrop of a deepening depression. As business confidence failed and the economy continued to worsen, Democratic resolve to follow through on their commitment to roll-back the rule of reason collapsed as well. As we will see in considerable detail, bad economic times prompted congressional Democrats to drastically scale-back the "Five Brothers," the party's initial and most radical antitrust program, and defer controversial regulatory legislation until the midterm elections of 1914 were safely behind them.

But economic conditions do not explain the Democrats' embrace of the Progressive party's regulatory trade commission idea. That decision came from the White House, and it was motivated by national party considerations. The legislative confusion produced by the worsening economy had the effect of augmenting Wilson's leadership within party policy councils. And Wilson was convinced that the party had to act resolutely on the reform promises of the 1912 election to neutralize Theodore Roosevelt's strident criticism of Democratic governance and draw supporters of the disintegrating Progressive organization into the Democratic camp. The president gambled that decisive action to pass the FTCA would not only shore up his party's midterm electoral support and return a congressional Democratic majority, it would lay the foundation for his own reelection in 1916. And each of these steps was critical if the Democratic party was to consolidate its electoral power and engineer a realignment in national politics.

The balance of this chapter proceeds as follows. The next section provides an overview of emergent and persistent patterns in American party politics at the high-water mark of the Progressive Era. In particular, I give sustained attention to significant structural changes in Democratic party organization since the passage of the Interstate Commerce Act: the emergence of presidential party leadership and the mechanism of the congressional party caucus. "Free and Unrestricted Competition" details the Democratic response to the Supreme Court's historic "rule of reason" decisions in 1911, in particular the party's explicit commitment to reinstate the *Trans-Missouri* doctrine by legislative action. "Agrarian Democrats at High Tide" carries this analysis into the chambers of Congress, where in 1914 the Democratic party in power undertook efforts to reinstate the doctrine of free and unrestricted competition into the meaning of the Sherman Act. "Toward the Progressive Party Regulatory Commission" examines the reasons behind the Democrats' final abandonment of the *Trans-Missouri* doctrine and their embrace of the Progressive regulatory commission idea.

From the Gilded Age to the Progressive Era: Emergent and Persistent Patterns in American Party Politics

The Persistent Historical Pattern

Key aspects of the politics of the FTCA provide continuity with my analysis of the Interstate Commerce Act (ICA). Most prominently, the antimonopoly agrarian tradition which had found expression in John H. Reagan's railroad legislation – the agrarian-styled regulatory bill – continued unabated within the Democratic party. Indeed, antimonopolist antagonism to the corporation and business concentration – best exemplified by the Bryanite wing of the Democratic party – had only deepened since the acrimonious realignment in 1896.[17] As discussed at the conclusion of the previous chapter, the sectional character of political conflict in the new party system – pitting an industrial Northeast against the agricultural and mining states of the South and West – effectively purged Mugwumps from the Democratic coalition. Indeed, Democratic support was decimated across much of the country's northeastern quadrant. As a result, much of the party's nationalist, state-building element either aligned itself with the Republicans or found its voice effectively silenced by the ascendant agrarian base. This newly intensified antimonopolism within the Democratic party was most consistently manifested in its unstinting support for a line of Supreme Court interpretations, beginning with *United States v Trans-Missouri Freight Association* (1897), which held the Sherman Anti-Trust Act to have enacted a congressional policy of government-enforced competition. This point will be extensively developed at a later point in this chapter. For the moment, it is sufficient to say that, as the Court interpreted the antitrust law, federal power had been placed in the service of "free and unrestricted competition" in interstate commerce.

A second and perhaps more momentous continuity with the previous chapter involves the structure of the electoral system through which agrarian Democrats were forced to channel the pursuit of their political goals. As we will see in some detail, the electoral constraints that acted upon Democrats in power after 1912, as in the case of railroad regulation, generated strong incentives to abandon the antimonopoly prescriptions of the party's agrarian base regarding the nation's burgeoning corporate economy, as party leaders maneuvered to maintain their hold on national power. As with the politics of the ICA, the

---

17. On the implications of the 1896 realignment for the makeup of major party coalitions, see Sundquist, *Dynamics of the Party System*, rev. ed., ch. 7.

contingent structure of national politics in the Progressive Era once again operated to discourage particular political options, with potentially significant implications for the trajectory of the American political economy.

The Emergent Historical Pattern

The Democratic Disadvantage in the System of 1896.   Despite these critical continuities, the politics of the FTCA does not simply replicate the analysis of the previous chapter. By the Progressive Era, the structural features of national party politics had undergone a tremendous change. After 1896, electoral college calculations would operate only indirectly on Democratic party leaders charged with crafting presidential electoral strategy. Of course parties continued to require an absolute majority of electoral college votes to win the presidency. But, as we will see, the lopsided character of the fourth-party system – the so-called System of '96 (1896–1928) – worked to militate against the explicit obsession with swing states so characteristic of Gilded Age presidential politics.

The reason was the precipitous decline in electoral competitiveness after 1896.[18] During the first stable phase of the fourth-party system (1896–1908), the number of competitive states needed to swing the presidential election outcome away from the Republicans typically exceeded the available set, a situation which proved an almost insurmountable obstacle to Democrats. Table 3.1 quantifies the hurdle that Democrats faced in trying to break the Republican lock on the electoral college. Using a standard measure of competitiveness (a victory margin of 5 percentage points or less), Table 3.1 indicates that the Republican hold on the White House was solidly in place by the reelection of William McKinley in 1900. Even using a less-stringent measure of competitiveness (a victory margin of 10 percentage points or less), the evidence is clear that Republican hold on the White House was daunting by the time of Theodore Roosevelt's landslide election in 1904.

Competitiveness in congressional elections also plummeted during the fourth-party system, once again to the detriment of the Democratic party. As Table 3.2 shows, during the first stable phase of the party system (1896–1908) the mean percentage of electorally competitive congressional districts nationwide fell from its Gilded Age level (1876–94) by

18. The percentage of state-level presidential contests yielding victory margins of 5 percentage points or less fell from 35.9 percent in the years 1876–92 to 13.3 percent during the years 1896–1908.

Table 3.1. *The "System of 1896" in the Electoral College:*
Competitive State Presidential Races Lost by Democrats, 1896–1908

Year	Measure of State Competitiveness	Number of Competitive States[a]	Number of Electoral Votes	Republican Electoral Vote Margin	Number Electoral Votes Sufficient to Swing Election to Democrats?
1896	5%	4	54	95	Yes
	10%	7	78		Yes
1900	5%	3	26	137	No
	10%	9	126		Yes
1904	5%	2	19	196	No
	10%	3	22		No
1908	5%	4	38	159	No
	10%	7	74		No

[a] This column lists only those competitive states in which the *Republican* candidate was victorious.
Source: ICPSR Study No. 7757; U.S. Bureau of the Census, *The Statistical History of the United States* (New York: Basic Books, 1976), series Y 79–83, series Y 84–134.

Table 3.2. *Percentage of All Congressional District Races Classified as Competitive, 1876–1928 (by Section)*

	Stable Phase 3rd-Party System 1876–94	Stable Phase System of '96 1896–1908	Progressive Split 1910–14	2nd Wilson Administration 1916–18	Stable Phase System of '96 1920–8
Northern Congressional Districts	30.3	17.9	26.1	18.3	10.4
Southern Congressional Districts	16.3	11.6	9.3	8.1	8.0

Note: A competitive race is one in which the winning candidate's margin of victory is 5 percentage points or less.
Source: ICPSR Study No. 7757.

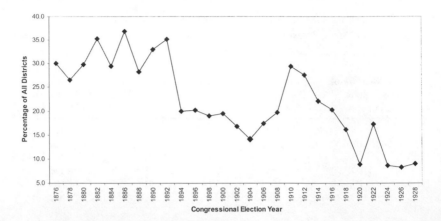

Figure 3.1. Electorally competitive congressional districts as a percentage of all districts, 1876 to 1928 (northern states only).

almost 38 percent.[19] In the North, the number of competitive districts declined from 30.3 percent of all districts to 17.9 percent; in the South, the numbers also fell, from an already low 16.3 percent of all districts to a still lower 11.6 percent (Table 3.2). The Democrats' minority status in the House of Representatives was predicated on their inability to effectively contest in districts outside the South. Figure 3.1 plots the dwindling percentage of competitive northern congressional races from 1876 to 1928. Besides identifying the 1894 midterm elections as a turning point in the structure of congressional elections, the figure provides initial evidence that Democratic control of Congress in the years 1912 to 1916 was made possible at least in part by a temporary upturn in the number of competitive northern races, a political condition that coincided with the brief rise of the Progressive party.

It took the open fissure of the Republican party in 1912 to give Democrats unified control of the federal government. But numerically, the Democratic party remained the nation's minority party.[20] At the presidential level, this is indicated by the simple fact that in no region outside

19. For the period 1876–94, the mean percentage of electorally competitive congressional districts nationwide was 25.8 percent. The equivalent figure for the period 1896–1908 was 16.0 percent. Figures are calculated based on data contained in ICPSR study no. 7757.

20. In the popular vote, Wilson actually polled 1.2 percentage points *less* than William Jennings Bryan in 1908.

Table 3.3. *Regional Percentage of 1912*
Presidential Vote

	Wilson %	Roosevelt %	Taft %
Northeast	37.7	29.4	27.0
Midwest	38.8	28.5	24.6
South	58.1	18.0	18.5
West	37.2	33.2	16.3

Table 3.4. *Number of States (by Region) in Which Wilson Vote Share Exceeds Combined Taft/Roosevelt Vote Share*

	Northeast	Midwest	South	West	*Total*
Wilson < Taft + TR	10	12	2	10	34
Wilson > Taft + TR	0	0	13	1	14
(N)	(10)	(12)	(15)	(11)	(48)

Note: "<" = less than; ">" = greater than.

of the South did Woodrow Wilson capture as much as 40 percent of the popular vote (Table 3.3).[21] Indeed, in only *one* northern state (Arizona) did Wilson's popular vote share in 1912 exceed the combined vote share of the Republican and Progressive candidates (see Table 3.4). A similar pattern holds at the congressional level. As noted earlier, stable Democratic control of the House required effective party competition in northern districts. But as Table 3.5 makes clear, the mean share of the northern Democratic congressional vote in 1912 remained essentially unaltered from preceding elections (41.1 percent), even as the Republican mean plummeted. Once again, it was the presence of progressive candidates of various stripes that cut heavily into the traditional Republican share of the congressional vote and gave Democrats control of the House.

In power, Democrats could not practice the more conventional politics of coalition maintenance. Rather, they were forced to occupy them-

21. In the South, Wilson took 58.1 percent of the popular vote.

Table 3.5. *Mean Party Percentage in Congressional Elections,*
1900–1920

Election Year	Southern Democrat	Northern Democrat	Northern Republican	Northern Progressive	(N)[a]
1900	69.1	42.5	54.5		
1902	78.4	43.5	53.8		
1904	71.7	37.0	58.6		
1906	77.3	40.2	54.2		
1908	73.5	41.6	53.4		
1910	78.4	42.8	50.0	20.4	(22)
1912	78.5	41.1	37.3	19.3	(228)
1914	79.1	39.6	46.0	8.9	(272)
1916	72.2	42.0	51.6	2.5	(94)
1918	82.8	42.6	56.4	0.4	(20)
1920	72.3	33.0	62.2		

[a] (N) = Number of Progressive third-party candidates.
Source: ICPSR Study No. 7757.

selves with the more difficult politics of coalition building – a politics that required Democrats to aggressively reach out beyond traditional constituencies to new blocs of voters and stabilize their hold on national power. Those voters who had left their traditional moorings in the Republican party to support the fledgling Progressive party offered the most coherent source of potential support for a new Democratic majority. At the presidential level, the Progressive party had been wildly successful, thanks in no small part to its magnetic candidate, former president Theodore Roosevelt. In 1912 Roosevelt outpolled the Republican candidate William Howard Taft in twenty-eight of forty-eight state races (see Table 3.6). Only in the industrial Northeast did Taft's mean electoral margin exceed Roosevelt's, though Roosevelt triumphed over Taft in key industrial states like Pennsylvania and New Jersey. It was this broad geographic distribution of Progressive support that lessened the need for Democratic strategists to make calculations explicitly based upon swing states. In thirty-four of the forty-eight state presidential races in 1912 (70.8 percent), the Progressive party vote was large enough to constitute a swing voting bloc in the event that the third party suffered an organizational collapse (Table 3.7 provides breakdowns for indi-

Table 3.6. *States in Which Roosevelt Vote Share Exceeds Taft Vote Share (by Region)*

	Northeast	Midwest	South	West	*Total*
Roosevelt < Taft	7	3	6	4	20
Roosevelt > Taft	3	9	9	7	28
(N)	(10)	(12)	(15)	(11)	(48)

Note: "<" = less than; ">" = greater than.

vidual states). Thus, Democratic electoral calculations in this chapter assume a more conventional Downsian character – as though appealing to a national median voter rather than a median state in the electoral college – because a successful appeal to this group promised to enhance Democratic chances in so many state contests.

The Reorganization of Democratic Party Government (I): The Emergence of the Presidency. A second discontinuity with the previous chapter concerns the transformed character of the Democratic party organization in government. This transformation was the result of changes in both the office of the president and the organization of Congress, as well as in the evolving pattern of interaction between these branches. As we saw in Chapter 2, presidential leadership was peripheral to the Democrats' embrace of the discretionary railroad commission. Rather, it fell to congressional party leaders to contain the antimonopoly impulse within their rank and file and demonstrate to their pivotal national coalition partner, business Mugwumps, the Democrats' capacity for responsible reform. In confronting the trust problem, the challenge facing Progressive Era Democratic leaders remained substantially unaltered: to contain agrarian antimonopolism and persuade Progressive party voters of the Democratic party's capacity for responsible reform. This time around, however, both presidential preferences and presidential action would be central to the final character of legislative choice.

Presidential practice had evolved considerably since the administration of Grover Cleveland. For one thing, by the Progressive Era nineteenth-century proscriptions against presidential electioneering were

Table 3.7. Comparison of Wilson-Taft Popular Vote Margin and Roosevelt Vote Share

State	Wilson-Taft Margin	TR	Swing Vote?[a]
VT	−12.7	35.2	+
UT	−4.9	21.5	+
MI	−0.2	38.9	+
ID	1.0	24.1	+
WY	1.8	21.8	+
NH	2.0	20.2	+
CT	3.3	17.9	+
RI	3.5	21.6	+
MA	3.6	29.1	+
WA	5.1	35.2	+
NM	6.7	17.1	+
ND	7.6	29.7	+
WI	8.4	15.6	+
OR	9.0	27.4	+
PA	10.0	36.5	+
OK	11.2	0.0	−
MT	11.9	28.3	+
MN	12.6	37.6	+
NY	12.6	24.5	+
IL	13.2	33.7	+
IO	13.3	32.8	+
DE	13.6	18.2	+
OH	14.1	22.1	+
MO	17.6	17.8	+
KA	18.9	32.8	+
ME	19.0	37.4	+
IN	19.9	24.7	+
NJ	20.6	33.5	+
WV	20.9	29.4	+
CO	20.9	26.9	+
NB	21.9	29.1	+
KY	22.9	22.4	+
NV	23.9	27.9	+
MD	24.9	24.9	tie
TN	28.8	21.4	−
AZ	30.9	29.3	−
AR	34.6	17.3	−
CA	41.3	41.8	+
SD	42.0	50.5	+
NC	47.3	28.3	−
VA	48.9	15.9	−
FL	61.1	8.9	−
AL	61.5	19.2	−
TX	63.3	8.8	−
LA	72.0	11.7	−
GA	72.4	18.1	−
MS	86.5	5.5	−
SC	94.9	2.5	−

Note: "+" indicates that a state's Roosevelt vote was large enough to swing the outcome to either Wilson or Taft in a two-way race.

[a] "+" = yes (N = 34); "−" = no (N = 13); "tie" (N = 1).

a thing of the past. Presidential campaign discourse, so evident in 1912, deepened the dependency of governmental action upon presidential initiative, strengthening the public perception of the presidential office as the federal government's vital center and – with the collapse of the Republican "czar" speakership – as its primary instrument for responsible party government. Woodrow Wilson enthusiastically seized the challenge of unifying governing institutions and directing them toward the dual vindication of progressive reform and Democratic party vitality. The story is often told of Wilson's decision to forgo the organization of a progressive coalition in Congress, choosing instead to work through traditional party leaders and mechanisms.[22] This was a significant political moment, for the new president had made the decision not simply to prove himself as a progressive leader. In addition, he would help rehabilitate the Democratic party in the public mind as an instrument of reform and, through it, engineer a realignment in national politics.

No doubt the differences we will observe between Wilson and Cleveland are to some extent the result of case selection. For example, Cleveland readily assumed a more prominent leadership role on issues like tariff reform and, in his second administration, the repeal of the Sherman Silver Purchase Act – programmatic areas (free trade, banking, and currency) in which nineteenth-century Democratic presidents had traditionally exercised party leadership.[23] But the sporadic character of Cleveland's leadership efforts throws into relief the *routinization* of legislative intervention that occurred under Wilson. Moreover, Cleveland's leadership posture still owed much to the nineteenth-century Jacksonian paradigm. Like Andrew Jackson during the Bank War and the conflict over removal, Cleveland preached the standard of personal conviction, intervening in the governing process according to his sense of moral right and constitutional propriety. Cleveland's political stances could be rigidly principled and even dogmatic, a position that rendered leadership even through nominal party majorities frustrating and explosively confrontational.[24]

22. Link, *Wilson: The New Freedom*, 153; Blum, *Woodrow Wilson and the Politics of Morality*, 66; Holt, *Congressional Insurgents and the Party System, 1909–1916*, 64–5.
23. On Cleveland's activities on behalf of tariff and currency reform, see Nevins, *Grover Cleveland: A Study in Courage*; and Koenig, *Bryan*.
24. Jacksonian leadership during the Bank War and the conflict over his determination to unilaterally remove federal deposits to state banks are covered in considerable detail in Remini, *Andrew Jackson: The Course of American Freedom, 1822–1832*; and Remini, *Andrew Jackson: The Course of American Democracy, 1833–1845*.

Wilson broke decisively with this Jacksonian model. In stark contrast to Cleveland, Wilson insisted on the importance of political opportunism and partisan comity to effective leadership.[25] "Power," Wilson had written, "consists in one's capacity to link his will with the purpose of others, to lead by reason and a gift for cooperation."[26] The progressive president would use the Democratic party as an instrument of collaborative leadership, participating actively in the programmatic direction of the party, but ready to trim his expectations to preserve party harmony. To be sure, Wilson possessed the advantage of negotiating with a party that, like him, was electorally vulnerable and dependent upon attracting sufficient numbers of Progressive party voters to sustain their majority hold on Congress. And as someone with his finger on the pulse of progressive opinion, this gave Wilson a peculiar advantage with his party that Cleveland never enjoyed. Congress would be more pliable before Wilson's will not simply because he could bring to bear the formidable patronage resources of the executive branch and not merely because of his talents as a public opinion leader. In the end, congressional Democrats would follow Wilson because he could lead them in a direction that promised the stabilization of Democratic power in Congress, and that was a potent instrument of presidential leadership.

As the above discussion implies, the commitment to work through the Democratic party required that Wilson accept the limitations of party government as well as its possibilities. In dealing with Democratic Congresses, Wilson was much more the pragmatist, much more an exponent of political opportunism than when he later confronted a Republican Senate majority in a showdown over the Treaty of Versailles. Indeed, for varying reasons, scholars often treat Wilson's wartime leadership under divided government as emblematic of his approach to congressional leadership per se.[27] But only once in the years 1913 to 1917 did Wilson challenge the judgment of congressional Democrats by taking his case

25. "The Ideals of Public Life": An Address to the Annual Dinner of the Cleveland Chamber of Commerce, November 16, 1907. In Link, ed., *The Papers of Woodrow Wilson* Vol. 17, 500.

26. Quoted in Blum, *Woodrow Wilson and the Politics of Morality*, 66.

27. Psycho-historians point to Wilson's handling of the Treaty of Versailles as evidence of deeply ensconced rigidities of personality, while students of the rhetorical presidency treat this same case as indicative of emergent presidential reliance on public opinion leadership to direct congressional processes according to their own lights. Each of these interpretations offers a poor fit of Wilsonian leadership under conditions of Democratic unified government. See George and George, *Woodrow Wilson and Colonel House*. Tulis, *The Rhetorical Presidency*.

directly to the public.[28] In seeking progressive reform in the Sixty-third Congress (1913–15), Wilson would push the party as far as it would go, engage with party leaders in endless rounds of negotiations, but ultimately defer to congressional leaders responsible for drafting legislation and husbanding it through the legislative process. Wilson accepted the loss of control over statutory details this sometimes entailed in the name of party unity. In this regard, it seems that Wilson was still bound by vestiges of the nineteenth-century norm of legislative deference, at least in comparison to the comparatively uncompromising exercise of unilateral party leadership we will confront in our next case chapter, in Franklin Roosevelt's fight to deal a "death sentence" to public utility holding companies.

The Reorganization of Democratic Party Government (II): The Democratic Caucus.   A final discontinuity with the previous chapter pertains to the organization of the Democratic party in Congress. As we will see later in this chapter, the passage of the FTCA was sustained by overwhelming Democratic majorities. This unity of party action points to a second shift in the modalities of national governing practice: the development of caucus discipline as a tool of party government. It was a unique moment in the history of American legislative organization, one as different from the competition between party leaders and committee chairman we saw under the Gilded Age leadership of Democratic Speaker John G. Carlisle (Chapter 2), as it would be from the system of seniority and committee comity we will observe in our study of the Public Utility Holding Company Act (Chapter 4).

Several features of Democratic caucus government deserve our consideration. In the first place, caucus power was asserted over traditional committee prerogatives. One rule, for example, authorized the caucus to "adopt [resolutions] forbidding [committee] reports on other than specified subjects, or by other than specified committees, without its explicit consent."[29] Other rules projected caucus power onto the floor. Thus, the Democratic caucus was empowered to issue instructions to the Rules Committee stipulating the terms upon which party legislation was to be disposed of on the floor.[30] But perhaps the most widely known caucus mechanism was the "binding resolution," by which a two-thirds vote of

---

28. The exception involved military and naval expansion in 1916. Link, *Wilson: The New Freedom*, 151–2.

29. Haines, "The Congressional Caucus of Today," 699.

30. Galloway, *History of the House of Representatives*, 173.

all Democrats present and voting in caucus committed the entire party contingent to the caucus position on all floor-related activities, from special orders of the Rules Committee, to amendments, recommittal motions, and votes of final passage. More stringent still was the caucus rule which "pledged the support of all Democrats to Ways and Means Committee bills."[31]

Compared to Cannonism, the more egalitarian thrust of caucus government seems clear. But it would be wrong to assume that caucus deliberations were immune to influence by powerful party leaders. Majority leader Oscar W. Underwood was particularly influential in this regard, emerging from the immediate post-Cannon era as the party's most influential leader. Underwood's power was anchored in his control of desired party resources. His position as chairman of the Ways and Means Committee and, therefore, his de facto chairmanship of the party's Committee on Committees, gave Underwood a particularly potent mechanism for rewarding and punishing caucus members, especially freshmen (who constituted almost 40 percent of the party in the Sixty-third Congress).[32] In addition to his power over committee appointments, Underwood (as chairman of Ways and Means) also possessed the right to be recognized at any time on the floor. As Haines has observed, the majority leader readily used this prerogative to "improvise . . . special rule[s] to restrict debate or to shut off amendments."[33] In this way, Underwood could play a decisive role in the process of floor deliberations in the House. As president, Woodrow Wilson understood the majority leader's influence over the disposition of House business under this new organization of Democratic party power. In order to harness that influence, he cultivated his relationship with Underwood. In particular, he deferred to the majority leader's choice of Texas Democrat Albert S. Burleson to be postmaster general and gave him control over "a generous share of the [executive] patronage."[34] In return, Underwood served as linchpin in the translation of administration preferences into legislative party action.[35]

Of necessity, Democrats sought exclusive partisan rights to the "progressive" label, and success in this endeavor required that they assert hegemony over chamber deliberations. In both chambers, Republicans –

31. Johnson, *Oscar W. Underwood*, 141.
32. Haines, "The Congressional Caucus of Today," 699; Peters, *The American Speakership*, 94.
33. Haines, "The Congressional Caucus of Today," 699.
34. Johnson, *Oscar W. Underwood*, 196–7.
35. Fleming, "Re-establishing Leadership in the House of Representatives: The Case of Oscar W. Underwood," 238–9.

progressive and otherwise – were barred from participation in the drafting and markup processes. Democrats would proceed solely upon caucus judgments. In committee, the Democratic contingent would caucus among themselves (the so-called miniature caucus) to determine which amendments, Democratic and Republican, were acceptable, and then "present a united front to the full committee."[36] At other times, caucusing among the entire party was the order of the day. Wholesale exclusion from the process of legislative deliberation took its toll on the minority parties. Both privately and publicly, Progressives and insurgent Republicans would blast "King Caucus" as merely Cannonism in a different guise.[37] Frustrated by their marginalized role, they would respond predictably – and perhaps with justification – condemning the Democrats' initial antitrust program for its sloppy drafting and ineffectual purpose. In one private exchange, Senator Robert M. La Follette, a progressive Republican, expressed his disenchantment with the Democratic usurpation of the progressive agenda for business reform.

> The fact is, the men who are working on these [antitrust] bills have tried to go ahead independently of Progressives who have spent years on these subjects. The Democrats have become slaves to the party caucus. They want every measure with a party brand on it for political capital. And most of them haven't been long enough interested in progressive principles, especially those involving economic issues, to be ready for the work. They have taken some bills introduced in the previous sessions by Progressive Republicans, and not wanting to follow literally, have cut and pieced without chart or compass, until their work is almost a joke.[38]

There is no need to exaggerate the extent to which Democratic leaders employed the caucus to bind party members into a cohesive floor unit. During Wilson's first administration the binding caucus resolution was employed in only four instances. But each of these occasions is instructive, for they involved actions to legislate the key planks of the party's 1912 Baltimore platform: the Underwood-Simmons Tariff Act, the Federal Reserve Banking Act, the Clayton Act, and the Federal Trade Commission Act – legislation deemed critical by Democratic leaders to vindicate the party as a responsible instrument of progressive reform and drive a realignment in national party politics.

36. Francis Newlands to Woodrow Wilson, 2/6/14. In Link, ed. *The Papers of Woodrow Wilson* Vol. 29, 227. See also Haines's discussion of the "miniature caucus" in "The Congressional Caucus of Today," 698.
37. Johnson, *Oscar W. Underwood*, 140.
38. Robert M. La Follette to Rudolph Spreckels, 2/16/14. In La Follette and La Follette, *Robert M. La Follette* Vol. 1, 488.

"Free and Unrestricted Competition"

Interpreting the Sherman Anti-Trust Act:
From Trans-Missouri to the "Rule of Reason"

With this section, we move from a consideration of electoral and party developments after 1896, to an examination of the regulatory attitudes manifested by agrarian Democrats on the so-called trust problem. The place to begin this discussion is with the Sherman Anti-Trust Act of 1890, the nation's first attempt to deal with the problems of business monopoly and anticompetitive trading practices in interstate commerce. In particular, agrarian preferences and political activity evolved in reaction to the federal antitrust law's interpretive history in the Supreme Court. By 1911, after more than twenty years of construction in the federal courts, the Sherman Act's prohibition against "every contract, combination . . . or conspiracy in restraint of trade or commerce" had acquired a settled meaning at law. The Supreme Court had repeatedly held that its provisions were to be read literally. In the Court's judgment, the Congress, exercising its plenary power in the field of interstate commerce, had declared a national policy of "free and unrestricted competition." As such, *every* direct restraint on competition in interstate commerce was illegal, whether or not such restraint had previously been considered reasonable at common law.

Agrarian Democrats were staunchly committed to the Court's construction of the Sherman Act and its underlying vision of the American political economy. For by this interpretation, Congress was held to have placed the weight of its authority in support of a policy of decentralized economic activity and property ownership. The seminal case was *United States v Trans-Missouri Freight Association*, in which Justice Rufus W. Peckham first delineated the policy intent behind the Sherman Act and its rule of enforced competition.[39] Speaking for the majority of the Court, Peckham set the Sherman Act against

> combinations of capital whose purpose in combining is to control the production or manufacture of any particular article in the market, and by such control dictate the price at which the article shall be sold; the effect being to drive out of business all the small dealers in the commodity, and to render the public subject to the decision of the combination as to what price shall be paid for the article.

Warming to his point, Peckham continued:

---

39. *United States v Trans-Missouri Freight Association* (1897) 166 U.S. 290.

In this light, it is not material that the price of an article may be lowered. It is in the power of the combination to raise it, and the result in any event is unfortunate for the country, by depriving it of the services of a large number of small but independent dealers, who were familiar with the business, and who had spent their lives in it, and who supported themselves and their families from the small profits realized therein. Whether they be able to find other avenues to earn their livelihood is not so material, because it is not for the real prosperity of any country that such changes should occur which result in transferring an independent business man, the head of his establishment, small though it might be, into a mere servant or agent of a corporation for selling the commodities which he once manufactured or dealt in; having no voice in shaping the business policy of the company, and bound to obey orders issued by others.[40]

The settled meaning of federal antitrust law after *Trans-Missouri* and just prior to the Supreme Court's "rule of reason" decisions was well stated by E. Henry Lacomb, Circuit Court judge for the Southern District of New York and author of its majority opinion in *United States v American Tobacco Company*.[41] The case involved the merger of American Tobacco with former competitors Continental Tobacco and Consolidated Tobacco. In the Court's opinion, it was irrelevant to inquire whether or not the merger had had a detrimental effect on prices or production. Equally irrelevant was a discussion of any economic efficiencies resulting from the merger. The only issue was whether or not the merger directly restrained competition between rivals. With evident dissatisfaction, Judge Lacombe reaffirmed the binding authority of the *Trans-Missouri* rule and held against the American Tobacco Company. The Sherman Act, in the judge's determination, was "no longer open to construction in the inferior federal courts." So bound, Lacombe simply invoked the *per se* rule and the national economic policy of "free and unrestricted competition" that informed the Sherman Act's prohibition against every direct restraint of trade:[42]

40. Ibid., 290, 324. Had this indeed been the policy intent behind the Sherman Act, Justice Oliver Wendell Holmes concluded, "I should regard calling such a law a regulation of commerce a mere pretense. It would be an attempt to reconstruct society." *United States v Northern Securities Company* (1904) 193 U.S. 197 (Justice Holmes, dissenting).
41. *United States v American Tobacco Company et al.* (1908) 164 F. 700.
42. The phrase "free and unrestricted competition" recurs repeatedly throughout Justice Peckham's opinion in *Trans-Missouri*. It was a phrase seized on by agrarian Democrats, and, as will be discussed in detail at a later point in the book, it was language that would reappear in the initial antitrust legislation introduced by the Democrats in 1914.

Disregarding various dicta and following the several propositions which have been approved by successive majorities of the Supreme Court, this language is to be construed as prohibiting any contract or combination whose direct effect is to prevent the free play of competition, and thus tend to deprive the country of the services of any number of independent dealers however small.[43]

Lacombe acknowledged the "revolutionary" impact of the statute as construed, adding parenthetically that such an impact did not necessarily prejudice the construction. Indeed, he continued:

When we remember the circumstances under which the act was passed, the popular prejudice against large aggregations of capital, and the loud outcry against combinations which might in one way or an other interfere to suppress or check the *full, free, and wholly unrestrained competition* which was assumed, rightly or wrongly, to be the very "life of trade," it would not be surprising to find that Congress had responded to what seemed to be the wishes of a large part, if not the majority, of the community, and that it intended to secure such competition against the operation of natural laws [emphasis added].[44]

The act was revolutionary, Lacombe continued, because it swept aside the ancient common law category of reasonable restraint.

The act may be termed revolutionary, because, before its passage, the courts had recognized a "restraint of trade" which was held not to be unfair, but permissible, although it operated in some measure to restrict competition. By insensible degrees, under the operation of many causes, business, manufacturing and trading alike, has more and more developed a tendency toward larger and larger aggregations of capital and more extensive combinations of individual enterprise. It is contended that, under existing conditions, in that way only can production be increased and cheapened, new markets opened and developed, stability in reasonable prices secured, and industrial progress assured. But every aggregation of individuals or corporations, formerly independent, immediately upon its formation terminates an existing competition, whether or not some other competition may subsequently arise. The act as above construed prohibits every contract or combination in restraint of competition. Size is not made the test: Two individuals who have been driving rival express wagons between villages in two contiguous states, who enter into a combination to join forces and operate a single line, restrain an existing competition; and it would seem to make little difference whether they make such combination more effective by forming a partnership or not.[45]

43. *United States v American Tobacco Company et al.* (1908) 164 F. 700, 701.
44. Ibid.
45. Ibid., 700, 701–2.

When, therefore, the Supreme Court announced its momentous "rule of reason" decisions in 1911, it fractured the legal status quo that had grown up around the antitrust law since 1896.[46] At once, the meaning of the Sherman Act was transformed. Its literal language was now to be read in the "light of reason," its legal sanctions applicable to "unreasonable" or "undue" restraints of trade only. For those opposed to the "rule of reason" decisions, as most agrarian Democrats were, the dissenting opinions of Justice John Marshall Harlan provided a potent rallying cry. For this reason, it is worth considering Harlan's remarks in some detail.

To Harlan, the meaning of the Sherman Act was crystal clear. He was indignant at the insinuation of Chief Justice White that earlier Court majorities had "grop[ed] about in the darkness" without the aid of the "light of reason."[47] As Harlan reminded his fellow justices, in *Trans-Missouri* and again in *United States v Joint Traffic Association* the Court had explicitly confronted the question whether the Sherman Act, properly construed, made special allowance for reasonable restraints of trade. Indeed, arguments in support of this interpretation had been presented by the most able corporation counsel in the country. And in each instance, the Court rejected such arguments as contrary to the "plain meaning" of the statute, declining to amend an act of Congress by judicial construction. "One thing is certain," Harlan wrote, "the 'rule of reason,' to which the court refers, does not justify the perversion of the plain words of an act in order to defeat the will of Congress."

> I beg to say that, in my judgment, the majority, in the former cases, were guided by the "rule of reason"; for it may be assumed that they knew quite as well as others what the rules of reason require when a court seeks to ascertain the will of Congress as expressed in a statute. It is obvious from the opinions in the former cases, that the majority did not grope about in darkness, but in discharging the solemn duty put on them they stood out in the full glare of the "light of reason," and felt and said, time and again, that the court could not, consistently with the Constitution, and would not, usurp the functions of Congress by indulging in judicial legislation. They said in express words, in the former cases, in response to the earnest contentions of counsel, that to insert by construction the word "unreasonable" or "undue" in the act of Congress would be judicial legislation.[48]

46. The "rule of reason" decisions are *United States v Standard Oil Company* (1911) 221 U.S. 1; *United States v American Tobacco Company et al.* (1911) 221 U.S. 106.
47. *United States v American Tobacco Company et al.* (1911) 221 U.S. 106, 192 (Justice Harlan, dissenting).
48. Ibid.

Quoting Justice Peckham's majority opinion in *Trans-Missouri*, Harlan asserted what he considered to be a cardinal rule of statutory construction: when Congress speaks directly, the "public policy of the government is to be found in its statutes." And in Harlan's judgment – a judgment consistent with fifteen years of Sherman Act rulings – Congress had spoken directly through the Sherman Act.

> The men who were in the congress [sic] of the United States at that time knew what the common law was about the restraint of trade. They knew what restraints of trade at common law were lawful and what were unlawful. But congress said: "The surest way to protect interstate commerce is not to start upon any distinctions at all as to the kinds of trade; 'every' contract in restraint of trade among the states is hereby declared to be illegal."[49]

Thus, by inserting the word "unreasonable" into the text of the Sherman Act's prohibition against every restraint of trade, Harlan wrote, the Court, by judicial legislation, "has not only upset the long-settled interpretation of the act, but has usurped the constitutional functions of the legislative branch of the government." In *Standard Oil*, Harlan wrote:

> [A]t every session of Congress since the decision of 1896, the lawmaking branch of the government, with full knowledge of that decision, has refused to change the policy it had declared, or to so amend the act of 1890 as to except from its operation contracts, combinations, and trusts that reasonably restrain interstate commerce.[50]

In *American Tobacco*, Harlan reiterated this point:

> By every conceivable form of expression, the majority, in the Trans-Missouri and Joint Traffic Cases, adjudged that the act of Congress did not allow restraint of interstate trade to any extent or in any form, and three times it expressly rejected the theory, which has been persistently advanced, that the act should be construed as if it had in it the word "unreasonable" or "undue." But now the court, in accordance with what it denominates the "rule of reason," in effect inserts in the act the word "undue," which means the same as "unreasonable," and thereby makes Congress say what it did not say; what as I think, it plainly did not intend to say; and what, since the passage of the act, it has explicitly refused to say. It has steadfastly refused to amend the act so as to tolerate a restraint of interstate commerce

49. This passage is excerpted from the written transcript of Justice Harlan's oral dissent, delivered in the *Standard Oil* case, 15 May 1911. That transcript can be found in *The Commoner*, May 26, 1911, 3.

50. *United States v Standard Oil Company* (1911) 221 U.S. 1, 92 (Justice Harlan, dissenting).

even where such restraint could be said to be "reasonable" or "due." In short, the court now, by judicial legislation, in effect amends an act of Congress relating to a subject over which that department of the government has exclusive cognizance.[51]

Harlan concluded his opinion in the *Standard Oil* case on a ominous note:

> After many years of public service at the national capital, and after a somewhat close observation of the conduct of public affairs, I am impelled to say that there is abroad in our land a most harmful tendency to bring about the amending of constitutions and legislative enactments by means alone of judicial construction. As a public policy has been declared by the legislative department in respect of interstate commerce, over which Congress has entire control, under the Constitution, all concerned must patiently submit to what has been lawfully done, until the people of the United States – the source of all national power – shall, in their own time, upon reflection and through the legislative department of the government, require a change of that policy. . . . The supreme law of the land, which is binding alike upon all – Presidents, Congresses, the courts and the people – gives to Congress, and to Congress alone, authority to regulate interstate commerce, and when Congress forbids any restraint of such commerce, in any form, all must obey its mandate. To overreach the action of Congress merely by judicial construction, that is, by indirection, is a blow at the integrity of our governmental system, and in the end will prove most dangerous to all.[52]

The Democratic Response to the "Rule of Reason"

The proposition that the "rule of reason" decisions expressed a cross-class, cross-party consensus on the legitimacy of reasonable restraint blinds us to the shockwaves these rulings sent through the Democratic party. Indeed, it is difficult to exaggerate the alarm voiced by agrarian Democrats in the wake of these decisions. Representative William C. Adamson of Georgia, for one, attacked the constitutionality of the Court's ruling. As chairman of the House Interstate Commerce Committee – the committee charged with drafting trade commission legislation in that chamber in 1914 – Adamson surmised that the late Mark Hanna's long-sought goal to distinguish legally between "good" and "bad" trusts was at long last a reality.

51. *United States v American Tobacco Company et al.* (1911) 221 U.S. 106, 192 (Justice Harlan, dissenting).
52. *United States v Standard Oil Company* (1911) 221 U.S. 1, 106 (Justice Harlan, dissenting).

The supreme court [sic] of the United States has no constitutional power to amend the Sherman law by writing into that statute the word "unreasonable." The trusts tried time and time again to amend the law in that way, by the insertion of that one word, but failed.

That was Mark Hanna's plan; he wanted the law to distinguish between good trusts and bad trusts, but congress [sic] declined to make the distinction. Now the supreme court takes on itself the power of legislation, which was expressly reserved to congress under the constitution, and proceeds to write into the law what congress refused to consider.[53]

Democrats reacted quickly to the *Standard Oil* ruling, announced on May 15, 1911, by introducing legislation in Congress to reinstate the *Trans-Missouri* prohibition against all restraints on competition. Indeed, in the two days following the Court's decision, a total of seven bills were introduced to expunge the rule of reason from the Sherman Act, six written by Democrats, mostly from the southern and western portions of the country and all outside the industrial Northeast. All sought specifically to clarify the first section's prohibition against "every contract, combination . . . or conspiracy in restraint" of interstate commerce or trade. For example, one such bill, introduced by Senator James A. Reed of Missouri, a member of the Senate Interstate Commerce Committee, read: "Every such contract, combination, or conspiracy is hereby declared to be unreasonable and illegal, and shall be so considered, taken, and held in all proceedings at law and in equity."[54] Another, sponsored by Senator Thomas P. Gore of Oklahoma, also a member of the Senate Interstate Commerce Committee, sought to ensure that "no contract, combination, or conspiracy of whatever kind or character in restraint of [interstate] trade or commerce . . . shall be construed or adjudged to be reasonable."[55] Still another was introduced by Senator Charles Culberson of Texas, chairman of the Senate Judiciary Committee in 1914 and in charge of shepherding the Clayton Act to passage on the floor of the upper chamber. In the wake of the rule-of-reason decisions, Culberson predicted a dramatic drop in the number of successful criminal prosecutions involving trusts, as future antitrust cases would turn on the "supposed intent of the conspirators rather than [being] con-

53. *The Commoner*, May 26, 1911, 6. Like Adamson, William P. Hamilton, editor of the *Wall Street Journal*, believed that the Supreme Court had acted unconstitutionally, violating the separation of powers and "[reading] into the Sherman act an amendment that never could have passed the Congress of the United States." Nevertheless, Hamilton counseled businessmen not to admonish the Court for its constitutional transgressions: "Why? Because you could never have got to pass through the Congress of the United States such a word as 'unreasonable' in the Sherman law, and you have got to get it into the law in order to save the business of the United States." The *New York Times*, May 18, 1911, 3.

54. 62d Cong., 1st sess., S.2374.   55. Ibid., S.2433.

fined to the issue of the actual existence of combination of monopoly."[56] His bill sought to remedy this situation, its first section stating: "Every contract, combination in the form of a trust or otherwise, or conspiracy, in restraint of trade or commerce . . . OF WHATEVER CHARACTER, is hereby declared illegal."[57]

But it was the Democratic party's titular leader, William Jennings Bryan, who was called upon most often to express his party's outrage at the Supreme Court decisions. In no uncertain terms, the headline in Bryan's political organ, *The Commoner*, announced to its agrarian readership: "The Trusts Have Won."[58] Bryan accused the Court of straining to rewrite the antitrust law. "The real-meat of the decision is to be found in the AMENDMENT of the anti-trust law to meet the demands of the trusts," the three-time Democratic presidential nominee wrote.

> For several years the trusts have been demanding the very amendment that the court [sic] has read into the law. There will be rejoicing in Wall street [sic], but there will be sadness in the homes of the masses who are now compelled to begin a campaign for the enactment of an anti-trust law so clear and explicit that the court can not repeal it by construction. . . . Now let those, republicans and democrats [sic], who are opposed to trusts, set to work to overcome the decision by legislation.[59]

Similarly, in an article written for the *North American Review*, Bryan characterized the rule-of-reason decisions as "revolutionary," telling the periodical's largely northeastern readership: "We may as well recognize that *we now have no criminal law against the trusts.*"[60]

> In crime the intent is everything, and the accused is entitled to the benefit of every reasonable doubt. What trust magnate could be convicted of criminal intent (with every reasonable doubt resolved in his favor) to *unreasonably* restrain trade when there is no legal definition of unreasonable restraint.[61]

As well, Bryan predicted that the "rule-of-reason" decisions would hobble civil proceedings brought under the antitrust law. For now that the Court had decided that each case must be decided upon the facts of the individual case, court rulings largely would be inapplicable in subsequent cases.[62]

---

56. *The Commoner*, June 21, 1911, 2.
57. 62d Cong., 1st sess., S. 2375 (emphasis in original).
58. *The Commoner*, May 26, 1911, 1.   59. Ibid.
60. Bryan, "The Reason." 21, 22. Emphasis in original.   61. Ibid., 21.
62. Bryan's analysis parallels the adverse report made in 1909 by Senator Nelson on behalf of the Senate Judiciary Committee, in reference to a bill to amend the antitrust act to allow reasonable restraints of trade. In that report Nelson stated: "The anti-trust act makes it a criminal offense to violate the law, and provides a punishment both by fine

Interviewed for *The Outlook*, and republished in *The Commoner* in early 1912, Bryan again reiterated his opposition to the rule of reason. Again he maintained the near impossibility of enforcing the antitrust law as construed by the White majority, expressing his belief that Congress "should at once declare by specific legislation that any attempt at restraint of trade should be considered unreasonable." Byran held that, "Such a law would repair the damage that the supreme court [sic] decision has done to the antitrust law."[63]

Bryan urged his agrarian readership in *The Commoner* to carefully study the opinions of Justice John Marshall Harlan in the *Standard Oil* and *American Tobacco* cases. Like Harlan, Bryan believed the Court had gone out of its way to reinterpret the antitrust law. The majority opinion in each case was pure *obiter dicta* – involving language and distinctions unnecessary to the decision of either case. Echoing Harlan's remarks, Bryan maintained that "in order to find the defendant companies guilty it was not necessary for the Court to discuss the question of reasonableness or unreasonableness[.]" That is to say, in both the *Standard Oil* and *American Tobacco* cases the defendants would have been found guilty under either interpretation of the Sherman Act.[64] Picking up on

and imprisonment. To inject into the act the question of whether an agreement or combination is reasonable or unreasonable would render the act as a criminal or penal statute indefinite and uncertain, and hence, to that extent, utterly nugatory and void, and would practically amount to a repeal of that part of the act.... And while the same technical objection does not apply to civil prosecutions, the injection of the rule of reasonableness or unreasonableness would lead to the greatest variableness and uncertainty in the enforcement of the law. The defense of reasonable restraint would be made in every case, and there would be as many different rules of reasonableness as cases, courts, and juries. What one court or jury might deem unreasonable another court or jury might deem reasonable. A court or jury in Ohio might find a given agreement or combination reasonable, while a court and jury in Wisconsin might find the same agreement and combination unreasonable. In the case of the *People v Sheldon* [(1893) 139 N.Y. 264], Chief Justice Andrews remarked: 'If agreements and combinations to prevent competition in prices are or may be hurtful to trade, the only sure remedy is to prohibit all agreements of that character. If the validity of such an agreement was made to depend upon actual proof of public prejudice or injury, it would be very difficult in any case to establish the invalidity, although the moral evidence might be very convincing.' ... To amend the antitrust act, as suggested by this bill, would be to entirely emasculate it, and for all practical purposes render it nugatory as a remedial statute. Criminal prosecutions would not lie, and civil remedies would labor under the greatest doubt and uncertainty. The act as it exists is clear, comprehensive, certain, and highly remedial. It practically covers the field of Federal jurisdiction, and is in every respect a model law. To destroy or undermine it at the present juncture, when combinations are on the increase, and appear to be as oblivious as ever of the rights of the public, would be a calamity."

63. *The Commoner*, January 12, 1912, 2.   64. Bryan, "The Reason," 14.

Harlan's theme of the judicial usurpation of congressional power, Bryan portrayed the decision as a clear example of institutional self-aggrandizement: "Nothing is more abhorrent to our institutions than an appointive legislative body," Bryan maintained.[65] Drawing upon core cultural assumptions, Bryan asserted the "natural tendency" of any political institution to enlarge the sphere of its own powers, "a tendency from which courts are not entirely free," and he counseled followers not to defer to the Supreme Court's judgment. Rather, Bryan prompted Democrats to restore the Sherman Act to its original vigor through legislation "specifically declaring that the [Sherman] law prohibits all restraint of trade – not merely unreasonable restraint":

> Under our Constitution the Court has the final word as to a law, and the only way in which the public can protest against judicial legislation is through the legislative branch of the government. While the Constitution divides the Federal Government into three branches, each independent of the other, it gives to the Supreme Court the power of interpretation, and this transcends for the time being the powers vested in the Legislature. But the people are not mocked; they can by legislation restrict the construction of the Court and prohibit a construction which will nullify a statute.[66]

Democratic Antitrust Politics and the Presidential Election of 1912

Against the claims of Martin J. Sklar, therefore, there is substantial evidence to suggest that agrarian Democrats put themselves in opposition

---

65. Ibid., 18.
66. Ibid., 17. Bryan's call for legislative repeal of the rule of reason can also be found in *The Commoner*, issues May 26, 1911, December 1, 1911, 1, and in an interview with C. M. Harger for the *Outlook*, reprinted in *The Commoner*, January 12, 1912, 2. Within the Democratic party, agreement was widespread that the restoration of the Sherman Act was, in itself, an insufficient remedy to the trust problem. Indeed, agrarian Democrats had advocated their own federal license system – the crucial antitrust plank of the Democrats' 1908 platform – for corporations engaged in interstate trade. Under the Democratic licensing scheme, any corporation in control of at least 25 percent of the product it dealt in would be required to obtain a federal license to engage in interstate trade. The purpose of the license system, Bryan explained, was to protect the public from watered stock and to ensure that such corporations sold "to all customers in all parts of the country on the same terms, after making due allowance for cost of transportation." More striking – because more threatening to big business – corporations controlling "more than 50 per cent of the total amount of any product consumed in the United States" would be denied a license, this as a way of checking the process of corporate concentration and maintaining a minimum of competition. *The Commoner*, May 26, 1911, 1; ibid., December 1, 1911, 1.

to the rule of reason, responding with legislative efforts to repeal its legal standing. That said, however, as our party system perspective would lead us to expect, the 1912 presidential election clearly complicated the Democratic party's stance towards reasonable restraint. Indeed, the nomination of Woodrow Wilson by the Democrats in 1912, like that of Grover Cleveland in 1884, 1888, and 1892, suggests a clear recognition of competitive party pressures and the need for a candidate with appeal beyond traditional voting blocs – one who could pull in disaffected members of the Republican party. To be sure, any candidate fielded by the Democrats in the three-way presidential campaign was likely to emerge victorious in 1912. But third parties are notoriously ephemeral in American electoral politics, and the failure to build bridges to disgruntled Republicans would render the Democrats long-term hold on national power short-lived. However, in selecting the progressive New Jersey governor and former political scientist Woodrow Wilson, the Democrats acquired a candidate out of step with many of the party's most deeply held convictions.

Wilson crafted his brand of Democratic progressivism to balance traditional party aspirations against the need to reach out to constituencies outside of normal party channels. Nowhere was this more apparent than in his stance on the trust question. In his speech accepting the Democratic nomination for president, Wilson readily endorsed the antitrust plank of the Baltimore platform, even as he was distancing himself from its more radical implications. That the antitrust plank proved amenable to different interpretations was in itself a short-term concession to national party victory, as it avoided an explicit call for repeal of the rule of reason. Nonetheless, the plank, largely written by Bryan himself, was pointed and retained a decidedly antimonopoly thrust. Specifically, it expressed the Democrats' "regret that the Sherman anti-trust law has received a judicial construction depriving it of much of its efficiency," and it committed the party to "the enactment of legislation which will restore to the statute the strength of which it has been deprived by such interpretation."[67]

Intentionally or not, Bryan and Wilson were able to exploit this ambiguity in a way that would allow them to tailor their appeals to different audiences. For example, while for the duration of the 1912 campaign it became the unstated policy of *The Commoner* to mute

---

67. *National Party Platforms, 1840–1960*, compiled by Porter and Johnson. The call for legislation supplemental to the Sherman Act, however, was couched in language less specific than that found in the 1908 platform's demand for the federal licensing of interstate corporations.

its hitherto persistent call for the statutory repeal of the rule of reason, Bryan nonetheless took the occasion of the publication of the party's Baltimore platform to instruct his largely agrarian readership on the meaning of its antitrust plank. Said Bryan: "Equally strong and felicitous is the plank on the supreme court [sic] decision which inserted the word 'unreasonable' in the anti-trust laws. The law must be restored to its former strength."[68] Moreover, on the stump for Wilson in the western states, Bryan was similarly pointed in his attacks on the rule of reason. There, he tore into President Taft for "laud[ing] the decision of the supreme court [sic] inserting the word 'unreasonable' into the criminal clause of the Sherman law." Bryan warned: "That is what the trusts have been after for fourteen years."[69] Equally indicative of agrarian Democratic regulatory attitudes, Bryan blasted Theodore Roosevelt's proposal to create an independent regulatory commission. Keeping in mind that the Democratic party would legislate this very same proposal only two years later, Bryan now characterized it as "the most dangerous plan ever presented to the American people":

> It is a step toward socialism, . . . and by placing power in the hands of a few men it would give the predatory interests still more powerful incentives to enter politics and elect a president.[70]

In accepting his party's nomination for president, Woodrow Wilson, like Bryan, sought to calm the trepidations of his agrarian base, invoking the shibboleth of competition and alluding to the collusive and arbitrary practices prevalent in the modern business world. Addressing himself to the tariff and the high cost of living, Wilson spoke of an emerging understanding of "at least some of the methods . . . by which prices are fixed."

---

68. *The Commoner*, July 12, 1912, 1.   69. Ibid., September 27, 1912, 6.
70. Ibid. Roosevelt, for his part, played on the public's perception of the Democratic party as a party of antiquarian ideas and ideals, the party of the economic and cultural hinterland. Roosevelt charged that the antitrust program of the Democratic party was unfit for the conditions of modern industrial America, branding Bryan's form of radical progressivism "a form of sincere rural toryism." Well-meaning but misguided, Bryanite agrarianism sought by the Sherman Law method "to bolster up an individualism already proved to be both futile and mischievous; to remedy by more individualism the concentration that was the inevitable result of the already existing individualism. They [see] the evil done by the big combinations, and [seek] to remedy it by destroying them and restoring the country to the economic conditions of the middle of the nineteenth century." Roosevelt, *Autobiography*. Excerpted in Resek, ed. *The Progressives*, 183.

We know that they are not fixed by the competitions of the market, or by the ancient law of supply and demand which is found stated in all the primers of economics, but by private arrangements with regard to what the supply should be and agreements among the producers themselves. Those who buy are not even represented by counsel. The high cost of living is arranged by private understanding.[71]

At the same time, however, Wilson took steps to distinguish between trusts and large-scale enterprise and to focus his attack on the former. He was not opposed to bigness per se, he explained; rather, he sought merely to break apart those corporate enterprises that had grown too large to be efficient. "Big business is not dangerous because it is big," Wilson asserted, "but because its bigness is an unwholesome inflation created by privilege and exemptions which it ought not to enjoy."

Up to a certain point (and only a certain point) great combinations effect great economies in administration, and increase efficiency by simplifying and perfecting organization, but whether they effect economies or not, they can very easily determine prices by intimate agreement, so soon as they come to control a sufficient percentage of the product in any great line of business; and we now know that they do.

In his acceptance speech, Wilson sought to negotiate a middle ground between agrarians and progressives, between tradition and modernity, between time-honored values of rugged individualism and the inescapable realities of corporate concentration. Speaking to Democratic agrarians, Wilson promised a "restoration," a "turning back from what is abnormal to what is normal."

[We] will see a restoration of the laws of trade, which are the laws of competition and of unhampered opportunity, under which men of every sort are set free and encouraged to enrich the nation.

However, as he continued his acceptance speech, Wilson began to speak beyond his party's traditional constituencies as if to broaden his base of support. He denied that his vision of the future was a simple yearning for the past.

I am not one of those who think that competition can be established by law against the drift of a world-wide economic tendency; neither am I one of those who believe that business done upon a great scale by a single organization – call it corporation if you will – is necessarily dangerous of the liberties, even the economic liberties, of a people like our own, full of intel-

71. The following discussion draws on Wilson's speech accepting the Democratic nomination of 1912, which is reprinted in full in The *Commoner*, August 16, 1912.

ligence and of indomitable energy. I am not afraid of anything that is normal.

As if to underscore the point, Wilson made his differences with the agrarian antimonopoly position explicit: "I dare say we shall never return to the old order of individual competition, and that the organization of business upon a great scale of co-operation is, up to a certain point, itself normal and inevitable." One more time, however, coalitional balancing seemed to pull Wilson back in the opposite direction. While continuing to hold out an olive branch to legitimate large business with one hand, Wilson nevertheless asserted that "the trusts . . . have gained all but complete control of the larger enterprises of the country." Even more ambiguously, he predicted that while "competition can not be created by statutory enactment, it can in large measure be revived by changing the laws and forbidding the practices that killed it, and by enacting laws that will give it heart and occasion again." Finally, Wilson criticized as largely ineffectual the "general terms of the present federal antitrust law, forbidding 'combinations in restraint of trade[.]'" The creativity of trust officials, the Democratic candidate continued, necessitated periodic revision of standing laws. And toward this end, he proposed to supplement the law with additional civil and criminal statutes as well as legislation rendering judicial processes more effective in bringing court cases to a rapid and successful conclusion.

As is well known, in 1912 Louis D. Brandeis was Wilson's principal advisor on antitrust matters. Brandeis articulated a sophisticated "theory of regulated competition," a policy prescription that sought to transcend the old dichotomy between enforced competition and administered markets. With Brandeis's help, Wilson instructed his audiences on the possibility and the efficacy of restoring economic competition without doing violence to legitimate large enterprise. It was a central postulate of the Brandeisian creed that "there are no natural monopolies to-day [sic] in the industrial world," that "in no American industry is monopoly an essential condition of the greatest efficiency."[72] In this view, what distinguished big business from trusts was that the former grew large from within, on the basis of economic efficiency and competitive strength. It was the product of natural evolution, an enterprise "that has survived competition by conquering in the field of intelligence and economy." Trusts, on the other hand, were made large

---

72. Brandeis, "Trusts, Efficiency, and the New Party," 14. See also, Brandeis, "Shall We Abandon the Policy of Competition," 435.

from without, "by combining competing businesses in restraint of trade." They were artificial creations – "an arrangement to get rid of competition" and preserve inefficiency. As such, Wilson maintained, through the statutory enumeration and proper enforcement of unfair trading practices, economic competition could naturally regulate the market *without* (again, contra Sklar) the creation of a powerful new regulatory institution.

With Brandeis's aid, Wilson searched for a position on the trust question that was electorally distinctive, substantively plausible, and attentive to coalitional needs. For our immediate purposes, however, the content of Brandeis's regulatory prescriptions is less important.[73] By most accounts, Wilson only imperfectly understood the subtleties of Brandeis's ideas. Besides, as we will see, Brandeis would play at best only a peripheral role in the development of Democratic antitrust legislation in 1914. More important than Brandeis's ideas was the selection of the Boston attorney himself to advise Wilson on the trust question. The selection is illuminating, for Wilson sought a program that would at once distinguish himself from Roosevelt and unite both Bryan Democrats and La Follette-led progressive Republicans. Brandeis was a bridge to La Follette progressives, a midwestern agrarian constituency Bryanites affectionately referred to as "Lincoln republicans," natural allies of "Jeffersonian democrats."[74] Brandeis was the perfect choice to counsel the Democratic candidate; for several years an intimate friend of Robert M. La Follette, Brandeis was also the Republican senator's principal advisor on antitrust matters.

Wilson's selection of Brandeis provides a window through which to view the coalition-building efforts that structured much of the Democratic strategy in 1912. At a minimum, Democrats hoped to obtain La Follette's tacit endorsement of Wilson's candidacy; at their most optimistic, they even hoped they might induce La Follette to break openly with the Republican party and align himself with a progressive Democratic party. The decision to pursue La Follette made eminent political sense. La Follette appeared to be ripe for the picking. Programmatically alienated from Taft conservatives, La Follette was also openly hostile to Theodore Roosevelt. To the Wisconsin senator, Roosevelt's progressivism was of dubious sincerity. Moreover, the apparent political opportunism Roosevelt had shown in derailing La Follette's own campaign for the

73. A nuanced and satisfying discussion of Brandeis's "theory of regulated competition" can be found in Berk, "Neither Markets nor Administration: Brandeis and the Antitrust Reforms of 1914," 24–59.
74. *The Commoner*, August 16, 1912, 2–3.

1912 Republican nomination left the latter with nothing short of animus for the fledgling Progressive party.[75]

La Follette eventually informed the Democratic campaign that he could not personally vote for Wilson, nor had he given up on the Republican party as a vehicle for reform. But, this said, La Follette worked vigorously behind the scenes to secure progressive Republican support for Wilson at the expense of Roosevelt's Progressive party. La Follette's campaign activity on behalf of Wilson was such that Roosevelt's running mate on the Progressive party ticket, Hiram Johnson, would comment: "Our chief danger in the next year will be this Congressional group, and particularly La Follette . . . who showed himself lacking in real courage when with all his mendacity and hatred he did not dare openly to come out for Wilson, but pretended he was still a Republican who preserved his party regularity, while all the time he was beseeching his friends and satellites to get into the open for Wilson."[76] The day following Wilson's election, Brandeis wrote La Follette to praise him for his effort on behalf of Wilson, telling the senator that "all true Progressives owe you a deep gratitude for yesterday's victory."[77]

75. Mowry, *Theodore Roosevelt and the Progressive Movement*, 183–206, 257, 263, 280. Wilson made overt appeals to La Follette supporters throughout the campaign, both to reopen the wounds between Roosevelt and La Follette and to minimize the distance between himself and the Wisconsin senator. An example is the following:

"Then there arose a sturdy little giant in Wisconsin who is now such an indomitable, unconquerable champion of progressive ideas all along the line. I mean Senator La Follette. Men who seek expediency rather than pursue principle took him up for a little while and pretended to follow him, and then rejected him, not because he was not the genuine champion of their principles, but because they apparently saw their interest lie in another direction. I do not believe there are many chapters of personal history in the records of parties in this country more difficult to reconcile with principles of honor than that. I feel myself close kin to these men who have been fighting the battle of progressive democracy, for no matter what label they bear we are of one principle.

"I remember hearing a story not long ago. I have told it a number of times but perhaps you will bear with me if I tell it again because it interprets my feeling. A very deaf old lady was approached by her son, who wanted to introduce a stranger to her, and he said, 'Mama, this is Mr. Stickpin.' 'I beg your pardon,' she said; 'what did you say the name was?' 'Mr. Stickpin.' 'I don't catch it,' she said. 'Mr. Stickpin.' 'Oh,' she said, 'it's no use; it sounds exactly like Stickpin.' Now, when I talk of men like La Follette's way of thinking in politics I feel like saying: 'I beg you pardon, what did you say you were?' 'A Republican.' 'A what?' 'A Republican.' 'No use; it sounds to me just like Democrat.' I can't tell the difference." Woodrow Wilson, "The Vision of the Democratic Party." In Davidson, ed. *A Crossroads of Freedom*, 260–1.

76. Doan, *The La Follettes and the Wisconsin Idea*, 72–3.

77. Louis D. Brandeis to Robert Marion La Follette, November 6, 1912. In Urofsky and Levy, eds. *The Letters of Louis D. Brandeis* Vol. 2, 710. Neither La Follette nor Brandeis were agrarian levelers on matters of regulatory policy; they accepted the

While Wilson worked to temper the image of his party as hostile to industrial concentration per se, he was nonetheless one with Bryanite Democrats in his firm opposition to a federal commission empowered to define and prohibit unfair trading practices. Far from embracing the regulatory commission idea, Wilson continually derided the Bull Moose solution to the trust problem. The Democratic candidate did support the creation of an information-gathering commission, as did Brandeis; one that would supplement the resources of the average individual in their legal battles with the trusts, and aid the courts in the effective administration of the antitrust laws. But Wilson objected vehemently to Roosevelt's proposal to grant discretionary power to an appointed board of experts – to supplant the rule of law with rule by individuals; to trade democracy for technocracy:

> What I fear . . . is a government of experts. God forbid that in a democratic country we should resign the task and give the government over to experts. What are we for if we are to be scientifically taken care of by a small number of gentlemen who are the only men who understand the job? Because if we don't understand the job, then we are not a free people.[78]

This position led Wilson to reject the independent regulatory commission as the solution to the trust problem:

> Sherman Act as reinterpreted by the rule of reason and channeled their energies both to clarify its substance and improve its procedure. Brandeis was the principal author of the La Follette-Lenroot bill of December 1911, which sought several changes in the federal antitrust law. First, it struck at court discretion in the definition of unfair competitive practices and unreasonable restraints of trade by defining and outlawing specific methods of unfair competition – cutthroat competition, tying contracts, the exclusion of competitors to essential raw materials, conducting business under assumed names or "fake independents," unfair advantages through railroad rebates, and "acquiring, otherwise than through efficiency, such a control over the market as to dominate the trade." Second, the La Follette-Lenroot program would strengthen the enforcement of the Sherman Act in the courts by 1) changes in the methods of dissolution decrees to ensure that stock ownership in each of the segments of the dissolved trusts were kept "separate and distinct," 2) allowing evidence obtained in successful government cases to be used in private suits for damages brought against the same defendants, and 3) stipulating that the statute of limitations shall not run out while a government suit is pending. Lastly, the program would create an administrative board or commission with strong powers of investigation and publicity. As Brandeis would explain to Wilson during the campaign, "We need the inspector and the policeman, even more than we need the prosecuting attorney." Louis D. Brandeis to Woodrow Wilson, September 30, 1912. In Urofsky and Levy, eds. *The Letters of Louis D. Brandeis* Vol. 2, 686–94.

78. Woodrow Wilson, "Labor Day Speech," address delivered in Braun's Park, Buffalo, New York, September 2, 1914. In Davidson, ed. *A Crossroads of Freedom*, 83.

Therefore, we favor as much power as you choose, but power guided by knowledge, power extended in detail, not power given out in the lump to a commission set up as is proposed by the third party and unencumbered by the restrictions of law, to set up a "constructive regulation," as their platform calls it, of the trusts and the monopoly.[79]

By contrast, Theodore Roosevelt and the Progressive party platform heartily endorsed the regulatory commission solution to the trust problem. Roosevelt Progressives were keenly aware of the power of large corporations to menace the public welfare. But whereas Wilson's yard-stick to distinguish between trusts and legitimate big business was organizational efficiency, Roosevelt's criteria turned on a determination of whether or not the public interest had been violated. The Progressive party's antitrust policy, Roosevelt explained, "would draw a line on conduct and not on size."[80] It would strike at the abuse of corporate power – natural resource monopolies, stock watering, unfair competition, and unfair privileges – not corporate power per se.

For his part, Roosevelt stressed the social efficacy of large economic units. He explained that "bigness brought relative freedom from competitive pressures, making it likely that large rather than small business could blend moral considerations into its operations and give serious attention to . . . 'corporate social responsibilities.' "[81] However, Roosevelt maintained, such a grant of power to large corporations was justified only in conjunction with strong regulatory controls to protect the public interest. Along these lines, the Progressive party platform proposed a system of "permanent active supervision" of corporate activity, with its centerpiece the creation of a "strong Federal administrative commission" with regulatory powers similar to those possessed by the Interstate Commerce Commission, minus the latter's power to set rates.[82]

We have actually made the Inter-State Commerce Law work. We have found by the test of actual work that the way to control the railways lies through increasing the power, and especially through increasing the application of the power of the Inter-State Commerce Commission, by regulating and controlling those railways, and not by any development of the Anti-Trust Law. Real control of the trusts can come only by the adoption of similar expedients. What I want to see done with our industrial concerns is to see an Inter-State Industrial Commission established, which shall handle the Stan-

---

79. Woodrow Wilson, "The Vision of the Democratic Party," In Wells, ed. *A Crossroads of Freedom*, 264–5.
80. Roosevelt, *Autobiography*. Excerpted in Resek, ed. *The Progressives*, 192.
81. Seltzer, "Woodrow Wilson as 'Corporate-Liberal,'" 197.
82. Porter and Johnson, *National Party Platforms*, 178; Roosevelt, "The Taft-Wilson Trust Programme," 105–7.

dard Oil, the Steel Trust, the Tobacco Trust, and every such big trust, through administrative action, just as the Interstate Commerce Commission handles the railways, and with a power extended beyond that of the Interstate Commerce Commission.[83]

Agrarian Democrats at High Tide: Toward the Reinstatement of the *Trans-Missouri* Rule

The presidential campaign of 1912 is important for what we learn about Democratic regulatory preferences as the party prepared to assume control of the national government. First, whatever else might be said, Democrats had not yet come to embrace the regulatory trade commission idea. As Wilson and Bryan's campaign comments reveal, Democrats agreed that the Progressive commission was unacceptable, attacking it as excessively statist and technocratic. In this, they espoused a long-standing Democratic conviction, one we earlier encountered with agrarian Democrats opposed to an independent railroad commission. But, of more immediate importance is the gap that appeared to separate Wilson from his party's agrarian wing over repeal of the rule of reason and the return to a policy of enforced competition. Throughout the presidential campaign, Wilson's remarks on trust policy were considerably more conciliatory toward business cooperation and large enterprise than the Bryanite position. How important were these differences? The new president's precise relationship to the party's Baltimore platform and its congressional leadership was as yet not defined. It remained unclear whether Wilson's campaign utterances represented statements of personal conviction or indicated a hard and fast presidential policy commitment, one that might set Wilson on a collision course with congressional Democrats over the direction of antitrust reform.

The Primacy of Party

The answer to such questions was soon apparent. Few things are as indicative of the nature of Democratic party government in the Progressive Era as the relationship that emerged between president and party on the subject of antitrust reform. Woodrow Wilson was not Franklin Roosevelt, and his legislative leadership was not the aggressive intervention of FDR on behalf of a unilaterally defined policy agenda, as we will observe in Chapter 4. While Wilson would be an active participant in

83. Roosevelt, "The Taft-Wilson Trust Programme," 105.

the framing of the Democrats' initial antitrust program, agrarian Democrats in Congress remained in firm control of its final substance. And substantively, agrarian Democrats remained committed to rolling back the rule of reason.

Wilson was an outspoken proponent of responsible party government, and he accepted the principles of the Baltimore platform as binding upon the policy actions of the Democratic party in power. Regardless of his personal convictions, it was in conjunction with the congressional Democratic party that the new president intended to govern. Wilson's deference to the Baltimore platform is revealed in an episode that occurred in the period between his November presidential victory and his inauguration in March. In one of the last important actions of his gubernatorial tenure, the president-elect pushed a series of corporation laws through the New Jersey state legislature – the so-called seven sisters. For our purpose here, this legislation is significant because of its orthodoxy regarding the *Trans-Missouri* rule. The most important of the seven statutes was the New Jersey Trust Definitions law. The content of the Definitions statute should have greatly allayed the concerns of agrarian Democrats by the way it closed the gap between Wilson's campaign utterances and his party's antimonopoly principles. Indeed, the Definitions law seemed to draw self-consciously on the phraseology of agrarian Democratic legislation introduced in the aftermath of the *Standard Oil* decision. Specifically, the statute made illegal:

> any agreement by which they [the trusts] directly or indirectly preclude *a free and unrestricted competition* among themselves, or any purchasers or consumers, in the sale or transportation of any article or commodity, either by pooling, withholding from the market, or selling at a fixed price, or in any other manner by which the price might be affected.[84]

Agrarian Democrats had a right to be pleased with the language of the New Jersey Trust Definition law. By its adherence to the principle of "free and unrestricted competition," the statute seemed to directly challenge the spirit of the rule of reason and its tolerance for the practice of reasonable restraint. Reaching back to the pre-*Standard Oil* status quo, it reaffirmed the party's deepest-held antitrust aspirations. Indeed, it even seemed to want to outdo the *Trans-Missouri* doctrine, outlawing actions that both directly and indirectly restrained competition. The consistency of Wilson's gubernatorial actions with the agrarian orthodoxy can be further gauged by comparing the language of the Definitions law with

---

84. Updyke, "New Jersey Corporation Laws"; *The New York Times*, January 21, 1914, 14 [emphasis added].

that of the Henry bill, antitrust legislation introduced late in 1911 by the Democratic chairman of the House Rules Committee, Robert L. Henry of Texas. Explicitly written to "legislate the 'rule of reason' out of the law," the Henry bill sought to prohibit any action that would "in any manner establish or settle the price of any article, commodity, or transportation between themselves or others *to preclude a free and unrestricted competition* among themselves or others in the sale or transportation of any such article or commodity"[85]

Outside of Democratic party circles, the implications of a national antitrust policy premised on the principles of the New Jersey Definitions statute did not go without comment. As Democrats turned seriously to take up the trust question early in 1914, former Attorney General George Wickersham, a Republican, was quick to warn that a Sherman Act definitions statute similar to the New Jersey law would effectively "abolish any rule of reason." "[S]o far from removing restraints upon the free course of trade and commerce among men," Wickersham continued,

> if enforced, they would effectually destroy the possibility of commercial intercourse, and, in Justice Holmes's picturesque phrase, "would make eternal the *bellum omnium contra omnes* and disintegrate society so far as it can into individual atoms." It can hardly be deemed possible that even under the most drastic caucus rule any such provisions as these should find their way onto the federal statute book.[86]

The passage of the New Jersey Trust Definitions law, therefore, is illuminating for what it suggests about Wilson's deference to party on the matter of antitrust principles. And within the party, agrarian antimonopoly goals continued to be ascendent. As the Democratic party assumed power, it remained committed to the *Trans-Missouri* rule of free and unrestricted competition, and that commitment would be plainly manifest when the party unveiled its antitrust reform package on January 22, 1914.

But while agrarian Democrats were clear about the policy direction in which they intended to move, they would not be able to legislate in a political climate of their own choosing. From Wilson's inauguration in March 1913 to the November 1914 midterm elections some twenty-one months later, the national economy would progressively worsen. Antitrust reform was to be the grand finale of the Democratic sixty-third Congress (1913–15), but by the time the party was ready to proceed,

85. Emphasis added. The Henry bill, including comments, can be found in *The Commoner*, November 24, 1911, 3.
86. *The Independent*, January 19, 1914, 90.

the economy was racing headlong toward depression. In the end, it would drive agrarian legislators into a full retreat from their most radical ambitions.

As the economy faltered, Progressive criticism of the Democrats' competence to govern sharpened, while the political atmosphere occasioned by the downturn threatened to render stillborn the much anticipated Democratic realignment. As we will see, bad economic times per se did not drive agrarian Democrats toward the Progressive party's trade commission plan. But it did eventually turn them away from their initial effort to reinstate a policy of free and unrestricted competition in interstate business transactions. In the end, what is striking is that they persisted as long as they did. Repealing the rule of reason was an action that would have tried party discipline under the best of circumstances. But the contingent rhythms of the national economy would fatally compromise the "five brothers" – the party's original antitrust program. The aspirations of agrarian reform would confront the constraints of business confidence, and the continuous slide toward economic depression would inject itself into the Democrats' political consciousness with increasing urgency. It was only at this point that political leadership would decisively pass to the president and the substance of antitrust reform would be thrown up for grabs.

Situating the Presidency in the Politics of Antitrust

Woodrow Wilson had ambitious plans for the Sixty-third Congress (1913–15). Democrats had not held unified control of the national government since 1895 and it was politically imperative that such power be exercised with vigor. As previously discussed, it was the new president's intention to vindicate the Democratic party as an activist reform party, one equipped to tackle the problems of a modern industrial economy. On March 5, 1913, the day following his inauguration, Wilson called congressional Democrats into special session. His intention was to keep the newly elected legislature in continuous session – if necessary right up to the November 1914 midterm elections – until the party had made good on each of the three main planks of its 1912 national platform: tariff revision, currency reform, and revision of the antitrust law.

Even before the political effects of the national economy had been fully registered, congressional Democrats were starting to chafe at the way Wilson was driving them. Congress had not yet passed the Federal Reserve Bank Act and newspapers were already reporting plans to begin antitrust reform, the final leg of the Democratic reform agenda. Wilson's frenetic legislative pace finally pushed one Democratic senator, John Sharp Williams of Mississippi, to the breaking point. Frustrated, the senator pleaded for presidential restraint, telling Wilson: "For heaven's sake wait until we get the currency bill through. Rome was not built in a day. Let us get through one thing at a time and then tackle the next thing in line." Sharp looked forward to antitrust reform, sensing that he and the president were in accord about the substance of antitrust legislation. But concern that Wilson's somewhat amateurish enthusiasm might compromise the party's most important reform item led the veteran senator to lecture the party's newest leader: "[P]lease do not precipitate [antitrust legislation] until we are through with other things. After all, it is the *pièce de résistance* of Democratic legislation, and must be husbanded."[87]

Antitrust action *was* the capstone of the Democratic program and Wilson remained anxious to begin the final leg of reform. By the time of his State of the Union Address on December 2, 1913, the president was ready to speak broadly about revisions to the antitrust law, leaving aside specific recommendations for a special message to Congress he planned for January. But with the economic downturn increasingly on his mind, Wilson chose to use that portion of his address to allay business trepidation about the next round of business reform. His language was overtly conciliatory:

> It is of capital importance that the businessmen of this country should be relieved of all uncertainties of law with regard to their enterprises and investments and a clear path indicated which they can travel without anxiety. It is as important that they should be relieved of embarrassment and set free to prosper as that private monopoly should be destroyed. The ways of action should be thrown wide open.[88]

His recommendations at this point, however, remained purposely vague, suggesting only that the Sherman Act be supplemented rather than directly amended, with new legislation directed toward the clarification of intent in the antitrust law and new machinery to facilitate its administration.

With the national economy worsening, many Democrats were starting to doubt the political prudence of a third round of new business regulations. After dining with one congressman in late 1913, Wilson-confidant

---

87. Woodrow Wilson to Henry D. Clayton, 10/20/13. In Link, ed. *The Papers of Woodrow Wilson* Vol. 28, 420; House diary, 11/13/13. Ibid., 532; John Sharp Williams to Woodrow Wilson, 11/17/13. Ibid., 560.

88. "First Annual Message." In Israel, ed. *The State of the Union Messages of the Presidents* Vol. 3, 2547–8.

Louis D. Brandeis commented on the air of "political apprehension" that seemed to permeate the House of Representatives. Former Minnesota representative "Moses Clapp used to be eloquent at prophesizing [sic] it," Brandeis observed. "The one pervading thought is re-election, even now at the beginning of the first regular session of the Congress."[89] But Congress was not the only place where Democrats were getting cold feet. Political apprehension had spilt over into the administration as well. Among Wilson's cabinet members, opinion divided over whether to proceed with antitrust reform or wait until after the 1914 midterm elections. Attorney General James C. McReynolds, Postmaster General Albert S. Burleson, and Secretary of War Lindley M. Garrison each counseled delay, arguing that it would give business an opportunity to accommodate itself to the new Democratic tariff and currency laws. On the other side, Treasury Secretary William Gibbs McAdoo and Secretary of State William Jennings Bryan "urged Wilson to go on and to fulfill the Democratic pledges on the trust."[90]

Brandeis concurred with Bryan and McAdoo. Lobbying from the outside, the Boston progressive wrote to Wilson's Interior Secretary Franklin K. Lane, formerly of the Interstate Commerce Commission, to urge the administration forward. Having been a part of the president's campaign effort, Brandeis understood the kind political argument that might strengthen Wilson's resolve to fight and he put this knowledge to work. Through Lane he insisted that action on antitrust reform was essential " 'to politically satisfy the demands of a very large number of progressive Democrats and *the near Democrats* who are beginning to express doubt" about the administration's political resolve. In the reform lawyer's judgment, the current recession was not likely to "be ended or lessened by any course which the administration may take." Brandeis concluded, "The fearless course is [therefore] the wise one."[91]

Wilson did not need to be persuaded to press forward on antitrust reform. In these early years, Wilson was particularly concerned that any sign of hesitation would kindle criticism from Progressive quarters and call into question the Democrats' vitality as a reform party. But with a sick economy on his hands, he became increasingly preoccupied with business confidence. Politically, he sought a course of action that was

89. Louis D. Brandeis to Alice Goldmark Brandeis, December 18, 1913. In Urofsky and Levy, eds. *The Letters of Louis D. Brandeis* Vol. 3, 224. Brandeis's dining companion was Congressman Raymond Stevens, a progressive Democrat from New Hampshire.

90. Urofsky and Levy, eds. *The Letters of Louis D. Brandeis* Vol. 3, 19; Link, *Wilson: The New Freedom*, 446.

91. Louis D. Brandeis to Franklin Lane, December 12, 1913. In Urofsky and Levy, eds. *The Letters of Louis D. Brandeis* Vol. 3, 20.

consistent with Democratic platform principles, satisfactory to progressive opinion, and still attentive to legitimate business interests. With these objectives in mind, Wilson instructed his commissioner of corporations, Joseph E. Davies, to undertake a survey of business opinion regarding antitrust legislation. The results of Davies's survey were relayed to Wilson in late December 1913, along with several legislative recommendations "made with the provisions of the [Democratic] platform distinctly in mind." For the most part, Davies's recommendations navigated these diverse political needs with impressive skill, and Wilson would use Davies's materials to craft the principles upon which he would conduct his antitrust negotiations with congressional leaders.[92]

Davies began his report by reiterating the same point Wilson had made in his State of the Union address: Any new legislation should be supplemental to the Sherman Act. In order to minimize the number of new legal ambiguities, Davies wrote, the administration should dissuade congressional leaders from directly tampering with the existing text of the law, except perhaps to strengthen criminal penalties. The commissioner of corporations then proceeded to outline his specific recommendations, organizing them into separate proposals for substantive, procedural, and administrative reform. Substantively, Davis argued that new legislation should be directed toward further reducing the uncertainty in the meaning of "restraint of trade." Three proposals were offered. First, he recommended that practices currently understood at law to constitute restraint of trade be enumerated in the new statute. Second, the Commissioner recommended new legislation to strike at anticompetitive practices and devices, such as predatory pricing, interlocking directorates, holding companies, stockwatering, and (his most radical proposal) placing a cap on corporate size – such as a 40 percent ceiling on the amount of industry output controllable by a single company.[93] Finally, Davies recommended an amendment to shift the burden of proof from the plaintiff to the defendant by making an indictment for restraint of trade prima facie evidence that restraint had in fact occurred.[94]

Procedurally, Davies recommended legislation to facilitate private litigation, such as extending the statute of limitations from three to five

92. Woodrow Wilson to E. M. House, 1/3/14. In Link, ed. *The Papers of Woodrow Wilson* Vol. 29, 99; Joseph E. Davies to Woodrow Wilson, 12/27/13, with enclosure. In Link, ed. *The Papers of Woodrow Wilson* Vol. 29, 78–85.

93. As noted earlier, the 1908 Democratic party trust plank had proposed to prohibit corporate control "of more than fifty per cent of the total amount of any product consumed in the United States."

94. Joseph E. Davies to Woodrow Wilson, 12/27/13. In Link, ed. *The Papers of Woodrow Wilson* Vol. 29.

years and making government findings conclusive as to fact in private actions involving the same defendants. More controversial were Davies's administrative reforms. In particular, he recommended the creation of an interstate trade commission. Davies conceded that a trade commission was not explicitly authorized by the 1912 Democratic platform, but he insisted that the authority to propose such a device derived implicitly from its effectiveness as a mechanism to secure platform goals. In addition, he argued, politically an interstate trade commission "would be received with great favor by the progressive thought of the country and as well by the business interests of the country." As to the specific powers such a trade commission might wield, Davies focused on areas of common ground among businessmen, southern Democrats, and northern progressives. The most important among these were powers of investigation and publicity, along with the authority to act as an arm of the court in executing dissolution decrees. An additional power, Davies conceded, was much more controversial. This involved clothing the new commission with broader, quasi-judicial powers, approaching those contained in the Progressive party's national platform. Specifically, Davies recommended giving the commission authority to make findings of fact and prescribe changes in business practices. For those businesses not in compliance after two months, the commission would be obliged to turn its findings and recommendations over to the Department of Justice for further action. Indicative of Wilson's thinking to this point in time, the proposal to clothe the new commission with broad regulatory powers (along with the suggestion to limit corporate size) was one of the few of Davies's recommendations that Wilson declined to follow as he fashioned his reform guidelines for upcoming party negotiations.[95]

On January 20, 1914, Wilson delivered his special message to Congress on antitrust reform. Here, as he had on earlier occasions, Wilson called on to Democrats in Congress to consider antitrust reform in a spirit of equanimity and legislate with due regard for the legitimate business interests. In a draft of his special message to Congress, Wilson wrote:

> What we are purposing [sic] to do, therefore, is, happily, not to hamper or interfere with business as enlightened business men prefer to do it, or in any sense to put it under the ban. The antagonism between government and business is over. We are now about to give expression to the best business judgement of America, to what we know to be the business conscience and honour [sic] of the land. The government and business men are ready to

95. Ibid.

meet each other half way in a common effort to square business methods with both public opinion and the law.[96]

Substantively, Wilson called for new legislation to clarify the policy and meaning of the Sherman Act, address the problems of unfair competition and interlocking directorates, direct the penalties and punishments of the antitrust law at individuals rather than businesses, and create an interstate trade commission with powers of information and publicity.[97] Two days after Wilson's special message to Congress, legislative leaders unveiled the Democratic antitrust program.

The Agrarian Program: The "Five Brothers"

The legislation introduced by Democrats on January 22, 1914, bears on the argument of this chapter in two special ways. First, it reveals the limits of Wilson's influence on the details of his party's antitrust program. Despite the faltering economy and the president's counsel of caution, the preferences of agrarian Democrats remained ascendent. Second, it provides compelling evidence of the absence of a cross-class, cross-party, corporate-liberal consensus on the legitimacy of reasonable restraint. Indeed, rather than signaling a rapprochement with economic elites, the Democratic package "was sweeping and severe enough to win the approval even of the ardent opponents of big business."[98] To be sure, in its overall structure, the legislation conformed closely to Wilson's antitrust message, as well as to most of the recommendations found in the Davies report. But, as we will see shortly, the devil was in the details, and its specific provisions sent shockwaves through the business community and set in motion an avalanche of progressive criticism.

The agrarian reform program was made up of five separate bills, which the press quickly dubbed the "five brothers." Programmatically, the legislation was a hodgepodge, drawing inspiration from multiple sources, including the Davies recommendations and the La Follette-Lenroot bill,[99] as well as Wilson's "seven sisters" and provisions from earlier Democratic antitrust bills, like the Henry bill. The provisions of the "five brothers" can be summarized as follows. The first bill, The Sherman Law Definitions bill, sought to clarify the Sherman Act's prohibitions against restraint of trade and monopolizing behavior by expressly outlawing

---

96. Baker, *Woodrow Wilson* Vol. 4, 370.
97. Chamberlain, *The President, Congress, and Legislation*, 36.
98. Link, *Wilson: The New Freedom*, 425.
99. See footnote 77 for a description of the La Follette-Lenroot bill.

specified business practices (to be discussed later). In addition, it made guilt personal, holding individual directors, officers, and agents criminally liable for corporate violations of the antitrust laws. A second bill, the Trade Relations bill, was intended to supplement Sherman Act prohibitions on predatory behavior by further outlawing specific forms of unfair competition, such as those involving injurious price discrimination, exclusive and tying contracts, and the arbitrary refusal of mine owners to sell their output to responsible parties. The legislation also extended the statute of limitations on the Sherman Act from three to five years, and provided new remedies for private parties seeking damages for violation of the antitrust laws. Individuals would be allowed to bring suits in equity against combinations in restraint of trade under the Sherman Act; they could also use court findings in government antitrust cases as conclusive evidence of facts and issues of law in private damage suits. Finally, the Trade Relations Bill would also provide injunctive relief to individuals "threatened or injured" by an unlawful combination.

A third piece of legislation, the Interlocking Directorates bill, made it illegal to be a director, officer, or employee simultaneously in two or more national financial institutions or in a state and national financial institution. It further prohibited any director, partner, or employee of a corporation engaged in the manufacture of railroad capital goods to be simultaneously a director, partner, or employee in any railroad or public service corporation engaged in interstate commerce. The most sweeping provision of the Interlocking Directorates bill was Section 4. It stipulated that two years after the passage of the bill, the presence of common directors on two or more corporations would *in itself* constitute conclusive evidence of the absence of competition. Additionally, if said corporations had ever been "natural competitors" – to be inferred from the nature of the business or the location of operations – such a condition would constitute an unreasonable restraint of trade. Both the Trade Relations and Interlocking Directorate bills specified stiff criminal penalties for the violation of their provisions.

The Democrats also unveiled an Interstate Trade Commission bill. This legislation conformed to Wilson's call for a national administrative body clothed with powers of "information and publicity." Indeed, judging by the scope of its proposed powers of surveillance, it is remarkable just how intrusive the Democrats' new national trade commission was designed to be. In the first instance, the bill did not limit the authority of the trade commission to large corporations; its powers would fall equally on *all* corporations operating in interstate commerce. In addition, the commission's information-gathering powers were virtually plenary. Not only was it empowered to compel witnesses, testimony, the production of regular reports, but it was to be allowed unfettered access to all manner of records, accounts, minutes, books, and papers. Thirdly, any information obtained by the commission could be made public at its discretion. Finally, the commission was empowered to investigate violations of the antitrust laws, either on complaint or on its own initiative, and submit its findings to the attorney general. It would also aid the courts as master in chancery, drawing up and overseeing dissolution decrees. The fifth and final bill, to be introduced at a later date, empowered the Interstate Commerce Commission to regulate the issuance of new securities by the railroads.[100]

The content of the five brothers and the fearful reaction it engendered from among the business community is perhaps the strongest evidence against Martin Sklar's claim that a cross-party, corporate-liberal consensus was in place by 1912. The Democratic package continued to reflect the stringent commitment to enforced competition first enunciated in *Trans-Missouri*. Criticism was immediately directed toward the Sherman Law Definitions bill. The purpose of the Definitions bill was to identify and prohibit certain specific offenses within the meaning of the phrase "every contract, combination in the form of trust or otherwise, or conspiracy in restraint of trade" and the word "monopolize." Section 1 contained four separate clauses in which prohibited actions were itemized. The first three sections mostly referred to business arrangements long void at common law:

> First – To create or carry out restrictions in trade or acquire a monopoly in any interstate trade, business or commerce.
> Second – To limit or reduce the production or increase the price of merchandise or of any commodity.
> Third – To prevent competition in manufacturing, making, transporting, selling, or purchasing of merchandise, produce, or any commodity.[101]

What concerned business leaders most was the section's fourth clause. Invoking the language of *Trans-Missouri*, this clause would make it illegal

> [t]o make any agreement, enter into any arrangement, or arrive at any understanding by which they, directly or indirectly, undertake to prevent a *free and unrestricted competition* among themselves or among any pur-

---

100. *The New York Times*, January 23, 1914, 1–2; Henry D. Clayton, "Trust Legislation," *The Commoner* (March 1914), 6–7.
101. The provisions of the Sherman law definitions bill are reprinted in full in *The New York Times*, January 23, 1914, 3.

chasers or consumers in the sale, production, or transportation of any product, article or commodity.[102]

In an article written for *The Commoner* and its Bryanite agrarian readership, Democrat Henry D. Clayton, chairman of the House Judiciary Committee, would characterize the Definitions bill as the most criticized and least understood of the five proposed bills.[103] Critics of the Definitions bill, however, were convinced they understood the implications of the Definitions bill only too well. Commenting on the fourth clause specifically, the noted Columbia economist Henry R. Seager remarked: "[t]he fourth formula seems to condemn every relaxation of cutthroat competition"; while *The New York Times* warned that the rule of reason would be "swept away by the bill's provisions."[104] Supporters of the Definitions bill seemed to understand the bill in terms no different than its opponents. One Ohio lawyer, for instance, was convinced that the "proposed amendments will be most helpful," adding with approval, "[t]hese supplemental statutes will effectually dispose of the rule of reason."[105]

In testimony before the House Judiciary Committee, which conducted hearings on the Democratic antitrust bills, William Draper Lewis and Herbert Knox Smith, members of the executive committee of the National Progressive party, expressed their belief that the essence of the Democratic trust program was to be found in Section 1, clause 4 – that "most extraordinary section" of the Definitions bill:

> The theory of the [Democratic] bills is that every man has got to compete with every other man, and that is going to carry the country back to the days of the blacksmith forge, the grist mill, and the cobbler's bench. . . .
>
> Competition may be either good or evil. . . . This bill would throw us back into the days of unbridled aggressive competition that was started a hundred years ago. That is the condition that has brought us to where we are to-day. That is the difficulty in my mind with the Clayton theory, that it proposes something that will throw us back into a condition where we lose efficiency in business, where we will gain nothing because we will have to go through the same process again.[106]

102. *The New York Times*, January 23, 1914, 3 (emphasis added).
103. Clayton, "Trust Legislation," 6.
104. Statement of Henry R. Seager, "Hearings before the Senate Committee on Interstate Commerce on Bills Relating to Trust Legislation," 63d Cong., 2d sess., 1246. (Emphasis added); *The New York Times*, January 24, 1914, 8.
105. Statement of E. C. Morton, lawyer, Columbus, Ohio, "Hearings before the Senate Committee on Interstate Commerce on Bills Relating to Trust Legislation," 1233.
106. Testimony of Herbert Knox Smith, "Hearings before the House Judiciary Committee on Trust Legislation," February 6, 1914, 63d Cong., 2d sess., 424. Smith was commissioner of corporations in the administration of Theodore Roosevelt. Accord-

Progressive supporters of an ICC-styled regulatory commission hammered away at what they perceived to be the antiquarian social and economic vision embodied in the Democratic bills. "The truth is," remarked *Collier's Weekly*, a leading progressive periodical, "there is in this country at the present moment a head-on collision between two ideas as to how big business units should be treated."

> The Democrats believe in breaking up big units by prosecution and in passing laws which shall enforce old-fashioned competition, and by arbitrary legislation keep all business in small units. The opposite view is that under modern conditions a business should be permitted to grow as large as it can grow and still be economically efficient, *but that these big units shall be sternly and drastically regulated* by a commission at Washington which shall have, roughly, the same power over ordinary corporations that the Interstate Commerce Commission has over railroads.[107]

The progressive vision of regulation, the magazine was quick to add, did not "contemplate industrial monopoly" or "the end of competition," as its Democratic detractors continually suggested. Rather, [o]ne of the chief duties of this [regulatory] commission would be *to preserve fair competition by forbidding and preventing unfair competition*, just as the Interstate Commerce Commission now prevents improper practices."[108] The real question, it concluded on another occasion, was whether the country was to embrace "a drastic return to enforced competition" favored by "old-fashioned, pronounced individualists," or adopt the program of "the more forward-looking believers in social cooperation," the progressive regulatory commission.[109]

To conclude this discussion, there is substantial historical evidence to suggest that as late as January 1914, when the Democratic party took up the trust question in earnest, an agrarian rapprochement with the corporate business community had not been negotiated – at least not on terms that clearly enshrined the legality of reasonable restraints of trade. I believe that there are two reasons Martin Sklar's analysis obscures this aspect of the history of the federal antitrust policy.

First, Sklar's own analysis focuses on the trade commission side of antitrust politics to the almost virtual exclusion of the five brothers and,

---

ing to William Draper Lewis, dean of the University of Pennsylvania Law School, the language contained in clause 4, section 1 of the Definitions bill, would do "what the Sherman Act avoided, it [would prevent] the formation of a partnership between two men who are in the same business, although their combined business may not represent one-thousandth of the industry." Ibid., 395.

107. *Collier's Weekly*, April 4, 1914, 16. See also, ibid., March 14, 1914, 12.
108. Ibid., April 4, 1914, 16.   109. Ibid., March 14, 1914, 12.

later, the omnibus Clayton bill. Because the five brothers were the original centerpiece of Democratic antitrust policy, Sklar is not well positioned analytically to assess the *shift* in Democratic policy toward the discretionary trade commission. From his vantage point, Sklar takes for granted what in fact needs to be explained, the transformation in Democratic antitrust policy in the middle of 1914.

Second, Sklar's analysis is incomplete because he too readily equates the preferences of the Democratic party to those of two allegedly corporate-liberal Democrats – Woodrow Wilson and Senator Francis G. Newlands of Nevada. However, legislation introduced by Newlands in the years prior to the passage of the FTCA suggest that the senator had no consistent public position concerning the powers of a trade commission. For instance, the last bill introduced by Newlands – on April 12, 1913, several months prior to the Democrats' taking up of the trust question – would have created a trade commission with substantial powers of investigation and publicity, but one without regulatory powers.[110] Nor was Newlands under any kind of illusion that his preferred solution to the trust question in any way represented the Democratic party organization more generally.[111] Likewise, as we have seen, Wilson was no friend of the regulatory commission idea. Nor, barring extraordinary circumstances, was he able to simply impose his own policy predilections on such a diverse coalition of interests as the Democratic party. As we have seen, Congress retained substantial discretion, within broadly stated

110. It was this type of political flexibility on Newlands's part that has led one scholar of the Federal Trade Commission Act to refer to the senator from Nevada – too cynically, I believe – as "the plastic Senator Newlands," that is, as lacking in a principled position on the solution to the trust question. That Newlands was "always anxious to please" is as much as anything testimony to his commitment to working within the confines of the Democratic party and its coalitional constraints. See Kolko, *Triumph of Conservatism*, 266.

111. This can be seen in the following statement, made on the floor of the Senate on May 16, 1911, immediately following the *Standard Oil* decision: "Now, Mr. President, I must admit that, so far as my own party in the Senate is concerned, the views which I entertain upon this subject have not made the headway I could wish. The Democratic party believes in keeping power as near as possible in the hands of the people in the various localities, in the states, and intrusting to the National Government only those powers which are necessary for the national defense and for national purposes and in carefully scrutinizing the granted powers with a view to preventing any enlargement of national jurisdiction within the boundaries of the states. So the traditions and the principles of the Democratic party have rather militated against the views which I have entertained, though I have absolute confidence of their correctness and am confident that these views will some time be incorporated in the laws of our country." Quoted in Darling, ed. *The Public Papers of Francis G. Newlands* Vol. 1, 410.

presidential parameters, to draw up the substance of party legislation.[112] And to a Democratic party organizationally rooted in the southern states, the idea of a strong regulatory commission was foreign and largely unwanted.[113] Indeed, opposition from his agrarian base would seem to be an important reason why Wilson hesitated to support a change of course on antitrust policy for so long, even when faced with a politically destabilizing economic downturn and mounting progressive opposition to the basic reform orientation of the Democratic party.

For these reasons then, the qualitative shift in Democratic party antitrust policy in early June 1914 from one of marked agrarian hostility to economic concentration to one that would facilitate the consolidation of corporate concentration, needs to be explained, not treated as a foregone conclusion by 1912. The embrace of the Progressive party trade commission was a critical turning point in both Democratic policy and the development of the American political economy. It is to the consideration of that transformation that we now turn.

Toward the Progressive Party Regulatory Commission

The "Privileged Position of Business" and the Gutting of the "Five Brothers"

It was not a cross-class, cross-party ideological consensus on the desirability of reasonable restraint that sealed the fate of the five brothers.

112. To his close friend Mary Ellen Hulbert, Wilson confided: "Editorially, the papers which are friendly to me (and some which are not) represent me, in the most foolish way, as master of the situation here, bending Congress to my indomitable individual will. That is, of course silly. Congress is made up of thinking men who want the party to succeed as much as I do, and who wish to serve the country effectively and intelligently. They . . . accept my guidance because they see that I am attempting only to mediate their own thoughts and purposes. I do not know how to wield a big stick, but I do know how to put my mind at the service of others for the accomplishment of a common purpose. They are using me; I am not driving them." September 21, 1913. In Link, ed. *The Papers of Woodrow Wilson* Vol. 28, 311.

Likewise, at a news conference in November 1913, Wilson commented on his upcoming trust program: "You know, my trust program is largely fiction. . . . I haven't had a tariff program. I haven't had a currency program. I have conferred with these men who handle these things, and asked the questions, and then have gotten back what they sent to me – the best of our common counsel. That is what I am trying to do in this case [the trust question]." November 3, 1913. Ibid, 487.

113. Illustrative of this antagonism to the regulatory commission idea is the letter to Wilson of William C. Adamson of Georgia, chairman of the House Interstate Commerce Committee, the committee in charge of the Interstate Trade Commission bill. In the letter, Adamson was furious at the efforts of progressives to persuade the pres-

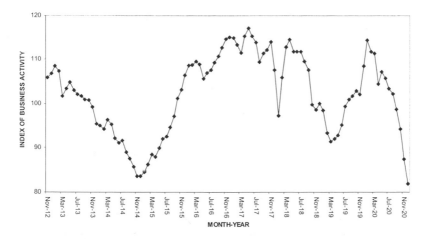

Figure 3.2. Monthy index of general business activity during the Wilson years (November 1912 to December 1920). *Source*: NBER Series 12002 (Index of General Business Activity).

Rather, it was the age-old political conviction that voters punish politicians for bad economic times. The recession did not push Democrats toward the Progressive trade commission – this lay several months in the future and coincided with Theodore Roosevelt's reemergence onto the political stage. But the economy did eventually cause Democrats to backpeddle frantically from any legislation that might further erode business confidence and cost them electoral support in November.

Congressional Democrats were in a state of political panic as the economy continued to worsen. The business contraction, which had started in March 1913 – the month Wilson took office – would continue unabated for twenty-two months. By the time the depression finally bottomed out in December 1914, business activity had fallen by nearly 25 percent against its previous peak. Figure 3.2 tracks general business activity during the Wilson years. It makes clear that the first two years of the Wilson administration were marked by almost uninterrupted economic decline, no doubt aided by the party's Bryanite antibusiness image and Congress's almost ceaseless reform activity. As measured by the

ident to reject his committee's information-gathering commission bill – the Covington bill – and embrace the Stevens's Regulatory Commission bill. See William C. Adamson to Woodrow Wilson (April 23, 1914). In Link, ed. *The Papers of Woodrow Wilson* Vol. 29, 496.

index of general business activity (series 12002) of the National Bureau of Economic Research, the volume of business transactions between January and December of 1913 fell from 108.4 to 95.4. But the period marked by congressional action on antitrust revision coincided with the worst phase of the economic down slide. Not until December 1914 would the volume of business transactions finally bottom out at 83.5.

The political impact of the depression on Congress was palpable. Legislators were preoccupied with off-year elections, and respectable opinion questioned the wisdom of further reform until safely past the midterm hurdle. Majority Leader Oscar Underwood was probably the most important House Democrat to favor postponing antitrust action. But as we will see, anxious Democrats could be found everywhere. The continued viability of the Progressive party organization was already being questioned, a development that underscored the potentially transitory nature of the current Democratic ascendancy. The business downturn held out the possibility of an even more rapid return to minority party status. To reelection-minded members of the party rank and file – of whom almost 40 percent were freshmen – careers that must have seemed promising only a few months earlier, now looked increasingly precarious. Among the measures contained in the original Democratic package, only the proposal for a trade commission with "sunshine" powers seemed relatively uncontroversial. The rest of the program was in a condition of political free fall.

While Democratic legislators were restive, Wilson remained firm in the conviction that Congress must enact an antitrust program before its members retired for the campaign season.[114] Wilson knew that the Progressive party leaders would turn the midterm elections into a referendum on his administration and, more broadly, on Democratic party governance. Therefore, in order to make the best case for returning a Democratic majority – and slow the migration of Progressive party voters back to the Republican party – the party needed to make good on the most important of its reform promises.

Wilson's commitment to legislative action, however, did not translate into public support for the five brothers, and he quietly began distancing himself from the specifics of the agrarian program. Indeed, officially the White House denied any connection with the bills, characterizing them as purely congressional legislation. As we have seen, the president's posture was somewhat disingenuous, as some of the most controversial provisions of the five brothers could be found in his "seven sisters" legislation. Still, not one administration official would testify in congres-

114. *The New York Times*, January 31, 1914, 7.

sional hearings held on the agrarian antitrust package, as the president – perhaps wisely – looked to keep his political options open, a posture that further fanned the political uncertainty growing in the House.[115] If anyone was privy to Wilson's thinking at this time it was probably Louis Brandeis. Thus is it suggestive that in speaking before the U.S. Chamber of Commerce in February 1914, Brandeis was adamant that the five brothers "are not Administration bills . . . they are the bills of House members who introduced them." "Free and unrestricted competition," Brandeis insisted, "was not the President's object, but rather regulated competition."[116]

Faced with presidential determination to keep Congress in session until the necessary legislation had been passed, party leaders began to look for ways to revise the program, expedite passage, and get back home.[117] The tension between the president's demand for action and Congress's desire to flee Washington ultimately forced the question of legislative tactics. Party leaders concluded that the carving up of the original program into five separate bills had been ill-conceived. The proliferation of legislation scattered institutional responsibility, weakened party authority, and diluted interest in the fate of any particular bill. A substantially scaled-back program, packaged as an omnibus bill, would more easily command caucus support and expedite final passage.[118] But a consensus on the specifics of the revised legislation was difficult to secure. The initial March 1 deadline for reporting the antitrust measures to the floor came and went as Democrats continued to whittle away at the program in the tense congressional atmosphere. The Definitions, the Trade Relations, and Interlocking Directorates bills came under heaviest scrutiny. Attorney General James C. McReynolds was reportedly displeased with the language of the Definitions and Trade Relations bills, while Majority Leader Underwood was particularly concerned with the Definitions bill. Never an enthusiastic supporter of the *Trans-Missouri* doctrine, Underwood could now argue that new uncertainties involving the Sherman Act would only delay economic recovery.[119]

Perhaps the recession's single greatest contribution to the politics of antitrust was to augment Wilson's programmatic leverage with congressional leaders, as presidential popularity was increasingly seen

115. Chamberlain, *The President, Congress and Legislation*, 39.
116. *The New York Times*, February 13, 1914, 2.
117. Ibid., January 31, 1914, 7.
118. Ibid., March 1, 1914, 12.
119. Ibid.; ibid., March 2, 1914, 6; Fleming, *Oscar W. Underwood*, 211–12.

as a critical variable in the Democrats' midterm success. As a result, Wilson was able to direct revisions to the antitrust program in a way he had not with the initial package, and it was clear that the president was in no mood for a Bryanite assault on business. Wilson met with Judiciary Committee members, with discussions centering on revisions to the Definitions, Interlocking Directorates, and Trade Relations bills. It was agreed that the first two bills would be "generally overhauled" and the language of the latter "modified."[120] Finally, at a March 15 press conference, Wilson announced that the Definitions bill would be cut from the party program, though curiously his explanation emphasized the concern that courts might treat its list of prohibited business activities as inclusive.[121]

Over the course of several more meetings with Clayton and his committee, Wilson pushed for further program modifications and insisted on an omnibus bill to expedite passage.[122] In successive press conferences Wilson was emphatic that trust legislation would not be postponed until after the midterm elections.[123] But the pressure to adjourn was now coming from all quarters. In a note to the president, William F. McCoombs, chairman of the Democratic National Committee, weighed in on the matter:

> As to matters political I receive a large mail every day and I am more and more convinced that an early adjournment of Congress seems highly advisable.
>
> It seems to me that the Party has reached high tide for the present and that the country is becoming restive over the uncertainties of [antitrust] legislation. It appeals to me that an adjournment to take up the legislative program in December is desirable. I think business would be better and our chances of returning a Democratic Congress would be greatly enhanced.[124]

In his response to McCoombs, Wilson was firm that political considerations required not *inaction*, but rather some form of *positive party action*, and that Congress should remain in session until an antitrust program had been passed.

---

120. *The New York Times*, March 10, 1914, 11.

121. "Remarks at a Press Conference," March 15, 1914. In Link, ed. *Papers of Woodrow Wilson* Vol. 29, 313.

122. *The New York Times*, March 17, 1914, 1–2.

123. "Remarks at a Press Conference," March 24, 1914. In Link, ed. *Papers of Woodrow Wilson* Vol. 29, 373–5; "Remarks at a Press Conference," March 26, 1914.

124. William F. McCoombs to Woodrow Wilson, April 4, 194. In Link, ed. *Papers of Woodrow Wilson* Vol. 29, 404.

As to the early adjournment of Congress, I feel that it would be very shocking to the party and to the country if we seemed to pause in our programme and adjourn at an earlier date than is customary even. I believe that the pending legislation . . . can be disposed of without very much fuss or controversy, and I think that it would enhance rather than decrease the confidence of the country in us if we continued to show absolute confidence in ourselves. I admit that the whole matter is debatable as to the question of political expediency, but I must say that it does not seem to me debatable as a question of party courage and energy.[125]

Reiterating this point at still another White House conference, Wilson expressed his "unqualified disapproval" to calls by Judiciary Committee members to abandon antitrust legislation for the current session. Legislation, he insisted, must be passed before adjournment and he threatened to keep Congress in Washington all summer if necessary to accomplish his ends.[126]

An omnibus antitrust bill – the Clayton bill – was finally reported to the floor of the House of Representatives on May 6, 1914. It retained the characteristic feature of agrarian economic regulation: court enforcement of legislatively determined, categorical prohibitions on specified business practices. For this reason alone, business leaders and progressives of Roosevelt's ilk – for whom administrative discretion and flexibility were crucial ingredients in any reform bill – were unlikely to be assuaged by the bill's alterations. But the new legislation was nonetheless of the utmost political significance. For it represented a formal severing by Democrats from their platform commitment to roll back the rule of reason. As Wilson had earlier announced, the Definitions bill was jettisoned in its entirety, thus assuring that the recently acquired legal supports for reasonable restraint would continue unencumbered. From the earlier Trade Relations bill, the omnibus Clayton bill incorporated several prohibitions on unfair competition, including unfair price discrimination and exclusive contracts. It also extended equitable and injunctive relief to individuals injured by illegal business combinations, and simplified the method for recovering triple damages for injury under the Sherman Act. The new legislation also contained qualified prohibitions against interlocking directorates and holding companies. The only new provision in the bill was one to bring labor unions out from under the purview of the Sherman Act. The change had been insisted on by the American Federation of Labor, and

125. Woodrow Wilson to William F. McCoombs, April 7, 1914. In Link, ed. *Papers of Woodrow Wilson* Vol. 29, 409.
126. *New York World*, April 14, 1914; *The New York Times*, April 15, 1.

union support was critical to the Clayton bill's overall chance of passage.[127]

The original trade commission bill fared no better in this atmosphere of congressional panic. A new commission bill had been written by a special subcommittee of the House Interstate Commerce Committee (HICC), which had emerged victorious in a jurisdictional dispute over trade commission legislation with Clayton's Judiciary Committee. Authored by Democrat James H. Covington of Maryland, the new commission bill represented a drastic modification of the Clayton committee's original measure. The Covington bill would limit the authority of the proposed commission to corporations capitalized at five million dollars or more. So restrictive was the commission's reach that, according to one estimate, less than 2,000 of the 350,336 corporations filing returns under the 1912 Corporation Tax Law would be subject to its authority.[128] The Covington bill also stripped the trade commission of its power of independent initiative; passed in this form, commissioners looking to investigate violations of the antitrust law would be dependent upon the attorney general for authorization. Finally, the bill also restricted the trade commission's access to certain categories of business books and papers and required commissioners to obtain presidential approval before making public certain types of business information.[129] In all, the changes made by the HICC were so extensive that Senate Democrats lashed out at the wholesale nature of the House retreat, vowing to reinstate the commission's powers when the initiative finally passed to their chamber.

The gutting of the trade commission bill was not simply the product of a reshuffling of House committee jurisdiction. The attack on the commission had Wilson's full backing, evidence that the president was still programmatically distant from the Progressive regulatory commission idea.[130] Attorney General McReynolds, for one, had expressed the fear that a commission with independent initiative would hamper policy initiative coming out of the Justice Department. Moreover, according to reports, the president was convinced that the current Bureau of Corporations already possessed "broad and effective powers," so that trade commission legislation could safely be limited to "a reorganization of

127. On labor and the Clayton bill, see Link, *Wilson: The New Freedom*, 426–31; Link, *Woodrow Wilson and the Progressive Era*, 68–9. On the labor policy of the Wilson years more generally, see Dubofsky, "Abortive Reform."

128. The calculation was made by *The New York Times*, March 17, 1914, 1, based on data supplied by the U.S. Commission of Internal Revenue.

129. *The New York Times*, March 16, 1914, 7.

130. Ibid.

the Bureau of Corporations ... without much more power than the bureau now possesses."[131] Democrats on the Senate Interstate Commerce Committee would not concede the president this much, derisively characterizing the Covington bill as "merely a weaker and more complicated Bureau of Corporations," and they awaited anxiously the opportunity to substitute their own commission bill.[132]

The Progressive Challenge and the Federal Trade Commission Act

The turn away from the five brothers, then, can be accounted for by the economic depression and a crisis of business confidence. But the turn *toward* the Progressive party's trade commission idea requires a different explanation: the reemergence of Theodore Roosevelt as the principal stump speaker for Progressive party candidates in the upcoming midterm elections. On May 30, 1914, Theodore Roosevelt fired his first salvo of the midterm season and it contained his strongest attack yet on Democratic antitrust policy: "Not the slightest progress has been made in solving the trust question," the Progressive leader exclaimed, directly indicting Wilson and the Democratic party. "The economic conditions are such that business is in jeopardy and the small business man, the farmer, and the industrial wage worker are all suffering because of those conditions." Democratic policies and Democratic incompetence, Roosevelt argued, constituted a permanent barrier to progress and economic recovery.

> [T]he only wise and sane propositions, the only propositions which represent a constructive governmental progressivism and the resolute purposes to secure good results instead of fine phrases, [are] the principles enunciated in the Progressive platform in connection with the trust and the tariff alike.[133]

The Progressive regulatory commission plan was the heart of Roosevelt's alternative strategy. It had been drafted by the National Legislative Reference Bureau of the Progressive Party, chaired by William Draper Lewis, dean of the law school of the University of Pennsylvania, and under the directorship of Donald Richberg, a Chicago attorney who had been active in local progressive politics before joining the national Progressive party. The functions of the Legislative Reference Bureau were to translate the planks of the Progressive party's 1912 plat-

131. *The New York Times*, February 17, 1914, 1; Link, *Wilson: The New Freedom*, 426.
132. *The New York Times*, March 17, 1914, 1.
133. Ibid., May 31, 1914.

form into detailed programs, draft bills based on these programs for introduction into Congress, and offer technical assistance to the bloc of Progressive congressmen in the House of Representatives. Legislative drafting served a purely political function, since the Progressive contingent in Congress wielded no institutional power. It was to publicize the Progressive party program to the nation from the floor of Congress, and, to the extent possible, help set the terms of policy debate. In making various party planks concrete, Lewis and Richberg had the help of such progressive notables as Jane Addams, James R. Garfield, Gifford Pinchot, Charles E. Merriam, Herbert Knox Smith, Benjamin Lindsay, and Walter Weyl.

Responsibility for drafting antitrust legislation fell specifically to Lewis, Richberg, and Herbert Knox Smith, the later having previously served as Roosevelt's commissioner of corporations. Roosevelt himself was also extensively consulted. The product of this collaboration was three bills (H.R. 9299, 9300, 9301) – the so-called Trust Triplets. The first bill established a federal trade commission with full powers of investigation and subpoena over corporations having "annual gross receipts exceeding three million dollars from business within the United States." The second bill empowered this commission further to define methods of unfair competition and issue orders, on its own initiative or through the courts, to compel corporate obedience. Finally, the third bill allowed the commission to regulate natural monopolies, defined broadly to include corporations that controlled natural resources, terminal or transportation facilities, financial resources, or any vital factor of production.[134]

For months Wilson's own circle of progressive advisors had urged him to repudiate the agrarian antitrust strategy and throw his support to a regulatory commission bill being sponsored in the House by Raymond Stevens, a freshman Democrat from New Hampshire. The Stevens bill had been authored by George Rublee, a New York attorney whose progressive interests had over the years brought him into close association with the likes of both Louis Brandeis and Theodore Roosevelt. Rublee had earlier assisted Brandeis in preparation for his testimony before a 1910 congressional inquiry investigating the Pinchot-Ballinger affair. More recently, Rublee had been a member of Theodore Roosevelt's original "brains trust" in the months leading up to the Republican

---

134. Gable, *The Bull Moose Years*, 162–5; Richberg, *My Hero*, 51; *The Outlook*, November 29, 1913, 677–8. The testimony of Draper, Smith, and Richberg can be found in U.S. Congress. House. Interstate Commerce Committee. Hearings on Trust Legislation 63d Cong., 2d sess., 1914, 241–301.

convention of 1912. In collaboration with Herbert Croly and Judge Learned Hand, Rublee helped "lay out the lines of the [Roosevelt] campaign for the Republican nomination."[135] Rublee had been converted to the idea of a trade commission with regulatory powers while attending congressional hearings on the five brothers. There he absorbed the testimony of Richberg, Lewis, and Smith, authors of the Progressive party's trade commission legislation. Rublee's bill, once it had been introduced by Stevens, merely put a Democratic face on the Progressive trade commission.

Sometime in April, Wilson appears to have sent out feelers to test Democratic reaction to the Stevens regulatory commission bill. Within the administration, the bill met with intense opposition from his attorney general, James C. McReynolds. In the House, William C. Adamson, chairman of the Interstate Commerce Committee, which had reported the Covington commission bill, was livid when informed that Rublee and Stevens had solicited the president's support for the Stevens bill. In an angry note to Wilson, Adamson flatly rejected any further consideration of the regulatory commission proposal. The chairman made it clear to the president that his committee had conducted a full set of hearings, "considered all the phases and suggestions mentioned in the letter," and was satisfied that the Covington bill – backed by the full committee, minus Stevens and the progressive Republican Lafferty of Oregon – was the correct approach to the problem.[136]

For months Rublee continued unsuccessfully to lobby the administration on behalf of the Stevens bill. There were some supporters. One was Interior Secretary Franklin Lane, the former chairman of the Interstate Commerce Commission. Lane privately endorsed the plan, believing it embodied the correct approach to the problem. However, Lane would offer Rublee little in the way of tangible assistance. Rublee likewise approached Commissioner of Corporations Joseph E. Davies.[137] Davies would likely head up any trade commission created by Congress. Thus, by emphasizing the extra authority that would accrue to him as chairman of a *regulatory* body, Rublee hoped to entice the commissioner into

135. See Rublee, "Reminiscences," 92–3.

136. William C. Adamson to Woodrow Wilson (April 23, 1914). In Link, ed. *The Papers of Woodrow Wilson* Vol. 29, 496.

137. Davies, "Informal Remarks," 104. Davies, a Wisconsin Democrat, had also managed Wilson's campaign in the Midwest in 1912. A progressive Democrat, Davies freely admitted that, barring Wilson's nomination at Baltimore, he would have thrown his support behind Roosevelt, adding that there were "a great many more of my age, particularly in the West, regardless of politics, who felt the same way about it." Ibid.

championing the Stevens bill from inside the administration. Indeed, as we saw earlier, Davies had floated the idea of a regulatory commission himself, only to have it fall on deaf ears. Perhaps for this reason, Davies was reluctant to press the case with the president again. As Rublee would later characterize it, Davies "was timid, he was afraid, didn't think there was any chance for it and wouldn't do anything about it." Not surprisingly, Rublee's proposal was rejected out of hand by Attorney General James C. McReynolds, who strongly disapproved of the plan. McReynolds urged Rublee to drop the whole thing, saying, as Rublee later recalled, "Why, my dear man . . . this is all settled. Everything is decided about this. There is nothing you can do about it. Why don't you give this up?"[138]

In the meantime, progressives of all stripes continued to heap criticism on the Clayton and Covington bills. Opponents blasted the Clayton bill for its inflexible prohibitions and the trade commission bill as simply useless. "Money Trust" expert Samuel Untermyer, for one, termed the Democratic antitrust program "lamentably weak and ineffective," calling the Covington trade commission "nothing more . . . than a Bureau of Information . . ." Senator Albert Baird Cummins of Iowa, a progressive Republican, agreed, and in committee proposed to give the trade commission strong regulatory powers. *The Outlook*, Theodore Roosevelt's official organ, condemned the omnibus Clayton bill as "devoid of a clear, effective principle for regulating instead of dissolving and exterminating" and dismissed the Covington bill as "worthless." In a similar vein, Norman Hapgood, progressive editor of *Harper's Weekly*, denigrated the technical competence of the Clayton bill's authors. "They mean well," Hapgood conceded, "but they do not represent the most expert knowledge available." Finally, from the floor of the House, Victor Murdock, leader of the chamber's small Progressive party contingent, ridiculed the Covington bill as a "weak, purely investigative" commission, destined to be "born a cripple"; while the Clayton bill, he argued, "persists in the attempt to make this country travel again the old, profitless circle which follows writing rigid inhibitions against big business, honest and otherwise, into law and leaving it to the long lingering delay which waits upon the interpretations of the courts."[139]

Against this backdrop, Roosevelt's reemergence on the political stage was catalytic. His attack on the antitrust program confirmed what

138. Rublee, "Reminiscences," 109–10.
139. Urofsky, *Louis D. Brandeis and the Progressive Tradition*, 83; Untermyer, "Completing the Anti-Trust Programme"; *Harper's Weekly*, June 6, 1914: 4; *The Outlook*, June 20, 1914: 375; *Congressional Record*, 63d Cong., 2d sess., 1914, 51, pt. 9: 8837.

Wilson had anticipated all along, that the Progressives intended to turn the midterm elections into a referendum both on the Wilson administration and the competence of the Democratic party to govern. With political strategies finally laid bare, the arguments of Wilson's progressive inner circle in support of the Stevens bill assumed a new persuasiveness and, in a momentous decision, the president finally threw his support behind the regulatory commission plan. "I think you will agree with me," Wilson instructed one progressive Democrat who continued to recommend the shelving of trust legislation until after the November elections, "that we cannot now, as we could not at any former stage, afford to show the least hesitation or lack of courage on this point which is going to be a point of attack during the campaign, as Mr. Roosevelt has kindly apprised [sic] us." Wilson did acknowledge that changes to the party's antitrust program would once again have to be made. But the president now seemed sanguine about the changes, believing they could be effected with little delay.

> I believe that we can by a combination of the measures now pending accomplish what it is necessary to accomplish at this session. What I have in mind is a little too intricate to be put into a hastily dictated letter, but conference will easily bring it out as we progress.
> ... The men you speak of, – Representative Stevens, Mr. Brandeis, and Mr. Rublee, – have themselves suggested, I hope a better way of dealing with the only really debatable part of the Clayton Bill. The rest of it seems to me rather plain sailing.[140]

A comparison of relevant congressional bills makes clear that the Democratic attempt to silence Roosevelt's criticism of their antitrust program was not limited simply to coopting the regulatory commission idea per se, but to coopting Roosevelt's regulatory plan in particular. How could Roosevelt criticize his own proposal? The key provisions of the Democrats' Federal Trade Commission bill, as introduced by Senate Democrats in June 1914, were transplanted almost verbatim from trust legislation drawn up by members of the national Progressive party organization the previous year. While officially it was Sections 10 to 12 of the Stevens bill that were incorporated as Section 5 of the Democrats' new regulatory commission bill (as introduced on June 13, 1914), the paternity of the Stevens bill is readily traceable to Sections 1, 2, 5, and 6 of the Progressive party's own regulatory commission bill (H.R. 9300), the second of three antitrust bills introduced in the House on November 23, 1913, by Victor Murdock, leader of the congressional

140. Woodrow Wilson to Henry F. Hollis, June 2, 1914. In Link, ed. *Papers of Woodrow Wilson* Vol. 30, 134.

Progressive Party. Table 3.8 reproduces the relevant sections of these bills.

Congressional debates on the FTCA underscore that participants were cognizant of the coalition-building imperatives that had prompted the president's decision to embrace the Progressive trade commission. These imperatives were most explicitly stated by Democrat Francis G. Newlands of Nevada, chairman of the Senate Committee on Interstate Commerce and himself a long time supporter of an ICC-styled trade commission. To dispel the attack of one agrarian Democrat who condemned the Democratic regulatory commission bill for its truckling to supporters of the Progressive party, Newlands invoked the imperatives of national party politics that hung over all Democrats' heads:

> The Senator will bear in mind that the Democratic Party at the last election was a minority party, and in order to be a majority party it has got to win from the opposing organizations. It seems to me that it can accept any suggestion that is right from the Progressive Party, which is pursuing substantially the same lines of reform that the Democratic Party has been pursuing, and that it might well adopt a suggestion that would be in the public interest.[141]

Driving his point home, Newlands continued:

> The Progressive Party now is in process of disintegration, and the question is whether the members of that party will return to the Republican Party . . . or whether they will join themselves with the Democratic Party. . . .
> I would gladly facilitate the latter process; and let me say that wherever we can harmonize our principles with the methods which they have approved in such a way as to draw into our organization men who have been preeminent in this reform we are serving the cause of the Democratic Party and Democracy throughout the entire country.[142]

Another agrarian Democrat, Senator James Reed of Missouri, condemned the new Democratic measure as "a betrayal of the Democratic party and of the country." The senator claimed to see "the doctrine of the Bull Mooser – not to destroy monopolies, but to regulate them, not to carry them to the courts of justice, but to a commission." Reed recalled for his Democratic colleagues their platform's pledge to redeem the Sherman Act from degradation by the Supreme Court's rule-of-reason decisions. "The very purpose of this legislation," he reminded his col-

---

141. *Congressional Record*, 63d Cong., 2d sess., 1914, 51, pt. 13: 12866. The agrarian Democrat to whom Newlands directed his remarks was Senator Charles Spalding Thomas of Colorado.

142. Ibid., 12867.

Table 3.8. *A Comparison of Three Regulatory Commission Bills*

Progressive Party Bill (H.R. 9300). Introduced 11/17/13.	Stevens Bill (H.R. 15560). Introduced 4/14/14.	Democratic Bill (H.R. 15631). Introduced 6/13/14.
Sec. 1. That unfair or oppressive competition in commerce among the several states and with foreign nations as hereinafter defined is hereby declared unlawful.	Sec. 10. That unfair or oppressive competition in commerce is hereby declared unlawful.	Sec. 5. That unfair competition in commerce is hereby declared unlawful.
Sec. 2. That the Interstate Trade Commission is hereby empowered and directed to prevent all corporations or associations subject to the jurisdiction of said commission from engaging in or practicing such unfair or oppressive competition.	The commission is hereby empowered and directed to prevent corporations engaged in commerce from using unfair or oppressive methods of competition.	The commission is hereby empowered and directed to prevent corporations from using unfair methods of competition in commerce.
Sec. 5. That whenever the interstate trade commission shall have reason to believe that any corporation or association subject to its jurisdiction has been or is engaging in unfair or oppressive competition it shall issue and serve upon said corporation or association a written order, at least 30 days in advance of the time set therein for hearing, directing said corporation or association to appear	Sec. 11. That whenever the commission shall have reason to believe that any corporation engaged in commerce has been or is using any unfair or oppressive method of competition it shall issue and serve upon said corporation a written order at least 30 days in advance of the time set for a hearing, directing said corporation to appear before the commission and show cause why an order shall not be issued	Whenever the commission shall have reason to believe that any corporation has been or is using any unfair method of competition in commerce it shall issue and serve upon such corporation a written order at least thirty days in advance of the time set therein for hearing, directing it to appear before the commission and show cause why an cause why an order shall not be issued by

Table 3.8. *(cont.)*

Progressive Party Bill (H.R. 9300). Introduced 11/17/13.	Stevens Bill (H.R. 15560). Introduced 4/14/14.	Democratic Bill (H.R. 15631). Introduced 6/13/14.
before said commission and show cause why an order shall not be issued by said commission restraining and prohibiting said corporation or association from such practice or transaction, and if upon such hearing the commission shall be of the opinion that the practice or transaction in question is prohibited by this act it shall thereupon issue such order restraining the same. The commission may at any time modify or set aside, in whole or in part, any order issued by it under this Act.	by the commission restraining and prohibiting said competition from using such method of competition, and if upon such hearing the commission shall find that the method of competition in question is prohibited by this act it shall thereupon issue an order restraining and prohibiting the use of the same. The commission may at any time modify or set aside, in whole or in part, any order issued by it under this Act.	the commission restraining and prohibiting it from using such method of competition, and if upon such hearing the commission shall find that the method of competition in question is prohibited by this act it shall thereupon issue an order restraining and prohibiting the use of the same. The commission may at any time modify or set aside, in whole or in part, any order issued by it under this act.
Sec. 6. That whenever the said commission, upon the issuing of such restraining order, shall find that said corporation or association has not complied therewith said commission may petition the District Court of the United States, within any district where the act in question took place or where the said corporation or	Sec. 12. That whenever the commission after the issuance of such restraining order, shall find that said corporation has not complied therewith, the commission may petition the district court of the United States, within any district where the method in question was used or where the said corporation is located or carries on business,	Whenever the commission, after the issuance of such order, shall find that such corporation has not complied therewith, the commission may petition the district court of the United States, within any district where the method in question was used or where such corporation is located or carries on business, praying the court to

Table 3.8. *(cont.)*

Progressive Party Bill (H.R. 9300). Introduced 11/17/13.	Stevens Bill (H.R. 15560). Introduced 4/14/14.	Democratic Bill (H.R. 15631). Introduced 6/13/14.
association is located or carries on business, asking said court to issue an injunction to enforce the terms of such order of the commission; and such court is hereby authorized to issue such injunction, and also, in case of any violation of such injunction, in the discretion of the court, to issue an order restraining and enjoining said corporation or association from engaging in commerce among the several States and with foreign nations for such time as said court may order.	asking said court to issue an injunction to enforce such order of the commission; and such court is hereby authorized to issue such injunction, and also in case of violation of such injunction in the discretion of the court to issue an order restraining said corporation from engaging in commerce for such time as said court shall order.	issue an injunction to enforce such order of the commission, and the court is hereby authorized to issue such injunction.

leagues, "was to redeem that platform pledge. It was to restore the strength of the statute and to make it more drastic and all embracing." Instead, the "bill has been emasculated. It has been rendered, in my opinion, so far as trust legislation is concerned, absolutely valueless."[143]

Congressional Republicans delighted in the obvious political irony surrounding the Democratic-sponsored FTC bill. One Massachusetts Republican taunted Senate Democrats for their party's obvious aboutface on antitrust policy. Reading aloud from Wilson's own campaign speeches, the senator reminded his partisan opponents of the president's

143. Ibid., pt. 16: 15862, 15821, 15819.

disparaging attacks on the Progressive party's regulatory commission proposal. The senator took further pleasure in drawing the similarities between the Progressive party plan and the new Democratic bill. President Wilson, the Senate was told, had come to the White House bound by his word to carry out the provisions of the Baltimore platform. "And yet this legislation is not intended, as I understand, to carry out the purposes of that declaration, but it is designed to do just what the President criticized the third party for advocating at the time."[144]

Similarly, outside of Congress, elite opinion circles were also quick to point out the strategic component that underlay the transformation of Democratic trust policy. Remarking on Theodore Roosevelt's "political declaration" of May 30, one leading periodical warned the Progressive party leader that his "plan of attack on the Wilson Administration" was likely to fall flat as a rallying cry for progressive supporters – an "uncertain trumpet" in the call to arms against the party in power. Referring to the Democrats' newly revamped trust policy, the periodical remarked:

> And as for the Democrats being clear off the track as regards dealing with the Trusts, the Colonel might rather have accused them of stealing his own idea. For are they not acting as if bent on legislating in order to carry out one of the planks of the Progressive platform? We mean the one promising "a strong Federal Administrative Commission," . . . doing for them [industrial corporations] . . . what is now done for the railroads by the Interstate Commerce Commission.[145]

Roll-Call Analysis

There exists no set of roll-call votes that will allow us to track the changing patterns of support for antitrust legislation from the Democrats' original proposals to the final FTCA. Neither chamber voted on the five brothers, only the House acted on the Covington trade commission bill (though with no recorded vote), and while both chambers voted on the final FTCA, roll-call data is available for the Senate action only. The paucity of roll-call data is genuinely disappointing. Nonetheless, with the evidence available we can make certain inferences about the powerful structuring role played by Democratic party leaders and the party caucus in the disposition of antitrust legislation. That evidence, both qualitative and quantitative, suggests the degree to which agrarian Democrats subordinated their distinctive vision of the American political economy to organizational discipline and national electoral victory. This claim is

144. Ibid., pt. 13: 12732.
145. *The Nation*, June 4, 1914, 655.

evident both from statements of betrayal expressed by agrarian *Republicans* on the floor of the House during the Clayton Act debates (agrarian Democrats were silent) and from the modest roll-call data at our disposal.

The remarks of Republican John M. Nelson of Wisconsin are representative of how agrarians less constrained by party organization reacted to the embrace of the regulatory commission by agrarian Democrats. To these legislators, the final Democratic trust program represented a straightforward surrender to advocates of corporate-liberalism – acquiescence to the principle of economic concentration and corporate power – all in the interest of party electoral victory. Like agrarian Democrats, Nelson was a strong believer in the reliance on strict legislative prohibitions on corporate behavior and stiff criminal penalties for their violation. On both accounts, and on the broader goal of limiting corporate power, the agrarian Republican found the shift in Democratic policy to be as devastating as it was opportunistic. "There is no hope in Democracy," Nelson lamented on the floor of the House.

> What we [Republicans] bolted was caucus rule and partisanship. But Democrats are the partisans of partisans and the slaves of the party caucus. [Y]ou can do nothing with a party that commits the unpardonable sin, the party that solemnly pledges itself to do the right thing and then deliberately and knowingly does the wrong, a party that will sacrifice the salvation of the American people, its deliverance from the yoke of monopoly, upon the altar of partisanship, for the sake of its one supreme god – party success.[146]

The "altar of partisanship" of which Nelson speaks is evident on almost every important vote for which data is available. Indeed, one of the things that is so striking about the operation of the Democratic caucus is the way it obviates the need for sophisticated roll-call techniques. When considering the voting behavior of Democratic legislators (our principal interest), party affiliation simply overwhelms any other consideration. The most significant of these occurrences took place in the House and concerns the Clayton legislation (see Table 3.9). On June 5, 1914, House Democrats voted 218 to 1 (71 not voting) to pass the first omnibus Clayton bill.[147] As noted earlier, this first version was emblematic of the agrarian approach to regulation in its inflexible prohibitions, criminal punishments, and reliance on court enforcement. So perhaps it is not so surprising that a party with such a large agrarian

---

146. *Congressional Record*, 63d Cong., 2d sess., 1914, 51, pt. 16: 16326–7.
147. The full House vote on the Clayton bill of June 5 was 277 to 54, with 104 not voting.

Table 3.9. *House Democratic Votes to Pass Clayton Bill*

	Yes	No	No Vote
1. Pass Clayton Bill 1 (June 5, 1914)	218	1	71
2. Pass Clayton Bill 2 (October 8, 1914)	216	0	74

Note: No recorded votes were taken in the House on either the Covington or the Stevens Trade Commission Bills.

contingent should have embraced that legislation so thoroughly, though the virtual unanimity is still worthy of note. But the final version of the Clayton Act, which passed the House on October 8, 1914, is another matter. This version had been shorn of the strict proscriptions on corporate behavior and stiff punitive sanctions that marked the agrarian version of the bill. "Flexibility" was the watchword of the final law – statutory prohibitions deliberately written to be open-ended – necessary to open up a broad, discretionary policy space for the newly created Federal Trade Commission. It is this direct interrelationship with the FTCA that allows us to see in the final vote on the Clayton Act a surrogate vote for or against the Progressive trade commission and the corporate-liberal solution to the trust problem. It is significant here, then, that Democrats were *unanimous* in their support, voting 216 to 0 (74 not voting) to pass this final version of the Clayton bill.[148] Agrarians who had earlier called for a return to the *Trans-Missouri* status quo and who had been instrumental in advancing the five brothers, now to a person fell into line to support an arrangement to facilitate the consolidation of the corporate economy. One would be hard pressed to find a more historically significant instance of the independent effect of party organization upon the policy preferences of House legislators. Even in the Senate, where individualism is generally more pervasive, Democratic votes on the Clayton Act and the FTCA were again remarkably unified (see Table 3.10).

Such variation as there was on the antitrust votes was generally due to Republicans. Republican voting patterns are important in this analysis for what they suggest about the underlying structure of district preferences, and therefore merit a brief consideration. Again, the most

---

148. The full House vote on the Clayton bill of October 8 was 245 to 52, with 138 not voting.

Table 3.10. *Senate Democratic Votes to Pass Clayton and Trade Commission Bills and Vote to Recommit Clayton Bill*

	Yes	No	No Vote
1. Pass Trade Commission Bill 1 (August, 5, 1914)	41	2	10
2. Pass Trade Commission Bill 2 (September 8, 1914)	34	0	19
3. Pass Clayton Bill 1 (September 2, 1914)	38	0	15
4. Recommit Clayton Bill 2 (October 5, 1914)	33	6	15
5. Pass Clayton Bill 2 (October 5, 1914)	34	3	16

significant votes were taken in the House on the Clayton bill. This discussion will utilize the trade-area boundaries classification scheme developed by Elizabeth Sanders and Richard Bensel to study regional patterns in American political development.[149] Trade areas are classified using U.S. Census measures of value added in manufacturing, and can be arrayed into three principal categories according to a particular unit's per capita level of industrialization. The Sanders/Bensel methodology is useful because it helps us to distinguish between district-level manufacturing ("core") and agricultural ("periphery") interests within each party, along with an intermediate category ("semi-periphery").[150] Applying the trade-area framework to Republican roll-call behavior yields significant patterns. Consider the House vote on the first Clayton bill. As

149. Sanders, "Industrial Concentration, Sectional Competition, and Antitrust Politics in America, 1880–1980," 142–214; Bensel, *Sectionalism and American Political Development, 1880–1980.*
150. Trading areas, Sanders argues, "comprise more logical economic units" of analysis than do states or congressional districts. Each unit has an integrity that derives from extensive economic interaction and the interdependence such activity fosters. Thresholds used to classify districts and states by trading area status are measures of per capita value-added in manufacturing (v.a.p.c.), and are intended to capture the level of industrialization in a given trading area: *periphery*, <$200 v.a.p.c.; *diverse*, $200–$299 v.a.p.c.; and *core*, ≥$300 v.a.p.c. Trade area boundaries employed in Sanders's analysis of the FTC and Clayton Acts are final 1921 Federal Reserve Branch Bank Territories, taken from the *Eighth Annual Report of the Board of Governors of the Federal Reserve* (Washington D. C., 1922), 693–9. Value-added in manufacturing was taken from the 1919 *Census of Manufacturing*, state-county tables. For a more extensive discussion of this methodology, see Sanders, "Industrial Concentration," 146–51; and, in particular, Bensel, *Sectionalism and American Political Development, 1880–1980*, 415–50. Data for coding districts and states by trading area status were graciously provided by Elizabeth Sanders.

Table 3.11. *Pattern of Republican Support for Agrarian and Corporate-Liberal Versions of Clayton Bill*

	Republican Core	Republican Semi-Periphery	Republican Periphery
Clayton Bill (1)	−26	−19	+29
	(46)	(37)	(48)
Clayton Bill (2)	−17	−16	−31
	(46)	(37)	(48)

Note: Cells scores are percentage point differences. Positive scores indicate a plurality in support of Clayton bill; negative scores indicate a plurality in opposition.

Clayton Bill (1) connotes agrarian version passed in the House on June 5, 1914. *Clayton Bill (2)* connotes corporate-liberal version passed in the House on October 8, 1914.

Table 3.11 indicates, although the differences are modest, such Republican support as there was for this version was concentrated among periphery (agrarian) Republicans. These legislators were 29 percentage points more likely to support than oppose the passage of the Democrats' first omnibus antitrust package. On the vote to pass the final Clayton bill, however, a different pattern of support emerges among Republicans. While manufacturing (core) and semi-periphery interests remain on balance opposed, periphery Republicans now emerge as the strongest *opponents* of the Democratic antitrust bill, the reverse pattern from that which was observed on the first vote. Overall, agrarian Republicans on this vote were 31 percentage points more likely to oppose than support the final Clayton bill.

As this pattern suggests, agrarian legislators less encumbered by party organization reacted strongly against the Democrats' final antitrust package. However, agrarians aligned with the chamber majority party cast their votes in ways that make their roll-call behavior an uncertain guide to underlying preferences. Agrarian Democrats came to power in the full flush of electoral victory, determined to make good on the antimonopoly plank of their Baltimore platform. Two years later, they stood before their constituents as the progenitors of a new institution foreign to both party ideology and interest. The political analyst Herbert Croly probably captured the irony of the political situation best when, in early 1915, he wrote: "The Trade Commission act represents a totally different approach [from the Sherman Act], a spirit strangely contradictory to the campaign theories of the President. . . . It is not the attitude anyone could have expected to see emerge from the tradition of the Democratic party. But nevertheless it did."[151]

Conclusion

This chapter has examined the ways in which the operation of the electoral and party systems placed effective constraints on the attainment of political objectives long articulated by the agrarian Democratic party. In the end, the very system of electoral democracy through which agrarian Democrats labored to achieve national power acted in concrete ways to shape and limit the possibilities in which that power could be exercised. The FTCA was surely, to borrow Herbert Croly's phrase, "an unseen reversal," in terms of the goals and aspirations long articulated by the agrarian Democratic party. Shunted aside were the promises of previous party platforms: to undo the rule of reason; to limit corporate size; to enumerate by statutory means the conditions under which corporations would be allowed to conduct their interstate business; and to inflict criminal punishment for their violation. More importantly, if the vision of agrarian democracy was predicated on the maintenance of small economic units, with ownership distributed widely among the citizenry, then the passage of the FTCA effectively brought down the curtain on that particular variant of the Jeffersonian vision.

The Democratic party was the minority party in the American party system. Progressivism effectively disrupted the traditional hegemony of the Republican party in national politics; while the pending disintegration of the Progressive party threw into relief the contingent nature of national Democratic ascendancy. The question foremost on the minds of most party leaders was well-articulated by Francis Newlands, who, from the floor of the Senate, wondered aloud which of the two traditional party organizations was to house the supporters of the Progressive party. The resolution of the trust question was, in an important sense, the first real litmus test of Democratic progressivism. While business conditions prodded Democrats to shelve antitrust legislation until more auspicious electoral times prevailed, progressive demands for a resolution to the trust problem propelled the party forward. No criticism of the agrarian five brothers was more harsh than that of the progressives; and the combination of progressive and business criticism doomed any chance of passage the original Democratic antitrust package might have had.

151. Croly, "An Unseen Reversal."

Shorn of crucial support, the agrarian package was swept aside in the heat of the political struggle.

Into this policy vacuum stepped supporters of the independent regulatory commission alternative. Supporters of the regulatory commission had developed extensive economic and legal arguments to buttress their claim that this strategy was an effective response to the trust problem. Good governance, they argued, demanded the creation of a regulatory commission. But in the eyes of Wilson and other party leaders the concept of "good government" went hand in hand with continued Democratic party governance. As a consequence, trust policy had to be justified not only on rational policy grounds but on rational political grounds. The regulatory commission idea made little headway within the Democratic party as long as it could not be justified on the basis of national political considerations. However, as the agrarian antitrust strategy revealed itself to be an ineffectual vehicle for Democratic party supremacy, party leaders began the process of searching for a policy that could not only resolve the nation's economic problems, but simultaneously alleviate their desperate coalitional deficit. The regulatory commission idea became increasingly attractive to Wilson and other Democratic leaders as it became apparent that the proposal had the support both of progressives and an important segment of the organized business community.

Yet, perhaps most striking was the apparent ease with which long-standing policy was transformed and deeply embedded doctrine was violated. Nor was this transformation an aberration, as demonstrated by the spate of progressive legislation passed in the wake of Woodrow Wilson's reelection bid. Reform followed upon reform in the summer of 1916: rural credits legislation, a workmen's compensation bill for federal employees, child labor legislation, the creation of a tariff commission, and the granting of the eight hour day to railroad labor. Whereas in 1912 Democrats denounced the Progressive party for trucking to socialism and for championing the vision of a strong and activist central state, by 1916 they were taunting the third party for its historical obsolescence, a relic of political aspirations largely attained.

> [Theodore Roosevelt] denounced the Democratic Party in 1912 as fatally incompetent, but he knows better now. He sees many of his own principles upon the statute in 1916 placed there by its legislation. He finds the Democratic platform of 1916 to be largely a transcript of his own, and he realizes that in this Republic two parties professing the same purposes can not endure.[152]

152. *Congressional Record*, 64th Cong., 1st sess., 1916, 54, part 10: 10062.

This fundamental change in Democratic policy and principle most likely would not have taken place absent the enormous structural pressures bearing upon the party, nor without the ability of the party organization in Congress to impose its will on the direction of policy development. If electoral constraints dictated which policy direction the Democrats would follow, effective party organization made more likely its success. But, in the case of the FTCA, party success was costly to agrarian Democrats who had waited for so long to wield national political power in defense of a way of life jeopardized by the concentrated economic power of a new industrial order and by social and political values that looked to centralized authority, government by experts and other nonelected decision makers, and the eradication of the nineteenth-century belief in a limited Constitution. Agrarians would never again wield the kind of power they held during the Wilson administration. By the time of Franklin Roosevelt's ascendance to the presidency in 1932, ongoing transformations in the structure of the American economy had rendered them a decided minority in American political life. It would be easy to overstate this point; for example, southern Democrats continued to wield substantial power in the committees of Congress. But the Jeffersonian vision was approaching exhaustion, leaving farmers to pursue discrete benefits and to stabilize their shrinking place in an increasingly urban and industrial America.

4

Progressive Republicans and the "Death Sentence" for Public Utility Holding Companies During America's Second New Deal

You give expression to a very firm belief that I have all along entertained, namely, that there be an amalgamation of the Republican-Progressives with the Democratic party, if the latter is to continue as a majority party in the years immediately ahead of us. So firmly am I convinced of this that I cannot understand the political short-sightedness of certain Democratic leaders who resent any recognition of the Republican-Progressives.

Harold Ickes to Raymond Moley[1]

[W]hat Mr. Roosevelt has done . . . is adopt neither Democratic nor Republican policies, but rather he has taken over the policies of that small group of so-called Progressive Republicans, typified by Senator Norris of Nebraska and Senator La Follette of Wisconsin. . . . In fact, easy as it has been to attribute the New Deal policies to the mysterious "Brains Trust," an analysis of the record will show that by far the larger part has sprung from the Progressives – that every feature of the New Deal program in years gone by has been urged by Progressive Republican Senators.

Frank R. Kent[2]

Introduction

Our consideration of the Public Utility Holding Company Act of 1935 must start earlier, with the alienation of progressive Republicans from the so-called First New Deal. Progressive Republicans were not only ardent supporters of Roosevelt for president in 1932, they were also his

1. Harold Ickes to Raymond Moley, October 2, 1933, *Harold Ickes Papers*, Box 227, Folder: Political (3), Manuscript Division, Library of Congress. Cited in Milkis, *The President and the Parties*, 329 fn. 17.
2. Kent, *Without Grease*, 10–11. Kent was a columnist for the *Baltimore Sun*, and a critic of the New Deal.

"staunchest friends and most effective supporters" in the early days of the New Deal.[3] But as the Seventy-third Congress wound to a close in June 1934, many of them stood ready to break with the Democratic president and his policies. Progressives were frustrated with Roosevelt's temporizing, his experiments with collectivism, and his lack of commitment to fundamental reform. Progressive disillusionment with the New Deal came to a head over Roosevelt's handling of the Wagner Labor Disputes bill, sponsored by Senator Robert F. Wagner, Democrat of New York.[4] Fearful of business opposition, Roosevelt had blocked consideration of the Wagner bill in Congress. In its place he substituted Senate Joint Resolution 143, a stop-gap labor measure, working with Republican leaders to secure a coalition of Democrats and conservative Republicans in support of the weak labor alternative.[5] The president's backroom maneuvering outraged Senate progressives, strong supporters of the Wagner bill, and they protested loudly the acquiescence of congressional Democrats – including Wagner himself – to Roosevelt's rival labor scheme. On the Senate floor, Robert M. La Follette, Jr., of Wisconsin, an ardent proponent of labor reform, chided liberal Democrats for subordinating principle to the president's political needs: "I was not brought up 'to march up the hill and march down again.'" "So far as I know, I have never started a fight in this body and quit." Senator Bronson Cutting of New Mexico more generally summed up the disaffection of progressive Republicans with the Democratic administration: "The new deal [sic]," he warned allies in the upper chamber, "is being strangled in the house of its friends."[6]

Frustration with the pace and character of Democratic reform helped fuel the formation of the Progressive party of Wisconsin in May 1934. The inspiration of Robert La Follette, Jr., and his brother Philip, the new party had as its immediate goal to contest the upcoming state and congressional elections. The platform of the Progressive party, however,

3. The description of progressive Republicans as Roosevelt's "staunchest friends and most effective supporters" comes from *The New Republic* 81 (December 12, 1934): 128. However, Harold Ickes aside, progressive Republicans refused to relinquish their separate identity in the Senate and their role as critics in national politics. They generally refused patronage, declined committee chairs, and rebuffed offers of administrative posts.

4. The Wagner Labor Disputes bill, forerunner to the National Labor Relations Act, sought to guarantee workers the right to organize and bargain collectively.

5. Senate Joint Resolution 143 authorized the creation of a board to investigate labor disputes, supervise elections, engage in mediation, and impose penalties for rules violations. The board, however, lacked broader powers to enforce compliance with its decisions. See Bernstein, *The New Deal Collective Bargaining Policy*, ch. 6 and p. 84.

6. *Congressional Record*, 73d Cong., 2d sess., 1934, Vol. 78, pt. 11: 12044, 12052. See also Huthmacher, *Senator Robert F. Wagner and the Rise of Urban Liberalism*.

betrayed national aspirations. It called for "a political realignment," one that would "place the exploiting reactionary on the one side and the producer, consumer, independent business and professional interests on the other." It advocated government ownership of public utilities, the central bank, and the munitions industries; jobs for the able-bodied unemployed; redistributive tax reform; a guarantee of labor's right to organize; and several welfare planks, including unemployment insurance, old age pensions, accident insurance, and financial aid to homeowners.[7]

In its first outing, the Progressive party showed tremendous vitality, not only installing Philip La Follette as governor and reelecting Robert La Follette, Jr., as senator, but also successfully contesting seven of ten Wisconsin congressional races. The success of the new party prompted several White House meetings between the La Follettes and Roosevelt, at which the main topics of discussion were the upcoming Seventy-fourth Congress and the 1936 presidential election. Roosevelt expressed his desire for progressive support in his own reelection bid. The La Follettes, for their part, promised to back the administration in the new Congress if Democrats pressed ahead with a truly progressive program, but in the long term they indicated their commitment to building a national Progressive party.[8] In public, the La Follettes hailed the Progressive party as a "permanent fixture" in American politics, and "the beginning of a political realignment."[9]

"It must never be forgotten," Rexford Tugwell would later write of Roosevelt, "that Franklin was first of all a practicing politician."[10] Despite his "natural inclination" to sympathize with the views of progressive Republicans, Roosevelt's political stance toward them was cooly calculated. From the beginning, Roosevelt had premised his actions on the assumption that progressive Republicans had little choice but to remain his "fast friends and uncritical supporters."[11] The president was convinced that there was simply no credible progressive alternative to the Democratic party. Consequently, he turned his attention to solidifying more ephemeral bases of support. With business opposition to the New Deal mounting rapidly, Roosevelt tailored policy considerations to subdue a growing "thunder on the right."[12]

But Roosevelt poorly judged the solidity of progressive Republican

---

7. Maney, *"Young Bob" La Follette*, 142–3.
8. Feinman, *Twilight of Progressivism*, 109.
9. Ibid., 84.
10. Tugwell, *The Democratic Roosevelt*, 327.
11. Ibid., 328; Sternsher, *Rexford Tugwell and the New Deal*, 311.
12. Burns, *Roosevelt*, ch. 12.

backing.[13] Their disenchantment and the emergence of a vigorous Progressive party complicated Roosevelt's initial calculus. "It is clear," Tugwell wrote, that Roosevelt "had made a fundamental error which he should try to correct."[14] Roosevelt's solution was to become "progressively orthodox": to shift style and substance to the left; to mount a radical agrarian-styled assault on corporate industrialists and finance capitalists. As Tugwell explained,

> The developments of 1934 led to the position Franklin had begun to assume during the campaign under the pressure of politics . . . [H]e was returning to an accepted version of the progressive position . . . This was the result, I think, of a number of combined estimates on his part. One of these was that the weight of the movement still lay with the older orthodox progressives. They believed in bearing down on big business and encouraging little business.[15]

Still, in itself the Democratic-progressive alliance was a volatile, and hence risky, electoral strategy. To Democratic party leaders, the only thing predictable about progressive Republicans was their ultimate unpredictability. Progressive Republicans, who had helped carry Woodrow Wilson to victory in 1916, swelled the ranks of the supporters of Warren G. Harding in the Republican landslide of 1920, then cast their vote for Robert La Follette, Sr., the Progressive party candidate in 1924. While crucial to a Democratic presidential victory in 1936, party strategists sought to augment their coalition base beyond progressive Republicans with inclusive appeals to additional groups.

13. In fact Roosevelt seems to have forgotten his own earlier assessments about the political character of these "progressives with a capital *R*." As recalled by Rexford Tugwell, Roosevelt observed: "They are wonderful people, but they did have the general characteristic of complete unreliability. They were individualists who never really granted leadership to anyone." Roosevelt continued: "When the Progressives had followed T.R. out of the Republican Party in 1912, . . . it had been a typical performance; they were always willing to quit something, and they were apt to become haughty and high-minded about it. When it came to giving anyone who represented them the leeway he had to have for maneuver or compromise in getting something done, they were almost sure to make a virtue out of demanding more. They were the best standers-on-principle we had. But the principle always turned out to be whatever happened to interest them as individuals – or maybe as politicians." Tugwell, *The Brains Trust*, 489–90.
14. Tugwell, *The Democratic Roosevelt*, 328. In March 1935 Roosevelt wrote to E. M. House: "Progressive Republicans like La Follette, Cutting, Nye, etc., . . . are flirting with the idea of a third party ticket . . . with the knowledge that such a third party would be beaten but that it would defeat us, elect a conservative Republican and cause a complete swing far to the left before 1940." (Roosevelt, *FDR: His Personal Letters*, 452–3). On progressives and antitrust thinking during the New Deal, see Hawley, *The New Deal and the Problem of Monopoly*.
15. Tugwell, *The Democratic Roosevelt*, 326.

Not long after the 1934 midterm elections, Roosevelt met with his chief
strategist, Edward J. Flynn of New York, to take stock of the party's
future. The two men agreed that the national Democratic party was
still "a rather ineffective force," with Democrats owing their current
prominence in national politics to the temporary effects of the depression on a still dominant Republican party. Speaking to Raymond Moley,
a former Roosevelt aide turned New Deal critic, Flynn recalled telling
the president:

> There are two or three million more dedicated Republicans in the United
> States than there are Democrats. The population, however, is drifting into
> the urban areas. . . . To remain in power we must attract some millions,
> perhaps seven, who are hostile or indifferent to both parties. They believe
> the Republican party to be controlled by big business and the Democratic
> party by the conservative South. These millions are mostly in the cities. They
> include racial and religious minorities and labor people. We must attract
> them by radical programs of social and economic reform.[16]

Progressive Republicans, labor, ethnic big-city machines, and the solid
South – this, in a nutshell, was the heart of Roosevelt's reelection coalition. Roosevelt's legislative agenda for the Seventy-fourth Congress was
intended to solidify the allegiance of these disparate and often contradictory social groupings, an agenda that in rhetoric and programmatic
content owed much to the Progressive party platform of May 1934.
Rhetorically, Roosevelt borrowed – in increasingly liberal doses – the language of class, corruption, and conspiracy, along with the dramatic
imagery of a frontal assault on the citadels of big-business power. Substantively, Roosevelt offered a program including social security, public
work relief, and the destruction of the "Power Trust." In response to the
electoral threat posed by Senator Huey P. Long of Louisiana, Roosevelt
would add the progressive demand for redistributive taxation. He would
also embrace, even if belatedly, state support for unionization and collective bargaining.[17] These measures formed the heart of the progressive
agenda, and in the spring and summer of 1935 they would become the
heart of the "second" New Deal.

This chapter focuses on one piece of legislation at the center of the
second New Deal: the Public Utility Holding Company Act of 1935
(PUHCA). For midwestern progressives and other foes of the Power
Trust the PUHCA was one of the singular political achievements of the

16. Moley, *The First New Deal*, 524–6.
17. Roosevelt was cautious in his solicitation of the labor vote. No champion of unions
    and no fan of union leaders, Roosevelt preferred to appeal to workers as consumers
    and as individual victims of the Great Depression.

New Deal.[18] It was also the federal government's most aggressive attempt to restructure national economic activity to date. In the words of one student of American business regulation, the PUHCA "was the most stringent corrective measure ever applied to American business. It went beyond any other in requiring the reorganization of corporate structures and in forcing divestment of property. It made the Securities and Exchange Commission a potent regulator of electric and gas holding companies."[19] In its final form, Title I of the PUHCA mandated the dissolution of all utility holding companies beyond the second "degree."[20] This was the "death sentence" provision, and its retention was at the heart of the battle over the PUHCA. Those holding companies left standing were required to register with the Securities Exchange Commission (SEC), submit detailed information concerning their holdings, and obtain SEC approval prior to undertaking a host of financial transactions.[21] The SEC was also empowered to write rules of conduct in such areas as proxy solicitation, intrasystem loans, intercompany transactions, service contracts, and accounting methods. Finally, after January 1, 1938, the SEC was to undertake the reorganization of existing holding companies into single integrated utility systems.[22] Title II of the PUHCA granted the Federal Power Commission the power "to regulate the rates, security issues, and financial transactions of operating companies engaged in the interstate transmission of electricity."[23]

18. Senator George Norris of Nebraska, who led the fight to break the economic and political power of the electric power industry, would later judge the PUHCA to be one of the few New Deal measures to greatly enhance the quality of American life. Norris, *Fighting Liberal*, 375.

19. Wilcox, *Public Policies Toward Business*, 590.

20. Most prominent utility holding companies contained several "degrees," "layers," or "stories" above the actual energy-generating companies. For example, the Associated Gas and Electric structure contained twelve such degrees. Indeed, by 1932 it is estimated that more than three-quarters of the nation's electricity was controlled by sixteen top holding companies. The final PUHCA left standing so-called Father and Grandfather holding companies (first and second degrees), prohibiting "remoter generations in the sequence of control." Roosevelt's first proposal required the compulsory dissolution of all utility holding companies above the first degree. The final compromise, as previously stated, ordered holding companies above the second degree to be dismantled. For a full discussion, see Wilcox, *Public Policies Toward Business*, 585–94.

21. These included the issuance or acquisition of new securities, amendments to existing security rights, dividend payments, and the making of allowances for depreciation or plans for reorganization, dissolution, liquidation, or receivership.

22. The SEC was also granted the discretionary authority to make exceptions where reorganization would result in the loss of substantial economies, prevent geographical integration, or where the retention of holding company structures did not impair localized management, efficient operation, and effective regulation.

23. Hawley, *The New Deal and the Problem of Monopoly*, 336.

The politics of the PUHCA shares important affinities with my earlier analysis of railroad regulation in the Gilded Age. Like the Interstate Commerce Act, the PUHCA case is centrally a study in party coalition maintenance. As we saw in Chapter 2, during the administration of Grover Cleveland, Democrats made issue concessions to New York Mugwumps traditionally aligned with the Republican party, this in order to keep a pivotal group in line and hold together the coalition that brought them to power in 1884. In a similar vein, New Deal Democrats sought to hold the allegiance of progressive Republicans whose active support was an important element in Roosevelt's 1932 election victory. As I will argue, Roosevelt's relentless push for the dissolution of public utility holding companies is best understood against the backdrop of efforts to retain the support of this critical coalition group, and in so doing, to ensure the Democratic party's continuing hold on national governing power.

The PUHCA also diverges in significant ways from each of our previous cases. In the case of both the Reagan bill under Grover Cleveland and the Clayton bill under Woodrow Wilson, agrarian political goals ultimately succumbed to more pressing party needs. In each case, the antimonopoly impulse among members of the Democratic party's core constituencies was pushed aside for policies targeting party allies with more tenuous political allegiances. By contrast, coalitional imperatives forced Franklin Roosevelt to align himself closely with this long-standing agrarian tradition. With regard to the electric power industry, administration leaders secured a political outcome considerably more radical than anything congressional Democrats would have embraced in the absence of persistent presidential pressure. Thus, rather than putting the brakes on agrarian radicalism, as previous Democratic administrations had sought to do, Roosevelt moved far to the left of his congressional party in pressing for the statutory dissolution of public utility holding companies. By taking up the antimonopoly mantel, Roosevelt hoped to demonstrate his commitment to progressive reform and thereby buttress flagging support among midwestern progressive Republicans.

A final point of distinction with previous chapters: By the coming of the "Age of Roosevelt," presidential party leadership had significantly supplanted congressional party leadership as an instrument of national coalition management. Thus while this chapter affirms the continued importance of electoral college and party system constraints on regulatory choice, it also serves notice that, with the advent of the New Deal, the particulars of our party-analytic framework have once again been substantially reworked. E. E. Schattschneider concluded his study of pressure groups and the tariff with the observation that "new policies create a new politics." One might add to this insight: so too do new institutions.[24] Prior party decisions to build up national administrative capacities helped precipitate changes among the key actors and standard practices of national party leadership by augmenting the power and prestige of the presidency.[25] The politics of the PUHCA almost perfectly captures this altered state of affairs. A unilateral administration initiative, the PUHCA illustrates a growing presidential independence from traditional party mechanisms of policy formation and legislative consensus building.[26]

Adding urgency to these developments, institutional changes in Congress had progressively undermined the influence of traditional party mechanisms in the process of legislation: for example, the dismantling of the House speakership as an instrument of party leadership, the decline of the party caucus as a consensus-building organ, and the rise of the seniority system as a mechanism for routinely distributing institutional assignments with minimal regard for the preferences of party leaders. Such changes eroded partisan unity in Congress, weakened institutional leadership, and promoted rank-and-file independence on policy matters. As a result, Roosevelt's controversial holding company bill lacked the effective party backing that had eased the passage of contentious legislation in the eras of Grover Cleveland and Woodrow Wilson. In the battle to pass the PUHCA, a more public and confrontational form of presidential leadership was manifest, one including protracted administration lobbying, extensive public relations efforts, and extended negotiations to meet the concerns of congressional power barons. None of these tactics was original to Franklin Roosevelt. What sets this case apart from our two previous analyses is Roosevelt's systematic reliance on such tactics to compensate for the absence of party discipline in the pursuit of a new Democratic majority. Such features are characteristic of the contemporary "bargaining" and "going public"

24. Schattschneider, *Politics, Pressures and the Tariff*, 288.
25. In the battle for New Deal reform, Roosevelt was able to draw on the institutional resources and/or individual talents of the Federal Power Commission, the Federal Trade Commission, the Interstate Commerce Commission, the Securities and Exchange Commission, the Reconstruction Finance Corporation, the Public Works Administration, the Federal Deposit Insurance Corporation, and the Home Owners Loan Corporation – not to mention the resources and talents of traditional executive departments, like Justice and Treasury.
26. An important recent study of the efforts and consequences of Franklin Roosevelt's desire to transcend traditional party constraints is Sidney Milkis, *The President and the Parties: The Transformation of the American Party System Since the New Deal*.

presidency and distinguish the traditional party-centered polity we have observed from an emergent president-centered polity.[27]

The rest of this chapter is organized in four sections. "Progressivism with a Capital *R*" examines the national electoral incentives that drove the Democratic party's persistent pursuit of progressive Republicans. This section also situates the antimonopoly impulse and progressive animosity toward the Power Trust within the context of Democratic electoral politics. "Discontent and Disillusionment" examines growing progressive Republican disenchantment with the cartelizing and conservative tendencies of the early New Deal. "The 'Death Sentence' for Public Utility Holding Companies" examines the development of the PUHCA within the executive branch as well as Roosevelt's embrace of the so-called death sentence for utility holding companies. "Presidential Party Leadership in the Making of a Second New Deal" analyzes presidential party leadership in Congress on behalf of the death sentence provision, highlighting the changing institutional context in which national party coalition politics was now conducted.

"Progressivism with a Capital *R*"

Marrying South to West: Resurrecting the Wilsonian Coalition of 1916

Woodrow Wilson would have instinctively recognized the electoral universe of 1932. Political alignments and elite divisions still conformed to the pattern set in motion in 1896. Republican hegemony in national politics remained its defining feature, while the central cleavage within the regime party continued to pit midwestern and western progressives against a conservative "Old Guard" located in the industrial Northeast. The Democratic party of Franklin Roosevelt instinctively relied on this electoral mapping to devise its campaign for the presidency. Its strategy was straightforward and yet, historically, had remained elusive: to resurrect Wilson's South–West coalition of 1916 through a series of issue-based appeals to progressive Republicans. "It was an old political idea," Roosevelt advisor Rexford G. Tugwell later recalled,

> . . . that of marrying the South to the West when the East could not be relied on, but in practice it had not often proved to be feasible. Bryan had not quite succeeded, Wilson hardly at all, and Smith had failed miserably. But Roosevelt meant to make the marriage; his courtship had begun long ago.[28]

27. On the bargaining presidency, see Neustadt, *Presidential Power*. On the "going public" presidency, see Kernell, *Going Public*.
28. Tugwell, *The Brains Trust*, 101. See also Lubell, *The Future of American Politics*, 57.

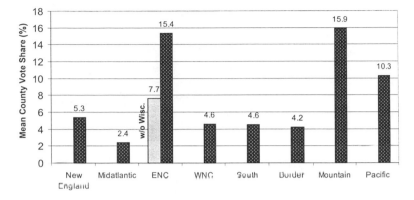

Figure 4.1. Regional support for Progressive party in 1924 presidential election.

While the Democrats could expect to benefit from the electorate's anti-depression, anti-Republican mood in 1932, party leaders nonetheless continued to look upon this South–West alliance as essential to solidifying their long-term hold on national power, when frustration with the Great Depression might be turned against the incumbent Democratic party.

Sowing the Seeds: Progressive Republicans, Al Smith, and the Presidential Election of 1928

To properly appreciate the relationship forged between progressive Republicans and the Democratic party in 1932, it is necessary to understand the ties laid down four years earlier. The presidential candidacy of Al Smith may have "failed miserably" as a national campaign, as Tugwell characterized it. But such an assessment overlooks the critical ways in which the Democratic campaign of 1928 helped condition the ground upon which Roosevelt's 1932 western strategy was built. In 1924, the run for the presidency by Robert La Follette, Sr., had laid bare the depth of western discontent within both of the major parties. As Figure 4.1 shows, La Follette's Progressive party ran particularly well in the Mountain and Pacific regions, as well as in the east-north-central states, even outside the candidate's home state of Wisconsin. The consequence was a precipitous decline in major party support in western progressive states. This decline is depicted in Figure 4.2, which shows that the mean county share of the 1924 Republican presidential vote in those states fell by a full quarter from its 1920 levels, from 68.5 percent to 51.5 percent.

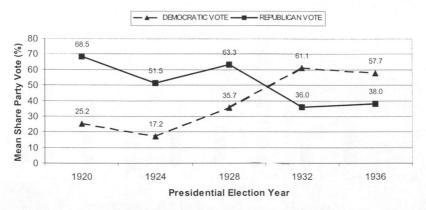

Figure 4.2. Mean county presidential vote share in progressive western states, 1920 to 1936.

Democrats were also hit hard. Their already meager county share shrunk by almost an additional one-third, from 25.2 percent to 17.2 percent. In a national campaign that could only be described as dismal, John W. Davis, the 1924 Democratic candidate, ran more than five percentage points *worse* in counties designated as progressive Republican than he did in those outside the region, even after controlling for a set of economic, demographic, and political variables (see first column, Table 4.1).

In response to La Follette's showing in 1924, Democrats took concrete steps to capitalize on western discontent, making a determined pitch for the western progressive vote in 1928. The Democratic platform of that year included not only a condemnation of the Republican party for its opposition to McNary-Haugen and its greater attentiveness to the economic problems plaguing industry than agriculture. It also committed the Democratic party to a program of price stabilization for agricultural products, the principle of parity, a federal farm marketing board, federal aid for the development of co-operative marketing associations, and a commitment to aggressively administer the federal rural credits program.[29] As James L. Sundquist wrote: After being rebuffed by Republican leaders at their national convention in Kansas City, western "agrarians were 'welcomed with open arms' in Houston. Their farm plank was accepted almost verbatim."[30] In addition, "not in a penny-pinching mood," Democratic National Committee Chairman John J. Raskob

29. Porter and Johnson, *National Party Platforms, 1840–1972.*
30. Sundquist, *Dynamics of the Party System,* 189.

Table 4.1. *Regression Estimates of County-level Vote for Democratic Presidential Candidates, 1924–1936*

	1924 John Davis	1928 Al Smith	1932 FDR	1936 FDR
Democratic Party Vote (1920)	0.9036** (.0107)	——	——	——
Democratic Party Vote (1924)	——	0.6973** (.0147)	——	——
Democratic Party Vote (1928)	——	——	0.7479** (.0138)	——
Democratic Party Vote (1932)	——	——	——	0.9696** (.0078)
1924 Progressive Party Vote	−0.1383** (.0139)	0.2373** (.0196)	0.0996** (.0123)	−0.0435** (.0130)
Progressive Republican States (1932)	−5.7090** (.4197)	4.0202** (.5635)	3.8309** (.4260)	−0.9095* (.4506)
% County Foreign Born	−0.3246** (.0419)	1.1611** (.4494)	−0.7091** (.0382)	0.1724** (.0370)
Per Capita Value Added in Mfg. ($1,000s)	−0.5896 (1.0478)	−2.0521* (1.0582)	−3.8924* (1.8375)	5.2937** (1.3771)
% County Rural Business	−0.0305** (.0107)	−0.0173 (.0148)	−0.0423** (.0129)	−0.0117 (.0092)
% County Rural Farming	0.1632** (.0105)	0.0783** (.0135)	0.0389** (.0144)	−0.0837** (.0084)
Per Capita Capital Intensity in Farming (in Dollars)	−0.0451** (.0039)	0.0110* (.0053)	−0.0015 (.0045)	−0.0267** (.0046)
Constant	2.2421** (.9131)	2.4362** (1.1043)	35.8256** (1.0949)	5.2817** (.8573)
(N)	(2,514)	(2,528)	(2,525)	(2,524)
Adjusted R²	.9125	.6421	.7219	.8739

** = p < .01; * = p < .05.
Note: Regression analysis performed using the method of ordinary least squares (with Huber Standard Errors in Parentheses).

approved expenditures totaling $500,000 to help organize the effort to swing the western farm vote. With Democratic money, independent agricultural leagues were organized in Illinois, Indiana, Ohio, Iowa, Missouri, Wisconsin, Nebraska, Minnesota, North Dakota, South Dakota, and Montana. While coordinating its activities with the

Democrats, these organs nonetheless operated "completely independent of local party control." As one study concludes, "Not often in the country's history had such a concentrated campaign been planned to influence a specific class of voters on a single issue in a definite area."[31]

The Democrats' selection of a "wet" Irish-Catholic as their 1928 presidential candidate ultimately imposed a heavy liability on the party's national electoral performance. Nevertheless, the final tally revealed encouraging trends for the Democrats out West. With La Follette removed from the field in 1928, both parties registered gains in western progressive states. But the Republican vote remained 5 percentage points below its 1920 level (see Figure 4.2). By contrast, Democrats not only recouped their 1924 losses, they registered gains almost 40 percent higher than they had in 1920, achieving a mean county share of 35.7 percent of the vote. Smith performed particularly well in counties that had gone for La Follette in 1924.[32] As Table 4.1 indicates, for every 10 percent increase in the county share of the 1924 Progressive party vote, the 1928 Democratic vote increased an additional 2.4 percent. Overall, Smith also ran four points better in counties located in the progressive West than in those outside the region.

At the elite level, progressive Republicans divided between the major parties in 1928. Among the western farm state leaders who rallied behind the Democratic party were George Peek, Chester Davis, Henry A. Wallace, and, most prominently, Senator George Norris of Nebraska. The acknowledged "dean" of western progressives, Norris would later term the 1928 presidential election his "political Rubicon." Norris had a long history of bolting the Republican party in support of progressive third-party candidates. He had thrown his support behind Theodore Roosevelt's Bull Moose bid in 1912 and he was an active supporter of Robert La Follette's Progressive party in 1924. But in crossing over to support a Democrat in 1928, Norris effectively severed his ties with the Republican party mainstream. A "power progressive" who for years had agitated on behalf of public-sponsored electrical energy development, Norris had acquired an "intense interest" in Al Smith's actions on behalf of water-power development as the governor of New York. Acting through his Secretary of State Robert Moses, Governor Smith would seek a conference with Norris to formalize the latter's support. Initially noncommittal, Smith's subsequent statements on behalf of the McNary-Haugen principle and government ownership and operation of federal

---

31. Fite, "The Agricultural Issue in the Presidential Campaign of 1928," 664.
32. This finding is consistent with those found in Fite, "The Agricultural Issue in the Presidential Campaign of 1928," 671.

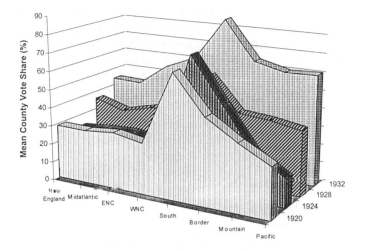

Figure 4.3. Regional vote for Democratic party, 1920 to 1932.

water power sites, and his denunciation of the Power Trust eventually earned the Democrat Norris's public endorsement.[33]

Reaping the Harvest: Progressive Republicans, Franklin Roosevelt, and the Presidential Election of 1932

While Smith's inroads into the progressive Republican West were significant, they were dwarfed by Roosevelt's depression-era accomplishments in the region. Figure 4.3 depicts graphically the magnitude of the Democrats' success in resurrecting Woodrow Wilson's South–West coalition in 1932, by comparing it to their regional inroads in the three previous presidential campaign efforts. Two trends are evident in Figure 4.3. First, the patterns highlight Al Smith's earlier success in the West. But more dramatically, it further makes clear the enormous Democratic gains achieved in 1932 relative to previous years. In progressive Republican states, the mean share of the county Democratic vote grew by more than two-thirds from 1928 levels to over 60 percent of the total vote – much of this no doubt fueled by the depression (Figure 4.2). Indeed, the decision to reconstruct the western progressive coalition seems strategically prescient in light of setbacks suffered in other areas. Multivariate analysis indicates that Roosevelt was unable to hold onto a sizable segment of Smith's support in counties with substantial foreign-born

33. Lowitt, *George W. Norris*, 410–11; Norris, *Fighting Liberal*, 287.

populations (Table 4.1).[34] Neither did the Great Depression appear to galvanize the Democratic vote in either urban or rural counties with sizable business communities. By contrast, Roosevelt ran almost 4 percentage points better in the counties of the progressive West that he did elsewhere, even after controlling for the 1928 Smith vote. His support was also positively correlated with the size of the county-level vote for Robert La Follette in 1924; the Democrat's county vote share increased by 1 percent for every 10 percent increase in support for the 1924 Progressive party. There seemed to be no denying that Roosevelt had won the West to the Democratic party, or at least to his presidency. The two questions that remain to be considered are: 1) How did Roosevelt accomplish it? And 2) What would it take to keep the West firmly in the Democratic party's orbit?

George Norris, the Power Trust,
and the Persistence of Agrarian Antimonopolism in
the American Political Tradition

Democratic success in the progressive West was in large part accomplished by the exodus of progressive Republican elites to the Roosevelt campaign, a mobilization far beyond anything Smith had been able to accomplish. Ensconced in Roosevelt's camp, western progressive leaders worked actively to mobilize the agrarian vote for the Democratic candidate. This cross-party elite movement was not simply the product of economic depression, though this was clearly a conditioning factor. More important, it was the culmination of a conscious strategy by Democrats in general, and Roosevelt in particular, to embrace themes and commitments that had long been a part of the progressive agenda. Few of these issues were more prominent than the economic and political dominance of the Power Trust, an issue that revealed the continuing salience of the ideology of agrarian antimonopolism in the American political landscape of the 1930s.

---

34. This is not surprising. In the first place, Roosevelt was not Smith. Smith was urban, ethnic, and Catholic. Roosevelt was a Yankee and a protestant patrician. On this ground alone, Roosevelt could not have the same appeal as Smith to immigrant voters. Moreover, Roosevelt ran an orthodox Democratic campaign in 1932, precisely because of Smith's disastrous showing in 1928. Roosevelt went back to the old formula of cultivating western Republicans, who were more protestant, rural, and native. Thus, immigrants would find less of interest in Roosevelt's substantive statements than they had with Smith, despite the former's antiprohibition stance. Roosevelt's appeal among immigrant voters would improve substantially in 1936, as his rhetoric and programmatic reorientation spoke more directly to their needs and experiences.

Among western progressive Republicans, George W. Norris and Robert La Follette, Jr., were at the pinnacle of prestige and influence in 1932. Between them, Norris best embodied the agrarian antimonopoly tradition we have tracked in this book, and he channeled his antipathy toward predatory bigness with particular fervor into an assault on utility holding companies. At the heart of Norris's career was a commitment to breaking apart the power monopolies, and his alienation from the Republican party arose in large part from its silence on this matter. In particular, Norris condemned utility holding companies as parasitic, their only function to "suck excess profits" from operating companies and consumers. In his own state of Nebraska, he had witnessed one such super-holding company, the Electric Bond and Share, extract $751,588 in dividends in one year, a return of 96.45 percent on its investment.[35] To be sure, La Follette was equally antagonistic to utility holding companies. But he was less enamored of the antimonopoly approach to business reform. In 1934, for example, his Progressive party would call for public ownership of public utilities as an alternative to the antimonopoly or trust-busting approach. While Norris was not averse to the principle of public ownership, he was convinced that such a solution was a nonstarter in American politics. Instead, Norris embraced the Brandeisian creed of decentralization, an ideology that the historian Ellis W. Hawley has succinctly characterized:

> Centralized wealth, centralized control, and centralized location, [Brandeisians] felt, were . . . all aspects of a broad general trend that should be reversed. . . . Large, monopolistic organizations, they held, were not the result of technological imperatives. They grew instead from the desire to avoid competition, the desire for promoters' profits, and the fact that "finance" simply went out and forcibly merged "a flock of little business concerns for milking purposes."[36]

As one manifestation of this decentralized vision of the American political economy, Norris called for legislation to dissolve public utility holding companies above the first degree – the so-called death sentence

35. Lief, *Democracy's Norris*, 391.
36. Hawley continues: "In most industries, [Brandeisians] argued, the size of greatest efficiency was reached at a comparatively early stage. Further growth depended upon financial manipulation, monopolistic devices, or the use of unfair practices. It followed that if such devices and practices were eliminated, huge corporations would not be created, or if created, they would not be successful. Competition, in other words, could and should be restored and maintained. The only exception was in dealing with 'natural monopolies,' with those few areas of economic endeavor where duplication of facilities was obviously wasteful. For such areas, government operation, or at least yardsticks, offered the best solution." Hawley, *The New Deal and the Problem of Monopoly*, 287.

as utility propagandists would label it during legislative action on the PUHCA in 1935.[37]

A good case could be made that an enlightened public policy should distinguish between "good" and "bad" holding companies, in much the same way that Theodore Roosevelt had insisted on differentiating between "good trusts" and "bad trusts." Holding companies could perform valuable functions. As two of the leading authorities of the day put it: "the holding company is the most effective device that has ever been invented for combining under a single control and management the properties of two or more hitherto independent corporations."[38] In the electric power industry, for example, holding companies facilitated centralize managerial control over local operating companies by skilled experts, they also unified their financial structure and provided greater access to capital markets, and they centralized voting control over subsidiaries with a minimum investment.

But by the 1930s, centralized control over the public utilities industry had become extreme, concentrated in the hands of "ten great groups of systems" controlling 75 percent of the country's electric light and power business – the most prominent among them being United Corporation, Electric Bond and Share, and the notorious Insull Utilities.[39] Within these utility groups, holding companies were stacked upon holding companies, sometimes reaching eight, ten, or even twelve layers high. It was impossible to justify the existence of such structures by the engineering or managerial efficiencies they brought to the generation and transmission of public power. Among power progressives and other critics, these holding company structures had more insidious designs. They allowed engineering and manufacturing groups to capture stable markets for their products and services at inflated prices; they facilitated financial sleights-of-hand like stock watering and asset overvaluation; and they allowed end-runs around state efforts to regulate operating companies. The result, almost everyone conceded, was a highly uneconomic form of consolidation: unwieldy regional or multiregional systems of noncontiguous, nonintegrated operating companies whose only unifying rationale seemed to be plunder from above at the expense of the power consuming public. To critics of the antimonopoly stamp, proposals to regulate

37. Roosevelt used the term "utility propagandists" to explain the origin of the term "death sentence," as applied to Section 11 of the Senate's Public Utility Holding Company bill calling for mandatory dissolution. See Rosenman, ed. *The Public Papers and Addresses of Franklin D. Roosevelt* 1938 vol., 549.

38. Bonbright and Means, *The Holding Company*, 4. The following discussion draws on their analysis of public utility holding companies.

39. Ibid., 91.

these entities were beside the point. The economic and political power wielded by the Power Trust made these structures a cancer on the body politic. No holding company above the first degree could be justified; all others should be exterminated, root and branch.

Franklin Roosevelt had courted power progressives like Norris for years. The task had been easy, in large part because Roosevelt took a genuine interest in the subject of public power and he had accumulated considerable expertise in the area. But Roosevelt was also an ambitious politician with national aspirations, and he believed that the key to placing a Democrat in the White House lay in the progressive West, especially in those states with strong traditions of independent or third-party politics, like the Wisconsin of Robert La Follette, Jr., Henrik Shipstead's Minnesota, and George Norris's own home state of Nebraska. Among Roosevelt and his political operatives, like James A. Farley, "there was never any question that Norris would use his enormous prestige to support the repeated efforts to establish a third party in the name of a new liberalism." Democrats therefore had to channel and exploit these reform impulses; that was the essence of "the politics of victory." The challenge facing Democrats "was not to *encourage* the protest and radicalism of the decade of depression," as one study of New Deal era party politics has observed, "but to use it or snuff it out if they could not."[40]

As governor of New York, Roosevelt openly courted a favorable reputation with power progressives by his aggressive stance toward the state utility companies. He was well aware "that the attitude many powerful Western leaders might assume toward [him] would depend in part upon his stand on power."[41] In his inaugural address as governor, on January 1, 1929, Roosevelt insisted:

> It is also the duty of our representative bodies to see that this power which belongs to all the people, is transformed into useable electrical energy and distributed to them *at the lowest possible cost. It is our power; and no inordinate profits must be allowed to those who act as the people's agents* in bringing this power to their homes and workshops. If we keep these two fundamental facts before us, half the problem disappears.[42]

In an effort to translate rhetoric into results, Roosevelt led the fight to create the New York Power Authority, a new state agency with the

40. Freidel, *Franklin D. Roosevelt: The Triumph*, 43–44; Newquist, "James A. Farley and the Politics of Victory: 1928–1936," Vol. 2, 442, 439 (emphasis added).
41. Freidel, *Franklin D. Roosevelt: The Triumph*, 43.
42. Roosevelt's gubernatorial inaugural address is quoted in King, *The Power Records of Hoover and Roosevelt*, Bulletin no. 157 (September 9), 15. Italicized passages are from the original.

authority "to finance, build, own, and operate generating facilities" on natural power sites like the St. Lawrence River. The governor asserted his preference to keep the transmission and distribution of water power in the hands of private enterprise, assuming the latter could limit themselves to earning a fair return on their investment. However, Roosevelt warned, if such arrangements did not satisfy the utility concerns, "then the State may have to go into the transmission business itself." Roosevelt's statements attracted national attention. And though power progressives considered it only a halting first step in a permanent solution to the power problem, Norris praised Roosevelt for taking a "very brave step in the right direction."[43]

The public power issue, then, was a vehicle upon which Roosevelt might channel western protest energies toward the Democratic party. In the late 1920s and early 1930s, the twin subjects of electric power generation and the Power Trust loomed large in the public mind. John Dewey termed the power issue "the most weighty single issue in the political field."[44] And, in a more important barometer of national political salience, fourteen western progressive senators signed a public declaration proclaiming "The Significance of the Power Question" to the 1932 presidential election.

> We regard the power question in its economic, financial, industrial and social aspects as one of the most important issues before the American people in this campaign of 1932.
>
>   Its political significance cannot be over estimated and must challenge the attention of those interested in any progressive movement or measure. The reason is plain. The combined utility and banking interests, headed by the Power Trust, have the most powerful and widely organized political machine ever known in our history. This machine cooperates with other reactionary economic, industrial and financial groups. It is strenuously working to control the nomination of candidates for the Presidency and the Congress of both dominant political parties.[45]

---

43. Rosen, *Hoover, Roosevelt, and the Brains Trust*, 8–10; Freidel, *Franklin D. Roosevelt: The Triumph*, ch. 8; Davis, *FDR: The New York Years*, 76–77.
44. Schlesinger, *The Crisis of the Old Order*, 124.
45. King, *The Power Records of Hoover and Roosevelt*, Bulletin no. 153 (March 18). The statement appears on the cover of the publication. It is signed by western Republican senators Smith W. Brookhart (Iowa), Bronson Cutting (N. Mex.), Lynn J. Frazier (N. Dak.), R. B. Howell (Nebr.), Hiram Johnson (Calif.), George Norris (Nebr.), and Gerald P. Nye (N. Dak.), and western Democratic senators Edward P. Costigan (Colo.), C. C. Dill (Wash.), Thomas J. Walsh (Mont.), and Burton K. Wheeler (Mont.). Three senators from southern Democratic states also signed the power statement: Thomas P. Gore (Okla.), Huey P. Long (La.) and Kenneth McKellar (Tenn.).

Roosevelt's struggles on behalf of cheap, publicly controlled electricity generation in New York ultimately earned him the support of power progressives. Norris himself took the lead in backing Roosevelt. The senator from Nebraska was adamant that "Roosevelt comes closer to representing the idea of standing for the people against monopoly than any other man who apparently has any show for the [Democratic] nomination."[46] Norris's own activities on behalf of Roosevelt's nomination were sufficiently aggressive that, in some quarters, he was charged with "trying to control the Democratic National Convention."[47]

Louis Howe, a Roosevelt strategist, approached Norris through intermediaries to obtain advice on the most effective ways to mobilize the progressive Republican vote for Roosevelt. Specifically, Howe asked about the necessity for an organization, detached from the regular party machinery, to reach out to independents.[48] The outgrowth of these conversations was the establishment of the National Progressive League (NPL) for the Election of Roosevelt and Garner. The NPL set up publicity offices in Washington, a national speakers' bureau, radio and finance operations in New York, and membership and fieldwork offices in Chicago. In the end, a national committee of both Democratic and Republican progressives representing three-fourths of the states was put together, though the organization remained in principle "a place for Republicans to hang their hats for FDR."[49] Norris was named NPL chairman, with progressive Democrat E. P. Costigan its vice-chair. Members of the NPL constituted a who's who of Theodore Roosevelt progressives and Wilsonian liberals, including Donald Richberg, Frederick C. Howe, Henry A. Wallace, Frank Murphy, Bainbridge Colby, Felix Frankfurter, Ray Stannard Baker, and Amos Pinchot. Progressive Republican senators Robert La Follette, Jr., Hiram Johnson, and Bronson Cutting also threw their support behind Roosevelt in 1932, and in latter days of the election the NPL played an active role in winning the West for Roosevelt.

Throughout the campaign Norris pushed Roosevelt to make strong public statements on power development and utility regulation as the most effective way to connect with rank-and-file progressive Republicans. Such themes, Norris assured Basil Manley, Roosevelt's advisor on power questions, would rally progressives more surely than any other issue. When only silence ensued, Norris wrote Manley in frustration that many "of the

46. Letter from George Norris to Norman Hapgood, (May 10, 1932). Norman Hapgood Manuscripts, Manuscript Division, Library of Congress.
47. Norris to Hapgood (May 10, 1932).
48. Lief, *Democracy's Norris*, 393.
49. Watkins, *Righteous Pilgrims*, 272.

Progressives have been somewhat disappointed with Roosevelt since his nomination because he has remained practically silent on the subject" of public power. From Muscle Shoals to utility holding companies, progressives waited for Roosevelt to issue a national power policy statement that would rally western Republicans to the Democratic standard.[50]

Roosevelt's most explicit statement on the public-power question finally came on September 21, during a campaign stop in Portland, Oregon. The Portland speech was important both for what it promised and for what it avoided. There the Democrat affirmed his party's platform call for a program of utilities regulation "to the full extent of federal power," offering an eight-point program that encompassed energy creation, rate regulation, and the problem of utility holding companies. Roosevelt's strongest statements involved his call for the development of federal water power sites and his support for government-owned and operated power stations, the latter to provide a yardstick to gauge fair rates and efficient service by private utility companies. His statements regarding the regulation of the power industry, on the other hand, were more cautious, an indication of the deep party divisions on the subject. The centerpiece of the Democratic regulatory plan was the "sunshine" principle – full publicity involving capital issues, capital investment, stock ownership, earnings, and intercompany contracts and services. Regarding holding companies specifically, Roosevelt called for "regulation and control . . . by [the] Federal Power Commission and the same publicity . . . as provided for the operating companies."[51] In discussing the power problem, Roosevelt liberally drew from the strongly seasoned rhetoric of western progressivism. Thus, at one moment he was positioning himself above the petty squabbling of partisan politics, telling his audience: "When questions like this are under consideration, we are not Democrats, we are not Republicans – we are a people united in a common patriotism." At the next moment, however, Roosevelt was at his demagogic best, condemning the "Insull monstrosity," inveighing against the "selfish interests," and promising the "positive and active protection of the people against private greed."[52]

50. Feinman, *Twilight of Progressivism*, 39–41; Schlesinger, *The Crisis of the Old Order*, 421–2; Freidel, *Franklin D. Roosevelt: The Triumph*, 352. Basil Manley, along with Harold Ickes, had been involved in organizing La Follette's third-party bid in 1924. Roosevelt would appoint Manley to the Federal Power Commission. Ickes would become secretary of the interior. On the 1924 presidential candidacy of Robert La Follette, Sr., see MacKay, *The Progressive Movement of 1924*.
51. *The New York Times*, September 22, 1932, 16; Rosenman, ed. *The Public Papers and Addresses of Franklin D. Roosevelt* Vol. 1, 737–9.
52. *The New York Times*, September 22, 1932, 16.

But significantly, at no time did he indicate support for either anti-monopoly goals or means, like Norris's call for the death sentence for public utility holding companies. Indeed, to many of his advisors, Roosevelt seemed at this time to be moving in the opposite direction, toward support for a national policy of cartelization and suspension of the antitrust laws as a corrective to depression-induced deflation and cut-throat competition. His unflinching embrace of agrarian antimonopolism still lay in the future, induced by growing progressive frustration with the New Deal and the need to consolidate a Democratic majority in national politics.[53]

"Discontent and Disillusionment": Western Progressives Confront the First New Deal

Progressive Republicans were crucial to Roosevelt's election in 1932 and they remained crucial to his reelection in 1936. But these Westerners were growing increasingly disenchanted with the New Deal of the First Hundred Days. Recovery programs like the National Industrial Recovery Act (NIRA) and the Agriculture Adjustment Act (AAA) were among the most prominent aspects of the First Hundred Days to come under attack by progressive Republicans. But these erstwhile allies also took aim at Roosevelt's seemingly weak commitment to fundamental economic and political reform, such as in the area of labor rights.

Business Appeasement and Cartelization in the First New Deal

To be sure, the NIRA carried the brunt of progressive criticism. In the Senate, where the progressive bloc was most powerful, opposition was vociferous. Progressive Republicans argued that the National Recovery Administration (NRA) promoted monopoly, crippled small business, neglected labor, and gouged consumers. Opposition to Title I of the NIRA,

---

53. In office, the Roosevelt administration attacked the Power Trust in several ways other than the PUHCA, through: 1) the creation of "yardsticks" such as the TVA, 2) PWA subsidies and loans to municipalities to construct their own power plants or distribution services, 3) the publication of comparative rate surveys by the FPC, 4) the development of national projects like the Bonneville and Grand Coulee dams, 5) the creation of the Rural Electrification Administration to provide funds to enable rural cooperatives to construct their own distribution services. As Ellis Hawley put it, progressives hoped that "in time, an abundance of cheap and easily accessible power might be forthcoming, power that would do more than any prohibitory law to promote decentralization, reinvigorate the hinterland, and encourage a society of small competitive units." See Hawley, *The New Deal and the Problem of Monopoly*, 328–9.

which included provisions for drafting industrywide codes of fair competition, was particularly strong. To most members of the Senate progressive bloc these codes were little more than government-sponsored agreements to fix prices and reduce output, a clear violation of the antitrust laws. Urban liberals like Senator Robert F. Wagner, Democrat from New York, were more supportive of arrangements to limit price competition. Wagner, who introduced the administration's recovery measure, insisted to his progressive critics that the NIRA sought to secure the traditional objectives of the antitrust laws, but by employing twentieth-century methods. Antimonopoly ideology was obsessed with size and breaking apart large enterprise. But where large enterprise proved more efficient as an engine for generating wealth, public policy required that political leaders seek ways to harness that capacity and "reap its full benefits" for the mass of Americans. Toward this end, Wagner maintained, restraints on competition such as those found in the NIRA, were necessary. They would help place business competition on a more constructive plane. They would help to stamp out cutthroat price wars and thereby secure material gains for labor in the areas of wages, hours, and working conditions. The NIRA did not do away with competition, Wagner argued, but rather "it purifie[d] and strengthen[ed] it."[54]

But the monopolistic implications of the NIRA were too much for most progressives to embrace. Idaho progressive William Borah was most vocal in his denunciations of the NIRA, predicting that big business would ultimately come to "regulate the regulators," and thereby come to dominate the industrial code drafting process.[55] The result would be a legally sanctioned regime of industrial monopoly, with dire consequences for small business, labor, and consumers. In the course of Senate debate on the NIRA, Borah had successfully inserted an amendment to Title I, one which explicitly prohibited NRA codes from "permit[ting] combinations in restraint of trade, price fixing, or other monopolistic practices."[56] Even with his amendment in place, however, Borah could not bring himself to support the passage of the bill. But other progressive Republicans were appeased, unanimously backing the amended recovery measure.[57] It was a different matter, though, when the conference version of the NIRA returned to the Senate *without* the Borah Amendment. In the end, the NIRA passed the Senate on a vote of 46 to

54. Huthmacher, *Senator Robert F. Wagner and the Rise of Urban Liberalism*, 148–50. Schlesinger, *The Coming of the New Deal*, 100; Hawley, *The New Deal and the Problem of Monopoly*, 30–1.
55. Hawley, *The New Deal and the Problem of Monopoly*, 30.
56. *Congressional Record*, 73d Cong., 1st sess., Vol. 77, pt. 6, June 6, 1933: 5246.
57. Ibid., 5424.

39. In this instance, however, progressive Republicans broke with the administration-backed cartelization scheme, voting 2 to 8 against passage.[58]

Progressive hostility to the NIRA only deepened with time. Senator Gerald Nye from North Dakota generally characterized the NRA's Blue Eagle as "a 'bird of prey' on the masses." William Borah and Senator Arthur Capper from Kansas took up the cause of small business, insisting that these economic entities were being suffocated by monopolistic codes that advantaged dominant firms in each industry, and they called for the reinstatement of the antitrust laws. Farmer-Labor senator from Minnesota Henrik Shipstead and New Mexico progressive Bronson Cutting offered a consumerist and labor slant to their critiques. Shipstead condemned the NIRA as a program of price-gouging, one that sanctioned the same monopolistic practices responsible for precipitating the Great Depression in the first place. Cutting faulted the NIRA for raising prices faster than mass purchasing power and for not extending to labor the same rights and protections granted employers. Even George Norris, who generally avoided open criticism of the Roosevelt administration over NRA codes, wrote in private:

> [T]he N.R.A. has not in my judgement been a success. The tendency has been to give the big fellow an advantage over the little fellow, and I think mistakes have been made in trying to enforce rules which have been adopted.[59]

Continued progressive Republican suspicion of the NIRA was evident in two subsequent Senate actions. The first involved a Senate resolution by Gerald N. Nye requiring that NRA Director General Hugh Johnson submit the names and business ties, past and present, of all individuals holding positions of responsibility within the NRA. By a vote of 41 to 33, the resolution was defeated when Arkansas Democrat Joseph Robinson moved to send the resolution back to the Finance Committee.[60] Voting 41 to 4, Democrats provided all the support for the Robinson motion to kill the Nye amendment. Progressive Republicans, on the other hand, were unanimous in support of Nye's effort to investigate monopolistic influence within the NRA.[61] The second action of note involved a

---

58. Ibid., 5861. Nor were populist Democrats happy with the NRA. Senator Huey P. Long of Louisiana, after a scathing denunciation of the recovery measure reminiscent of William Jennings Bryan, declared "The Democratic Party dies tonight, Mr. President. We will bury it." Quoted in Schlesinger, *The Coming of the New Deal*, 101.

59. Feinman, *Twilight of Progressivism*, 72.

60. *Congressional Record*, 73d Cong., 2d sess., Vol. 78, pt. 3, June 6, 1933: 2845.

61. Eastern Republicans were also unanimous in opposition, no doubt hoping for partisan advantage by embarrassing the administration.

rider to a joint resolution on relief appropriations, offered by Borah, which sought to "restore the antimonopoly and antitrust laws suspended under the National Recovery Act." Among progressive Republicans, this vote was considerably more contentious than the final passage of the NIRA, in part because the intensity of the antimonopoly impulse varied across progressives, but more likely because Borah's rider might derail a much needed emergency relief bill. The amendment ultimately failed on a Senate vote of 33 to 43, but progressives continued to side with Borah on balance, voting 6 to 4 to reactivate the antitrust laws.[62]

Briefly, the Agricultural Adjustment Act also came in for its share of progressive criticism in the months leading into the November 1934 midterm elections. The deliberate destruction of crops and animals in order to inflate prices appalled many progressives. Former governor of Wisconsin Philip La Follette termed the destruction of wealth a "cock-eyed" strategy for ending hard times. A number of progressives criticized the administration's reliance on an underlying theory of overproduction to explain the depression and prescribe its solutions. It was this preoccupation with the supply side of the equation that led Roosevelt to embrace programs to restrain initiative, restrict output, and destroy crops. The real problem, progressives maintained, were underconsumption and problems of distribution. Borah held that farmers should be encouraged to produce more, not less. "Limitation of production," he asserted, "is death to any industry." Norris likewise criticized the immorality of crop destruction at a time when deprivation was so rampant in the country.

Business Appeasement and the Failure to Support Fundamental Structural Reform

Finally, as we saw at the top of this chapter, Roosevelt's heavy-handed handling of labor legislation also brought forth sharp criticisms from progressives. Senator Robert Wagner's Labor Dispute Act of 1934 was popular with both progressive Republicans and liberal Democrats alike. It sought to create a labor board with the power to compel testimony and information, resolve representational disputes, arbitrate management–labor conflicts, issue cease-and-desist orders, and enforce its orders in court. Progressives saw the Wagner bill as consonant with their commitment to both recovery and structural reform. Unionization and collective bargaining would help resolve the problem of underconsumption and thereby promote economic recovery. On the other hand,

62. *Congressional Record*, 74th Cong., 1st sess., Vol. 79, pt. 4, June 6, 1933: 4183.

it would also right the imbalance in political power between management and workers and promote greater equity and democracy in the workplace.

Roosevelt's silence on the issue worried both liberal Democrat and progressive Republican friends of fundamental labor reform. Moving into the 1934 elections, Roosevelt seemed to be bending over backwards to quell growing business disenchantment with the New Deal. The version of Wagner's bill finally embraced by the White House gutted virtually all of Wagner's most important features. In this new bill, intervention by the Labor Board would be authorized only at the behest of the labor secretary. More limiting still, intervention would be authorized only in the case of a strike or the threat of a strike. To make matters worse, the administration version dropped Wagner's prohibition on company unions, while the refusal of employers to bargain with the certified representatives of workers was dropped from Wagner's list of unfair labor practices.

The *coup de grace* for progressives, however, was Roosevelt's decision to back away from even this watered-down measure. Instead, Roosevelt substituted Senate Resolution 143, a stop-gap labor measure, which would give the president the statutory authority for one year to create fact-finding labor boards to "investigate issues, facts, practices or activities of employers or employees in any controversies arising under Section 7(a)," the labor section of the NIRA. Having already passed the House unanimously, Roosevelt next secured Wagner's support for the resolution. The low point for Senate Democrats occurred when La Follette took to the Senate floor to initiate a fight for Wagner's *original* measure. "[O]ne of the most embarrassing moments of [Wagner's] whole political life," the New York Democrat found himself uncomfortably situated in between his loyalty to the administration and his commitment to progressive labor reform. Wagner sought to rationalize the delay to progressives, arguing that the hectic pace of New Deal innovation required a respite, in order to assess the effectiveness of existing programs and to allow an opportunity for "the processes of learning and understanding to catch up with the social program that has been inaugurated." But Roosevelt's timidity on behalf of labor reform, along with the willingness of even staunch liberal Democrats like Robert Wagner to fall into line with administration positions, generated substantial bitterness on the part of the Senate progressive Republican bloc.[63] The conservative nature of Roosevelt's stop-gap measure and the party discipline exhibited by Senate Democrats on behalf of the measure called into question the

63. Huthmacher, *Senator Robert F. Wagner and the Rise of Urban Liberalism*, 160–71.

commitment of the Roosevelt administration and the Democratic party to lasting economic and political reform.

Western Progressive Disaffection and the Elections of 1934

Evidence of western progressive dissatisfaction with the New Deal is suggested by the off-year election returns of 1934. Political scientists generally remember 1934 as the only midterm election of the twentieth century in which the president's party actually *gained* seats in Congress (nine in this instance). And while this is clearly a significant achievement, a closer look at the data reveals that all was not well in the states of the progressive West. Election returns show pattens of declining support adding fuel to concerns in the Roosevelt camp about eroding political support amongst progressives for the president's party in Congress. To be sure, congressional Democrats were never as strong in the West as Roosevelt had been. For example, Democratic congressional candidates registered no statistically significant gains in 1932 over 1930 in the counties comprising the progressive Republican West. At the same time, these same Democrats also ran about 12 percentage points behind Roosevelt in these counties. In this context, what is significant about the 1934 midterm elections is that Democratic support in the progressive West continued to decline. Controlling for a range of demographic and economic factors, Democrats in 1934 ran more than 6 points worse in western progressive counties than they did in 1932.[64] In part, these losses stemmed from the successful debut of the Wisconsin Progressive party, where Robert and Philip La Follette's third-party organization successfully contested seven of ten House races and decimated the local Democratic party. But even when Wisconsin is removed from the analysis, the overall trend remains strong. Democratic candidates running in these remaining progressive Republican states still ran almost 4 points behind their 1932 figures.

Against the backdrop of the 1934 midterm results, Roosevelt's invitation to Robert and Philip La Follette to visit the White House, discussed at the outset of this chapter, takes on additional significance. As will be recalled, on the subject of the 1936 presidential election, the brothers were noncommittal, unwilling to abandon the new party they had just successfully test run in Wisconsin. But they assured the president that progressive Republicans would continue to rally to his standard if he were to embrace a truly progressive agenda. Roosevelt indicated the necessity of progressive support to the success of the New Deal and

64. See Table 4.1 for the list of control variables used.

promised to seek their input in the "formation of an advanced progressive program." Roosevelt also made clear his desire for the support of the La Follettes in his own reelection bid.

The "Death Sentence" for Public Utility Holding Companies

Roosevelt's conversion from regulation to abolition of public utility holding companies, then, should be seen against the backdrop of the 1934 midterm elections, progressive Republican frustration with the monopolistic tendencies and weak-kneed reformism of the early New Deal, and Roosevelt's own growing preoccupation with reelection in 1936. As we have also seen, Roosevelt's public utterances during the 1932 presidential campaign contained no break with the holding company plank contained in the Democratic platform. An examination of Roosevelt's public utterances in 1933 and 1934 only serves to underscore this point. But all of this changed in early 1935. With the campaign to institute the death sentence, Roosevelt seized the mantle of antimonopolism in an effort to reenergize his progressive Republican support and preempt the possible formation of a liberal third party in 1936.

This should not be read to imply that Roosevelt harbored no independent commitment to reform the power industry. But the particular challenges he was willing to issue, the rhetoric he was willing to employ, and the enemies he was willing to make – these, by and large, were forged in the heat of the political moment, by exploiting the opportunities and possibilities that lay scattered in the crisis environment of the mid-1930s.

That said, the politics of the PUHCA did not unfold as neatly as these initial statements suggest. Far from it. Roosevelt faced substantial resistence from both the business community and rank-and-file Democrats in Congress, whose preferences still conformed to the 1932 platform. As a result, Roosevelt also moved cautiously. Until business openly broke with the New Deal, the Roosevelt administration moved in fits and starts on the death sentence. It was an ironic political stance for Roosevelt to stake out, as his insistence on the wholesale leveling of utility holding companies would hasten the final break with business.[65] Equally

---

65. The Chamber of Commerce's denunciation of the New Deal in May 1935 included strong criticism of the PUHCA. The chamber said in part: "The Utility Bill of 1935, as introduced in Congress, not only would seek to super-impose Federal regulation upon State regulation of operating companies, but would undertake to destroy utility holding companies, which have had a substantial part in the development of our electric and gas utilities and which have undoubtedly conferred upon large areas benefits

important, once the fight had been joined, the president's recalcitrance and his aggressive party leadership would also contribute to an erosion of the mastery he had hitherto exhibited over Congress. The Democratic coalition ruptured badly over the death sentence, in ways that anticipated the rise of the conservative coalition in Roosevelt's second term.[66]

But in the final analysis, Roosevelt's problems were as much institutional as they were ideological. Executive leadership was complicated by a revolution in congressional organization that had been put in place over the preceding generation. As we will see, the routinization of the seniority system, coupled with changing House norms and more fortuitous changes in the composition of Democratic leadership, all robbed Roosevelt of valuable congressional party assistance as the struggle over the death sentence intensified in the spring and summer of 1935. Developmentally, institutional changes in Congress would compel Roosevelt to exploit more systematically the possibilities of executive power, and in the process contribute to the redesign of national party leadership in an increasingly president-centered political system.

Policy Development and Party Leadership in the White House

If procedural change in Congress necessitated greater efforts at presidential policy leadership, the parallel growth of the executive branch considerably enhanced the president's capacity to aggressively seize that role. Institutionally, the executive establishment was a more densely populated environment in the 1930s than it had been at the time Wilson assumed office. In drafting legislation to address the problem of public power, Roosevelt could rely on the expertise, budget, and accumulated information bases of the Federal Power Commission (FPC), the Federal

which they otherwise would have lacked. . . . The destruction of enterprises not only will mean violation of fundamental principles but inevitable losses to millions of innocent investors. Even threat of destruction brings disadvantage to many communities through postponement of services they need for their development, and causes national loss through withholding from those industries most affected by unemployment, orders for construction and equipment that would afford a large aggregate of work." See *The New York Times*, May 3, 1935, 4.

66. Of the PUHCA, James Patterson wrote: "The vote on this bill was one of the most significant of the New Deal Years, for it revealed major Democratic defections from the administration. Having left the New Deal on one key issue, these Democrats were to find it easier to do so again and again. The public utilities holding-company bill thus marked an important milestone in the shift of essentially conservative Democratic senators from unhappy loyalty to open opposition." Patterson, *Congressional Conservatism and the New Deal*, 41.

Trade Commission (FTC), the Interstate Commerce Commission (ICC), and the newly created Securities and Exchange Commission (SEC), as well as the traditional departments like Treasury and Interior. The proliferation of departments, commissions, and agencies within the federal administrative apparatus also squared well with Roosevelt's managerial temperament, as he was a firm believer in delegating policy-making authority to multiple administrative units. What might be lost in the efficient and harmonious coordination of scarce executive resources, Roosevelt believed, was more than recouped in the larger quantity of information and the greater range of policy options that flowed upward in the ensuing bureaucratic competition for presidential attention.[67]

The genesis of the PUHCA reflected Roosevelt's capacity for policy development and his predilection for harnessing multiple and competing lines of authority. On July 5, 1934, Roosevelt created the National Power Policy Committee (NPPC), mandating it to coordinate governmental efforts to develop a unified national power policy and make electrical energy "more broadly available at cheaper rates to industry, to domestic and, particularly, to agricultural consumers."[68] Roosevelt appointed his interior secretary, Harold L. Ickes, to chair the NPPC. Ickes's appointment was symbolically important. A charter member of the National Progressive League, Ickes was among those progressive Republicans who had worked actively for Roosevelt's election in 1932. He was also one of the few progressive Republicans who had been willing to compromise their independence by accepting a position in the new Democratic administration. Ickes's appointment established a visible link between progressive Republicans and administration power policy. In establishing the NPPC, Roosevelt put Ickes on notice that the time was at hand to put before Congress "legislation on the subject of holding companies and for the regulation of electric current in interstate commerce." Ickes was instructed to take the lead in identifying "what lines should be followed in shaping this legislation."[69]

It soon became apparent to Ickes and other NPPC members, however, that their mandate to coordinate a public power policy was being

---

67. Neustadt, *Presidential Power and the Modern Presidents*, 131–2.
68. Rosenman, ed. *The Public Papers and Addresses of Franklin D. Roosevelt*, Vol. 4, 339, Letter to Secretary of the Interior Harold L. Ickes establishing the National Power Policy Committee. Hawley writes that the committee included Morris L. Cooke, Robert Healy, David Lilienthal, Edward Markham, Frank McNinch, Elwood Mead, and T. W. Norcross. Hawley, *The New Deal and the Problem of Monopoly*, 331, fn. 6.
69. Hawley, *The New Deal and the Problem of Monopoly*, 340.

undercut by Roosevelt's own actions. Without indicating as such, Roosevelt had given the green light to the FPC, the FTC, and the Treasury Department to develop their own approaches for dealing with utility holding companies and electrical energy prices. The most serious challenge to NPPC leadership came from Treasury, which put forward a graduated taxation scheme to streamline and eliminate intermediate holding company structures. An intercorporate dividend tax was to be levied "in proportion to the holdings of one company in others and the amount of income that such a company derived from its subsidiaries."[70] By comparison, the plan pushed by the NPPC substituted direct planning for indirect tax inducements and, more critically, it embraced *regulation* over Treasury's emphasis on the *elimination* of utility holding companies. Drafted by counsel Benjamin V. Cohen and White House aide Thomas Corcoran, the NPPC approach would reorganize and oversee existing holding companies with an eye toward simplification and eventual consolidation of the utilities industry into integrated and geographically contiguous regional power systems. Holding companies would survive, but under strict federal scrutiny. They would also be allowed to continue holding the securities and properties of other systems, but only where the SEC judged such actions consistent with the public interest.[71] In a memorandum to Ickes, Cohen outlined the philosophy undergirding the NPPC draft bill. Cognizant of FDR's antimonopoly rumblings on this issue, Cohen took pains to assert the plan's consistency with "the Brandeisian distrust of big business" and its contribution to the restoration of local control and regulation. However, undercutting his own position, Cohen insisted that "the bill did not fragment economic conglomerates simply because they were large, but only where greater size resulted in inefficiency, the restriction of competition, or the wielding of unbridled economic and political power."[72]

Cohen's emphasis on the regulation of holding companies put the NPPC scheme squarely at odds with the president's immediate political

---

70. Ibid., 331.
71. Funigiello, *Toward a National Power Policy*, 56; Hawley, *The New Deal and the Problem of Monopoly*, 331.
72. Funigiello, *Toward a National Power Policy*, 56. Funigiello writes: "Cohen did not contemplate total elimination of the holding company, but its strict regulation; for the industry was a very real actuality today, having large amounts of capital invested in it that could not be readily untied." Writing to Healy, Cohen continued: "[T]he bill does not outlaw the holding company but regulates and restricts the use of the holding company form and provides a mechanism through which, over a period of time, existing holding company structures may be simplified, and their field limited to a sphere where their economic advantages may be demonstrable." Ibid., 50.

interests. As early as late November 1934, at a meeting in Warm Springs, Georgia, Roosevelt had made clear his intention to pull utility holding companies up by their roots. No proposal could get the president's support without such a provision included.[73] As a result, Roosevelt was drawn to the Treasury plan. Use of the tax code to directly eliminate a large number of intermediate holding companies appealed both to Roosevelt's political imagination and to his sense of public drama. The NPPC proposal was a nonstarter on both counts. At the Warm Springs meeting, Roosevelt was adamant that "a holding company which exists for the control of operating companies was against the public interest and, since it [can't] be regulated, should be abolished."[74] In subsequent conversations, Roosevelt would concede the need to spare holding companies that performed managerial functions, "providing they are paid for the service of management only; and provided they do not hold stock in any of the companies in which they manage."[75] But the emphasis remained abolition, not regulation.

We know now that, at this point in time, Roosevelt was in the midst of a political juggling act. Anxious to lead a crusade against the Power Trust and rally progressive Republicans to his standard, Roosevelt also sought to check business defections from the New Deal and forestall the mobilization of the power industry until after legislation could be safely introduced in Congress. A subtle balancing politics ensued, as was manifest in Roosevelt's State of the Union address of January 4, 1935. There, to powerful effect, the president proceeded to trip over his prepared text. Copies of the text, which had been circulated earlier, referred simply to the need to restore "sound conditions to the electric power industry through abolition of the *evil features* of holding companies."[76] But in speaking before Congress, Roosevelt's stated goal was transformed into one to "'abolish the *evil* of holding companies.'"[77] In subsequent conversations with reporters, Roosevelt maintained that he couldn't recall his exact phrasing, but that he had meant to say "the *evils*" or "the *evil features*" of holding companies, suggesting, like his uncle Theodore,

---

73. Parrish, *Securities Regulation and the New Deal*, 154. See also, Leuchtenburg, *Franklin D. Roosevelt and the New Deal*, 154–5; Schlesinger, *The Politics of Upheaval*, 305–6.

74. Funigello, *Toward a National Power Policy*, 53; Lilienthal, *The Journals of David E. Lilienthal*, 42–3, 45. It is reported that neither Cohen, Ickes, or Healy attended the Warm Springs meeting. See Funigello, *Toward a National Power Policy*, 53, fn. 66.

75. Funigello, *Toward a National Power Policy*, 54.

76. Annual Message to Congress, January 4, 1935. In Rosenman, ed. *The Public Papers and Addresses of Franklin D. Roosevelt* Vol. 4, 23. (Emphasis added).

77. Funigello, *Toward a National Power Policy*, 57. (Emphasis added).

that he distinguished between "good" and "bad" holding companies.[78] Whether or not he personally held to this distinction, Roosevelt was clearly dissembling in his comments to the press. His decisive role in ensuring the inclusion of the death-sentence provision in the as yet unreleased PUHC bill makes this clear. Moreover, in the immediate aftermath of his State of the Union address, administration officials and allies took to the stump with strong populist rhetoric to drum up public support for the death sentence. Speaking before the Economic Club of New York, for example, Tennessee Valley Authority administrator David Lilienthal blasted utility holding companies as financial parasites that a proper federal power policy should seek to eliminate. Likewise, the FTC rushed to publish a report in which it would conclude that the elimination of utility holding companies was one of several "reasonably effective solution[s] to the holding company problem." In Congress as well, Sam Rayburn, a Texas Democrat, who along with Senator Burton Wheeler, also a Democrat, had attended White House strategy sessions, labeled the holding company "a conspiratorial instrument of Wall Street lawyers to enslave the country."[79]

Roosevelt's State of the Union address stoked the desire of power progressives to finally resolve the utility holding company problem. As *The New Republic* observed, Roosevelt's recently articulated stance toward the Power Trust "undoubtedly went a long way toward restoring friendly feelings" with progressive Republicans who, only "a few weeks ago . . . were greatly distressed over what they considered the trend of the President toward the right."[80] Pressure from progressives made Roosevelt increasingly anxious to place some form of holding company bill before Congress quickly. At a White House meeting on January 21, Roosevelt again indicated his preference for the Treasury's more dramatic tax plan. But after prolonged arguments with Cohen, Corcoran, and Ickes, Roosevelt finally agreed to the NPPC strategy, with one critical alteration. Embracing the NPPC's plan to construct an integrated and geographically contiguous power system, Roosevelt's nevertheless insisted that "a mandatory 'death sentence' for utility holding companies" be written into the final administration bill. All holding companies were to "be dissolved within a five year period unless the Federal Power Commission certified that their continuance was necessary for the operation of an economic unit in contiguous states," and in any such

---

78. Roosevelt Presidential Press Conference Number 191 (January 4, 1935). *Complete Presidential Press Conferences of Franklin D. Roosevelt* Vol. 5, 5–6.

79. Funigiello, *Toward a National Power Policy*, 58.

80. *The New Republic*, January 9, 1935, 244.

case, "the remaining holding companies would be limited to a single tier."[81] Roosevelt also ordered the NPPC draftsmen to "rewrite the language of the first section to include a violent denunciation of the holding company abuses condemned in the FTC report."[82]

Roosevelt's blanket insistence on the death sentence for utility holding companies was part of a political calculus to embrace the rhetoric and substance of antimonopolism. Swept aside were all arguments regarding the economic benefits of holding companies, such as their ability to diversify risk, raise capital, and provide both cheaper and better engineering and management services. Also dismissed were worries about the possible negative impact on securities prices, on investors, and on the savings of widows and orphans. This was to be a war waged on bigness, a battle between good and evil, in which extermination was the only feasible political goal. Writing some months later, *New York Times* columnist Arthur Krock would ascribe Roosevelt's unyielding insistence on the death sentence to his need for the support of western progressive Republicans in 1936. "This group is hot for the killing," the journalist wrote, "and he must stand by them to the end."[83] Politically, the fight for the death sentence was one in which the administration's political resolve might actually prove to be more important than the final goal itself. Indeed, in the end, progressives would judge Roosevelt and his allies more on their effort and determination than on the legislation actually secured.[84]

The public utility holding company bill was first introduced in Congress on February 6, 1935. Fearful of a congressional backlash against the submission of controversial legislation penned entirely in the White House, steps were taken to create the illusion that the NPPC bill had originated in Congress, under the sponsorship of Wheeler and Rayburn, the respective chairmen of the Senate and House committees on interstate commerce. As Cohen explained it at the time, "it is always helpful if Congress feels that the particular bill is their bill

81. Hawley, *The New Deal and the Problem of Monopoly*, 331–2; Funigiello, *Toward a National Power Policy*, 62.
82. Funigiello, *Toward a National Power Policy*, 63.
83. Quoted in Funigiello, *Toward a National Power Policy*, 88–9.
84. Of the final PUHC bill Norris himself remarked, "I am going to vote for the conference report. I believe that I do not disagree with [administration forces] on anything which ought to be in it. I am firmly of the belief, however, that this is a conference report which [administration forces were] induced to sign because [they] realized [they] could not get anything better. I am confident that [they are] not satisfied with it, and I also realize that in conference reports there must always be a compromise." Norris proceeded to state his continued opposition to the existence of holding companies beyond the first degree. *Congressional Record*, 74th Cong., 1st sess., 1935, 79, pt. 12: 14470.

and not the bill of the executive. Everyone may know that the executive branch has been very active when it is presented, still there is
that condition."[85] In the end, NPPC members agreed to submit their
own observations on the holding company problem in a separate report
to Congress.

As it turned out, the facade of congressional authorship served
Roosevelt well, for in the weeks following the introduction of the PUHC
bill in Congress, presidential leadership was weak and vacillating. In fact,
the more heated the controversy over the death sentence became, the
more Roosevelt seemed to recede into the political background. With
hindsight we now know that Roosevelt's coalition-building strategy was
still in a state of flux. Conscious of the need to swing his party to the
left to maintain the support from reform groups like the progressive
Republicans, Roosevelt was not yet ready to jettison business support
for the New Deal on the right. Unwilling to publicly endorse the death
sentence without a clearer sense of its political viability, Roosevelt
exploited the fiction that the bill was a congressional measure for all it
was worth. At a news conference conducted in the middle of February,
for instance, Roosevelt deflected questions designed to elicit his position
on the pending PUHC bill, telling reporters he had not yet seen the bill,
and that, besides, it was his policy not to comment on pending congressional legislation.[86] Perhaps more brazenly, Roosevelt used the fiction
of congressional origins to deflect political heat away from himself and
onto Democratic leaders in Congress. Informed by one Senate colleague,
James Byrnes, that his insistence on the death sentence was "putting the
President on the spot," Burton Wheeler, the PUHC bill's Senate sponsor,
explained that he "was not putting FDR on the spot because the death
sentence was his idea, not mine." When Byrnes responded, "Well I've
talked to the President and had him talked out of it but he said he was
standing behind you," an exasperated Wheeler insisted, "He isn't standing behind me – I'm standing behind him." For weeks such scenes appear
to have continued, until Wheeler finally confronted Roosevelt, telling the
president not to "give the impression you're willing to change because
this is your bill." While Roosevelt declined Wheeler's request that he
issue a statement of public support at that time, he did give the senator
a handwritten note in which he affirmed his commitment to the terms

85. Quoted in Funigiello, *Toward a National Power Policy*, 60. See also "Minutes of a
Meeting of the National Power Policy Committee," January 17, 1935; and Benjamin
Cohen to Robert Healy, January 9, 14, 1935, in ibid.
86. Roosevelt Presidential Press Conference Number 184, February 15, 1935. *Complete
Presidential Press Conferences of Franklin D. Roosevelt* Vol. 5, 113.

of the PUHC bill, telling Wheeler to use it in Congress if he needed it to assuage doubts.[87]

With Roosevelt initially unwilling to make full use his office, the PUHC bill languished in Congress. Finally, the president could no longer avoid declaring himself one way or the other regarding the death sentence. It was a turning point in the politics of the public utilities bill. On March 12, 1935, the NPPC issued its report to Congress on the development of a unified policy on power matters. Appended to the report was a message from the president that was inflammatory in its rhetoric, potent in symbolism, and uncompromising in its stated goals. In it, the patrician Roosevelt began his political metamorphosis into William Jennings Bryan. Roosevelt attacked what he termed the "private empires" that had been amassed by the Power Trust, and he defended plans for their immediate dissolution. The president invoked potent symbols to amass support, such as in his condemnation of utility holding companies for their "unwarranted and intolerable powers over *other people's money.*" Here, the president tapped the prestige of progressive icon Louis D. Brandeis, whose popular book *Other People's Money and How the Bankers Use It* had earlier attacked the activities of the Finance Trust. Simultaneously, he referenced the column "Other People's Money," a regular feature in *The New Republic*, whose author, John T. Flynn, easily equaled Roosevelt in his hostility toward utility holding companies. Locating the holding company devise outside the bounds of "American traditions of law and business," Roosevelt asserted that regulation "has small chance of ultimate success against the kind of concentrated wealth and economic power which holding companies have shown the ability to acquire in the utility field." They have "built up in the public utility field what has justly been called a system of private socialism which is inimical to the welfare of a free people."[88]

Roosevelt concluded his message to Congress with this antimonopolist manifesto.

Most of us agree that we should take the control and the benefits of the essentially local operating utility industry out of a few financial centers and give back that control and those benefits to the localities which produce the business and create the wealth. We can properly favor economically independent business, which stands on its own feet and diffuses power and responsibility among the many, and frowns upon those holding companies

87. Wheeler, *Yankee from the West*, 311–12.
88. "A Recommendation for the Regulation of Public Utility Holding Companies," March 12, 1935. In Rosenman, ed. *The Public Papers and Addresses of Franklin D. Roosevelt* Vol. 4, 101.

which, through interlocking directorates and other devices, have given tyrannical power and exclusive opportunity to a favored few. It is time to make an effort to reverse that process of the concentration of power which has made most American citizens, once traditionally independent owners of their own businesses, helplessly dependent for their daily bread upon the favor of a very few, who, by devices such as holding companies, have taken for themselves unwarranted economic power. I am against private socialism as much as I am against governmental socialism. The one is equally as dangerous as the other; and destruction of private socialism is utterly essential to avoid governmental socialism.[89]

Presidential Party Leadership in the Making of a Second New Deal

Executive branch domination of the PUHCA drafting process is only the first indication of the changed institutional context in which party leaders had traditionally acted. As we observed in Chapter 2, the Interstate Commerce Act was purely a creature of Congress, with national party leadership almost exclusively the province of congressional party leaders. Even in the Progressive era, for all its documented innovations in presidential leadership, Woodrow Wilson still acted principally as first among equals with congressional draftsmen in the framing of the "Five Brothers." Wilson articulated principles of action, but left it to the House Judiciary Committee to craft legislation that was consistent with both national party goals and congressional party needs. Roosevelt abandoned this Wilsonian protocol almost entirely, drafting the PUHCA within the executive branch and pressing a reluctant Democratic Congress to accept its most salient features as written.

It might be argued that the above characterization is overdrawn, that a more apt comparison is between Franklin Roosevelt and the Woodrow Wilson of the League of Nations fight. Certainly Wilson's intransigence on the final language of the Treaty of Versailles and his public campaign on behalf of that language is more reminiscent of Roosevelt's recalcitrant stand on the death sentence and his rhetorically charged statements in defense of that provision. The critical difference, however, is that Wilson's intransigence and public utterances were targeted against a Republican-dominated Senate. Roosevelt, by contrast, was working with a Democratic Congress of landslide proportions. It is this public

89. "A Recommendation for the Regulation of Public Utility Holding Companies," March 12, 1935, in ibid. The Jackson, Mississippi, *Daily News* asserted that the PUHC bill was being used by Roosevelt as "a vehicle for reelection." *The New York Times* believed the measure represented both "personal conviction" and "essential politics." Both papers are cited in Funigiello, *Toward a National Power Policy*, 73.

campaign against *his own* congressional party that makes Roosevelt's leadership actions appear so quintessentially modern.[90] While politically induced, intraparty adjustments to regulatory legislation were characteristic features of all three episodes we have examined, such intraparty adjustments now assumed a more public and more confrontational character, more characteristic of what Samuel Kernell has labeled the leadership technique of "going public," with its emphasis on the mobilization of public pressure by a popular president to *coerce* congresspersons – and most significantly, I am arguing, the president's own legislative party – to accede to legislation they might not otherwise accept.

Executive branch policy leadership, then, is one key feature of the altered institutional context in which the politics of national party leadership was now played out. But a second and equally consequential development had taken place in Congress, one that in fact helps clarify Roosevelt's seemingly antiparty actions. Especially in the House, the organization of the chamber had undergone a dramatic transformation, encompassing most notably the institutionalization of the seniority system, the separation of the Rules Committee from party leadership, and the development of norms of comity and deference in the relationship between chairmen and their committee. The cumulative result was to undercut the capacity of legislative party leaders and their agents to advance national party goals in Congress. As legislation to eliminate utility holding companies advanced through the House a series of eruptions took place: The Interstate Commerce Committee revolted against its chairman, Texas Democrat Sam Rayburn, over the inclusion of the death-sentence provision; the Rules Committee revolted over a special order to require a roll-call vote on the death sentence and therefore to force the issue of party loyalty on the floor; and most broadly, a large portion of the Democratic party revolted against White House leadership on the floor of Congress, over the aggressive intrusion of the executive into realms of traditional legislative prerogative.

It was something of a "Catch-22." On the one hand, the intrusiveness of Roosevelt's party leadership was almost wholly responsible for the divisiveness that PUHCA politics engendered within the Democratic party rank and file. On the other hand, the disorganization of congressional Democratic leadership virtually ensured an increasingly intrusive leadership role for Roosevelt to manage national coalition concerns. Functionally speaking, institutional changes in Congress made it likely

90. As Jeffrey Tulis notes, even Theodore Roosevelt's public campaign to strengthen national railroad regulation stopped once the Republican Congress began its deliberations on the Hepburn bill. Tulis, *The Rhetorical Presidency*, ch. 4.

that presidents would step into the breach to fill the need for national party direction. And it was rational that Roosevelt would seek to fill this void. Such needs were, after all, also coincident with the president's own personal political interests. But the resultant blurring of presidential and party needs on the part of both Roosevelt and congressional Democrats only magnified the sense of institutionally separate interests hard-wired into the Constitution. Presidents could not be expected to press national party considerations with the same sensitivity to congressional needs as legislative leaders because their electoral self-interest was directly implicated in the outcome. It was also more likely to raise conflict over issues of traditional legislative prerogative, as Roosevelt inserted himself into policy processes historically the preserve of Congress. As long as Congress was content to pass the political initiative to the White House to lead the nation out of the Great Depression, the consequences of new institutional environment for executive–congressional relations would not be fully apparent. But once Roosevelt started to push legislation that undercut a complex national platform compromise, placing congressional Democrats in an electorally vulnerable position, the political and institutional stakes of presidential party leadership became increasingly clear.

Balance of Power Politics in the Senate: Progressive Republicans and the Retention of the Death Sentence

The strategic complications of this new congressional environment asserted themselves early on. Initially, Roosevelt had hoped to originate consideration of the PUHCA in the House of Representatives. But soon he was forced to turn away from the House and pin his hopes on the Senate. Both Rayburn and Montana Democrat Burton Wheeler, the chairman of the Senate Interstate Commerce Committee, had been present in White House strategy sessions during the bill's drafting stages. But early on, Roosevelt seemed to place greater stock in Rayburn's personal commitment to the death sentence and his eagerness to press that provision against opponents both in committee and on the floor. So much did this seem to be true, that Wheeler came away from these White House meetings convinced that Roosevelt was ignoring him. Writing of this experience some years later, Wheeler could only recall that he "was not in too good grace with FDR at the time." At first glance, this seems odd because Wheeler was something of a political asset in Roosevelt's dealings with Senate progressive Republicans. The Montanan had been the vice-presidential running mate of Robert La Follette, Sr., on the Progressive Party ticket in 1924, and still had considerable credibility with western progressives. But, on the other hand, Wheeler appears to have had his own ideas concerning PUHC legislation, with provisions that were considerably less stringent than those gaining ascendancy in the White House. Earlier we observed Roosevelt's distance from the regulatory proposal of the NPPC, a policy-making body of his own creation. It should not come as a surprise therefore that Wheeler could walk away from these White House meetings feeling similarly marginalized.

Left without a clear role to play in the unfolding strategy of the White House, Wheeler decided to pursue his own course in the Senate independent of House proceedings. Perhaps Roosevelt got wind of this. For soon thereafter, White House emissaries Cohen and Corcoran called on Wheeler, asking him to sponsor the administration bill after it had passed the House. Wheeler agreed even though, as earlier noted, Roosevelt's plan to dismantle utility holding companies was stronger than anything found in his legislation. Wheeler did acknowledge, however, that the administration bill "was more carefully crafted than mine." Finally, for reasons that will become clear later, it became certain that Rayburn would be unable to report the PUHC bill with the death sentence intact. At this point, the White House again approached Wheeler, this time asking the senator to initiate the legislative process on behalf of the administration's bill.[91]

Wheeler would later write that Senate passage of the administration's PUHC bill tested his "influence and ability . . . in the fine art of legislating," adding as well that "no test could have been more severe than the administration's bill." Putting these somewhat self-flattering comments to one side, it is clear that Senate Democrats were under tremendous pressure to break with Roosevelt on the mandatory elimination clause. The utilities industry had undertaken a massive lobbying campaign to induce members of Wheeler's Interstate Commerce Committee to drop the death sentence from the PUHC bill. This pressure included not only a massive letter and telegram writing campaign, but also the mobilization of prominent constituents from committee members' home states.[92] In all, it was a well-financed, well-organized effort to impress upon senators the deleterious impact of the administration bill upon their political fortunes back home. Utility industry lobbyists clearly sensed their power to swing enough members of Wheeler's committee to delete the death sentence, even without Wheeler's help. This was made clear when one lobbyist, apparently not impressed with the chairman's committee

91. Wheeler, *Yankee from the West*, 307–8.
92. Funigello, *Toward a National Power Policy*, ch. 4.

influence, inquired somewhat presumptuously of Wheeler, "Suppose the committee doesn't go along with you?"[93] But when the Senate Interstate Commerce Committee (SICC) reported its bill in early June, Section 11 of the administration bill (which included the death-sentence provision) remained intact. Moreover, adding salt to the wounds of the utilities executives, Wheeler purposely incited the antimonopoly enthusiasm of Senate progressives with a majority report that breathed fire, insisting that the goal of the PUHCA was "to *atomize* the unwieldy, concentrated political and financial power of holding companies and to affect savings for the consumers."[94]

Why was Wheeler able to protect the administration bill in committee and report it out with the death sentence intact? The critical element in his success – and an essential difference between the politics of the PUHCA in the Senate and the House – seems to have been the balance-of-power position wielded by progressive Republicans on the SICC. While there is no direct evidence of the alignments that shaped committee decision making on the PUHC bill, recurrent patterns on two key Senate floor votes to amend Section 11, as well as the vote to pass the PUHC bill, offer strong evidence of the Democratic–progressive Republican coalition that sustained the death sentence in Wheeler's committee.

The strongest assault on Section 11 was initiated by Illinois Democrat William H. Dieterich. Dieterich, an SICC member, introduced an amendment that would delete Section 11 in its entirety. A second crippling amendment to Section 11 was offered by another SICC Democrat, Senator Augustine Londergan of Connecticut. The Londergan amendment would have required both that a specific complaint be lodged with the Interstate Commerce Commission against a holding company and that a finding of guilt be issued before divestiture could proceed. On each of these two amendments, SICC members narrowly supported the death sentence by voting 9 to 10 against their adoption. A breakdown of these votes demonstrates the crucial role that progressive Republicans played. Democrats weakly but consistently opposed these two amendments, 5 to 8, while *nonprogressive* Republicans voted 4 to 0 in support. The two committee progressives (progressive Republican James Couzens of Michigan and Farmer-Laborite Henrik Shipstead of Minnesota) played the pivotal role, shifting the balance in favor of the death sentence by one vote. On the vote to pass the PUHC with Section 11 intact, the same pattern essentially held. In all, these voting patterns strongly indicate

93. Wheeler, *Yankee from the West*, 309.
94. Funigiello, *Toward a National Power Policy*, 83 (emphasis added); Wheeler, *Yankee from the West*, 306–9.

Table 4.2. *Importance of Senate Progressives to Retention of Roosevelt's "Death Sentence" Provision*

A. Dieterich Vote to Delete Section 11 (the "Death Sentence").

	Democrats	Progressive Republicans	Other Republicans	Total
Yes	29	0	15	44
No	35	10	0	45

B. Londergan Vote to Provide for Due Process for Holding Companies.

	Democrats	Progressive Republicans	Other Republicans	Total
Yes	28	0	15	43
No	35	10	0	45

C. Vote to Pass Public Utility Holding Company Bill (with Section 11 Intact).

	Democrats	Progressive Republicans	Other Republicans	Total
Yes	45	11	0	56
No	18	0	14	32

that progressive Republicans occupied the balance of power in SICC deliberations, giving Wheeler the critical support necessary to report the administration bill with Section 11 intact.

Progressive Republican support was not only pivotal to Wheeler in committee, it was equally determinative of administration success on the floor. Roosevelt had correctly gauged the mood of Senate progressive Republicans, and to a person they were standing behind the death-sentence provision. The Dieterich and Londergan amendments were narrowly defeated in the full Senate, 44 to 45 and 43 to 45, respectively. As Table 4.2 shows, on each vote progressives voted as a bloc, supplying the margin of victory to pass the administration bill without undermining the antimonopoly thrust of Section 11. In addition, progressive Republicans votes, while less pivotal to the final passage of the PUHC bill, were nonetheless essential to providing the administration a comfortable margin of victory.

A Rule-laden House and the Struggle for the Death Sentence

Compared with the Senate, House Republicans from progressive states possessed neither the numbers nor the inclination to play the balance-

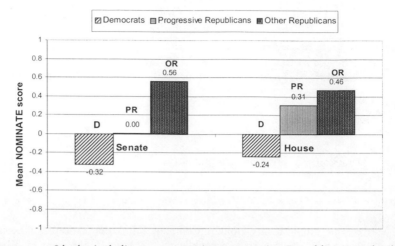

Figure 4.4. Ideological distance separating progressive Republicans and other Republicans and Democrats.

of-power role on the death sentence. In the first place, population-based apportionment limited the relative size of the midwestern and western Republican contingent in the House. But more important, these Republicans were not nearly as polarized ideologically from their eastern party colleagues as were their Senate analogues. This, in a nutshell, was the first structural challenge faced by Democratic leaders in the House of Representatives. Without a progressive Republican contingent on the House Interstate Commerce Committee to act as a swing group, Rayburn would be dependent upon Democratic party unity to get the death sentence out of committee. And once on the floor, House leaders would again have to rely on party unity to defend the death sentence. In each instance, the unprecedented lobbying effort of the utilities industry, both in Washington and in congressional districts, placed tremendous pressure on rank-and-file Democrats to break ranks with Roosevelt.

Figure 4.4 utilizes Poole and Rosenthal first-dimension D-NOMINATE scores to measure the degree of ideological heterogeneity both within the Republican party and between these two Republican groups and the Democratic party.[95] As the table indicates, in the House, the ideological distance separating the mean progressive Republican from nonprogressive Republican was substantially smaller than in the Senate. In addition,

95. A discussion of the D-NOMINATE measure can be found in Poole and Rosenthal, "A Spatial Model for Legislative Roll Call Analysis."

the mean House Republican from the progressive bloc of states was ideologically much further from chamber Democrats than in the Senate. In all, we would not expect the same alliance between Democrats and Republicans from progressive states in the lower chamber that we observed in the Senate.

Comity. Because of intense lobbying pressure and the absence of a progressive Republican swing group, the ability of party leaders to use the institutional levers of the House on behalf of the administration's PUHC bill would be decisive. Such institutional support, however, would not be forthcoming. This was immediately apparent as the House Interstate Commerce Committee (HICC) organized itself to consider the PUHC bill, just passed by the Senate. It will be recalled that in the Sixty-third Congress (1913–15) House Democrats had explicitly excluded Republicans from executive sessions of the Judiciary Committee during the drafting stages of its antitrust legislation. In this way, the Democrats kept control over the substance of the bill that had been worked out in caucus and in consultation with Woodrow Wilson. By comparison, what strikes the analyst in this instance is the radically different atmosphere in which committee chair Rayburn now appeared to operate. Rather than pursuing caucus, administration, or even personal legislative goals, Rayburn's actions betray a heightened preoccupation with the preservation of committee comity and the broad pursuit of balance: partisan balance, balance in committee status, ideological balance, and to a little lesser extent regional balance. In the pursuit of committee harmony, Rayburn reduced the likelihood that specific policy goals could be aggressively pursued. And in the end this is what happened, as the HICC reported the administration's public utility bill out without the death sentence provision.

What seems so striking in light of our previous chapter is how this preoccupation with bipartisanship and balance is so starkly evident at every step of the committee process. There were twenty-seven members of the HICC in 1935, nineteen Democrats and eight Republicans. The disproportionate representation of Democrats on the committee reflected the lopsided ratio of partisan representation in the full chamber (319 to 103), suggesting that, absent other constraints, a wide degree of latitude was available to the chair to organize the committee strategically in support of the death sentence. Rayburn divided the administration bill into three sections and appointed three ad hoc subcommittees, one for each section, each with the responsibility to examine the provisions under its jurisdiction and report back its recommendations to the full committee. It was therefore critical which subsets of committee members

Table 4.3. *Appointment Structure of Senate Ad Hoc Subcommittees Created to Consider Public Utility Holding Company Bill*

Subcommittee # 1: Title I (pp. 1–77).

Name	Party	Rank	Seniority	State
Rayburn	D	1	12	TX
Huddleston	D	2	11	AL
Pettengill	D	10	3	IN
Eicher	D	16	2	IO
Mapes	R	2	12	MI
Wolverton	R	3	5	NJ

Subcommittee # 2: Title II (pp. 77–103).

Name	Party	Rank	Seniority	State
Crosser	D	4	10	OH
Corning	D	5	7	NY
Kenney	D	12	2	NJ
Martin	D	15	4	CO
Wadsworth	R	8	2	NY
Reece	R	7	7	TN

Subcommittee # 3: Title II/III (pp. 103–178).

Name	Party	Rank	Seniority	State
Lea	D	3	10	CA
Bulwinkle	D	6	7	NC
Cole	D	9	4	MD
Monoghan	D	14	2	MT
Cooper	R	1	11	OH
Merritt	R	6	9	CT

Source: Committee on Interstate Commerce. Executive Session minutes, 74th Congress. Records of the U.S. Senate, National Archives, Washington, D.C.

Rayburn chose for these assignments. And it is here that we can see the constraint of committee norms pull upon Rayburn's choices.

Firstly, not only were Republicans not excluded from participation in the PUHC markup process as they had been in the Wilson era, but, at each stage in the formation of workgroups, Rayburn was scrupulous in preserving the chamber ratio of partisan representation. As Table 4.3

shows, eighteen HICC members were assigned to work on the PUHC bill, twelve Democrats and six Republicans. On each of the three ad hoc subcommittees Rayburn formed, four Democrats and two Republicans were assigned. While Rayburn always preserved the Democrats' 2:1 chamber ratio on each subcommittee, the advantage gave the White House little consolation because it only required one Democratic defection to kill any portion of the PUHC bill.[96] This point is critical because, secondly, Rayburn was equally scrupulous in distributing senior Democrats to each of the three subcommittees. Though we are forced to speculate at this point, all indications are that Rayburn sought to satisfy the subcommittee assignment preferences of ranking Democrats. But whatever his criteria, the end result was that Representative George Huddleston of Alabama, the HICC's second-ranking Democrat, and an ardent foe of the death sentence, was assigned to the subcommittee with responsibility for passing on the mandatory elimination provision (Rayburn chaired this subcommittee).[97] Huddleston's appointment was pivotal, as his presence effectively killed any chance that the death-sentence provision would emerge from the subcommittee intact.

What was the breakdown of support and opposition for the death sentence on the HICC? I have been unable to locate the records of any committee vote on this provision. What I have done instead is to utilize the vote to reinstate the death sentence in the full House as a proxy for voting patterns in committee. This vote was taken in the House Committee of the Whole on July 1, 1935. Here, we find that, like the Democrats in the Senate, House Democrats splintered over the retention of the controversial provision to eliminate utility holding companies. Among Democratic HICC members the vote was 8 to 7 to restore Section 11 to its original form. Democrats on Rayburn's subcommittee, which had responsibility for Section 11, voted 2 to 2, indicating that the mandatory elimination provision likely never made it out of subcommittee. This is because Republicans were a solid phalanx, exhibiting nothing of the ideological split so central to the success of the administration bill in the Senate. Republican HICC members voted 0 to 8 against the death sentence, while in Rayburn's subcommittee their vote was 0 to 2. Finally, one indication of the centrality of the death sentence in generating divisions among Democrats is that the amended bill – *without* the death sentence – passed the full subcommittee 12 to 6, on a strictly partisan

96. For purposes of subcommittee deliberation, a tie vote was considered a vote against the bill or provision in question.
97. Data on subcommittee assignments pertaining to the PUHC bill can be found in the minutes of the executive session meetings of the HICC housed in the National Archives.

vote. Roosevelt's leadership was plainly splitting the House Democratic party in two.

Deference. A second indication of the distance we have traveled in the evolution of House norms is manifested in the different responses to committee revolt evinced by New Deal chairman Sam Rayburn and Gilded Age chairmen like John Reagan, chairman of the HICC, and Richard Bland, the chairman of the House Coinage Committee. As we saw in the cases of railroad regulation and free coinage of silver, these Gilded Age chairmen were willing to employ the prerogatives of their position to mobilize the floor against committee decisions in pursuit of their preferred legislation. By the 1930s, however, Rayburn's actions reveal a chairman who understood the institutional expectations of his role to be that of an "agent" acting on behalf of a committee "principal" – even when facing a committee with preferences at odds with his own and those of his party's national leader. Rayburn deferred to his committee and its decision to report the PUHC bill without the death sentence. Indeed, in committee Rayburn's actions conveyed no indication of opposition to the final provisions of the committee bill.[98] Likewise, and unlike Reagan and Bland, there would be no motion to substitute the Senate (administration) bill for the HICC bill on the floor of the House. In fact, Rayburn would make the opening remarks on the floor *on behalf* of the committee bill and act as the bill's floor manager, although as we will see, not nearly in strong enough terms to satisfy the drafters of the committee provisions.

The constraints operating upon Rayburn ultimately forced the Roosevelt administration to find another agent to work on its behalf as the PUHC bill moved through the House. That job fell to Edward C. Eicher, a second-term Iowa representative and a junior Democratic member of the HICC. A dissenting report issued under Eicher's name would accompany the HICC majority and minority reports on the PUHC bill. In it, Eicher would reprise the administration's position on the importance the death-sentence provision to any successful conclusion of the power problem. Eicher would also press the White House's case before the full House and assume the role of administration whip on the floor, mobilizing Democratic supporters of the death sentence to ensure a maximum turnout on votes considered crucial to the president.

Autonomy and Seniority. If comity and deference were two measures of the changing environment in which party leaders and their agents

98. *Congressional Record*, 74th Cong., 1st sess., Vol. 79, pt. 9: 10353.

pursued national party goals, yet another critical change was the consolidation of the House Rules Committee as an autonomous political body. In Chapter 2 we saw how the Rules Committee could be used by party leaders to defend national party interests against a committee chair asserting a personal agenda. In this case, by comparison, we will find the Rules Committee asserting its own independence against agents of the national party. This was a critical roadblock, one with roots in the Speaker's removal from the Rules Committee in 1910–11 as part of the progressive attack on "Cannonism." With party leaders proscribed from membership on the Rules Committee, and with the Democratic caucus no longer the binding force it had been during the sixty-third Congress, the relationship of Rules to party leaders depended critically upon the ideological and personal proclivities of its chair and members.

The rise of the Rules Committee as an independent chamber force would prove to be an almost insurmountable obstacle to the White House and the passage of its holding company legislation. This can be seen in the following episode. One way by which Roosevelt had hoped to reinstate the death sentence was by forcing a roll-call vote on an amendment to restore the original provisions of Section 11. Democrats would then be forced to publicly declare their support for a popular president on a vote the White House deemed critical. It would fall to Edward Eicher, the White House's HICC ally, to formally move the amendment in the House Committee of the Whole.[99] In order to pull this maneuver off, though, Roosevelt needed a special order from the Rules Committee requiring a recorded vote upon the amendment. At the president's insistence, Rayburn went to the Rules Committee to press for such an order. Under the leadership of its former chairman, Alabama Democrat William Bankhead, the Rules Committee had been a strong administration ally, issuing so many special orders to limit debate and amendments that Republicans quickly labeled them "gag rules."[100] But death in the ranks of congressional party leaders, coupled with the operation of a largely routinized seniority system – the final institutional change crucial to this analysis – effectively severed this cooperative working relationship between Rules and Roosevelt. When Speaker of the House Henry T. Rainey died on August 19, 1934, toward the end of the seventy-third Congress, a process was initiated in which Majority Leader Joseph W. Bryns assumed the Speaker's chair and Bankhead became the new majority leader, a move that required the latter to relinquish his chairmanship of the Rules Committee. In his place, seniority dictated

99. Ibid., pt. 10: 10509.
100. Patterson, *Congressional Conservatism and the New Deal*, 53.

that the second-ranking Democrat on the Rules Committee, John J. O'Connor of New York, assume the chair. While O'Connor had heretofore supported much of the New Deal legislation, he was wholly out of sympathy with the death-sentence provision of the PUHC bill, possessing considerable personal animosity toward Roosevelt to boot.[101] As chair, O'Connor would exercise the influence at his disposal to persuade committee members already reluctant to support the death sentence to deny Rayburn his request for a special order. With Rayburn unsuccessful, the vote to retain the Senate's version of Section 11 would have to proceed by way of a more anonymous teller vote.

Throughout the consideration of the PUHCA, Rayburn remained in an awkward position: an administration ally constrained by norms of House behavior. In his opening remarks, Rayburn was careful to avoid direct criticism of the committee product, observing that no bill had "had any longer, more conscientious, and, with the ability of the members of the committee, a more real consideration than this bill has had." While the chairman had nothing but praise for the committee's hard work, he also took the occasion to note that he had "not changed [his] opinion on the essential aspects of the bill as originally introduced." Unwilling to criticize the committee bill, Rayburn took aim directly at the utilities industry itself. The chairman blasted the industry for unleashing an avalanche of propaganda "in the mail, by telegrams, and by advertisements in the newspapers," information in which they had misrepresented "the facts with reference to this bill."[102] He also vilified utility holding companies as "soulless, impersonal, intangible, immoral, and well-nigh all-powerful" masters of the American people. To Rayburn, these corporate structures served no other purpose than to allow "a few men in the top holding company [to] enrich themselves and their families and favorites[.]" Holding companies were "just as necessary to the public welfare as piracy on the high seas or as robbery on the land." Continuing, Rayburn explained the motivation that sparked his interest for reform:

> What I want to do is to take from the backs of the clean, honestly operated operating companies of this country these leeches and bloodsucking holding companies, who perform no service, but who are milking to death the local operating companies under their control and are milking to death

---

101. Ibid. Patterson observes that O'Connor's brother Basil, a former law partner of Roosevelt's in New York, represented Associated Gas & Electric, one of the nation's largest utility holding companies (53, fn. 48).

102. *Congressional Record*, 74th Cong., 1st sess., Vol. 79, pt. 9: 10316.

those who have invested their hard-earned money in the securities of these local operating companies.[103]

Not waiting to see whether Rayburn's opening remarks would resonate with the wavering legislators, opponents of the death sentence on both sides of the aisle moved quickly to neutralize his words. Republican Jennings Randolph, representative from West Virginia, for one, sought to exploit the division between Rayburn and his committee, giving voice to the rumor that the chair was "in favor of the Senate [administration] bill and in disagreement with the bill reported by his committee." Rayburn, however, was quick to voice his disagreement. "That is not true at all," the chairman replied, though he vaguely acknowledged that both House and Senate bills had provisions to recommend them. Republican William Henry Wilson, representative from Pennsylvania, continued the attack, seeking to fuel a growing Democratic antipathy toward Roosevelt's aggressive leadership. Wilson reminded the chamber that no House member had been involved in the drafting of the bill originally introduced by Rayburn. Rather, it had been penned by "the smart young men in our Government bureau," brain trusters who could now be observed viewing the House proceedings from the chamber gallery, sitting along "one long row which was classified as 'intelligentia [sic] row.'"

Wilson condemned the administration for its unwillingness to pursue a more constructive regulatory course, one that would rectify abuses "without ruthlessly and deliberately destroying the lifetime savings of hundreds of thousands of our citizens." One of the chamber's most conservative members, Wilson also saw a communistic plan of government ownership lurking behind the administration bill, an "un-American" scheme in which the destruction of utility holding companies was but a first step, and he pointed to the 1932 Socialist platform as evidence of this intention. More important to our consideration, however, the congressman also located the animating principles of the administration bill in the Progressive party platform of 1924, and proceeded to list a number of members of the Progressive "resolution committee and framers of the platform of 1924" who had taken up positions in the administration, many of whom, like Donald Richberg, Basil Manley, and Frederic C. Howe, had also been active in the 1932 NPL (National Progressive League) efforts to elect Roosevelt.[104]

Things only got worse for Rayburn when Democratic HICC members took the floor. George Huddleston, representative from Alabama and the second-ranking Democrat on the committee, criticized the chairman

103. Ibid.   104. Ibid., 10330–4.

for not presenting a more vigorous defense of the committee bill, noting the "extraordinary parliamentary situation" in which a bill was being reported to the floor without a real sponsor. Insisting that the bill had been orphaned by the chair, Huddleston designated himself as the bill's de facto sponsor, chiding Rayburn with words that exposed the norms undergirding House committee operations.

> It is a committee bill; it is entitled to the support of those who want to be "regular" – of those who want to follow the committee. Those who undertake to change it cannot be of the "regular" Democrats but of those who are "off the reservation."[105]

The arguments Huddleston proceeded to make on behalf of the committee bill deserve notice in themselves, not only for the way he sought to wrest committee leadership away from Rayburn, but for what they reveal of the ideological development of the Democratic party since the 1880s – indeed, since 1914. For here we find a remarkable reversal of situations, with a southern Democrat taking the lead in arguing for a strong regulatory body with the discretionary authority to dismantle private enterprises. Not only would Huddleston argue on behalf of positions articulated by the Progressive Theodore Roosevelt in 1912 and the Republican Shelby Cullom in 1886, he did so by arguing against the anti-monopoly tradition represented by the likes of agrarian Democrats William Jennings Bryan and John Reagan. The issue, Huddleston declared, was "whether we will regulate or whether we will destroy." His position, and that of many Democrats both on the HICC and off, was that utility holding companies "should be rigidly and sharply regulated." Huddleston claimed authority for his position from the 1932 Democratic platform, which, as we saw earlier, explicitly advocated the *regulation* of holding companies selling securities in interstate commerce "to the full extent of Federal power." Upon reading the national party plank to the assembly, Huddleston stated firmly: "Upon that plank I stand," adding,

> Those who advocate destruction cannot quarrel with me for my Democracy. No Democrat can find fault with me for standing upon the Democratic platform of 1932. Socialists, radicals, and what not, of whatever stripe – they have the right to quarrel with me, but no Democrat dare challenge me on that.[106]

Democrats, it would seem, had taken their contemporary place as promoters and boosters of the American regulatory state.

It soon became apparent that the "Socialists, radicals, what not"

105. Ibid., 10353.   106. Ibid., 10354.

Huddleston had in mind – were once again those brain trusters who had attached themselves to the Roosevelt White House. Like the Republican Wilson earlier, Huddleston sought to drive a wedge between House Democrats and the Roosevelt administration over the defense of traditional legislative prerogatives. But the separation of powers issue was secondary. Rather, Huddleston hoped to check any movement of House Democrats to reinstate the death sentence. "This bill was written by Mr. Benjamin Cohen and Mr. Thomas Corcoran," Huddleston remarked, "two bright young men brought down from New York to teach Congress 'how to shoot.' Some of us were here when both were yet in short pants. But these are days when experience and fidelity in public service or in business life are exceedingly 'disqualifying.' "[107]

As the debate on the PUHC bill continued, the heart of the issue always remained Title I, Section 11, the death sentence. As proposed by the administration and passed by the Senate, Section 11 specified that the existence of any holding company was contingent upon its importance to "the operation of a 'geographically and economically integrated public-utility system.' " And in all cases, holding companies above the first tier would be eliminated by 1938. In contrast, Huddleston explained, the committee's regulatory bill would lodge discretion with the Securities and Exchange Commission to determine whether the existence of a particular holding company was "detrimental to the public interest." A holding company would be required to divest itself of its assets only upon the judgment of the SEC. As Huddleston summed it up, employing modes of argument formerly employed by the Republican Roosevelt:

> What is the difference between the two sections[?] The public interest is made the test in the House provision. The public interest is made the guide by which the Commission will know how to proceed. The Senate bill would go after this situation with a meat ax and would destroy good, bad, and all, except those particular companies which happen to be in the peculiar situation to fit in with the arbitrary and capricious provision which was adopted. That is the issue on this provision of the bill. Alice in Wonderland has come to Washington.
> *"Let the jury consider their verdict,"* the King said.
> *"No,"* said the Queen, *"sentence first, verdict afterward."*[108]

Like Rayburn, Huddleston condemned the torrents of outside pressure that were beating upon the Congress. Its effect was "to disturb and to thwart sound judgment and careful reasoning" and "prevent fair and just decisions in the public interest." But Huddleston's villains were not

107. Ibid.   108. Ibid., 10355.

the utility holding companies against which Rayburn had inveighed. Rather, they were the propaganda activities systematically undertaken by executive branch institutions and public officials. Citing what he characterized as reliable information, Huddleston accused the Federal Trade Commission of issuing "somewhere near 300 newspaper releases in the form of publicity stuff, telling the people of the country what they had found wrong with the utilities."

> So they whipped up the country into a rage; they formed a public opinion, especially among those who had the least information and hence are most suspicious; they raised this public opinion to a fever heat. Demagogues grasped their opportunity and agitators saw that the time was ripe for them. So, like vultures riding the storm, they mounted upon this wave of ill will and opinion against the utilities. They have continued to ride right down to this time.[109]

The Tennessee Valley Authority, as well, came in for attack by Huddleston, accused of initiating a "program of propaganda slipped into school literature and put out to the people through their publicity agencies." The Democrat had equally harsh words for Roosevelt for having "repeatedly thrown his all-powerful influence into the scale," while Rayburn was also rebuked for having "mounted the radio and 'radioed' from one end of the country to the other, telling the people how bad the utilities are and how much this kind of legislation was needed." Concluding his defense of the committee's bill, Huddleston remarked, "Let us have done with this talk of propaganda. Both sides are guilty. Both have interfered with a fair and just decision upon the part of Congress."[110]

With Rayburn's hands effectively tied, it fell to Eicher to make the White House pitch for the restoration of Section 11. In his dissenting report, appended to the HICC majority report on the PUHC bill, Eicher had already made clear the administration's view that the "substitute bill reported by the committee departs radically from the policy recommended by the President and fails completely to meet the vital and irrepressible issues presented by the unregulated growth of the utility-holding companies." The HICC bill, Eicher had argued at that time,

> ... helplessly accepts as permanent a situation which those [holding company] groups have created, and attempts theoretically to regulate conditions that ought not exist and that as a matter of experience cannot be regulated. It fatalistically condones and perpetuates a system of private paternalism in the most important of our industries based on greed, destruc-

109. Ibid.   110. Ibid.

tive of independent competitive enterprise, and incompatible with political and economic liberty.[111]

Now on the floor of the House, Eicher developed further the administration line of thought. The Iowa Democrat pressed the antimonopoly line for all it was worth, arguing that "we are in fact engaged in a battle between giants . . . On the one front are arrayed the forces of the Federal Government . . . On the other front stand the forces concentrated economic and political power, which, while the people slept, invaded practically every business avenue, and now reach with their tentacles of interrelated and interlocking control into every fiscal activity in the Nation." Continuing his attack, Eicher reiterated the statements Roosevelt had attached to the March 12 NPPC report.

> No reasonable mind that has given sustained thought to the extent and significance of these developments can deny the serious import of the President's conclusion that there has been built up in the public-utility field a system of private socialism which is inimical to the welfare of a free people. The opportunity for private profit has become so intriguing, the continued exercise of centralized economic power is so appealing that no surprise need be felt, human ambitions being what they are, over the stout resistance the Government is encountering in its endeavor to dislodge the privileged few from the citadel of citadels out of which they manipulate their effective controls, to wit, the holding company device.[112]

Having failed to extract a roll-call vote on the death sentence from a resistant Rules Committee, Rayburn had followed up with a request to extend the time governing debate on Eicher's proposed amendment to reinsert the death sentence into Section 11. Under House rules, debate on amendments in the Committee of the Whole was governed by the five-minute rule: five minutes apiece were allotted to both supporters and opponents of the death sentence. Rayburn sought a special rule that would allow debate on Section 11 for a total of three hours and grant control over the one and one-half hours allotted to supporters of the death sentence to Eicher. But again the Rules Committee turned down Rayburn's request, declining to accommodate the president's interests.[113]

Rayburn's remaining option was to seek unanimous consent for his request before the Committee of the Whole. Of course, it took only one objection to quash Rayburn's request, and such objection was quickly

111. U.S. Congress. House. Committee on Interstate and Foreign Commerce. 74th Cong., 1st sess., Report No. 1318, "Public Utility Act of 1935: Additional Views of Mr. Edward C. Eicher," 44–5.
112. *Congressional Record*, 74th Cong., 1st sess., Vol. 79, pt. 9: 10358.
113. Ibid., pt. 10, 10512.

made by both Republicans and Democrats. Mississippi Democrat John Rankin helped clarify the political stakes in the upcoming debate on the death sentence. "As everyone knows," Rankin observed, "this is the crux of the bill. This is the section of the bill the administration is interested in."[114] Rankin, who supported the death sentence, was nonetheless unwilling to support Rayburn's motion, for fear that Eicher's control over Democratic time allotments would limit the number of members who wanted to get their position on the record. Rules Committee chairman John J. O'Connor also objected to Rayburn's proposal. O'Connor's reasons were procedural, insisting that the delegation of control over Democratic time by a bill's floor manager violated House practice. Both Rayburn and Lindsay Warren of North Carolina, the temporary chairman of the Committee of the Whole, disagreed with O'Connor's reading of chamber rules. But unfortunately for Rayburn, the rules governing unanimous consent did not require that the Rules Committee chairman issue a well-founded objection, only that he object. In the end, O'Connor would propose to cut the difference with Rayburn, but in a way that neutralized the administration's voice in the Committee of the Whole. He proposed that a total of two and one-half hours be allocated for debate on the Eicher amendment to restore the death sentence, but with a five-minute rule imposed on each speaker and floor recognition under the control of Chairman Warren.[115] The administration would therefore not be able to control debate on the Democratic side, with Eicher obtaining the floor for only one five-minute bloc in the period after the O'Connor compromise was accepted by the House.

The Defeat of the Death Sentence in the House Committee of the Whole

Rayburn's inability to secure a recorded vote for the Roosevelt administration may have weakened the pull of party loyalty and public pressure to support a popular president. But fortunately for scholars, it does not impede our ability to analyze the choices these legislators made. Reporters for the Scripps-Howard newspaper chain undertook their own head count when the amendment finally came up for a vote in the House Committee of the Whole on July 1, 1935.[116] The results were a severe

---

114. Ibid., pt. 10: 10510.
115. Ibid., 10514.
116. The figures presented are taken from the results of the Scripps-Howard count printed in *The New York Times* on July 2, 1935, as amended by corrections published in the *Times* the following day on July 3, 1935. Four votes were unaccounted for by the Scripps-Howard team, all of them Democrats.

Table 4.4. *Logit Estimation of Support for Eicher Amendment to Reinstate the "Death Sentence" in the House Committee of the Whole*

Variables	Support for Eicher Amendment
Party	2.102**
	(.528)
Progressive States	0.935**
	(.372)
Value-added in Mfg. (Per Capita)	−0.152
	(.729)
Rural Farming Areas	0.021**
	(.008)
New Dealers	0.601*
	(.294)
Level of District Competition (Democrats)	0.007†
	(.004)
Constant	−3.439**
	(.577)
−2 Log Likelihood	378.3
% Correctly Predicted	70.6
(N)	(359)

** = p < .01; * = p < .05; † = p < .10.
Note: A description of variables used in this analysis can be found in the Appendix to this chapter.

setback for the administration. The vote on Eicher's amendment to reinstate the death sentence was easily defeated, 152 to 225, with 49 not voting. Republicans formed a unified opposition to the amendment, 7 to 92, with 4 not voting. Democrats also defected from the administration position in scores, with the party barely able to marshal a majority on behalf of the Eicher amendment (135 to 133 with 45 not voting). Table 4.4 reports the results of LOGIT analysis on the Eicher amendment, employing several economic and political variables of particular interest to this analysis. A number of findings here warrant our consideration. First, while the model demonstrates the statistically significant effect of party on the vote, it is clear from the aggregate party breakdown presented earlier that this was principally driven by the behavior of House Republicans. Of more importance to this analysis, looking only at Democrats, positive coefficients indicate that representatives from progressives states, those from rural farming districts, and those we might label New Dealers (Democrats in their first or second term) were

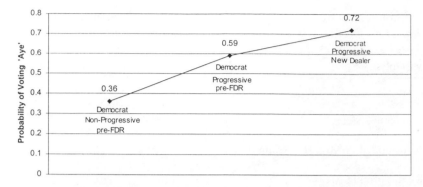

Figure 4.5. Probability of "Ideal Type" Democratic support for Eicher amendment.

more likely to support the administration position (in support of the death sentence) than other Democrats.

How large were the effects of western progressivism, rural farming constituencies, and New Dealer status on the likelihood a Democrat supporting the Eicher amendment? Because LOGIT coefficients in themselves cannot tell us the size of their effect on voting behavior, Figure 4.5 converts these statistics directly to probability scores. Holding the value of the remaining variables at their mean, we see that a Democrat whose district was located *outside* the progressive states and whose legislative career started *prior* to 1932 had the lowest probability of supporting the Eicher amendment (.36). Analytically relocating that representative to a progressive state increases the probability of support to .59, while making her a New Dealer raises the probability of support to .72, exactly double the likelihood of our initial estimate.

Figure 4.6 extends this analysis further, assessing the differential impact of district agrarianism on both progressive New Deal Democrats and on nonprogressive, pre-FDR Democrats. The figure shows an increase of roughly .20 in the probability of both types of Democrats supporting the death sentence as we move from districts with a low percentage of rural farming activity to those with a high percentage. But perhaps more interesting, the table further indicates the primacy of political over economic variables. For example, looking strictly at districts with a low percentage of rural farming activity, the probability of a New Deal Democrat from a progressive state supporting the Eicher amendment was .36 greater than a pre-FDR Democrat from a nonprogressive state. Likewise, among districts with high levels of rural farming, the probability of a progressive state, New Deal Democrat supporting

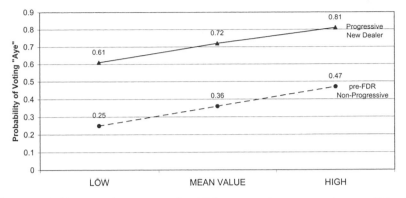

Figure 4.6. Democratic support for Eicher amendment to reinstate "Death Sentence," controlling for level of district agricultural production. Note: "Low" = 1 standard deviation below mean value; "High" = 1 standard deviation above mean value.

the death sentence was .34 greater than a nonprogressive, pre-FDR Democrat.

Finally, although significance levels indicate that these results should be interpreted with caution, our findings also suggest that electoral competitiveness actually had a slight negative impact on Democratic support for the death sentence (these probability scores are not shown). That is to say, the probability of a Democrat supporting the administration's position *increased* as the electoral pressures he or she faced decreased. This is an unexpected finding, one that suggests that it may actually have been fortunate for Roosevelt that Rayburn was unable to secure a roll-call vote on the Eicher amendment, since a more highly publicized vote would have likely induced more defections among Democrats from competitive districts. This finding also reminds us that the position staked out by the administration was not generally a popular position with Democratic constituents. Rather, it was a commitment made by Roosevelt to maintain the support of electorally influential progressive Republicans in the Senate. Congressional Democratic support for the death sentence was sufficiently unpopular that it required a degree of electoral insulation before a representative was willing to stand by the president and the national party interest.

On July 2, 1935, the House of Representatives formally voted to substitute the weakened HICC bill for the stringent Senate bill. The vote was an easy 258 to 147 in favor of substitution. Republicans again voted 92 to 7 in support of the HICC bill. This time around, Democrats could not even muster a majority against the substitute, voting 166 to 130 to

Table 4.5. *Logit Estimation of Support to Substitute HICC Weak*
PUHC Bill for Senate Bill with "Death Sentence"

Variables	Support for HICC Substitute
Party	−2.245**
	(.510)
Progressive States	−0.963**
	(.370)
Value-added in Mfg. (Per Capita)	−0.623
	(.638)
Rural Farming Areas	−0.019**
	(.007)
New Dealers	−0.520*
	(.269)
Level of District Competition (Democrats)	0.001
	(.004)
Constant	3.588
	(.555)
−2 Log Likelihood	423.72
% Correctly Predicted	68.1
(N)	(386)

** = $p < .01$; * = $p < .05$.
Note: A description of variables used in this analysis can be found in the Appendix to this chapter.

accept the HICC bill. The ten members of the Progressive and Farmer-Labor parties were unanimous in their support of the administration-backed Senate version, giving us some measure of progressive Republican preferences on the matter. As Table 4.5 indicates, voting patterns largely followed the vote on the Eicher amendment. Once more, although the party coefficient is statistically significant, it is largely a function of a unified Republican vote. Likewise, the table further indicates that, as before, New Deal Democrats, representatives from progressive states, and those from rural farming areas threw their support behind Roosevelt and the stronger Senate PUHC bill.

Intensification of Presidential Pressure and the Passage of
a Modified Death Sentence

Roosevelt administration forces employed a number of additional tactics in an effort to restore the death sentence to the PUHCA. From the manipulation of Senate conference committee assignments and the use of administration emissaries to influence conference deliberations, to congressional investigations and political strong-arming – few stones were left unturned as Roosevelt undertook steps to secure compulsory dissolution. The passage of the final PUHCA, with its slightly more restricted version of the death sentence, was almost exclusively the product of executive-branch pressure on congressional Democrats. It was also additional evidence of the difficulties of presidential party leadership in an increasingly fragmented and rule-laden congressional environment.

On the Senate side, the administration was assured that its position would be maximally represented in the conference committee. Four of the five senators selected to confer on the PUHC bill had supported the death sentence, a proportion out of sync with the closeness of the vote on the Dieterich amendment.[117] In addition, what is most significant about the composition of the Senate delegation is how it once again highlights the typically neglected role of the vice president as a national party agent. In our discussion of the Interstate Commerce Act we saw how the vice president, in his capacity as president of the Senate, possessed the discretion to shape the composition of certain types of committees. In the case of Thomas Hendricks, Grover Cleveland's vice president, it had been the composition of the Select Committee on Interstate Commerce. In this instance, Roosevelt's vice president, John Garner of Texas, the former Democratic Speaker of the House of Representatives, pushed aside traditional Senate protocol to seize control of the conference committee selection process.[118] As early as the previous April, Garner had announced his intention to disregard both seniority and the preferences of committee chairmen in favor of his own discretion in the appointment of conference committees. Senior Democrats on the Interstate Commerce Committee were furious as Garner passed them up for membership on the Senate PUHC bill delegation. Ellison D. Smith of South Carolina, the second-ranking Democrat on the committee, expressed his displeasure in a brief exchange with Garner. "I desire to know," Smith inquired, "if the custom and rule of nearly 150 years have been abrogated and set aside in the matter of appointing conferees on the part of the Senate?" Smith, who had earlier voted against the death

117. Garner selected Democrats Burton Wheeler, Alben W. Barkley of Kentucky, Fred H. Brown of New Hampshire, and Farmer-Laborite Henrik Shipstead of Minnesota, all of whom had supported the death sentence by voting against the Dietrich amendment. Only Republican Wallace H. White of Maine was appointed to the conference committee as an opponent of compulsory dissolution.

118. Not only did Garner hand pick the Senate PUHCA delegation, he also instructed them to stand firm on the issue of compulsory dissolution.

sentence, was particularly incensed about his exclusion. To Garner he remarked: "I notice that conferees were appointed who were notoriously in favor of a certain controversial provision of the bill." "On the PUHC conference committee on the utilities bill I think there was but one member who had been a member of the committee for any considerable time."[119]

To reinforce Garner's actions in the Senate, Roosevelt sent "expert advisors" Benjamin Cohen, who had helped draft the original PUHC bill, and Dozier Devane, of the Federal Power Commission, to accompany the Senate conferees. Their responsibility was to help induce Democratic House conferees to accept the Senate version of the bill. They were also instructed to use their influence to ensure that Rayburn did not independently pursue his own compromise. However, all of this additional leverage was not enough; in the end, the administration tactics failed to bring recalcitrant House conferees into line. The House delegation voted 3 to 2 against the administration-backed Senate bill, with Huddleston and the two House Republicans holding out for the House bill. The ensuing conference committee deadlock over the issue of compulsory dissolution would last for two months.[120]

Roosevelt persisted. Perhaps the most elaborate administration effort to break the conference stalemate involved efforts to publicly expose the excesses of the utility lobby in the recently concluded congressional fight on the PUHC bill. At Roosevelt's prompting, Senator Hugo L. Black of Alabama sought and obtained Senate authorization to form a special committee to investigate improper influence by the utility lobby.[121] The Black committee understood its mandate from the White House as one to so scandalize the utilities lobby that House conferees would be forced by mounting public pressure to yield to the Senate on the death sentence.[122] As *Time* magazine put it, the purpose of the Black committee was "to turn up a first-rate Power lobby scandal which might move House-Senate conferees to reinstate the Utility Bill's 'death sentence.'" More broadly, the weekly reported that Black's committee had been allocated the money and the mandate "to investigate not only Utility

119. Garner responded in part that he had "appointed conferees recently in only two cases," both involving power matters. Besides the PUHC bill, Garner had appointed George Norris to be a conferee on a bill amending the Tennessee Valley Authority Act. Haynes, *The Senate of the United States*, 323; *Congressional Record*, 74th Cong., 1st sess., Vol. 79, pt. 10: 11091–3.
120. Funigiello, *Toward a National Power Policy*, 93.
121. Freyer. *Hugo L. Black and the Dilemma of American Liberalism*, 61; Funigiello, *Toward a National Power Policy*, 99–100. At the time, Black was chairing a similar investigation of lobbying tactics involving air and ocean mail contracts.
122. Funigiello, *Toward a National Power Policy*, 113.

Bill lobbying but also 'all efforts to influence, encourage, promote or retard . . . any other matter or proposal affecting legislation.' " In effect, the popular periodical concluded, Black had been "armed with a mighty blackjack which he could swing at will on anyone who dared oppose Administration bills."[123]

With adequate time, this latest gambit might have stood a reasonable chance of success. But Rayburn, who was heading up the delegation of House conferees, moved too quickly to force Huddleston's hand. With revelations of utility lobby excesses just coming to light, Rayburn moved that the House instruct its conferees to accept the death-sentence provision in the Senate bill. Playing on the still-smoldering Democratic resentment against administration pressure tactics, Huddleston countered with a motion to instruct House conferees to exclude administration "lobbyists" Cohen and Devane from future committee deliberations. On both counts Roosevelt suffered major setbacks. The House rejected the death sentence a second time by a vote of 209 to 155, with 65 not voting. Indeed, the results were particularly demoralizing for the administration, for the vote patterns indicated very little change from the first death-sentence vote in the Committee of the Whole.

While hindsight is always 20–20, political observers such as the *St. Louis Post-Dispatch* concluded that Rayburn acted too hastily in his attempt to exploit the revelations of the Black committee. The paper speculated that if "the impetuous Rayburn had delayed one or two days . . . he would have had the newspaper accounts working for the administration's side." Instead, with the conference committee still in deadlock, the paper predicted that "the chances were against any bill" in this session of Congress.[124]

The cumulative effect of Huddleston's intransigence in conference, Rayburn's tactical mistakes, and the spectacle of a second round of Democratic defections on the death sentence finally forced Roosevelt to seek a compromise. The president insisted on retaining the death-sentence form, but he was now willing to limit compulsory dissolution of holding companies to those above the *second* degree (so-called father and grandfather holding companies situated just above utility operating companies). The SEC would be further empowered after January 1, 1938, to reorganize the remaining companies into a single, integrated public utility system. The SEC would also be given the authority to grant exceptions to this reorganization goal, if simplification entailed loss of

---

123. *Time*, July 22, 1935; McGeary, "Congressional Investigations During Franklin D. Roosevelt's First Term." Chairman John J. O'Connor would also use the Rules Committee to offer a sympathetic forum to holding company executives and lobbyists being excoriated by the administration-backed Black committee in the Senate.

124. Hardeman and Bacon, *Rayburn*, 193.

substantial economies, if present organization facilitated geographical integration, or if these holding companies were not too large for localized management, efficient operation, and effective regulation.[125]

On August 18, Roosevelt held a strategy session with House allies and the Senate conferees. Concerned about the possible political repercussion among progressives, the president made it clear to participants that "he would not shoulder the responsibility for abandoning the death sentence."[126] Vice President Garner requested the task of dealing with opposition Democrats in the House. On August 21 Garner met with congressional leaders, who had been mixed in their support of compulsory dissolution. Rules Chairman O'Connor and Democratic whip Patrick J. Boland of Pennsylvania had voted against the Eicher amendment in the Committee of the Whole, while the Speaker of the House, Joseph W. Byrns of Tennessee, had voted in favor.[127] Garner informed them that they faced the choice of mobilizing support for the compromise provision or accepting the prospect that Congress would remain in session indefinitely.[128]

The administration was not out of the woods yet. In conference Senator Alben Barkley of Kentucky introduced the administration's compromise bill and it was summarily rejected by Huddleston and the House Republican delegation.[129] The administration's last hope hinged on efforts to secure another House motion, this one instructing House conferees (really, Huddleston) to accept the Barkley modified death sentence. On the floor of the House, Huddleston was adamant that a vote for the Barkley compromise was a vote "for the death sentence in only a slightly different form." The amendment, he maintained, merely juggled enough words "to afford any weak kneed [Democrats] an opportunity to recant."[130] John G. Cooper of Ohio, a Republican House conferee, warned opponents of the Senate bill that the Barkley amendment "represents all that they originally asked for." To Rayburn, Cooper was equally direct: "Do not think anyone will be deceived by this different shroud of language in which death has been newly wrapped."[131] In response Rayburn stressed the added leniency of the Barkley compromise, and for added effect Rayburn

125. Hawley, *The New Deal and the Problem of Monopoly*, 335–6.
126. Funigiello, *Toward a National Power Policy*, 96, fn. 99.
127. Technically, Bryns stepped down from his role as Speaker once the House dissolved into the Committee of the Whole, which, as noted earlier, was presided over by Lindsay Warren of North Carolina.
128. Funigiello, *Toward a National Power Policy*, 96.
129. The compromise had been drafted in the White House by Felix Frankfurter, though it would be known to participants as the Barkley amendment.
130. *Congressional Record*, 74th Cong., 1st sess., Vol. 79, pt. 13: 14166.
131. Ibid., 14165.

read to the chamber a message from Roosevelt stating his conviction that the Barkley compromise represented "a greater recession from the Senate bill than I would like to see made," though, in the interest of mutual adjustment, he urged its passage.[132]

The motion to instruct House conferees to accept the Barkley amendment was successful, passing 219 to 142 with 69 not voting. Republican opposition continued to be strong, 7 to 83 with 14 not voting. This time around, however, rank-and-file Democrats fell into line behind Roosevelt, 203 to 59, with 54 not voting. In reporting the "lopsided vote of 203 Democrats," the *New York Times* concluded that "many opponents ran to vote on orders of the Democratic high command." Whether this, the continuing revelations of the Black committee upon constituency opinion, or the desire to bring this long session of Congress closer to an end, House Democrats embraced Roosevelt's modified death sentence proposal, deserting Huddleston and the Republican opposition.[133]

With the passage of the Barkley amendment further opposition from the House collapsed. The PUHCA passed the House by a vote of 222 to 113 with 95 not voting, with support patterns falling substantially along party lines. Democrats supported the final bill by a vote of 204 to 44, with 68 not voting. Republicans opposed the PUHCA 6 to 68 with 27 not voting. In the Senate, the final compromise passed without a recorded vote and was signed into law on August 26, 1935.

Conclusion

Despite the final compromise and Roosevelt's difficulty in extracting it from Congress, it would be a mistake not to see the passage of the PUHCA, with its modified death sentence, as a significant victory for antimonopoly agrarian goals. In an industry in which the pyramiding of holding companies could reach the tenth and even twelfth degree, the PUHCA ordered the compulsory dissolution of all holding companies above the second level. It further empowered the SEC to dissolve holding companies above the first degree where the commission found them to be inconsistent with the public interest. Additionally, this degree of agrarian success – especially in the pitched fight over the Dieterich amendment – would have been impossible without the unified action of Senate progressive Republicans. Still, as we have seen, a focus on the legislative behavior of progressives ignores the most important contextual point.

132. Hardeman and Bacon, *Rayburn*, 196.
133. Third-party representatives supported the Barkley compromise 9 to 0, with 1 not voting.

The passage of the PUHCA with even a modified death-sentence provision would not have taken place without the almost ceaseless activity of Roosevelt forces both inside and outside of Congress. In his efforts to convince progressive Republicans that the Democratic party was an appropriate vehicle for the attainment of their substantive goals, Roosevelt pressed forward on multiple fronts to secure a PUHC bill with little leniency toward holding companies. In the end, if there was an irony to the Public Utility Holding Company Act it was that antimonopoly agrarianism had achieved one of its most significant political triumphs in the field of economic regulation at a time in American political history when both that tradition and its core constituency were in eclipse.

Nevertheless, the agrarian victory was not complete, and Roosevelt's failures in the PUHCA battle are as illuminating as his successes. In particular, intense constituency pressures, along with fragmentation and institutional change in the House of Representatives, both facilitated and legitimated the defection of congressional leaders from national party goals being sponsored out of the White House. All of this points to the emergence of a contemporary world of district-looking, reelection-minded congresspersons and a president-centered polity.

The remarkable lobbying effort organized by utility holding companies convinced many in Congress that constituents were opposed to the frontal assault that Roosevelt had launched on these corporate structures. Such a conviction no doubt took on added force in northern districts and states, where the electoral longevity of Democratic legislators representing traditional Republican districts was of particular concern. But southern Democrats also defected in large numbers, perhaps fearing for their region's future economic development. Indeed, it appears that Roosevelt was willing to alienate virtually all important elements of the Democratic coalition in pursuit of the antimonopoly agrarian demand for complete holding company dissolution. Such resolute initiative suggests the force with which party system constraints and coalition-building incentives operated on this elected leader.

Finally, the contemporary era was about to be ushered in along another front as well. The 1936 election was a watershed moment in the history of the Democratic party, an election that fundamentally altered the psychology, and hence the political and legislative behavior, of southern Democrats. As we have seen, since at least the 1890s, and arguably since the end of Reconstruction, the largely southern and agrarian Democratic party had been the minority party in American politics. Not only was it virtually impossible for agrarian Democrats to win the presidency without appealing to new and different constituencies, but the absence of such support, especially after 1896, made it difficult to retain control of Congress as well. Thus southerners had numerous reasons to support the programmatic agenda of Roosevelt's second New Deal in its attempt to capture the allegiance of defection-prone progressive Republicans and pull the urban immigrant working class into a new majority coalition. Not only did southerners obtain the advantages of patronage and the policy advantages that unified government control brought them, but, more importantly, they benefited disproportionately in terms of the allocation of power within Congress. The seniority system made it likely that southerners would dominate positions of institutional leadership whenever congressional Democrats obtained a majority of seats, but such a majority remained contingent on the influx and continued reelection of nonsouthern Democrats from traditionally Republican areas. And as long as northern Democratic tenure was insecure, southerners had a strong incentive to support issue positions at odds with their own preferences; as long as Democratic loyalty among nonsouthern voters could not be assured, southern support for liberal reform was a precondition for their own institutional power.

All this changed with the election of 1936, consolidating as it did the Democrats' strong showing in the midterm elections of 1934. A Democratic majority coalition had finally been born. New Democratic loyalties had been forged in the North that would secure the power base of southern Democrats in the Congress. As much of the character of liberal legislation threatened the institutional pillars of southern society, and as the threat of minority party status was now a less credible counterargument to southern policy proclivities, southern Democrats were emboldened to move into open opposition to the New Deal, and to form a conservative alliance with similarly predisposed Republicans to block liberal Democratic initiatives in the future. A long chapter in the history of the Democratic party was finally at a close.

Appendix: Definition and Operationalization of Variables Used in Multivariate Analyses

Table 4.4 presents a statistical model of the vote on the Eicher amendment in the Committee of the Whole, using both constituency and political variables (the same model is used in Table 4.5). The political variables are PARTY, PROGRESSIVE STATES, NEW DEALERS, and LEVEL OF DISTRICT COMPETITION (DEMOCRATS). PARTY takes the value of 1 for Democrats and 0 for Republicans. I expect that Democrats will be more likely than Republicans to support the death sentence. PROGRESSIVE STATES represents the ten midwestern and western states sending progressive Republicans to the Senate in 1932. It takes the value of 1 if a member of Congress represents a district located in one of these states and o if not. Given the association of these states with New Deal era progressivism, I expect both Republicans and Democrats from these states to demonstrate greater support for the death sentence than legislators from outside those states. NEW DEALERS is a dummy variable that identifies Democrats elected in either 1932 or 1934 and whose House career therefore coincides with Roosevelt's time in office, Democrats most likely to see their electoral fate most closely tied to Roosevelt's personal popularity and political success. NEW DEALERS takes the value of 1 for all Democrats who in the seventy-fourth Congress were in their freshman or sophomore terms and o for all else. I expect New Deal Democrats to be more likely to support the death sentence than those Democrats whose legislative careers predate the Roosevelt presidency. LEVEL OF DISTRICT COMPETITION (DEMOCRATS) is an interaction term, and is intended to measure the effect of district electoral competitiveness on Democratic support for the death sentence. It takes the value of a representative's margin of victory in the 1934 midterm election if he or she is a Democrat and a value of o if the representative is a Republican. It is predicted that Democrats from competitive districts will be less likely to cross a popular president with long coattails, and would therefore be more likely to support the death sentence. Finally, economic constituency variables are VALUE-ADDED IN MFG. (PER CAPITA) and RURAL FARMING AREAS. VALUE-ADDED IN MFG. (PER CAPITA) is a continuous variable that measures a district's per capita value added in manufacturing. It allows us to interpret the support for the death sentence among legislators representing industrial interests. It is expected that support for the death sentence will vary inversely with the amount of a district's industrial activity, the rationale being that business interests should generally oppose legislation supporting the right of the federal government to trample on property rights by forcing the liquidation of corporations whose existence is deemed contrary to the public interest. RURAL FARMING AREAS, another continuous variable, measures the percentage of a district comprised of rural farming communities. It is expected that support for the death sentence will increase among legislators as the agrarian character of their districts increases.

5

Conclusion: Parties and the American Regulatory State

The Party System Perspective and American Regulatory State Development, 1884–1936

The Democratic party was centrally involved in the construction of a modern American regulatory state. In this book, I have argued that the passage of the Interstate Commerce Act, the Federal Trade Commission Act, and the Public Utility Holding Company Act cannot be adequately explained through the use of conventional pressure-group frameworks or district-driven models of legislative choice. Rather, political party efforts to retain control of the presidency set the terms of Democratic decision making. In addition to this – and contrary to contemporary theories of legislative party organization – I have shown that party regulatory choices cannot be understood by reference to the median preference of the congressional Democratic caucus. Across the three historical periods I have examined, structures of party organization and levels of party discipline have substantially varied. But in each of the cases analyzed, party leaders emerge as central players in the definition of legislative choice. Whether railroad regulation, business regulation, or the "death sentence" for public utility holding companies, party policy choices did not emanate from the majority party's rank and file. Indeed, as we have seen, rank-and-file Democrats repeatedly fell in line behind choices that repudiated their own strongly held policy preferences. In order to understand the regulatory choices of Democrats in power we need to move beyond rank-and-file preferences to the preferences of party leaders. And we cannot understand the preferences of party leaders without factoring into the analysis the importance of the presidency as a much-desired party resource.

I have termed the analytic framework of this book a "party system perspective" on the creation of American regulatory institutions. I have chosen this appellation because my analysis relies upon the structure of national party competition and the imperatives of national coalition building in the electoral college to explain the content of legislative choice. I have argued that in the years 1884 to 1936, Democrats faced a "Downsian dilemma," and I have depicted this dilemma as essentially a Hobson's choice – a choice affording no real alternatives. In confronting the problems of industrial capitalism, Democrats were forced to choose between the short-term desire to enact policies consistent with the long-standing party commitments, or jettison these commitments in deference to the preferences of electoral groups whose political support was pivotal to the consolidation of governing power. It was a Hobson's choice because in the world of democratic politics, the stabilization of a winning electoral coalition was a precondition for anything else the Democratic party might reasonably hope to accomplish in office.

The pursuit of swing states and pivotal groups by Democratic leaders was, therefore, the controlling force behind each of the regulatory choices considered in this book. In each instance, the need to fashion a stable majority coalition in the electoral college – to reach out programmatically to groups traditionally outside the national Democratic coalition – defined the acceptable range of regulatory alternatives acceptable to party leaders. Regulatory choice reflected the preferences of groups considered essential to the building of a new Democratic majority, prompting intervention in the legislative process to secure policy outcomes consistent with these coalitional constraints. While such intervention did not always result in the continuation of Democratic party governance, the choices made did prove consequential for the formation of the American regulatory state in its critical developmental stages. For under the pressures of building a new majority party, an agrarian Democratic party with historic antistatist and antimonopoly commitments turned its governing power to the expansion of national administrative power and the consolidation of corporate capitalism.

From the Party-Centered Polity to the President-Centered Polity

This book has also sought to place the operation of electoral college politics and national coalition-building imperatives within a broader context of institutional development. Between the presidencies of Grover Cleveland and Franklin Roosevelt, amid otherwise similar party system constraints, shifting relationships took place between parties, presidents, and legislators – alterations that challenged the capacity of traditional party leaders to act effectively in the policy process on behalf of presidential electoral needs. Changes in the institutional mechanisms by which the national legislature adjusted to party system demands – the supplanting of well-articulated legislative party processes with the techniques of modern presidential leadership – transformed relationships between Congress and the executive. In particular, the decline of congressional party government reinforced basic differences of interest between institutions, deepening the constitutional separation of powers and yielding a legislative decision-making process better able to resist the exigencies of national coalition building.

As we saw in Chapter 4, Franklin Roosevelt's efforts to secure the death sentence for utility holding companies at times seemed to resemble a naked contest of wills between otherwise independent branches of government. Of course, it was substantially more than that. Roosevelt's coalitional ambitions were not simply personal. They were consistent with coalitional strategies that had been pursued by national Democratic leaders for years. Moreover, Roosevelt sought to build a *party* coalition in Congress, one which involved key Democrats in most stages of the planning process. But the differences with our first two cases are nonetheless striking. The divergence of substantive preferences within the Democratic party was no less intense in the politics of railroad and business regulation. Yet, whether measured by roll-call votes or the public statements of leading players, the politics of the Interstate Commerce Act and the Federal Trade Commission Act are striking for the degree of interinstitutional comity party leaders were able to maintain as they scrapped long-standing party commitments for national electoral advantage.

With the politics of the Public Utility Holding Company Act (PUHCA), a president-centered polity emerges. A commonplace term, the notion of a president-centered polity is both illuminating and misleading. It is illuminating for the way it captures the new regime's reliance on the presidency for party leadership in Congress. By the age of Roosevelt, party mediation of policy relations between the legislature and the executive is beginning to recede before a presidential office with its own organizational and political resources to command. As party leader in title and in fact, FDR stood ready to do battle with Democrats in Congress for national policy supremacy. In the case of the PUHCA, modern techniques of presidential leadership were central to the character of the party system politics that ultimately unfolded. It was Roosevelt's decision to reach beyond his party's consensus, as embodied in the Democratic party platform of 1932, and to seek the death sentence for utility holding companies. Likewise, it was within the confines of the Roosevelt White House that the substance of holding-company legislation was devised and drafted, legislation subsequently presented to Congress as a fait accompli. Finally, it was largely through the concerted effort of the president, administration "lobbyists," and assorted public-relations gambits – as well as the aid of key party loyalists in Congress – that Roosevelt was able to secure the degree of holding-company dissolution he eventually did. Presidential elections have been a crucial part of the politics in each of the three cases we have examined in this book. But, as the analysis in Chapter 4 makes clear, the politics of national coalition building in the 1930s had become decidedly centered around the president.

Still, as just suggested, the label *president-centered polity* is also misleading. It overstates the power of the modern presidency to secure national party goals in light of the period's other major development: the emergence of the autonomous legislator, one substantially less constrained by the dictates of parties and presidents. Beyond the centrality of presidential leadership, in the politics of the PUHCA we observed the deleterious effects of changing congressional rules on the cohesiveness of the legislative party. The most important of these changes was the institutionalization of the seniority system. By automatically elevating members with long and unbroken tenure to positions of institutional authority, the seniority system played havoc with party policy influence, awarding committee power to members out of sync with party and administration goals, and insulating them from party discipline. In Chapter 4, we saw the policy consequences flowing from the elevation of conservative New York Democrat John J. O'Connor to the chairmanship of the House Rules Committee. Firmly ensconced in this position, O'Connor, an ardent opponent of the death sentence, stymied Roosevelt's efforts to secure a closed rule to protect his PUHC bill from damaging floor amendments. O'Connor would also use the Rules Committee to mount an investigation of the lobbying tactics used by the administration in the PUHCA battle. The chairman's aim was to counter the political effects of an administration-backed Senate investigation into the lobbying tactics of the utilities industry, a last-ditch effort by Roosevelt forces to mobilize public support behind holding-company dissolution.

The years after Franklin Roosevelt, of course, have witnessed the full flowering of the president-centered polity. Presidential electoral organizations have grown increasingly centered around the candidate. As well, the decentralization of authority to subcommittees in Congress has further increased the ability of legislators to secure electoral advantage and institutional power on their own initiative. Finally, the persistence of divided government since the 1950s has only exacerbated the sense of institutional difference structured into presidential–congressional relations by the Constitution. As a result, congressional willingness to accommodate electoral college concerns in the policy process has diminished accordingly. With the virtual institutionalization of Democratic legislative majorities until 1994, presidents of both parties would find it difficult to tend to their coalitional needs through legislative initiatives. Scholars would eventually come to diagnose the problems of the modern presidency in a way that took account of these altered institutional arrangements: Presidents are now said to exert national policy leadership in a context in which public expectations of presidential performance vastly exceed the capacity for successful action.[1] Necessity is the mother of innovation, however, and presidents in turn have sought the organizational capacity to build ad hoc legislative coalitions, to undertake unilateral administrative initiatives, and to exploit campaign-style public-relations techniques.[2]

The Republican Party and the Downsian Dilemma

One question that naturally arises from this study of electoral incentives and policy choice concerns the behavior of the Republican party. Why, it might be asked, do Democrats alone seem to respond to Downsian coalitional pressures as our theory expects them to? Conventional models of two-party politics suggest that each party faces the same incentive to converge on the preferences of the median voter, and yet in this book only Democrats seem to have behaved in a recognizably Downsian fashion. I am inclined to discount the possibility that this divergent behavior springs from intrinsic differences in the cultural character of the Republican and Democratic parties, differences perhaps rooted in their unique origins and developmental paths. Historical changes in the programmatic content of the Republican party on matters like race, regulation, and federalism give lie to the proposition that this party is less susceptible to such electoral pressures. It is more likely the case that these behavioral differences originated not in the nature of the Republican and Democratic parties. Rather, they derived from the parties' relative status within the party system – that is to say, whether they are locked into place as the nation's majority or minority party.

Throughout this book we have seen that the idea that political parties are motivated by a simple thirst for the perquisites of office caricatures American parties. Republican and Democratic parties are electoral and

1. Lowi, *The Personal President*; Moe, "The Politicized Presidency"; Skowronek, *The Politics Presidents Make*.
2. Wayne, *The Legislative Presidency*; Nathan, *The Administrative Presidency*; Kernell, *Going Public*.

governing organizations with deeply held policy positions and ideological commitments, programmatic affinities that, when fused with the political interests of coalition partners, are difficult to shake. It is only under extreme electoral duress that parties are likely to shed their historic commitments and beliefs, and such stress is much more likely to be the province of the minority party in the party system. Before 1884, for example, Republicans had to go back to 1856 – the first presidential election ever contested by their party – to recall a time they failed to emerge victorious in a national contest. Against this historical backdrop, Republican leaders could simply afford to remain aloof and refuse to cater to the candidate preferences of reformers in their party. If the past was any guide, Republicans would find a way to pull the election out of the hat one more time. But even if they did not, party leaders expected to find themselves quickly returned to power as the electorate became disenchanted with government under the party of "rum, Romanism, and rebellion."

Such electoral self-confidence only magnified with time. By 1912, Republicans could say with justifiable pride that they had lost the presidency to the Democrats on only three occasions (and to only two Democratic candidates) in their almost sixty-year history. Under such conditions, it becomes explicable that Republican elites would rather cut loose the progressive wing of their party and face certain electoral defeat, than succumb to the pressure of Roosevelt and his followers to jettison Taft and alter the programmatic direction of the party. Many Republicans continued to believe, once again, that a brief flirtation with Democratic government would bring voters to their senses and return the Republican party quickly to power. Exactly the same thing can be said about national politics in the early 1930s. While there was probably little the Republican party could have done to win in the depression-driven environment of the 1932 presidential election, many observers still believed that they lived in a Republican world and that the return of better times would bring with it a return of the Republican party to power. Consider the following comments of one contemporaneous news periodical:

> The broad trend of American politics for three quarters of a century has been clear and undebatable. The Republicans have been the dominant party. They have nearly always won – with the three exceptions of Grover Cleveland, Woodrow Wilson and Franklin Roosevelt. Each of these widely separated Democratic administrations lasted two terms, although Cleveland's did not run consecutively. Each was a reform administration that followed a temporary lapse in Republican prestige. Both Cleveland and Wilson gave way to long periods of Republican rule.

From these facts arise the accepted tradition that this is a Republican country; that the Republicans alone can bring prosperity; that the voters merely chastise them occasionally, but always restore them to favor after a brief, unsatisfactory experience with the Democrats.[3]

With such perceptions firmly locked into place, the majority party in the American party system had little to lose of long-term importance by hunkering down and refusing to act as a Downsian opportunist.

Democrats could never afford the same level of electoral complacency as their historic rivals, especially when it was largely political happenstance that brought them to power in the first place. It was truly a Republican era in the years between 1884 and 1932, and the nullification of contingent political circumstances – the return of Mugwumps or Progressives to the Republican fold; the return of economic prosperity – threatened Democrats in power with a return to their traditional position as the out-party in the American two-party system. Faced with such severe environmental constraints, Democrats responded rationally, *as if* they were "single-minded seekers of reelection."[4] But such behavior was situationally induced. It goes without saying that political parties are populated with agents endowed with free will; as such, a party may elect to ignore structural dictates. But they do so under pains of adverse selection. And where adverse selection meant the possibility of yet another prolonged return to the electoral wilderness, Democrats found themselves induced to make programmatic choices that would stabilize their hold on national power, even as it set their party along a different developmental course, a course that would finally result in a transformation of the Democratic party itself.

The Democratic Imprint on American Regulatory State Development

The Sherman and Clayton Acts have become as much a part of the American way of life as the due process clause of the Constitution.

President Franklin D. Roosevelt[5]

This book has principally sought to examine the partisan pressure to co-opt opposition policies in competitive electoral contexts. In this concluding section, I would like to consider the consequences for

3. Mallon, "The Party Line-Up for 1936."
4. Mayhew, *Congress: The Electoral Connection.*
5. Letter to Secretary of State Cordell Hull, September 6, 1944. Quoted in Thorelli, *The Federal Antitrust Policy*, iii (title page).

American regulatory state development resulting from the enactment of non-Democratic regulatory proposals by the Democratic party. The question is: Did the Democrats leave their own unique stamp on the character of American business regulation even as they were enacting the policies of Republican Mugwumps, Progressives, and progressive Republicans? The answer is, decidedly, yes.

Democrats and the American Antitrust Tradition

Substantively, numerous scholars have noted the peculiar culture of antitrust that pervades American business regulation and differentiates it from the regulatory strategies of most other advanced industrial countries.[6] Perhaps the central tenet of this American antitrust tradition is the idea that market competition is an essential "countervailing power" to the economic and political power of big business.[7] Animating this proposition, in turn, is the conviction that political restraints on big business are essential to the preservation of a widespread ownership of productive property – historically, a critical American social and political value. Many of these same scholars have also located this unique American tradition, with its procompetition, antibigness biases, in the political aspirations of America's expansive agricultural and small-business sectors.[8] This book has sought to demonstrate that, by and large, this historical impulse – which I have characterized as agrarian and antimonopolist – has been borne in national politics by the Democratic party. As a result, even as Democrats in power deployed the intellectual materials of their political rivals to construct a national regulatory apparatus, they were building a new American state decidedly more skeptical of the value of economic concentration and business cooperation, and more antagonistic toward corporate power, than would likely have occurred under the auspices of Republican party leadership.

The Interstate Commerce Act. This Democratic party imprint on the American regulatory state is apparent from the start, with the provisions of the Interstate Commerce Act (ICA). As we saw in Chapter 2, although

6. Thorelli, *The Federal Antitrust Policy*; Horn and Kocka, eds. *Law and the Formation of Big Enterprises in the Nineteenth and Early Twentieth Centuries*; Lustig, *Corporate Liberalism*, ch. 2; Sanders, "Industrial Concentration," 142–214; Sklar, *The Corporate Reconstruction of American Capitalism*; Freyer, *Regulating Big Business*.

7. On the notion that the antitrust laws are properly employed as a countervailing power to holders of "original market power," see Galbraith, *American Capitalism*.

8. For example, see Sanders, "Industrial Concentration"; Freyer, *Regulating Big Business*.

the agrarian contingent within the Gilded Age Democratic coalition finally acquiesced to the demand for a railroad commission, they insisted on and got an antipooling provision as part of the final settlement. This provision expressly forbade the railroads to restrain competition by the use of cooperative agreements to divide freight or revenue. The Democrats' antipooling provision imported the culture of antitrust – with its fear of collusion against the public interest by large corporate enterprises – into the heart of the ICA. It mandated railroad competition and criminalized efforts to promote stable, cooperatively determined pricing schedules because of the implicit potential for corruption. As we saw in Chapter 2, the inclusion of this provision into the final ICA induced a majority of Senate Republicans to try to kill the final regulatory legislation. It has likewise forced some scholars to conclude that the Interstate Commerce Commission "was stillborn" in 1887. By this interpretation, what was begun as a "practical desire for a stable rate structure" became distorted by a "deep-seated mistrust, hatred, and fear of large, insulated aggregations of power."[9] Indeed, the historian Albro Martin maintains that for all the talk of new administrative machinery and expert policymaking, the real purpose of the ICA was negative, not positive.

> [It] was . . . to strip the railroads of the enormous economic power which they had attained through voluntary pooling and to end all attempts to clothe the railroads with the power to establish legally enforceable pools or cartels – arrangements which would have subordinated government to an intolerable economic juggernaut.[10]

In sum, even as they were yielding to electoral pressures for a railroad commission, the antimonopoly core within the Democratic party was drawing a line in the sand, refusing to delegate the authority to this expert body to craft a transportation policy around government-supervised railroad cartels. In the end, the agrarian prohibition on cooperative railroad behavior would inject an almost unworkable tension into American transportation policy. Railroad discrimination against shippers and locales stemmed in large part from the fierce competition for available traffic. As such, the agrarian Democratic insistence on still more competition only ratcheted up the economic pressures that made such discriminations endemic to the railway industry. Moreover, as transportation costs rose over the course of the late nineteenth century and early twentieth century, a national policy of enforced railroad competition pushed secular railroad revenues downward, bringing the American

9. Martin, "The Troubled Subject of Railroad Regulation," 370.
10. Ibid., 343.

transportation system to the brink of crisis by the time of the United States' entry into World War I.[11]

The Sherman Act. The Democratic party was also active early on in efforts to make the Sherman Act into an instrument of forced business competition. In doing so, they directly challenged the intent of the act's Republican authors, who had consciously crafted the language of that act to be consistent with well-settled common-law regulatory principles – principles that looked benignly upon voluntary business combinations to restrain competition. The collision between Republican common-law leanings and the Democrats' more radical antimonopoly goals were most clearly manifested during legislative actions to repeal the Bland amendment to the Sherman Act. Introduced by Missouri Democrat Richard Bland, this amendment would have explicitly placed business actions to restrain competition within the meaning of Sherman Act prohibitions against "restraint of trade." The crucial showdown occurred over a vote to instruct House conferees to recede from Bland's procompetition amendment. With House Republicans in the majority, the vote to recede readily carried the chamber. But for our purposes, what is significant is that the vote on the Bland amendment broke along strict party lines, with Democrats endorsing a national policy of enforced competition (by voting *not* to recede from the Bland amendment) 0 to 96, and Republicans voting to remove the provisions of the Bland amendment from the Sherman Act (by voting to recede) 105 to 1.[12]

Of course, while Democrats lost this battle, they ultimately won the war – at least for a while. As we saw in Chapter 3, the transformation of the Sherman Act into a national competition policy occurred in 1897, when the Supreme Court found "free and unrestricted competition" to be the true intent behind the antitrust law.[13] But here again, what is critical for our purpose is the fact that in declaring a national policy of free and unrestricted competition, the Supreme Court was concurring in arguments made before it by Democratic Attorney General Judson C. Harmon. It is for this reason that the *Trans-Missouri* rule is best understood against the backdrop of sustained Democratic party efforts to subordinate big business to a regulatory regime premised on mandatory competition.[14] In the following years, the Democratic party was the most

---

11. Skowronek, *Building a New American State*, chs. 3, 6; Orren, *Belated Feudalism*, ch. 5.

12. James, "Prelude to Progressivism."

13. *United States v Trans-Missouri Freight Association* (1897) 166 U.S. 290.

14. In making this claim, I differ with Martin Sklar, who sees the *Trans-Missouri* decision as a willful act of judicial policy making, one which shattered a prior institutional

vocal defender of the Court's *Trans-Missouri* declaration of free and unrestricted competition. It was also the most vocal opponent of the Supreme Court's "rule of reason" decisions in 1911. But the new rule-of-reason standard did not constitute a return to the old common-law status quo. Certain forms of cooperative pricing arrangement, regardless of their voluntary status, continued to remain illegal under the Sherman Act. Thus, despite its newfound permissiveness, it might be said that from this point on, a procompetition bias had been institutionalized in the Sherman Act, a vestige of persistent Democratic efforts to reshape the principles of American antitrust law.

The Clayton Act and Its Amendments. The Clayton Act of 1914 further strengthened the procompetition, antibigness bias in the national antitrust law. While Chapter 3 focused on the Democrats' embrace of the Progressive trade commission idea, its companion legislation nevertheless continued to infuse the new American regulatory state with a statutory mandate to break apart certain forms of business combination and attack anticompetitive practices that promoted concentrated market power. Specifically, the Clayton Act outlawed interlocking directorates among competing corporations with an aggregate value greater than $1,000,000. In addition, the new law made it illegal to engage in inter-corporate stockholding, create holding companies, and utilize certain anticompetitive business devices, (such as tying contracts and exclusive dealing arrangements), where the effect of any of these activities was "to substantially lessen competition or to tend to create a monopoly in any line of commerce."[15] Of course, it fell to the Federal Trade Commission (FTC) and the courts to determine what constituted substantially lessened competition or a tendency to create a monopoly, which left the tangible effect of the new law unclear. This said, the Clayton Act did nevertheless require in effect that the FTC concern itself with these practices in an ongoing manner by singling them out in the statute.

To round out this discussion, subsequent amendments to the Clayton Act under Democratic presidents Franklin Roosevelt and Harry Truman would further deepen the association of the antitrust law with the protection of small business and the desire to restrain corporate size. The Democratic Robinson-Pateman Act (1936) amended Section 2 of the

consensus between Congress, the executive, and the lower federal courts on the common law meaning of the Sherman Act. My research leads me to conclude that the executive branch was never a part of this institutional consensus. For an extended treatment of this issue, see James, "Prelude to Progressivism."

15. Holt, *The Federal Trade Commission*, 11; Stevens, "The Clayton Act," 39–41.

Clayton Act, which dealt with price discrimination, to substantially limit the ability of businesses to charge lower prices to large customers than they did to smaller ones.[16] The Celler-Kefauver Anti-Merging Act (1950), on the other hand, expanded Section 7 prohibitions against acquiring stock in competing corporations to cover mergers by purchase of assets as well.[17]

Undercutting Institutional Prestige: Concurrent Jurisdiction

The Democrats' co-optation of opposition regulatory proposals also had implications for the authority and stature of the commissions they subsequently created. While admittedly speculative, it seems clear that the same statutes that created the Interstate Commerce Commission and the Federal Trade Commission also contributed to the diminution of institutional prestige that each of these commissions experienced in the years immediately after their founding. Clearly these bodies would have faced stiff resistance to their assertions of administrative authority even under the best of circumstances. Their novelty, their peculiar mixture of legislative, executive, and judicial powers, and the deep inroads they made into traditional judicial prerogatives – each of these factors made it likely that the courts would react to commission power and policy judgments with considerable skepticism. It was therefore imperative that Congress send the courts clear statutory signals of commission preeminence in the fields of endeavor for which they had been designed. But Congress did not do this – and for reasons traceable to the suspicion Democrats traditionally harbored toward the very institutions they had helped to create. The specific manifestation of this agrarian antagonism was a provision inserted into both the ICA and the FTCA, one that provided for alternative (and *rival*) institutional mechanisms of dispute resolution. In each instance, "concurrent jurisdiction" – competing sources of policy authority – was written into the law as a hedge against the possibility that these insulated experts would prove unwilling or unable to enforce the regulatory laws vigorously.

Consider first the Clayton Act. This Democratic statute (in conjunction with the FTCA), did not merely empower the FTC to initiate action against businesses engaging in unfair competitive practices, issue cease-and-desist orders, and make preliminary rulings as to the meaning of anticompetitive practices contained in the act. It simultaneously granted the attorney general this same power of initiation, while conferring upon

16. Hovenkamp, *Federal Antitrust Policy*, 58.
17. Wilcox, *Public Policies Toward Business*, 62–3.

the district courts similar authority to render judgments regarding the statute's substantive provisions. In sum, both the FTC and the courts were conferred equal status as policymakers in the application of the Clayton Act. The source of the problem lay in Section 15, which provides

> That the several district courts of the United States are hereby invested with jurisdiction to prevent and restrain violations of this Act, and it shall be the duty of the several district attorneys of the Untied States, in their respective districts, under the direction of the Attorney General, to institute proceedings in equity to prevent and restrain such violations. Such proceedings may be by way of petition setting forth the case and praying that such violation shall be enjoined or otherwise prohibited.[18]

Complicating these interpretive lines of authority further, the Clayton Act lodged final review of FTC orders with the Circuit Courts of Appeal, while final review of district court orders came under the immediate purview of the Supreme Court.[19]

This Democratic preference for concurrent jurisdiction was not peculiar to the Clayton statute. Section 9 of the ICA afforded shippers the option of initiating suits on their own behalf in federal court rather than lodging their complaint with the newly constituted ICC. Section 9 reads:

> That any person or persons claiming to be damaged by any common carrier subject to the provisions of this act may either make complaint to the Commission as hereinafter provided for, or may bring suit in his or their own behalf for the recovery of the damages for which such common carrier maybe liable under the provisions of this act, in any district or circuit court of the United States of competent jurisdiction; but such person or persons shall not have the right to pursue both of said remedies, and must in each case elect which one of the two methods of procedure herein provided for he or they will adopt.[20]

The implication, of course, was that the ICC had no greater claim to superior policy judgment than any federal court in the land, a situation that could only have stiffened the determination of the courts to scrutinize closely the assertions of power and jurisdiction made by the new commission.

The price paid for concurrent jurisdiction was heavy. If Congress was unwilling to make clear its conviction that the ICC and the FTC possessed a peculiar capacity for regulatory policymaking – implying instead that courts were the equal of commissions in rendering informed regu-

---

18. Stevens, "The Clayton Act," 46.   19. Ibid., 47.
20. *United States Statutes at Large*, 49th Cong., 2d sess. Ch. 104. February 4, 1887.

latory judgments – then it was not likely that the courts would assert this prerogative on the commissions' behalf. Indeed, as the subsequent history of each institution suggests, concurrent jurisdiction merely emboldened the courts to treat these commissions as superfluous bodies, duplicating the work of the courts and possessed of no real value beyond the performance of fact-finding tasks for their judicial superiors. As one scholar perceptively queried soon after the passage of the Clayton and FTC Acts: "[I]s it possible to escape the conclusion that this increased administrative authority [invested in the FTC] is and will be, at least to a considerable extent, nullified by the provisions . . . investing the judicial branch of the government with a concurrent jurisdiction in that enforcement?"[21]

The years after the creation of the FTC saw the Supreme Court attack that institution's policy-making powers with purpose. In *Federal Trade Commission v Gratz*, the Supreme Court held that the courts, and not the commission, would determine the meaning of the words "unfair methods of competition."[22] The Court reached a similar conclusion in *Federal Trade Commission v Curtis Publishing Company*, this time in regard to the meaning of the phrase "substantially lessen competition or tend to create a monopoly."[23] The erosion of institutional authority that the FTC suffered at the hands of the Court was such that one scholar, writing in 1924, was forced to conclude: "The implication is that . . . the Commission is only a 'fact finding' body in a very restricted sense, with authority to make conclusive findings only as to the existence or non-existence of physical facts. All question of economic or business judgment would thus be for the courts to decide."

> The question is of great importance, for if the Commission is, by these decisions, shorn of all power to exercise administrative discretion in matters of unfair competition or of restraint of trade or monopoly, it has become little more than a subordinate adjunct of the judicial system.[24]

The fledgling ICC suffered an even more humiliating fate at the hands of the Supreme Court, which refused to be bound by either the ICC's findings of fact or its interpretive conclusions.[25] In *Cincinnati Railway*

---

21. Stevens, "The Clayton Act," 47.
22. *Federal Trade Commission v Gratz*, 253 U.S. 421 (1920).
23. *Federal Trade Commission v Curtis Publishing Company*, 260 U.S. 568 (1923).
24. Henderson, *The Federal Trade Commission*, 102.
25. *Cincinnati Railway Company v Interstate Commerce Commission*, 162 U.S. 184 (1896); *Interstate Commerce Commission v Alabama Midland Railway Company et al.*, 168 U.S. 144 (1897). The following paragraph is culled from discussions in Sharfman, *The Interstate Commerce Commission*; Hoogenboom and Hoogenboom, *A History of the ICC*; and Skowronek, *Building a New American State*, 154–60.

Company v ICC, and *ICC v Alabama Midland Railway Company*, the Court declared its willingness to hear new evidence in cases on appeal from the commission, adding that it would set aside the commission's findings of fact as it saw fit. The Court then challenged the commission's policy judgments and attacked its substantive powers. In *Texas and Pacific Railway Company v ICC* (the so-called Import Rate case) the Supreme Court challenged the ICC's judgment regarding the meaning of "unjust discrimination" in Section 2 of the ICA.[26] In *ICC v Alabama Midland Railway Company* the Court reversed the ICC's judgment that the existence of competition in itself did not relieve the railroads from the ICA's prohibition against long haul–short haul discriminations.[27] Similarly, in *ICC v Cincinnati, N.O.&T.P.R. Company* (the Maximum Freight Rate case), the Court denied the ICC the authority to prescribe reasonable rates as a corrective to those judged to be unjust or unreasonable.[28] Finally, the Court overturned the judgment of the ICC that railroad rate associations – cooperative mechanisms used to stabilize freight rates without dividing freight or revenue – were not in violation of the ICA's antipooling clause, adding that they ran afoul of the Sherman Act to boot.[29]

The early administrative history of the ICC and the FTC recalls to mind the origins of these novel institutions in years of Democratic party rule. It also helps to remind us of the deep-seated aversion that agrarian Democrats had traditionally harbored toward the commission form of government, with its reliance on regulatory policy making by independent experts. As I have argued in this book, the pressures of presidential politics had forced Democrats into choices of regulatory form and substance they would have been otherwise loathe to make. Electoral college constraints and coalitional imperatives yielded programmatic appeals to groups located far outside the substantive and ideological commitments of the Democratic party. The difficult choice between short-term electoral needs and long-term policy goals was reluctantly resolved in favor of the stabilization of Democratic governing power, but with durable consequences for the trajectory of American regulatory state development. For out of the drive to fashion

26. *Texas and Pacific Railway Company v ICC*, 162 U.S. 197 (1896).
27. *Interstate Commerce Commission v Alabama Midland Railway Company et al.*, 168 U.S. 144 (1897).
28. *Interstate Commerce Commission v Cincinnati, N.O.&T.P.R. Company*, 167 U.S. 479 (1897).
29. *United States v Trans-Missouri Freight Association*, 166 U.S. 290 (1897); *United States v Joint Traffic Association*, 171 U.S. 505 (1898).

a stable majority coalition, a party with a historic antipathy to both federal and business power had put the instruments of government in service to national administrative capacity and the consolidation of the corporate economy. That these outcomes were the product of strategic considerations and not party ideology is indicated by the radical anti-monopoly line pursued by Franklin Roosevelt in his battle to dissolve public utility holding companies, a clear indication of what party leaders are willing to champion when party system incentives are aligned in the appropriate direction.

Still, as the last several pages have elucidated, the agrarian Democratic cast to these historic state-building episodes must also be kept in view. The aspirations and concerns of agrarians might be sublimated for national electoral objectives, but they could not be wholly expunged. The willingness of Democrats to multiply lines of policy-making authority as a hedge against commission corruption may have helped to placate a suspicious agrarian base, but it compounded the difficult battle these new regulatory authorities would be forced to fight as they sought to establish their administrative preeminence in the new American political economy. Nor could the deeper antagonism of agrarian Democrats to corporate power be wholly submerged by national party considerations. Agrarian commitments to preserving market competition and checking business concentration were stamped and restamped onto the emerging character of American regulatory state, an impulse that directly fed this country's novel antitrust tradition and a characteristic that remains today a defining feature of American business regulation.

Bibliography

Government Documents

Congressional Directory
Congressional Record
Statistical Abstract of the United States
United States Congress. House. 1914. *Hearings before the House Judiciary Committee on Bills Relating to Trust Legislation*, 63d Cong., 2d sess.
United States Congress. House. 1935. Committee on Interstate and Foreign Commerce. *Report of the National Power Policy Committee*, 74th Congress, 1st sess.
United States Congress. Senate. 1886. Select Committee on Interstate Commerce. *Report*. 2 vols. 49th Cong., 1st sess.
United States Congress. Senate. 1914. *Hearings before the Senate Committee on Interstate Commerce on Bills Relating to Trust Legislation*, 63d Cong., 2d sess.

Primary Sources and Memoirs

Baker, Ray Stannard. *Woodrow Wilson* Vol. 4 (Garden City, N.Y.: Doubleday, Doran & Company, Inc., 1931).
Bancroft, Fredric, ed. *Speeches, Correspondence and Political Papers of Carl Schurz* Vol. 4 (New York: G.P. Putnam's Sons, 1913).
Cleveland, Grover. *Letters, 1850–1908*. Allan Nevins, ed. (Boston: Houghton Mifflin Company, 1933).
Cleveland, Grover. *Papers* (microfilm edition).
Congressional Quarterly. *Guide to Congress* 2d ed. (Washington, D.C.: Congressional Quarterly Press, 1976).
Congressional Quarterly. *Guide to U.S. Elections* (Washington, D.C.: Congressional Quarterly Press, 1975).
Darling, Arthur B., ed. *The Public Papers of Francis G. Newlands* (Washington, D.C.: W. F. Roberts Company, Inc., 1931).
Davidson, John Wells, ed. *A Crossroads of Freedom: The 1912 Campaign Speeches of Woodrow Wilson* (New Haven: Yale University Press, 1956).

Freedman, Max. *Roosevelt and Frankfurter: Their Correspondence, 1928–1945* (Boston: Little, Brown, 1967).

Hapgood, Norman. *The Changing Years* (New York: Farrar and Rinehart, 1930).

Hapgood, Norman. *Papers*. Manuscript Division, Library of Congress.

Ickes, Harold L. *Papers*. Manuscript Division, Library of Congress.

Ickes, Harold L. *The Secret Diary of Harold L. Ickes: The First Thousand Days, 1933–1936* (New York: Simon and Schuster, 1953).

Israel, Fred L., ed. *The State of the Union Messages of the Presidents* 3 vols. (New York: Chelsea House, 1966).

Link, Arthur S., ed. *The Papers of Woodrow Wilson* 69 vols. (Princeton, N.J.: Princeton University Press, 1966–94).

Louchheim, Katie. *The Making of the New Deal: The Insiders Speak* (Cambridge: Harvard University Press, 1983).

McPherson, Edward. *Handbook of Politics* Vols. 2–3 (reprint, New York: Da Capo, 1972).

Morison, Elting E., ed. *The Letters of Theodore Roosevelt* (Cambridge: Harvard University Press, 1954).

National Democratic Convention. *Official Proceedings*.

National Executive Committee of Republicans and Independents. *Report* (New York: Burr Printing House, 1885).

Parsons, Stanley B., Michael J. Dubin, and Karen Toombs Parsons. *United States Congressional Districts, 1883–1913* (New York: Greenwood Press, 1990).

Peterson, Merrill D., ed. *The Portable Thomas Jefferson* (New York: Penguin Books, 1987).

Polk, James K. *The Diary of James Knox Polk* (Chicago: A.C. McClure and Company, 1910).

Porter, Kirk H., and Donald Bruce Johnson (compilers). *National Party Platforms, 1840–1960* (Urbana: University of Illinois Press, 1961).

Richberg, Donald. *My Hero: The Indiscreet Memoirs of an Eventful but Unheroic Life* (New York: G.P. Putnam's Sons, 1954).

Roosevelt, Elliot, ed. *FDR: His Personal Letters, 1928–1945* Vol. 3 (New York: Duell, Sloan and Pearce, 1950).

Roosevelt, Franklin D. *Complete Presidential Press Conferences* Vols. 5–6 (New York: Da Capo Press, 1972).

Roosevelt, Theodore. *Autobiography* (New York: Charles Scribner's Sons, 1913).

Rosenman, Samuel I., ed. *The Public Papers and Addresses of Franklin D. Roosevelt* (New York: Random House, 1938).

Rublee, George. "Reminiscences," Columbia University Oral History Project, microfilm.

Seymour, Charles. *The Intimate Papers of Colonel Edward M. House* 2 vols. (Boston: Houghton Mifflin Company, 1926).

Straus, Oscar. *Under Four Administrations: From Cleveland to Taft* (Boston and New York: Houghton Mifflin Company, 1922).

Urofsky, Melvyn I. and David Levy, eds. *The Letters of Louis D. Brandeis* Vols. 2–3 (Albany: State University of New York Press, 1975).

Periodicals

Chicago Tribune
Collier's Weekly
The Commoner
Current History
Current Opinion
Harper's Weekly
The Independent
Investor America
The Irish World and Industrial Liberator
Journal of United Labor
La Follette's Magazine
Literary Digest
The Nation
New Republic
New York Herald Tribune
The New York Times
New York World
North American Review
The Outlook
Saturday Evening Post
The Wall Street Journal
Washington Evening Star

Court Cases

Cincinnati Railway Company v Interstate Commerce Commission, 162 U.S. 184 (1896).
Federal Trade Commission v Curtis Publishing Company, 260 U.S. 568 (1923).
Federal Trade Commission v Gratz, 253 U.S. 421 (1920).
Interstate Commerce Commission v Alabama Midland Railway Company, 168 U.S. 144 (1897).
Interstate Commerce Commission v Cincinnati, N.O. & T.P.R. Company, 167 U.S. 479 (1897).
People v Sheldon, 139 N.Y. 264 (1893).
Texas and Pacific Railway Company v Interstate Commerce Commission, 162 U.S. 197 (1896).
United States v American Tobacco Company et al. 164 F. 700 (1908).
United States v American Tobacco Company et al., 221 U.S. 106 (1911).
United States v Joint Traffic Association, 171 U.S. 505 (1898).
United States v Northern Securities Company, 193 U.S. 197 (1905).

United States v Standard Oil Company et al., 221 U.S. 1 (1911).
United States v Trans-Missouri Freight Association, 166 U.S. 290 (1897).
Wabash, St. Louis and Pacific Railway v Illinois, 118 U.S. 557 (1886).

Books and Articles

Abrams, Richard M. "Woodrow Wilson and the Southern Congressmen, 1913–1916." *Journal of Southern History* 22 (1956): 417–37.

Aldrich, John. *Why Parties? The Origin and Transformation of Political Parties in America* (Chicago: University of Chicago Press, 1995).

Aldrich, John, and David W. Rohde, "The Transition to Republican Rule in the House: Implications for Theories of Congressional Politics." *Political Science Quarterly* 112 (4) (1997–8): 541–67.

Alexander, DeAlva Stanwood. *Four Famous New Yorkers: The Political Careers of Cleveland, Platt, Hill, and Roosevelt* Vol. 4 (New York: Holt, Rinehart and Winston, 1923).

Amar, Akhil Reed. "A Constitutional Accident Waiting to Happen." *Constitutional Commentary* 12 (Summer 1995): 143–5.

Archon, Guy. *The Invisible Hand of Planning: Capitalism, Social Science, and the State in the 1920s* (Princeton, N.J.: Princeton University Press, 1985).

Argersinger, Peter H. *Structure, Process, and Party: Essays in American Political History* (Armonk, N.Y.: M.E. Sharpe, Inc. 1992).

Ball, William J., and David A. Lenthold. "Estrimating the Likelihood of an Unpopular Verdict in the Electoral College." *Public Choice* 70 (May 1991): 215–24.

Bawn, Kathy. "Congressional Party Leadership: Utilitarian versus Majoritarian Incentives." *Legislative Studies Quarterly* 23 (2) (May 1998): 219–43.

Beard, Charles A. *The Economic Basis of Politics and Related Writings* (New York: Vintage Books, 1957).

Bensel, Richard Franklin. *Sectionalism and American Political Development, 1880–1980* (Madison: University of Wisconsin Press, 1984).

Bensel, Richard Franklin. *Yankee Leviathan: The Origins of Central State Authority in America, 1859–1877* (New York: Cambridge University Press, 1990).

Benson, Lee. *Merchants, Farmers, and Railroads: Railroad Regulation and New York Politics, 1850–1887* (Cambridge: Harvard University Press, 1955).

Benson, Lee. "Research Problems in American Political Historiography." In Mirra Komarovsky, ed. *Common Frontiers of the Social Sciences* (Glencoe, Ill.: The Free Press, 1957).

Berk, Gerald. *Alternative Tracks: The Constitution of American Industrial Order, 1865–1917* (Baltimore and London: Johns Hopkins University Press, 1994).

Berk, Gerald. "Constituting Corporations and Markets." *Studies in American Political Development* 4 (1990): 130–68.

Berk, Gerald. "Neither Markets nor Administration: Brandeis and the Antitrust

Reforms of 1914." *Studies in American Political Development* 8 (1) (1994): 24–59.

Berkhoff, Robert F. "The Organizational Interpretation of American History: A New Synthesis." *Prospects* 4 (1979): 611–29.

Berman, William C. "Civil Rights and Civil Liberties." In Richard S. Kirkendall, ed. *The Truman Administration as a Research Field* (Columbia: University of Missouri Press, 1967).

Berns, Walter. "Third Party Condidates Face a High Hurdle in the Electoral College." *American Enterprise* 7 (January–February 1996): 48.

Bernstein, Barton J. "The Ambiguous Legacy: The Truman Administration and Civil Rights." In Barton J. Berstein, ed. *Politics and Policies of the Truman Administration* (Chicago: Quadrangle Books, 1970).

Bernstein, Irving. *The New Deal Collective Bargaining Policy* (Berkeley and Los Angeles: University of California Press, 1950).

Berthoud, John E. "The Electoral Lock Thesis: The Weighting Bias Component." *PS: Political Science and Politics* 30 (June 1997): 189.

Binkley, Wilfred. *American Political Parties: Their Natural History* (New York: Knopf, 1943).

Blodgett, Geoffrey. *The Gentle Reformers: Massachusetts Democrats in the Cleveland Era* (Cambridge: Harvard University Press, 1966).

Blum, John Morton. *Joe Tumulty and the Wilson Era* (Boston: Houghton Mifflin Company, 1951).

Blum, John Morton. *The Progressive Presidents* (New York: W.W. Norton & Company, 1980).

Blum, John Morton. *Woodrow Wilson and the Politics of Morality* (Boston: Little, Brown and Company, 1956).

Bonbright, James C., and Gardiner C. Means. *The Holding Company: Its Public Significance and Its Regulation* (New York: McGraw-Hill, 1932).

Brams, Stephen J. *The Presidential Election Game* (New Haven: Yale University Press, 1978).

Brandeis, Louis D. "Shall We Abandon the Policy of Competition." *Case and Comment* 18 (February 1912): 494–6.

Brandeis, Louis D. "Trusts, Efficiency, and the New Party." *Collier's Weekly* 49 (September 1912): 14–15.

Brooks, Robert C. *Political Parties and Electoral Problem* (New York: Harper and Brothers, 1923).

Bryan, William Jennings. "The Reason." *North American Review* 194 (July 1911): 10–24.

Bryce, James. *The American Commonwealth* rev. ed., 2 vols. (New York: The Macmillan Company, 1911).

Buck, Solon J. *The Granger Movement: A Study of Agricultural Organization and Its Political, Economic and Social Manifestations, 1870–1880* (Cambridge: Harvard University Press, 1913).

Buenker, John D. *Urban Liberalism and Progressive Reform* (New York: Charles Scribner's Sons, 1973).

Burner, David. "The Election of 1924." In Arthur M. Schlesinger, Jr., and Fred L. Israel, eds. *History of American Presidential Elections, 1789–1968* (New York: Chelsea House Publishers, 1971).

Burner, David. *The Politics of Provincialism* (Cambridge: Harvard University Press, 1967).

Burnham, Walter Dean. *Critical Elections and the Mainsprings of American Politics* (New York: W.W. Norton & Company, Inc., 1970).

Burnham, Walter Dean. "Party Systems and Political Process." *The Current Crisis in American Politics* (New York: Oxford University Press, 1982).

Burnham, Walter Dean. *Presidential Ballots, 1836–1892* (Baltimore: Johns Hopkins University Press, 1955), 249.

Burnham, Walter Dean. "The System of 1896: An Analysis." In Paul Kleppner, ed. *The Evolution of American Electoral Systems* (Westport, Conn.: Greenwood Press, 1981).

Burns, James MacGregor. *Roosevelt: The Lion and the Fox* (New York: Harcourt Brace Jovanovich, 1956).

Chamberlain, Lawrence H. *The President, Congress, and Legislation* (New York: Columbia University Press, 1946).

Chandler, Alfred D., Jr. "The Large Industrial Corporation and the Making of the Modern American Economy." In Stephen E. Ambrose, ed. *Innovations in Structure and Process* (Baltimore: Johns Hopkins University Press, 1967).

Clayton, Henry D. "Trust Legislation." *The Commoner* (March 1914): 6–7.

Clifford, Clark. *Counsel to the President. A Memoir* (New York: Random House, 1991).

Clubb, Jerome M., and Howard W. Allen, "Party Loyalty in the Progressive Years, 1909–1915." *Journal of Politics* 29 (1967).

Clubb, Jerome M., William H. Flanigan, and Nancy H. Zingale. *Partisan Realignment: Voters, Parties, and Government in American History* (Beverly Hills, Calif.: Sage Publications, 1980).

Colleta, Paulo E. "The Democratic Party, 1884–1910." In Arthur Schlesinger, Jr., ed. *History of American Political Parties* (New York: Chelsea House Publishers, 1973).

Coolidge, Louis A. *An Old-Fashioned Senator, Orville H. Platt* (New York: G.P. Putnam's Sons, 1910).

Cox, Gary W., and Mathew D. McCubbins. *Legislative Leviathan: Party Government in the House* (Berkeley and Los Angeles: University of California Press, 1993).

Crafts, W. A. "Is the Railroad Problem Solved?" *The Atlantic Monthly* 60 (1887): 76–84.

Craig, Douglas B. *After Wilson: The Struggle for the Democratic Party, 1920–1934* (Chapel Hill: The University of North Carolina Press, 1992).

Croly, Herbert. "An Unseen Reversal." *The New Republic* 1 (January 9, 1915): 7–8.

Cuff, Robert D. "American Historians and the Organizational Factor." *Canadian Review of American Studies* 4 (1973): 19–31.

Cullom, Shelby M. *Fifty Years of Public Service* 2d ed. (Chicago: A.C. McClurg & Company, 1911).

Cummins, Albert B. "The President's Influence a Menace." *The Independent*, June 1, 1914, 350–51.

Cushman, Robert E. *The Independent Regulatory Commissions* (New York: Oxford University Press, 1941).

Davidson, John Wells, ed. *A Crossroads of Freedom: The 1912 Campaign Speeches of Woodrow Wilson* (New Haven: Yale University Press, 1956).

Davies, Joseph E. "Informal Remarks." *New York State Bar Association Antitrust Law Symposium* (Chicago: Commerce Clearing House, Inc., 1955), 104.

Davis, Kenneth S. *FDR: The New Deal Years* (New York: Random House, 1979).

Davis, Kenneth S. *FDR: The New York Years, 1928–1933* (New York: Random House, 1985).

Doan, Edward N. *The La Follettes and the Wisconsin Idea* (New York: Rinehart and Company, 1947).

Dobson, John M. "George William Curtis and the Election of 1884: The Dilemma of the New York Mugwumps." *New York Historical Society Quarterly* 52 (1968): 215–34.

Dobson, John M. *Politics in the Gilded Age: A New Perspective on Reform* (New York: Praeger Publishers, 1972).

Domhoff, G. William. *The Higher Circles: The Governing Class in America* (New York: Vintage Books, 1973).

Donald, David Herbert. *Lincoln* (New York: Simon and Schuster, 1995).

Downs, Anthony. *An Economic Theory of Democracy* (New York: Harper and Row, 1956).

Dubofsky, Melvyn. "Abortive Reform: The Wilson Administration and Organized Labor, 1913–1920." In James E. Cronin and Carmen Sirianni, eds. *Work, Community and Power: The Experience of Labor in Europe and America, 1900–1925* (Philadelphia: Temple University Press, 1983).

Durkheim, Emile. "The Concept of the State." In Anthony Giddens, ed. *Durkheim on Politics and the State* (Stanford, Calif.: Stanford University Press, 1986).

Eaton, Dorman. "Parties and Independents." *North American Review* 144 (June 1887): 549–64.

Epstein, Leon. *Political Parties in the American Mold* (Madison: University of Wisconsin Press, 1988).

Evans, Peter B., Dietrich Rueschemeyer, and Theda Skocpol, eds. *Bringing the State Back In* (Cambridge: Cambridge University Press, 1985).

Feinman, Ronald L. *Twilight of Progressivism: The Western Progressive Senators and the New Deal* (Baltimore: Johns Hopkins University Press, 1981).

Fine, Sidney. *Laissez-Faire and the General Welfare State: A Study of Conflict in American Thought, 1865–1901* (Ann Arbor: University of Michigan Press, 1956).

Finegold, Kenneth, and Theda Skocpol. "State, Party, and Industry: From Business Recovery to the Wagner Act in America's New Deal." In Charles C. Bright and Susan F. Harding, eds. *Statemaking and Social Movements: Essays in History and Theory* (Ann Arbor: University of Michigan Press, 1984).

Fiorina, Morris P. "Group Concentration and the Delegation of Legislative Authority." In Roger G. Noll, ed. *Regulatory Policy and the Social Sciences* (Berkeley and Los Angeles: University of California Press, 1985).

Fiorina, Morris P. "Legislative Choice of Regulatory Forms: Legal Process or Administrative Process?" *Public Choice* 39 (1982): 33–66.

Fiorina, Morris P. "Legislator Uncertainty, Legislative Control, and the Delegation of Legislative Power," *Journal of Law, Economics and Organization* 2 (1986): 33–51.

Fite, Gilbert C. "The Agricultural Issue in the Presidential Campaign of 1928." *Mississippi Valley Historical Review* 37 (4) (March 1951): 653–72.

Fleming, E. McClung. *R.R. Bowker: Militant Liberal* (Norman: University of Oklahoma Press, 1952).

Fleming, James S. "Re-establishing Leadership in the House of Representatives: The Case of Oscar W. Underwood." *Mid-America* 54 (4) (October 1972): 234–50.

Flick, Alexander C., ed. *History of the State of New York* (New York: Columbia University Press, 1935).

Follett, Mary Parker. *The Speaker of the House of Representatives* (New York: Longmans, Green and Company, 1902).

Freidel, Frank. "The Election of 1932." In Arthur M. Schlesinger, Jr., and Fred L. Israel, eds. *History of American Presidential Elections, 1789–1968* (New York: Chelsea House Publishers, 1971).

Freidel, Frank. *FDR and the South* (Baton Rouge: Louisiana State University Press, 1965).

Freidel, Frank. *Franklin D. Roosevelt: Launching the New Deal* (Boston: Little, Brown and Company, 1973).

Freidel, Frank. *Franklin D. Roosevelt: The Triumph* (Boston: Little, Brown and Company, 1956).

Freyer, Tony. *Hugo L. Black and the Dilemma of American Liberalism* (Glenview, Ill.: Scott, Foresman/Little, Brown, 1990).

Freyer, Tony. *Regulating Big Business: Antitrust in Great Britain and America, 1880–1980* (New York: Cambridge University Press, 1992).

Funigiello, Philip J. *Toward a National Power Policy: The New Deal and the Electric Utility Industry, 1933–1941* (Pittsburgh: University of Pittsburgh Press, 1973).

Gable, John Allen. *The Bull Moose Years: Theodore Roosevelt and the Progressive Party* (Port Washington, N.Y.: Kennikat Press, 1978).

Galambos, Louis. "The Emerging Organizational Synthesis in Modern American History." *Business History Review* 44 (Autumn 1970): 279–90.

Galambos, Louis. "Technology, Political Economy, and Professionalism: Central Themes of the Organizational Synthesis." *Business History Review* 53 (Winter 1983): 471–93.

Galbraith, John Kenneth. *American Capitalism: The Concept of Countervailing Power* (Boston: Houghton Mifflin Company, 1952).

George, Alexander L., and Juliette L. George. *Woodrow Wilson and Colonel House: A Personality Study* (New York: J. Day Company, 1956).

Gilligan, Thomas G., William J. Marshall, and Barry R. Weingast, "Regulation and the Theory of Legislative Choice: The Interstate Commerce Act of 1887." *Journal of Law and Economics* 32 (April 1989): 35–61.

Ginsberg, Benjamin, and Martin Shefter. "The Presidency and the Organization of Interests." In Michael Nelson, ed. *The Presidency and the Political System* 2d ed. (Washington, D.C.: Congressional Quarterly Press, 1988).

Glad, Paul W. *The Trumpet Soundeth: William Jennings Bryan and His Democracy, 1896–1912* (Lincoln: University of Nebraska Press, 1960).

Goldman, Ralph M. *Search for Consensus: The Story of the Democratic Party* (Philadelphia: Temple University Press, 1979).

Goodwyn, Lawrence. *The Populist Moment: A Short History of the Agrarian Revolt in America* (New York: Oxford University Press, 1978).

Graham, Otis L., Jr. "The Democratic Party, 1932–1945." In Arthur M. Schlesinger, Jr., ed. *History of U.S. Political Parties* Vol. 3 (New York: Chelsea House Publishers, 1973).

Grantham, Dewey W. "Southern Congressional Leaders and the New Freedom, 1913–1917." *Journal of Southern History* 13 (1947): 439–59.

Greenstone, J. David. *The Lincoln Persuasion: Remaking American Liberalism* (Princeton, N.J.: Princeton University Press, 1993).

Hadley, Arthur T. "American Railroad Legislation." *Harper's Monthly* 57 (June 1887): 141–50.

Haines, Wilder H. "The Congressional Caucus of Today." *American Political Science Review* 9 (4) (November 1915): 696–706.

Hamilton, Virginia Van der Veer. *Hugo Black: The Alabama Years* (Baton Rouge: Louisiana State University, 1972).

Harbeson, Robert W. "Railroads and Regulation, 1877–1916: Conspiracy or Public Interest." *Journal of Economic History* 27 (June 1967): 218–39.

Hardeman, D. B., and Donald C. Bacon. *Rayburn: A Biography* (Austin: Texas Monthly Press, 1987).

Hattam, Victoria C. *Labor Visions and State Power: The Origins of Business Unionism* (Princeton, N.J.: Princeton University Press, 1993).

Hawley, Ellis. *The New Deal and the Problem of Monopoly* (Princeton, N.J.: Princeton University Press, 1966).

Haynes, Frederick Emory. *James Baird Weaver* (Iowa City: The State Historical Society of Iowa, 1915).

Haynes, George H. *The Senate of the United States: Its History and Practice* 2 vols. (Boston: Houghton Mifflin Company, 1938).

Hays, Samuel P. "The New Organizational Society." In Jerry Israel, ed. *Building the Organizational Society: Essays on Associational Activities in Modern America* (New York: Free Press, 1972).

Hays, Samuel P. "Political Parties and the Community-Society Continuum." In William Nisbet Chambers and Walter Dean Burnham, eds. *The American*

Party Systems: Stages of Political Development 2d ed. (New York: Oxford University Press, 1975).

Hays, Samuel P. *The Response to Industrialism* (Chicago: University of Chicago Press, 1957).

Hechler, K. W. *Insurgency: Personalities and Politics of the Taft Era* (New York: Columbia University Press, 1940).

Henderson, Gerard C. *The Federal Trade Commission: A Study in Administrative Law and Procedure* (New Haven: Yale University Press, 1924).

Hillman, Jordan Jay. *Competition and Railroad Price Discrimination* (Evanston, Ill.: The Transportation Center at Northwestern University, 1968).

Hilton, George W. "The Consistency of the Interstate Commerce Act." *Journal of Law and Economics* 19 (October 1966): 87–133.

Hinich, Melvin J., and Peter C. Orjeshook. "The Electoral College: Spatial Analysis." *Political Methodology* 1 (Summer 1974): 1–29.

Hofstadter, Richard. *The Age of Reform* (New York: Vintage Books, 1956).

Hollingsworth, J. Rogers. "The United States." In Raymond Grew, ed. *Crises of Political Development in Europe and the United States* (Princeton, N.J.: Princeton University Press, 1978).

Hollingsworth, J. Rogers. *The Whirligig of Politics: The Democracy of Cleveland and Bryan* (Chicago: University of Chicago Press, 1965).

Holt, James. *Congressional Insurgents and the Party System, 1909–1916* (Cambridge: Harvard University Press, 1967).

Holt, W. Stull. *The Federal Trade Commission: Its History, Activities and Organization* (New York: D. Appleton and Company, 1922).

Hoogenboom, Ari, and Olive Hoogenboom. *A History of the ICC: From Panacea to Palliative* (New York: W.W. Norton and Company, 1976).

Horn, Norbert, and Jurgen Kocka, eds. *Law and the Formation of Big Enterprises in the Nineteenth and Early Twentieth Centuries* (Göttingen: Vanderhoek & Ruprecht, 1979).

Hovenkamp, Herbert. *Enterprise and American Law, 1836–1937* (Cambridge: Harvard University Press, 1991).

Hovenkamp, Herbert. *Federal Antitrust Policy: The Law of Competition and Its Practice* (St. Paul, Minn.: West Publishing Company, 1994).

Huthmacher, J. Joseph. "Urban Liberalism and the Age of Reform." *Mississippi Valley Historical Review* 49 (1962): 231–41.

Huthmacher, J. Joseph. *Senator Robert F. Wagner and the Rise of Urban Liberalism* (New York: Atheneum, 1971).

Israel, Jerry, ed. *Building the Organizational Society: Essays on Associational Activities in Modern America* (New York: The Free Press, 1972).

Jaenicke, Douglas Walter. "Herbert Croly, Progressive Ideology, and the FTC Act." *Political Science Quarterly* 93 (1978): 471–93.

James, Scott C. "Building a Democratic Majority: The Progressive Party Vote and the Federal Trade Commission." *Studies in American Political Development* 9 (2) (Fall 1995): 331–85.

James, Scott C. "A Party System Perspective on the Interstate Commerce Act:

The Democracy, Electoral College Competition, and the Politics of Coalition Maintenance." *Studies in American Political Development* 6 (1) (Spring 1992): 163–200.

James, Scott C. "Prelude to Progressivism: Party Decay, Populism, and the Doctrine of 'Free and Unrestricted Competition' in American Antitrust Policy, 1889–1897." *Studies in American Political Development* 13 (2) (Fall 1999), forthcoming.

James, Scott C., and Brian L. Lawson. "The Political Economy of Voting Rights Enforcement in America's Gilded Age: Electoral College Competition, Partisan Commitment, and the Federal Election Law." *American Political Science Review* 93 (1) (March 1999): 115–31.

Jefferson, Thomas. "Manufactures" (from *Notes on the State of Virginia*). In Merrill D. Peterson, ed. *The Portable Thomas Jefferson* (New York: W.W. Norton & Company, 1980).

Jensen, Richard. *Grass Roots Politics: Parties, Issues, and Voters, 1854–1983* (Westport, Conn.: Greenwood Press, 1983).

Johnson, Evans C. *Oscar W. Underwood: A Political Biography* (Baton Rouge and London: Louisiana State University, 1980).

Keller, Morton. *Affairs of State: Public Life in Late Nineteenth Century America* (Cambridge, Mass.: Belknap Press, 1977).

Keller, Morton. *Regulating a New Economy: Public Policy and Economic Change in America* (Cambridge: Harvard University Press, 1990).

Kent, Frank R. *The Democratic Party* (New York: The Century Company, 1928).

Kent, Frank R. *Without Grease* (New York: William Morrow and Company, 1936).

Kernell, Samuel. *Going Public: New Strategies of Presidential Leadership* 2d ed. (Washington, D.C.: Congressional Quarterly Press, 1993).

Key, V. O. *Politics, Parties and Pressure Groups* 3d ed. (New York: Thomas Y. Crowell, 1952).

Kiewiet, D. Roderick, and Mathew D. McCubbins. *The Logic of Delegation: Congressional Parties and the Appropriations Process* (Chicago: University of Chicago Press, 1991).

King, Judson. *The Power Records of Hoover and Roosevelt* (Washington, D.C.: The National Popular Government League, 1932).

Kirkland, Edward C. *Industry Comes of Age: Business, Labor and Public Policy, 1860–1897* (Chicago: Quadrangle Books, 1961).

Kleppner, Paul. "Coalitional and Party Transformations in the 1890s," In Seymour Martin Lipset, ed. *Party Coalitions in the 1980s* (San Francisco: Institute for Contemporary Studies, 1981).

Kleppner, Paul. *Continuity and Change in Electoral Politics, 1893–1928* (Westport, Conn.: Greenwood Press, 1987).

Kleppner, Paul, ed. *The Evolution of American Electoral Systems* (Westport, Conn.: Greenwood Press, 1981).

Kleppner, Paul. *The Third Electoral System, 1853–1892* (Chapel Hill: University of North Carolina Press, 1979).

Kloppenberg, James T. *Uncertain Victory: Social Democracy and Progressivism in European and American Thought, 1870–1920* (New York: Oxford University Press, 1986).

Koenig, Louis W. *Bryan: A Political Biography of William Jennings Bryan* (New York: Putnam, 1971).

Kolko, Gabriel. *Railroads and Regulation, 1877–1916* (Princeton, N.J.: Princeton University Press, 1965).

Kolko, Gabriel. *The Triumph of Conservatism* (New York: The Free Press, 1963).

Kousser, J. Morgan. *The Shaping of Southern Politics: Suffrage Restriction and the Establishment of the One-Party South, 1880–1910* (New Haven: Yale University Press, 1974).

Krehbiel, Keith. "Are Congressional Committees Composed of Preference Outliers?" *American Political Science Review* 84 (1) (March 1990): 149–63.

Krehbiel, Keith. *Information and Legislative Organization* (Ann Arbor: University of Michigan Press, 1992).

Krehbiel, Keith. "Where's the Party?" *British Journal of Political Science,* 23 (1993): 235–66.

Ladd, Everett Carll, Jr. *American Political Parties: Social Change and Political Response* (New York: W.W. Norton & Company, Inc., 1970).

La Follette, Belle Case, and Fola La Follette. *Robert M. La Follette, June 14, 1855–June 18, 1925* 2 vols. (New York: Macmillan, 1953).

La Follette, Robert M. "Presidential Appointments." *La Follette's Magazine* 7 (January 1915): 3.

Lambert, John R. *Arthur Pue Gorman* (Baton Rouge: Louisiana State University, 1953).

LaPalambara, Joseph, ed. *Bureaucracy and Political Development* (Princeton, N.J.: Princeton University Press, 1963).

LaPalambara, Joseph, and Myron Weiner, eds. *Political Parties and Political Development* (Princeton, N.J.: Princeton University Press, 1966).

Letwin, William. *Law and Economic Policy in America: The Evolution of the Sherman Antitrust Act* (Chicago: University of Chicago Press, [Phoenix edition], 1981).

Leuchtenburg, William E. "The Election of 1936." In Arthur M. Schlesinger, Jr., and Fred L. Israel, eds. *History of American Presidential Elections, 1789–1968* (New York: Chelsea House Publishers, 1971).

Leuchtenburg, William E. *Franklin D. Roosevelt and the New Deal* (New York: Harper and Row, 1963).

Leuchtenburg, William E. *In the Shadow of FDR: From Harry Truman to Bill Clinton* 2d ed. rev. (Ithaca, N.Y.: Cornell University Press, 1993).

Lief, Alfred. *Democracy's Norris: The Biography of a Lonely Crusade* (New York: Stackpole Sons Publishers, 1939).

Lilienthal, David E. *The Journals of David E. Lilienthal: The TVA Years, 1939–1945* Vol. 1 (New York: Harper and Row, 1964).

Lindblom, Charles. *Politics and Markets* (New York: Basic Books, 1977).

Link, Arthur S. "The South and the 'New Freedom': An Interpretation." *American Scholar* 20 (1951): 314–24.

Link, Arthur S. *Wilson: The New Freedom* (Princeton, N.J.: Princeton University Press, 1956).

Link, Arthur S. *Wilson: The Road to the White House* (Princeton, N.J.: Princeton University Press, 1947).

Link, Arthur S. *Woodrow Wilson and the Progressive Era, 1910–1917* (New York: Harper Torchbooks, 1954).

Link, Arthur S., and Richard L. McCormick. *Progressivism* (Arlington Heights, Ill.: Harlan Davidson, Inc., 1983).

Lippman, Walter. *Drift and Mastery: An Attempt to Diagnose the Current Unrest* (Englewood, N.J.: Prentice-Hall, 1961).

Longley, Lawrence D., and James D. Dana. "The Biases of the Electoral College in the 1990s." *Polity* 25 (Fall 1992): 123–45.

Lowi, Theodore. "Party, Policy, and Constitution in America." In William Nisbet Chambers and Walter Dean Burnham, eds. *The American Party Systems* 2d ed. (New York: Oxford University Press, 1975).

Lowi, Theodore. *The Personal President: Power Invested, Promise Unfulfilled* (Ithaca, N.Y.: Cornell University Press, 1985).

Lowitt, Richard. *George W. Norris: The Triumph of a Progressive, 1933–1944* (Urbana: University of Illinois Press, 1978).

Lubell, Samuel. *The Future of American Politics* 3d ed. rev. (New York: Harper and Row, 1965).

Luce, Robert. *Legislative Procedure: Parliamentary Practice and the Course of Business in the Framing of Statutes* (Boston and New York: Houghton Mifflin Company, 1922).

Lustig, R. Jeffrey. *Corporate Liberalism: The Origins of Modern American Political Theory, 1890–1920* (Berkeley and Los Angeles: University of California Press, 1982).

Lynch, Denis Tilden. *Grover Cleveland: A Man Four-Squared* (New York: Horace Liveright, Inc., 1932).

Mack, Shelley C. *The Permanent Majority: The Conservative Coalition in the United States Congress* (University: The University of Alabama Press, 1983).

MacKay, Kenneth Campbell. *The Progressive Movement of 1924* (New York: Columbia University Press, 1947).

Macy, Jesse. *Party Organization and Machinery* (New York: The Century Company, 1918).

Mallon, Paul. "The Party Line-up for 1936." *Current History* 42 (July 1935): 337.

Malone, Preston. "The Political Career of Charles Frederick Crisp" (Ph. D. dissertation, University of Georgia, 1962).

Maltese, John Anthony. *Spin Control: The White House Office of Communications and the Management of Presidential News* (Chapel Hill: University of North Carolina Press, 1992).

Maney, Patrick J. *"Young Bob" La Follette: A Biography of Robert M. La Follette, Jr., 1895–1953* (Columbia: University of Missouri Press, 1978).

March, James G., and Johan P. Olsen *Rediscovering Institutions: The Organizational Basis of Politics* (New York: The Free Press, 1989).

Marcus, Robert D. *Grand Old Party: Political Structure in the Gilded Age, 1886–1896* (New York: Oxford University Press, 1971).

Martin, Albro. "The Troubled Subject of Railroad Regulation." *The Journal of American History* 62 (2) (September 1974): 339–71.

Marx, Karl, and Friedrich Engels. "The German Ideology." In Robert C. Tucker, ed. *The Marx-Engels Reader* 2d ed. (New York: W.W. Norton and Company, 1978).

Mayhew, David R. *Congress: The Electoral Connection* (New Haven: Yale University Press, 1974).

McCormick, Richard L. *From Realignment to Reform: Political Change in New York State, 1890–1910* (Ithaca, N.Y.: Cornell University Press, 1981).

McCormick, Richard L. *The Party Period and Public Policy* (New York: Oxford University Press, 1986).

McCormick, Richard P. *The Party Game: The Origins of American Presidential Politics* (New York: Oxford University Press, 1982).

McCown, Ada. *The Congressional Conference Committee* (New York: Columbia University Press, 1927).

McCoy, Drew. *The Elusive Republic: Political Economy in Jeffersonian America* (New York: W.W. Norton & Company, 1980).

McCraw, Thomas K. *Prophets of Regulation: Charles Francis Adams, Louis D. Brandeis, James M. Landis, Afred E. Kahn* (Cambridge, Mass.: Belknap Press, 1984).

McDonagh, Eileen Lorenzi. "Representative Democracy and State Building in the Progressive Era." *American Political Science Review* 86 (4) (December 1992): 938–50.

McFarland, Gerald W. *Mugwumps, Morals, and Politics, 1884–1920* (Amherst: University of Massachusetts Press, 1975).

McFarland, Gerald W. "Partisan of Non-Partisanship: Dorman B. Eaton and the Genteel Reform Tradition." *Journal of American History* 54 (4) (March 1968): 806–22.

McGaughey, Elizabeth P. "Democracy at Risk: The Dangerous Flaws in the Electoral College." *Policy Review* 63 (Winter 1993): 79–81.

McGeary, M. Nelson. "Congressional Investigations During Franklin D. Roosevelt's First Term." *American Political Science Review* 31 (4) (August 1937): 680–94.

Miliband, Ralph. *The State in Capitalist Society* (New York: Basic Books, 1969).

Milkis, Sidney. *The President and the Parties: The Transformation of the American Party System Since the New Deal* (New York: Oxford University Press, 1993).

Miller, George H. *Railroads and the Granger Laws* (Madison and Milwaukee: University of Wisconsin Press, 1971).

Minor, Henry. *The Story of the Democratic Party* (New York: The Macmillan Company, 1928).

Moe, Terry M. "The Politicized Presidency." In John E. Chubb and Paul E. Peterson, eds. *The New Direction in American Politics* (Washington, D.C.: The Brookings Institute, 1985).

Moley, Raymond. *After Seven Years* (New York: Harper and Brothers, 1939).

Moley, Raymond. *The First New Deal* (New York: Harcourt, Brace and World, Inc., 1966).

Morgan, H. Wayne. *From Hayes to McKinley: National Party Politics, 1877–1896* (Syracuse, N.Y.: Syracuse University Press, 1969).

Mowry, George E. *The Era of Theodore Roosevelt and the Birth of Modern America, 1900–1912* (New York: Harper & Row, 1958).

Mowry, George E. *Theodore Roosevelt and the Progressive Movement* (Madison: University of Wisconsin Press, 1946).

Mueller, John E. *War, Presidents and Public Opinion* (New York: John Wiley and Sons, 1983).

Mulder, Ronald A. *The Insurgent Progressives in the Senate and the New Deal, 1933–1939* (New York: Garland Publishing, Inc., 1979).

Nash, Gerald D. "Origins of the Interstate Commerce Act of 1887." *Pennsylvania History* 24 (July 1957): 181–90.

Nash, Gerald D. "The Reformer Reformed: John H. Reagan and Railroad Regulation." *Business History Review* 29 (June 1955): 189–97.

Nash, Gerald D. "Selections from the Reagan Papers: The Butler-Reagan Ticket of 1884." *The Journal of Southern History* 21 (3) (August 1955): 379–86.

Nathan, Richard P. *The Administrative Presidency* (New York: John Wiley & Sons, 1983).

Neilson, James W. *Shelby M. Cullom, Prairie State Republican* (Urbana: University of Illinois Press, 1962).

Neustadt, Richard E. *Presidential Power: The Politics of Leadership* (New York: John Wiley & Sons, Inc., 1960).

Nevins, Allan. *Grover Cleveland: A Study in Courage* (New York: Dodd, Mead & Company, 1934).

Newquist, Gloria. "James A. Farley and the Politics of Victory: 1928–1936" (Ph. D. dissertation, University of Southern California, 1966).

Norris, George. *Fighting Liberal: The Autobiography of George W. Norris* (Lincoln and London: University of Nebraska Press, 1972).

Orren, Karen. *Belated Feudalism: Labor, the Law, and Liberal Development in the United States* (New York: Cambridge University Press, 1992).

Orren, Karen. *Corporate Power and Social Change* (Baltimore: The Johns Hopkins University Press, 1974).

Orren, Karen, and Steven Skowronek. "Beyond the Iconography of Order: Notes for a 'New' Institutionalism." In Lawrence C. Dodd and Calvin Jillson, eds. *The Dynamics of American Politics: Approaches and Interpretations* (Boulder, Colo.: Westview Press, 1994).

Ostrogorki, Mosei. *Democracy and the Organization of Political Parties* 2 vols. (New York: The Macmillan Company, 1902).

Panebianco, Angelo. *Political Parties: Organization and Power* (New York: Cambridge University Press, 1988).

Parrish, Michael E. *Securities Regulation and the New Deal* (New Haven: Yale University Press, 1970).

Parrish, Michael E. *Felix Frankfurter and His Times: The Reform Years* (New York: The Free Press, 1982).

Parsons, Stanley B., Michael J. Dubin, and Karen Toombs Parsons. *United States Congressional Districts, 1883–1913* (New York: Greenwood Press, 1990).

Patterson, James T. *Congressional Conservatism and the New Deal: The Growth of the Conservative Coalition in Congress, 1933–1939* (Lexington: University of Kentucky Press, 1967).

Peters, Ronald M., Jr. *The American Speakership: The Office in Historical Perspective* 2d ed. (Baltimore: Johns Hopkins University Press, 1997).

Phillips, Cabell. *The Truman Presidency: The History of a Triumphant Succession* (New York: Macmillan, 1966).

Pika, John A. "Reaching Out to Organized Interests: Public Liaison in the Modern White House." In Richard W. Waterman, ed. *The Presidency Reconsidered* (Itasca, Ill.: F.A. Peacock Publishers, Inc., 1993).

Plotke, David. "The Wagner Act, Again: Politics and Labor, 1935–37." *Studies in American Political Development* 3 (1989): 105–56.

Poggi, Gianfranco. *The Development of the Modern State: A Sociological Introduction* (Stanford, Calif.: Stanford University Press, 1978).

Polsby, Nelson, Miriam Gallagher, and Barry Rundquist. "The Growth of Seniority in the House of Representatives." *American Political Science Review* 63 (3) (1969): 148–68.

Poole, Keith T., and Howard Rosenthal. "A Spatial Model for Legislative Roll Call Analysis." *American Journal of Political Science* 29 (2) (May 1985): 357–84.

Procter, Ben H. *Not Without Honor: The Life of John H. Reagan* (Austin: University of Texas Press, 1962).

Przeworski, Adam, and John Sprague. *Paper Stones: A History of Electoral Socialism* (Chicago and London: University of Chicago Press, 1986).

Purcell, Edward A. "Ideas and Interests: Businessmen and the Interstate Commerce Act." *Journal of American History* 54 (December 1967): 561–78.

Radosh, Ronald, and Murray N. Rothard, eds. *A New History of Leviathan: Essays on the Rise of the Corporate State* (New York: Dutton, 1972).

Ramsey, M. L. *Pyramids of Power: The Story of Roosevelt, Insull and the Utility Wars* (Indianapolis: The Bobbs-Merrill Company, 1937).

Ray, P. Orman. *An Introduction to Political Parties and Practical Politics* 3d ed. (New York: Charles Scribner's Sons, 1924).

Remini, Robert V. *Andrew Jackson: The Course of American Democracy, 1833–1845* (Baltimore: Johns Hopkins University Press, 1998 [1984]).

Remini, Robert V. *Andrew Jackson: The Course of American Freedom, 1822–1832* (Baltimore: Johns Hopkins University Press, 1998 [1981]).

Resek, Carl, ed. *The Progressives* (Indianapolis and New York: The Bobbs-Merrill Company, Inc., 1967).

Richardson, James A., ed. *A Compilation of the Messages and Papers of the Presidents* (New York: Bureau of National Literature, 1911).

Ripley, William Z. *Main Street and Wall Street* (Boston: Little, Brown and Company, 1929).

Ritter, Gretchen. *Goldbugs and Greenbacks: The Antimonopoly Tradition and the Politics of Finance in America* (New York: Cambridge University Press, 1997).

Robinson, Edgar E. *The Presidential Vote, 1896–1932* (Stanford, Calif.: Stanford University Press, 1934).

Robinson, Edgar Eugene. *The Roosevelt Leadership* (Philadelphia and New York: J.B. Lippincott Company, 1955).

Rohde, David W. *Parties and Leaders in the Postreform House* (Chicago: University of Chicago Press, 1991).

Roosevelt, Theodore. "Autobiography." In Carl Resek, ed. *The Progressives* (Indianapolis and New York: The Bobbs-Merrill Company, Inc., 1967).

Roosevelt, Theodore. "The Taft-Wilson Trust Programme." *The Outlook*, September 21 (1912): 105–7.

Rosen, Eliot A. *Hoover, Roosevelt, and the Brains Trust* (New York: Columbia University Press, 1977).

Rothman, David J. *Politics and Power: The United States Senate, 1869–1901* (Cambridge: Harvard University Press, 1966).

Rublee, George. "The Original Plan and Early History of the Federal Trade Commission." *Proceedings of the Academy of Political Science* 11 (1926): 114–20.

Salvatore, Nick. *Eugene V. Debs: Citizen and Socialist* (Urbana and Chicago: University of Illinois Press, 1982).

Sanders, Elizabeth. "Industrial Concentration, Sectional Competition, and Antitrust Politics in America, 1880–1980." *Studies in American Political Development* 1 (1986): 142–214.

Sanders, Elizabeth. *Roots of Reform: Farmers, Workers, and the American State, 1877–1917* (Chicago: University of Chicago Press, 1999).

Sarajohn, David. "Democratic Surge, 1905–1912: Forging a Progressive Majority" (Unpublished dissertation: University of California, Los Angeles, 1977).

Sarajohn, David. *The Party of Reform: Democrats in the Progressive Era* (Jackson and London: University Press of Mississippi, 1989).

Satz, Debra, and John Ferejohn. "Rational Choice and Social Theory." *Journal of Philosophy* 91 (February 1994): 71–87.

Savage, Sean J. *Roosevelt: The Party Leader, 1932–1945* (Lexington: University Press of Kentucky, 1991).

Schattschneider, E. E. *Politics, Pressures and the Tariff* (New York: Prentice-Hall, 1935).

Schickler, Eric. "Institutional Change in the House of Representatives, 1867–1986: A Test of Partisan and Median Voter Models" (manuscript).

Schlesinger, Arthur M., Jr. *The Coming of the New Deal* (Boston: Houghton Mifflin Company, 1958).

Schlesinger, Arthur M., Jr. *The Crisis of the Old Order, 1919–1933* (Boston: Houghton Mifflin Company, 1957).

Schlesinger, Arthur M., Jr., ed. *History of U.S. Political Parties* Vol. 2 (New York: Chelsea House Publishers, 1973).

Schlesinger, Arthur M., Jr. *The Politics of Upheaval* (Boston: Houghton Mifflin Company, 1960).

Seltzer, Alan L. "Woodrow Wilson as 'Corporate-Liberal': Toward a Reconsideration of Left Revisionist Historiography." *Western Political Quarterly* 30 (June 1977): 183–212.

Sharfman, Isaiah L. *The Interstate Commerce Commission: A Study in Administrative Law and Procedure* (New York: The Commonwealth Fund, 1931).

Shefter, Martin. "Party, Bureaucracy and Political Change in the United States." In Martin Shefter, *Political Parties and the State* (Princeton, N.J.: Princeton University Press, 1994).

Shepsle, Kenneth A., and Barry R. Weingast, "Political Solutions to Market Problems." *American Political Science Review* 78 (1984): 417–34.

Sheplse, Kenneth A., and Barry R. Weingast, eds. *Positive Theories of Congressional Institutions* (Ann Arbor: University of Michigan Press, 1995).

Sinclair, Barbara. *Legislators, Leaders, and Lawmaking: The U.S. House of Representatives in the Postreform Era* (Baltimore: Johns Hopkins University, 1995).

Sinclair, Barbara Deckard. *Congressional Realignment, 1925–1978* (Austin: University of Texas Press, 1982).

Sklar, Martin J. *The Corporate Reconstruction of American Capitalism, 1890–1916* (New York: Cambridge University Press, 1988).

Sklar, Martin J. *The United States as a Developing Country: Studies in U.S. History in the Progressive Era and the 1920s* (New York: Cambridge University Press, 1992).

Skocpol, Theda. "Bringing the State Back In: Strategies of Analysis in Current Research." In Peter B. Evans, Dietrich Rueschemeyer, and Theda Skocpol, eds. *Bringing the State Back In* (Cambridge: Cambridge University Press, 1985).

Skocpol, Theda. "Political Responses to Capitalist Crisis: Neo-Marxist Theories of the State and the Case of the New Deal." *Politics and Society* 10: 155–201.

Skocpol, Theda. *Protecting Soldiers and Mothers: The Political Origins of Social Policy in the United States* (Cambridge, Mass.: The Belknap Press, 1992).

Skocpol, Theda, and Kenneth Finegold. "Explaining New Deal Labor Policy." *American Political Science Review* 84 (December 1990): 1297–304.

Skowronek, Stephen. *Building a New American State* (New York: Cambridge University Press, 1977).

Skowronek, Stephen. "Notes on the Presidency in the Political Order." *Studies in American Political Development* 1 (1986): 286–302.

Skowronek, Stephen. *The Politics Presidents Make: Leadership from John Adams to George Bush* (Cambridge: Harvard University Press, 1993).

Skowronek, Stephen. "Presidential Leadership in Political Time." In Michael Nelson, ed. *The Presidency and the Political System* (Washington, D.C.: Congressional Quarterly Press, 1984).

Sproat, John G. *The Best Men: Liberal Reformers in the Gilded Age* (New York: Oxford University Press, 1968).

Stanwood, Edward. *A History of the Presidency* 2d ed. (New York: Houghton, Mifflin and Company, 1900).

Steinmo, Sven, Kathleen Thelan, and Frank Longstreet, eds. *Structuring Politics: Historical Institutionalism in Comparative Perspective* (New York: Cambridge University Press, 1992).

Sternsher, Bernard. *Rexford Tugwell and the New Deal* (New Brunswick, N.J.: Rutgers University Press, 1964).

Stevens, W. H. S. "The Clayton Act." *American Economic Review* 5 (1) (March 1915): 38–54.

Sundquist, James L. *Dynamics of the Party System* 2d ed. (Washington, D.C.: The Brookings Institution, 1983).

Thomas, Harrison Cook. *The Return of the Democratic Party to Power in 1884* (New York: Columbia University Press, 1919).

Thompson, Margaret Susan. *The "Spider Web": Congress and Lobbying in the Age of Grant* (Ithaca, N.Y.: Cornell University Press, 1985).

Thorelli, Hans B. *The Federal Antitrust Policy: Origination of an American Tradition* (Baltimore: Johns Hopkins University Press, 1955).

Tugwell, Rexford G. *The Brains Trust* (New York: The Viking Press, 1968).

Tugwell, Rexford G. *The Democratic Roosevelt: A Biography of Franklin D. Roosevelt* (Garden City, N.Y.: Doubleday and Company, Inc., 1957).

Tulis, Jeffrey. *The Rhetorical Presidency* (Princeton, N.J.: Princeton University Press, 1987).

United States Congress. House. Committee on House Administration. *History of the House of Representatives, 1789–1994* (Washington, D.C.: Government Printing Office, 1994).

Untermyer, Samuel. "Completing the Anti-Trust Programme." *North American Review* 199 (April 1914): 528–39.

Updyke, F. A. "New Jersey Corporation Laws." *American Political Science Review* 7 (4) (November 1913): 650–2.

Urofsky, Melvyn I. *Louis D. Brandeis and the Progressive Tradition* (Boston: Little, Brown and Company, 1981).

Urofsky, Melvyn I. "Wilson, Brandeis and the Trust Issue, 1912–1914." *Mid-America* 49 (1967): 3–28.

Uslander, Eric M. "Pivotal States in the Electoral College: An Empirical Investigation." *Annals of the New York Academy of Sciences* 219 (November 1973): 61–76.

Uslander, Eric M. "Spatial Models of the Electoral College: Distribution Biases and Assumptions." *Political Methodology* 3 (Summer 1976): 335–81.

Vagts, Detlev F. "Railroads, Private Enterprise and Public Policy – Germany and the United States, 1870–1920." In Norbert Horn and Jurgen Kocha, eds. *Law and the Formation of Large Enterprises in the 19th and Early 20th Centuries* (Gottingen, West Germany: Vandenhoeck and Ruprecht, 1979), 604–16.

Watkins, T. H. *Righteous Pilgrim: The Life and Times of Harold Ickes, 1874–1952* (New York: Henry Holt, 1990).

Watters, George Wayne. "Isham Green Harris: Civil War Governor and Senator From Tennessee, 1818–1897" (Ph. D. dissertation, Florida State University, 1977).

Wayne, Stephen J. *The Legislative Presidency* (New York: Harper & Row, 1978).

Weber, Max. "Bureaucracy." In Guenther Roth and Claus Wittich, eds. *Economy and Society* 2 vols. (Berkeley and Los Angeles: University of California Press, 1978).

Weber, Max. "Bureaucracy and Political Leadership." In Guenther Roth and Claus Wittich, eds. *Economy and Society* 2 vols. (Berkeley and Los Angeles: University of California Press, 1978).

Weber, Max. "Parliamentary Government and Democratization." In Guenther Roth and Claus Wittich, eds. *Economy and Society* 2 vols. (Berkeley and Los Angeles: University of California Press, 1978).

Weiner, Myron, and Samuel P. Huntington, eds. *Understanding Political Development* (Boston: Little, Brown and Company, 1987).

Weingast, Barry R., and William Marshall. "The Industrial Organization of Congress: Or Why Congress, Like Firms, Are Not Organized As Markets." *Journal of Political Economy* 96 (1988): 132–63.

Weinstein, James. *The Corporate Ideal in the Liberal State, 1900–1918* (Boston: Beacon Press, 1968).

Weinstein, James. *The Decline of Socialism in America, 1912–1925* (New Brunswick, N.J.: Rutgers University Press, 1984).

Welch, Robert E., Jr. *George Frisbie Hoar and the Half-Breed Republicans* (Cambridge: Harvard University Press, 1971).

Wheeler, Burton K. *Yankee from the West* (Garden City, N.Y.: Doubleday and Company, Inc., 1962).

Wiebe, Robert. *Businessmen and Reform* (Cambridge: Harvard University Press, 1962).

Wiebe, Robert H. *The Search for Order, 1877–1920* (New York: Hill and Wang, 1967).

Wilcox, Clair. *Public Policies Toward Business* (Chicago: Richard C. Irwin, Inc., 1955).

Wilson, Woodrow. *Congressional Government* (Boston: Houghton Mifflin Company, 1885).

Wolfskill, George. *The Revolt of the Conservatives: A History of the American Liberty League, 1934–1940* (Boston: Houghton Mifflin Company, 1962).

Yarnell, Allen. *Democrats and Progressives: The 1948 Presidential Election as a Test of Postwar Liberalism* (Berkeley and Los Angeles: University of California Press, 1974).

Index